Placing the Poet

Placing the Poet

Badr Shakir al-Sayyab and Postcolonial Iraq

Terri DeYoung

STATE UNIVERSITY OF NEW YORK PRESS

Published by
State University of New York Press, Albany

Printed in the United States of America

For information, contact State University of New York Press, Albany, NY
www.sunypress.edu

Production by Cathleen Collins
Marketing by Nancy Farrell

Library of Congress Cataloging in Publication Data

DeYoung, Terri.
Placing the poet : Badr Shakir al-Sayyab and postcolonial Iraq /
Terri DeYoung.
p. cm.
Includes bibliographical references and index.
ISBN 0-7914-3731-0 (alk. paper). — ISBN 0-7914-3732-9 (pbk. :
alk. paper)
1. Sayyāb, Badr Shākir, 1926–1965—Criticism and interpretation.
I. Title.
PJ7862.A93D49 1997
892'.716—dc21 97-23836
CIP

10 9 8 7 6 5 4 3 2 1

Contents

Preface

In late 1990 when the tensions leading up to the Gulf war were at their height, an anonymous Iraqi dissident ended his memoir of torture and suffering in Saddam Hussein's prisons[1] with the following lines from "Al-Mabghā" (The Whorehouse), a 1960 poem by Badr Shākir al-Sayyāb:

Baghdad is a great whorehouse
(The songstress' glances are
Like a clock ticking on the wall
Of a waiting room in a train station)...

Baghdad is a nightmare (a disgusting carnage
Swallowed by the sleeper
Whose hours are days, whose days are years, with the year a yoke:
The year is a wound smoldering in the soul).

The wild cow's eyes between Ruṣāfa and the bridge[2]
Are bullet holes that embellish [like the dots of letters] the flat white
surface of the full moon...

Is this Baghdad?
Or has Gomorrah
Returned, and the [time of] return was
A death? But in the jingling of chains
I sense . . . what? The sound of a waterwheel
Or the cry of the sap in the roots?

Although the article's author ultimately rejects the possibility of Sayyāb's hopeful conclusion—that something good will eventually arise from the ashes of the misery he has endured—the very fact that it was this poem that he remembered and chose to quote when speaking of the most harrowing and emotionally traumatic experiences of his life shows very graphically how much Sayyāb's poetry still speaks to his fellow Iraqis as somehow summative of their experiences in this century, especially the experience of the enormous changes wrought by the coming of the Western version of modernity to their land in the last one hundred years.

Furthermore, Sayyāb's reputation, over thirty years after his death in 1964, continues to resonate beyond the borders of Iraq into all parts of the Arab world. In Egypt, for example, where I had the chance to spend some time in the 1970s and 1980s, many people could quote poems of his from memory, and many friends and acquaintances—including a number who would probably not class themselves as aficionados of things literary or as intellectuals—have shared with me their admiration for a poet whom they felt (almost without exception) "spoke from his heart" in words whose rhythms, while seemingly simple and clear, magically evoked the power of Arabic and its magnificent literary tradition at its most dignified and eloquent levels of expression. Few other modern poets could make the claim to have written poetry so universally respected and admired by those around them.

Yet Sayyāb is virtually unknown in the West. Like almost all other modern Arab poets, he has been represented by a handful of articles and a few isolated translations in the Western languages. My original intention, then, in conceiving this project was simply to make the work of at least one major modern poet from the Arab world accessible to Western readers in a venue where they could appreciate its complexity, as well as its development over time. Along the way, however, I have had the pleasure of discovering new insights into Sayyāb's poetry through a concurrent—and initially unrelated—immersion in the work of postcolonial literary theorists and the writings of authors from other countries that have been subject, like Iraq, to the often dubious advantages of "the colonial experience." What I found forced me to rethink my project in midstream, but the results of this unsettlement have been greatly rewarding in a number of ways. In particular, it showed me how important the aspect of place is in Sayyāb's poetry—as a literal and metaphoric ground for battling with the demons of colonialism—which led to my engagement with the issues outlined in the first part of the present study. I can only hope that the resulting discussion in the pages that follow can convey some of the excitement and magic that Sayyāb's poetry seems to have brought to the audience he first offered it to so many years ago, and still conveys to the Arab public today.

Acknowledgments

The completion of a book project, especially a first one, implies that some sort of academic milestone has been reached. This is especially true for me in the case of this book, because I have been involved in engagements with Sayyāb's work, in one way or another, since my junior year in college. Along the way, I have encountered many individuals who have helped me in one way or another with my search for an understanding of what Sayyāb's work has meant, both to himself and others—so many, in fact, that it would be impossible to express my gratitude and appreciation to them all.

Nevertheless, there are some people who have played an important role in both my general education and this project in particular, to whom I would like to express special thanks for their unselfish commitment and willingness to help a younger scholar who would have found herself hopelessly "at sea" without their guidance. At Princeton, I was fortunate to be introduced to the study of Arabic language and literature by Andras Hamori and Roy Mottahedeh, whose patience and exemplary integrity as academic role models I have tried subsequently to emulate, often with (I am afraid) lesser rather than greater success. At the American University in Cairo, where I received my MA degree, Muhammad Nowaihi and Sami Badrawi were similarly instrumental in guiding me to a deeper and broader knowledge of Arabic literature and the cultural background out of which it emerges. Finally, my dissertation director, Mounah Khouri, and James Monroe, as an advisor and extremely valued member of my Ph.D. committee at Berkeley, took up where their predecessors had left off and showed me just how many riches in the field were still waiting to be discovered.

In more recent times, I have benefited from the special help of two colleagues at the University of Washington, Farhat Ziadeh and Walter Andrews, both of whom read the manuscript of this work, each from his own perspective of expertise, with exemplary care and attention. Without their valuable insights and support at crucial junctures in the writing, I suspect this project might never have come to a conclusion and certainly not as soon as it did. In the same vein, special thanks are due to Issa Boullata of McGill University and Sasson Somekh of Tel Aviv University for graciously making available to me documents relating to Sayyab's work that would have otherwise been unobtainable, and whose lack would have impoverished this study greatly.

The University of Washington has generously allowed me support to pursue the writing of this book in the form of two grants, one from the Graduate School for Summer Quarter 1992 and one from the Royalty Research Fund in Summer Quarter 1995 and Spring Quarter 1996.

Earlier versions of material used in chapters 1, 5 and 7 of this study appeared in the following articles: "A New Reading of Badr Shākir al-Sayyāb's 'Hymn of the Rain,'" in *The Journal of Arabic Literature* 24, no. 1 (March 1993): 39–61; and "Mu'ārada and Modern Arabic Poetry: Some Examples from the Poetry of Badr Shākir al-Sayyāb," *Edebiyāt* 5 (1994): 217–245. I am grateful for permission to quote from them here. "The Waste Land" and "Portrait of a Lady" from *Collected Poems 1909–1962* by T.S. Eliot, copyright 1936 by Harcourt, Brace & Company, copyright © 1964, 1963 by T.S. Eliot, are reprinted by permission of the publishers. Acknowledgment is made to Harcourt Brace & Company and to Faber and Faber for their kind permission to quote from both the above referenced poems here.

CHAPTER ONE

Empty Spaces and Unveiled Placeholders

Locating Southern Iraq

> And I looked, and behold a pale horse: and his name
> that sat on him was Death, and Hell followed with him.
> And power was given unto them over the fourth part of
> the earth, to kill with the sword, and with hunger,
> and with death, and with the beasts of the earth.
>
> —Rev. 6:8

It may seem odd to begin a study devoted to the consideration of how insights generated by postcolonial literary theory might apply to the verse of Iraqi poet Badr Shākir al-Sayyāb with a chapter highlighting the apocalyptic element in his work. As is abundantly clear from even the most casual perusal of apocalyptic writings, their dominant focus is always on temporality: the representation of the end of things as they have been, with perhaps a hopeful gesture toward a renewed and better future. When Sayyāb avails himself, as he does in many of his most successful poems—like the famous "Unshūdat al-Maṭar" (Hymn of the Rain)—of apocalyptic categories, this temporal element is never absent, but hovers over the trajectory of the poem like a vengeful specter waiting for the appropriate opportunity to emerge.

In postcolonial literary theory, in contrast, as in postmodernism, the tropes of "place," "space," and "spatialization" have become *the* privileged signifiers in the creation of analytical constructs, though perhaps this parallel development has not occurred for entirely the same reasons in both cases. In postmodernism, and in the allied critical discourse of poststructuralism, the emphasis on spatial metaphors and figures of speech seems to have come to the fore at least partially under the pressure of attempts to think beyond, or against the grain of, the modernist valorization of temporality.[1] As Fredric Jameson says in his landmark study of postmodernism, "a certain spatial turn has often seemed to offer one of the more productive ways of distinguishing postmodernism from modernism proper, whose experience of temporality—existential time, along with deep memory—it is henceforth conventional to see as a dominant of high modernism."[2]

On the other hand, in colonial and postcolonial writing—and postcolonial theory—the focus on space may indeed relate to an antitemporality, but it can also be said to represent at the base something more tangible: space is quite literally (as well as metaphorically) the location where colonizer and colonized engage in struggles for power. The matter of who possesses the *place*, the land, becomes important not only terms of imaginative representation and what it might assert as possible but also in terms of quite specifically who can *do* what to whom. As Edward Said has recently said, speaking from the perspective of the colonized, ". . . anti-imperialist resistance . . . literature develops quite consciously out of a desire to distance the native African, Indian, or Irish individual from the British, French, or (later) American master. Before this can be done, however, there is a pressing need for the recovery of the land that, because of the presence of the colonizing outsider, is recoverable at first only through the imagination."[3] Elsewhere in the same essay, Said notes that this tactic of "recovery of the land," is usually formulated as part of a direct response to deterritorializing strategies of the colonial powers already in play, such as redrawing national boundaries (or instituting them in the first place), building new cities or renaming old ones, instituting Western practices for recording land ownership, and even carrying out construction projects, such as the building of roads or ports, and agricultural schemes.

It may be useful to sketch out briefly some of the possible typologies for this struggle in order to come to grips with their implications for the representation of place in the literature of colonialism. The extreme case, for instance, might be located in the practices of settler colonialism—where the land is physically taken away from the people who had formerly lived there. This would then be seen as the most devastating form of colonial usurpation, one that generates enormous ambivalences and anxieties, not only for the dispossessed but for those who do the dispossessing.[4]

Adjacent to settler colonialism, and often interfacing with it, one could speak of colonialisms where the educational system for the "natives" was completely dominated and directed by the European power, as was the case in the Arab world in the portion of the Maghrib under French control. Even in those places where British sway held—and there was less formal control of the educational system—there were various attempts at interference.[5] Because education includes lessons on geography and history—the two elements most widely recognized as constructing an individual with a sense of a "national" identity, of belonging to a "nation"—it can act as an extraordinarily powerful tool in the hands of whoever runs it.[6]

Thus we can see that even for colonized groups who remained in physical possession of the land, loss of control over their governing institutions constituted a deracinating experience of imperialist power that could destabilize their relationship to this land and transform it into what Richard Terdiman has usefully phrased, in another context, a "problem," "a site and source of cultural disquiet."[7] In other words, what is often most important in tracing the trajectory of a thematics or style of expression, such as a preoccupation with descriptions of nature or a penchant for tropes dependent on spatialization, is not so much pinpointing its origin, the instant when it first occurs, but in recognizing when—and in what ways—it seems to become the index for a trauma, a crisis, something that forms a source of anxiety for a large number of the members of a given cultural group. It becomes equally important, then, to pay close attention as well to the context in which that anxiety is expressed and made explicit.

As an example of how this contextual way of looking at a recurrent theme can be heuristically useful, one could posit postmodernism's tendency toward spatialization not only as a countermove against the temporalist bias of modernism but also as a sign of an increased anxiety about the subject's spatial relations: not only the self's relation to a particular place or location but relations with "others" from different places and different cultures who are contending for the same place or the same recognition. This could then be used to set up a further contrast with modernism, where the characteristic anxiety might be portrayed as being over the self's relationship to the past and to "others" from history. To put it in an authorial context, T.S. Eliot's anxiety would have been more over his relationship to predecessors from English and American literature than to his contemporaries writing poetry in other countries, while Steven Spielberg's anxiety as a postmodernist storyteller would not be over his "place" vis-à-vis Charles Dickens or even D.W. Griffith, but François Truffaut or Akiro Kurosawa or Satayajit Ray.

In the same register of looking for recurrences and then contextualizing them as anxieties, one might consider European romanticism's obsession with organic metaphors as not only a reaction against the mechanistic theories of the immediately preceding period[8] but also as index of an anxiety over new ways of thinking about organism, about the new discoveries problematizing the nature of life and living beings that are exemplified so perfectly in Mary Shelley's *Frankenstein*. In a similar sense, then, the themes of land, space, and geography would seem to form an anxiety or "problem" for all colonial and postcolonial writers, whether settlers or indigens, and it should not be surprising for us to find these themes highlighted in their writing.[9]

In light of the foregoing, then, it should hold a special interest for us that the importance of place in the works of the Iraqi poet Badr Shākir al-Sayyāb is singled out in virtually every critical evaluation of his writings, often yoked in an uneasy juxtaposition with acknowledgment of its apocalyptic bent. All of the earliest commentators to deal with the young Sayyāb's poetry, for instance, specifically fix at one point or another in their discussions upon the role played by "the Iraqi environment (*bī'a*),"—as one of them puts it—as a defining characteristic of his work, something setting it apart from that of his contemporaries.[10] In virtually the first evaluation of Sayyāb's writing, penned by the noted Iraqi journalist and man of letters Rafā'īl Buṭṭī in an introduction he wrote for Sayyāb's first collection of poems, we find the following description of the poet: "He is the happy son of the Iraqi countryside, with all of [its] wide open spaces laid out before him."[11] The date-palm groves surrounding Sayyāb's home village of Jaykūr became, in another early critic's view, "fields of passion and a home ground for inspiration, where Sayyāb stood enchanted, wondering and jubilant."[12] At the other temporal extreme, in an appreciation written shortly after Sayyāb's death, the eminent Egyptian critic Lewis 'Awaḍ would go even further, saying that Jaykūr had become in the poet's final years "a symbol of salvation," and "a last refuge from the hell of the present,"[13] a focal point around which the process of composition revolved.

This response has become, if anything, significantly more pronounced in recent works.[14] It may even have determined the global strategies used in writing Sayyāb's life in the works undertaken by his two major biographers, 'Īsā Bullāṭa and Iḥsān 'Abbās.[15] Both writers begin with exceptionally long and detailed descriptions of the village where Sayyāb was born before proceeding to the more conventional topics, like the subject's family background and upbringing, usually addressed at the beginning of biographies.[16]

It becomes even more worthy of note that we find Sayyāb constantly revisiting the landscape as a reference point from which to theorize an identity and come to terms with the issues of self and other as they relate to his own existence once we recall that his life roughly parallels the period when Britain controlled Iraq, first through a mandate from the League of Nations and later through a succession of sweetheart treaties with nominally independent Iraqi governments, which allowed the British to maintain a military and commercially dominant presence on Iraqi soil. Thus it would seem more than advisable, in any approach to understanding Badr Shākir al-Sayyāb's poetry, to make at least an attempt to visualize something of this land from which he came and where he lived, on and off, for the larger part of his life.

To attempt to get a handle on this question of place, then, one might begin, rather conventionally, as follows. Badr Shākir al-Sayyāb was born in 1926 in southern Iraq, not far from the Iranian border and the Persian Gulf. His birthplace was a tiny village, Jaykūr, with a population of less than 500. It lies on the banks of the Shaṭṭ al-'Arab, as the confluence of the Tigris and Euphrates rivers is known once they join together at the town of Qurna, about 100 miles from the sea. Although Jaykūr rarely appears on maps, modern or otherwise, it lies not very far from the large "capital city" of the south, Baṣra, where Badr received his secondary schooling.

The group of statements given above would constitute the first step in forming an inventory of "facts" about Jaykūr and about Sayyāb's life there, without which it would be impossible to proceed. But even such a modest beginning raises questions. For instance, to recite them is to begin to develop a "discourse" in Michel Foucault's sense of the term: an organized linkage, or "apparatus" (to again use Foucault's terminology) of words that, properly groomed, pruned, sorted, and arranged, will allow us to constitute for ourselves an "episteme" (though a very minor one, to be sure)—literally, a knowledge system or coordinated understanding—of Sayyāb's life and career as poet. The question of epistemes and discourses is a very complicated one that I will treat in much more detail in a moment. For now, let me simply emphasize that epistemes function by *excluding* as well as including information.

The specific impasse I would seek to highlight here is related to, but to a degree also separate from, the previous point. It revolves around the fact that any such attempt to delineate these places, inventory the "facts" about them, and seek a point of entry into Sayyāb's world creates a special difficulty for Western readers because they have at hand, ready-made, another very powerful interpretive episteme of the space known as "southern Iraq," one that differs markedly from the one operative in Sayyāb's works. Nowadays this Western discourse of southern Iraq has become inextricably bound up with geopolitical concerns, with questions of national power and conflicting interests whose end point has been expressed in war. The power this discourse now has, because of its pervasiveness, to overwhelm—and thus to exclude—any other that might be ranged against it is difficult to deny.

This is where another aspect of Foucault's analysis concerning the nature of discourse becomes productive. In his studies of various apparatuses of social power and their sites of articulation—the clinic, the madhouse, and the prison—Foucault became increasingly drawn to the examination of the contending forces that drive the dialectical relationship of knowledge and power—a relationship he then sought to isolate, externalize, and map in as much detail as possible. Increasingly over time this process came to express its terms through metaphors of war.[17] Eventually, however, Foucault seems to have come to the conclusion that the relationship between knowledge and power appears to be, of necessity, a symbiotic one of mutual dependence. As he himself put it, "the exercise of power itself creates and causes to emerge new objects of knowledge and accumulates new bodies of information. . . . It is not possible for power to be exercised without knowledge, it is impossible for knowledge not to engender power."[18] A major vehicle for disseminating this knowledge/power nexus is through what Foucault calls a discourse, the structure of words (oral or written) in which we find the articulation of what can—and cannot—be said about any subject, always within the implicit parameters set down by the dual apparatus of knowledge/power.

It is this aspect of Foucault's work, how it applies to the formation of discourses, that seems to have held the greatest relevance—and certainly the greatest interest—for the early developers of postcolonial literary theory, since one of its major effects was to refocus critical attention on the question of just how disinterested or "objective" any piece of writing can be. And what they were discovering was that the colonial enterprise was as much a textual construction as it was the result of applications of armed force.[19] Of course, one may protest that knowledges or epistemes may not be consciously created to exercise power. But Foucault's answer would be, I think, that the potential for utilizing knowledge for the purposes of power is always there and may be seized on and so deployed at times and in places far removed from their first articulation. How those potentials may be actualized should therefore be seen as a subject worthy of attention and study, rather than identifying it as an unimportant or "subjugated" knowledge, ignoring its existence, and thus allowing it to operate unexamined. In point of fact, a salutary example of how the knowledge/power relation works in practice to control the development of an episteme (what can and cannot be said about a certain subject) can be given ample illustration by recounting the story of how a discourse actualizing "southern Iraq" in the minds of Americans in the 1990s came to be formed.

For most of this century the operation of conceptualizing the Iraqi landscape in the minds of those ordinary Westerners who were called upon, for one reason or another, to do so could easily be likened to that of the youthful Joseph Conrad, who is reported to have himself enacted in the 1860s the same scene he would so memorably father upon his character Marlow in *Heart of Darkness*: the young boy who imperiously plants his finger on what he perceives as a "blank spot" upon the globe and confidently declares, "One day, when I grow up, I shall go there."[20] What is implied by this "mapping" operation, of course, is that only with the arrival of the "civilizing," "sovereign" subject of Western rationalism and humanism will this spot be rescued from its blankness and come to exhibit a topography of meaning, order, and coherence.[21] Southern Iraq, to the ordinary inhabitant of Europe or America could be said to occupy a similar "blank spot"—an area of absence waiting to be invested with meaning.

What is especially interesting about Conrad's story—at least for our purposes in speaking of the creation of a space the West now knows as "southern Iraq"—is that once the adult Marlow performs his self-appointed task, he creates a landscape that exhibits certain submerged but markedly apocalyptic overtones. The constant display of a chiaroscuro description of light and darkness in *Heart*, relieved only by the fitful illumination of baleful fires glowing cherry-red, the sudden appearance of strange beasts and the gradual breakdown in the descriptions of the boundaries between man and beast, the strange characters who, when encountered, speak in the same maddeningly ambiguous riddles as the angels in Revelation (like the runaway Russian sailor to whom Marlow gives Towson's *An Inquiry into some Points of Seamanship*), the splitting of the major female characters into a duality of good and evil (the Intended vs. Kurz's African native mistress, recalling the biblical division between Babylon the Whore and the mother who flees with her child into the wilderness), and finally a confusion of temporality coupled with a doubling that makes it difficult to differentiate the events of creation, of Genesis, from those of the end, of Armageddon—all these make it easy to understand why, when Francis Ford Coppola chose to use *Heart of Darkness* as his scaffolding for interpreting the Vietnam war, he titled the resulting film *Apocalypse Now*. Similarly, Kurz's final cry, "the horror, the horror"—which to a certain extent became the rallying cry of Anglo-American modernism early in this century—gains a large portion of its evocative resonance from its resemblance to what one might imagine the cry of the damned on the Day of Judgment would be. Even more provocative is Homi Bhabha's comment made during a discussion of Conrad's story as a paradigm for representations of the colonial experience: "Marlow keeps the conversation going, suppresses the horror, gives history the lie—the white lie—and waits for the heavens to fall."[22] In this last phrase, "waiting for the heavens to fall," Bhabha seems to point to without being explicit, an ambivalence evident in Conrad's use of apocalyptic in *Heart of Darkness*: for Marlow, "the horror" is real, he constantly reiterates his obscure premonitions of some dramatic, irreversible dénouement, but the events the narrative itself recounts read as a parody of real apocalypses, especially the Book of Revelation in the Bible. When the end finally does come, then, in Marlow's interview with the Intended, it is Chicken Little waiting for the sky to fall, not Armageddon.

What makes this linkage between a narrative recounting a colonial journey into an unmapped space and the apocalyptic even more interesting is that apocalyptic is an essentially "placeless" discourse—since to be everywhere, as the Judgment Day will be, is to be no special place in particular. While apocalyptic language is saturated with markers of temporality (even though that temporality may be confused), its lack of readily recuperable place markers is equally characteristic. Even when particular places are mentioned, like Babylon or Jerusalem in the Book of Revelation, they are clearly not referents to real physical locations, but are either allegorized and/or metonymically transformed through rhetorical devices like personification. Thus when "Babylon" is mentioned, it appears before us in the form of a woman, upon whose head is written the legend: "mystery, Babylon the great, the mother of harlots and abominations of the earth" (Rev. 17:5). This city-turned-woman is then implicitly contrasted, shortly thereafter, with "the new Jerusalem," that St. John witnesses "coming down from God out of heaven, prepared as a bride adorned for her husband" (Rev. 21:2).

It would be an interesting critical project to explore further the general relationship between apocalyptic categories and the narratives of colonialism. For now, however, let me limit myself to pointing out that it is through those very same apocalyptic categories that the "blank spot" known as southern Iraq has, especially in the last two decades, received a meaning in the West. This process could be said to begin, in one sense, as early as the last half of the nineteenth century, when Western archaeologists started to conduct extensive excavations in the area, largely with an eye to establishing the historical validity of biblical narrative. Much of this investigation was oriented toward notions of origin—the development of the first cities and the like—but the archaeologists' interest in recovering evidence of the destructive natural events that they believed lay behind certain biblical stories, like Noah's flood or Abraham's departure from the city of Ur, lent a certain eschatological tinge to the project. Perhaps even more to the point, there were attempts to identify exact locations for events from the Babylonian captivity of the Jews, like the site of Nebuchadnezzer's fiery furnace, or his son Belshazzer's palace, where the handwriting appeared upon the wall and the prophet Daniel had his apocalyptic visions. Thus, the categories linking Iraq to punishment stories, disaster motifs, and even the earliest apocalyptic book in the Bible were there, provided with a venerable pedigree, waiting to be exploited at the beginning of the war that broke out between Iraq and Iran in the early 1980s.

There is an intermittent emphasis in Western accounts of the Iran–Iraq war on details that underscore its possible recuperability within an apocalyptic framework. Mostly these details are situated in the cultural space of the demonized Iranians: the famous fountain in Tehran that ran red with water dyed to simulate the blood of martyrs, the repeated emphasis on describing the Iranian attacks as consisting of "human waves" of untrained recruits, usually characterized as "barefoot boys" seeking martyrdom.[23] In general, however, the telltale features of apocalyptic discourse are skirted, approached, but not fully appropriated. There are many comparisons, for example, to the trench warfare of World War I (itself a war frequently described using an apocalyptic code, though with ambivalent referents—it is "endless," the slaughter is "indiscriminate"—that form discontinuities rather than cohesions), including claims of widespread use of poison gas in both conflicts.[24] A more telling point in this regard, then, might be the recurrent references in many accounts of the war to the Shi'ī-Sunnī divide in Islam, centered on speculation concerning how it might affect the outcome of the war, and the religious overtones implied by such a structuring of the conflict. An interesting illustration of how this works is provided by Anthony Cordesman's *The Iran–Iraq War and Western Security 1984–87*, where he says:

> The war has exposed the darkest side of religion. Like similar periods of stress in the Christian West, and in ancient Israel, conflict and social change in Iran have combined with religious faith to create a new Shi'ite ideology that often glorifies xenophobia and religious prejudice and which transforms opposition into the forces of 'Satan.'[25]

This slippage into the religious discourse that is a prerequisite for the turn to apocalyptic is all the more noticeable because Cordesman generally eschews obvious tropologies that might more easily accommodate the highly wrought figuration of apocalyptic speech—in keeping with his positioning of himself within "military expert" discourse.

An even more notable example of how these different discourses may be shaped so as to converge ultimately upon apocalyptic can be found in Kanan Makiya's (a.k.a. Samir al-Khalil's) *Republic of Fear*. This book also provides a significant transition point from the Iran–Iraq war to the Gulf war in 1991 because it was first published during the former conflict but only became a best-seller during the latter. Although Makiya's presentation in *Republic of Fear* and his other books of the political implications of events in the recent history of Iraq has proved intensely controversial, no one could fail to grant that he possesses a highly developed awareness of the symbolic fault lines that run throughout modern discourse—both internally and externally generated—relative to the Arab world. The concluding paragraph of his book reveals a marked ability to use the power of apocalyptic categories as the invisible ground for his rhetorical strategy:

> On the face of it, the Iraq–Iran war presents itself, both in its origins and in what has sustained it, as the titanic clash of two men locked in a fight to the finish. This does not go far enough only because the dominant political attribute of each man is his unprecedented concentration of authority deriving in the one case from fear and in the other from faith. Fear and faith are among the most elemental and primordial of all human drives; under certain circumstances they have the force to make men die in droves for no other reason than that they cannot imagine doing otherwise. They have conferred onto the personal will of these two men the deadly power unleashed by the decisions of this war. The final meaning of a war like this, one it shares with the Lebanese civil war but none of the Arab–Israeli wars, resides in the simple truth that its mere occurrence has taken away from all of us yet another chunk of an already battered humanity.[26]

Not only is there the reference to Khomeini and Saddam Hussein as "titanic" figures whose power goes beyond the merely human (thus invoking parallels with the "Beast" in Revelation, who has been consistently linked to political leaders through the ages, from the Roman emperor Nero to Oliver Cromwell and, in our own century, Stalin and Hitler); there is as the paragraph unfolds a gradually heightened set of references to origins (thus "fear and faith" become "elemental" and "primordial," for example) mingled inextricably with "ending codes" (the two leaders are "locked in a fight to the finish," "a war like this" has "a final meaning" in its destruction of the "humanness" of humanity). Probably the key gesture in the direction of apocalyptic teleology is found in the middle of the paragraph, where Makiya asserts that "fear and faith . . . have the force to make men die in droves,"[27] thus heightening the destructiveness of the event in order to make it representable in apocalyptic terms—and this is because the men "cannot imagine doing otherwise": that is, their actions are determined by the power of a vision outside themselves, not by their own wills—the same kind of presupposition that is underwritten by the inexorable course of the apocalyptic vision.

In this paragraph, what we see is in many ways a preparation for the much more decisive turn toward apocalyptic we find in discourse about the 1991 Gulf war, where such symbolism becomes almost universal as the ground for engagement with war events in both prowar and antiwar rhetoric. It is as though all of the apocalyptic vocabulary developed during the cold war, once so useful in representing all the imagined (or unimaginable) possibilities of nuclear holocaust but now, with the end of the Soviet Union, temporarily homeless, finds a new refuge in that triangle bounded by Baghdad, Basra, and Kuwait City. Other discourses founded on apocalyptic idiom relating to past Western wars also made their contributions to this turn. For George Bush, of course, Saddam Hussein became Hitler (the twentieth century's most ubiquitous stand-in for the Beast of Revelation), and he was to catapult this into an extremely effective rhetoric representing the war as a quasi-religious "crusade" against evil, eliding its more prosaic origins in a struggle over the control of an essential industrial resource: oil.

On the left we might picture the extreme edge of the discourse as being marked out by predictions of a global ecological catastrophe that was to ensue on the heels of the retreating Iraqi army's firing of the oil wells in Kuwait. Not untypical is the paragraph introducing an article entitled "For Generations to Come: The Environmental Catastrophe," most notable now because its inclusion in *Beyond the Storm: A Gulf Crisis Reader* has ensured that it will continue to reach a broader audience in time as well as space than the more ephemeral discourse of newspapers and magazines:

> The coalition forces have stopped fighting and Kuwait has been "liberated." The emir has been restored but the country has not. A new human nightmare has emerged. The specter of exploding oil wells, day indistinguishable from night, black rain, a massive oil spillage, thousands of tons of toxic chemicals released into the atmosphere, the tragic plight of the Kurdish and Iraqi peoples mean that the misery and suffering will linger on, perhaps for decades. It has been estimated that spending a day in Kuwait City is equivalent to smoking 250 cigarettes. Only now, is the world waking up to the terrible price being paid for engaging in military hostilities in Gulf. The world's ecology is very fragile.[28]

Here—in the catalog of reversals of natural phenomena especially, like the "black rain," the inability to distinguish night from day, or the transformation of the Gulf waters into oil, as well as the globalization of its effects—the overtones of apocalyptic are unmistakable. No one should doubt that such a discourse had its uses for both sides. Not the least, it was effective in underscoring the seriousness of their claims. But apocalyptic is also a radically dehumanizing, totalizing discourse that, in the case of "southern Iraq" at least, ends up legitimating images of this place, this location, as a kind of theater where the spectacle of battle, destruction, and death are naturalized: not only made possible but "logical," "rational," and even "necessary" in order to fulfill the apocalyptic presuppositions. As Edward Said noted shortly after the end of the war: "From early on there was an overriding sense of inevitability, as if George Bush's apparent need to get down there and, in his own sporty argot, "kick ass" *had* to run up against Saddam Hussein's monstrous aggressiveness. . . . The public rhetoric, in other words, is simply undeterred, uncomplicated by any considerations of detail, realism or cause and effect."[29] The temporality invoked here is precisely that of the apocalyptic. What Said seems to have failed to notice, or at least chooses not to mention, is that the deterministic, hyperbolized, eschatological language used by Bush was echoed in the discourses of those who opposed the war, and this may well have inadvertently led to a reinforcement—rather than an undermining—of the notion that this war was inevitable.

One should not, on the other hand, see this particular discourse as something essentially foreign to a number of discursive precedents familiar to the Iraqis themselves. Apocalyptic in this case is not an interpretive pattern exclusively imposed on a subaltern, colonized people from without. The Koran, still a primary source of cultural authority in the Islamic world just as the Bible is in the West, contains many suras that exploit eschatological imagery, compatible with the Islamic teaching that there will be a Last Day and a Final Judgment when all mankind will be called to account for their deeds on earth. One of the most intensely wrought and frequently quoted of these passages is in Sūra 81:

1) When the sun shall be wrapped up into a bundle
2) When the stars shall stoop like hawks from the heavens
3) When the mountains shall be set in motion
4) When the camels about to birth shall be left to wander alone, unattended
5) When the wild beasts come together in droves
6) When the seas shall spill over their banks
7) When the souls shall be coupled
8) When the baby girl buried alive shall be asked
9) For what sin she was killed
10) When the scrolls shall be unrolled
11) When the roof of heaven shall be stripped off
12) When the fires of hell shall be stirred to life
13) When the Garden shall draw near
14) The soul shall realize what it has brought.[30]

Vividly rendered scenes of destruction are here clearly coupled with references to a time of Judgment and a millennial return to Eden or Paradise, all themes familiar to anyone even minimally conversant with the apocalyptic prophecies of Christianity and Judaism, as a good portion of Muhammad's original audience undoubtedly was. These eschatological aspects of the Koran have tended to be de-emphasized by most later Islamic thinkers, however, in keeping with their emphasis on Islam as a life-affirming religion that concerned itself with people's relationships—with one another as well as with God—indelibly woven into the fabric of their existence in this world, as much as it did with their relationship solely to God in the next. Early Muslims generally emphasized a position that called for Islam to redress what was perceived as an imbalance in these relationships generated by the kind of monastic Christianity that flourished in the area prior to the rise of Islam. For them, the contemporary Christianity's fixation on the hereafter, and its tendency to consider achievement of a virtuous life in this world as an impossibility (at least without separation from the ordinary run of humanity by retreat into a monastery) represented an extreme of behavior that, if used as the basis for social formation, would impede the fashioning of the bonds needed to bind the group sharing religious beliefs (the *umma*, or "community") together, and might even eventually undermine the benefits that human society offered to the individual by undermining the presuppositions on which "society," as a concept, rested.

As with the evidence from nineteenth-century archaeological excavations in southern Iraq for Westerners, however, the Koran-created categories of apocalyptic could be seized upon by Muslims and exploited when the time was right. The invasion of Iraq by the Mongols in 1258 A.D., which resulted in the destruction of the city of Baghdad, the extermination of the Abbasid dynasty, and caused widespread havoc in the system of irrigation that supported agriculture in the Tigris–Euphrates valley, has been frequently portrayed in apocalyptic terms—in Arabic histories as well as in Western recountings of the events drawing upon those sources—as bringing utter destruction to the structures undergirding classical Arab/Islamic civilization. Similarly, in an even more specifically Iraqi context, the "triple tragedy" of 1831—when Baghdad was struck by an epidemic of plague, a flood, and the depredations of a punitive expedition sent by the Ottomans to depose one of their governors who had shown too many independent tendencies, all taking place in the space of scarcely more than a month—was deployed to account for the supposed backwardness of Iraqi economic and social development in the nineteenth century. The "triple tragedy" increasingly was portrayed as apocalyptic[31] because it was a convenient stand-in, in less detailed accounts of Iraqi history, for a complex array of factors that had made that country slower to appropriate Western technology than some of its neighbors, like Egypt and Syria. Thus apocalyptic was not only naturalized in the society where Sayyāb grew up, under the authoritative sign of the Koran, it was also underwritten and supported by some powerfully appealing readings of history.

More recently, it should perhaps not be surprising to find Saddam Hussein himself quite capable of appropriating certain echoes of these same apocalyptic categories during the Iran–Iraq war. Even as late as the speech he made at his last meeting with the U.S. ambassador before the invasion of Kuwait, he twice remarks that the Iraqis deserve special consideration from the United States and their other allies in the region because they shed "rivers of blood," during the Iran–Iraq war. This reference fits quite comfortably within the lexicon of apocalyptic imagery, whether of the biblical or the Koranic variety.

Had Badr Shākir al-Sayyāb lived long enough to have seen how deeply the Iran–Iraq war and, more especially, the Gulf war would inscribe the apocalyptic upon the landscape of his beloved southern Iraq and its inhabitants, he probably would have been troubled, but it is unlikely that he would have been surprised. More than once he had written that very same narrative into his own work. For example, in one of the few public lectures he gave during his lifetime outlining his concept of poetry and the role of the poet in society, he begins by saying that what distinguishes the poet of modernity from his predecessors is precisely his resemblance to Saint John the Divine, the author of the Book of Revelation in the Bible. Like Saint John, in Sayyab's opinion, the modern poet's "eyes have been ravaged by his visions and he perceives the seven sins pervading the world like a terrifying monster."[32] In his bold use of such a comparison, there can be no more direct evidence of precisely how important the apocalyptic categories could be for Sayyāb, especially as they underwrite his concept of the poet as inspired visionary, one that would be familiar to most students of Western romanticism.

Given this context, one should give special attention to the fact that Sayyāb's first widely recognized poem, "Unshūdat al-Maṭar" (Hymn of the Rain)—still considered by many to be among his best—contains the following lines:

> 53) I can almost hear Iraq storing up the thunder
> 54) And massing the lightning in the mountains and the plains,
> 55) Until, when men tear away their seal
> 56) The winds from Thamud will not leave
> 57) Any trace in the valley.[33]

According to Sayyāb himself, the poem was written early in 1953 when he was living temporarily in Kuwait as a political exile.[34] He was being sought by the Iraqi police for his role in demonstrations that had broken out late in 1952. These were aimed at toppling the Iraqi government, which had just signed a treaty with Britain allowing that country to keep troops indefinitely on Iraqi soil and to maintain its special rights and privileges, particularly those related to the oil industry, upon which Britain had grown increasingly dependent in the postwar years. These demonstrations and riots had failed to topple the British-supported regime of Nūrī al-Sa'īd, as had a similar outbreak in 1948, but hundreds had been arrested, and hundreds more, like Sayyāb, were being sought.

In "Hymn of the Rain" the speaker[35] is represented as standing on the shore of the Persian Gulf, looking northward to Iraq. He is racked with despair over what he sees as the failure of his fellow Iraqis to achieve real freedom, and he has a vision of them trapped in an eternal sterile seasonal cycle where the superficial change from winter to spring brings in reality only the endless recurrence of repression and famine as their harvest is taken from them by oppressors. He then imagines the apocalyptic scenario just quoted as an alternative temporality, one where the destruction of the apocalypse would lead to a final and permanent "spring," when social justice would prevail.

The specific imagery of the passage relies heavily on apocalyptic discourse as it appears in the Koran. This is signaled most explicitly by the mention of "Thamūd," which was a pre-Islamic tribe destroyed by God for refusing to listen to a prophet who was sent to them. Sayyāb's use of the allusion, however, has two features particularly worth mentioning as distinguishing it from the typical apocalyptic eschatology that is at the core of these scenarios in the Bible and the Koran. First, the punishment story of Thamūd refers not to an event at the end of history, but something very early in history—preceding the appearance of Islam. Thus it is not concerned with the universal end of all things, but posits a time beyond that end, potentially a time of new beginnings. Sayyāb's stress on this can be seen even more clearly in some of his later poetry, like "Madīna Bi-lā Maṭar" (City Without Rain, 1958), where he depicts the impending destruction of the city of Babylon (standing in for modern-day Baghdad, which is located close to the site of ancient Babylon), but the apocalyptic scenario is short-circuited by the bold appropriative gesture made by a young girl in a procession of children who have come to pray to Ishtar for intercession

73) And the sky flashed lightning, as though a lily of fire
74) Was opening above Babylon and illuminating our valley.
75) A glow penetrated to the depths of our land, and stripped it bare,
76) With all its seeds and roots, with all its dead.
77) And clouds—beyond the walls and ramparts Babylon had raised
78) Around its fever and around its thirsty soil—
79) Were pouring down rain—if not for those walls, they would have
quenched our thirst!
80) In the eternity of listening between one thunderbolt and the next
81) We heard, not the rustling of palm tree under a torrential cloudburst
82) Or the wind whispering among the wet trees
83) But the pounding of hands and feet
84) A murmur, and the "Ah!" of a little girl as she seized with her right
hand
85) Upon a moon fluttering like a moth, or upon a star,
86) Upon a gift from the cloud,
87) Upon a tremor of water, a drop in which a breeze whispered,
88) So that we may know that Babylon will be cleansed of its sins![36]

With this last line of the poem and the mention of "cleansing sins," the signifier "Babylon" is suddenly revealed as "overdetermined," acting as a referent pointing to more than one discursive formation. It has links both to the overt coding of "ancient world" Babylon, where the fertility religions that form the poem's ostensible subject were practiced, and to "Babylon, the whore" found in Revelation. The "whore" element of sin, further, is precisely negated by the gesture of the "innocent" young girl, which converts the "destructive torrent" of apocalyptic coding into the "cleansing water drop" that will bring new life. Thus there is a time beyond the destruction: the time of real (but final) rebirth that is tied neither to the inexorable teleology of linear human time nor to the unvarying—and therefore ultimately sterile—cycle of seasonal time, which brings rebirth in the spring only to have it snatched away by death in the winter.

Such millennialism contrasts with the kind of reading of apocalyptic that many observers have found increasingly prevalent in popular Western culture of the late twentieth century, where the emphasis in apocalypse—undoubtedly influenced by the desacralized representations of a nuclear holocaust—is placed on the catastrophe itself, the finality of the end, with no millennial expectations allowed. As Christopher Sharrett, in speaking of filmic representations of the apocalyptic genre, says, "the apocalypse of postmodernity is almost always couched in that popular misuse of apocalypse not as revelation[37] but doomsday, disaster, the end."[38]

This way of realizing apocalyptic categories has had—and continues to have—a powerful influence on current Western, and especially American, conceptualizations of Iraq. One such representation, that has formed a kind of counterpoint to my own work in writing and revising this chapter in the early months of 1995, is a PBS announcement that is part of a series—scheduled, fortuitously or not, just in time to influence the current debate in Congress over the funding of the PBS corporation—highlighting the achievements and importance of public television in providing material for public viewing that would be otherwise inaccessible because commercial television networks would not provide it (each spot ends with the sentence displayed on the screen: "If PBS doesn't do it, who will?"). There are a number of installments dealing with relatively unproblematic PBS documentary portrayals of famous American individuals and events: the Civil War ("PBS: Historian"), Amelia Earhart ("PBS: Storyteller"—"She was missing for over fifty years. Only PBS could bring her back the way she really was . . ."), Lou Gehrig ("PBS: Observer of the American Scene").

But for the piece devoted to highlighting the achievements of the MacNeil-Lehrer News Hour, the "jewel in the crown" of the network's public affairs programming, the creators of the campaign have chosen to focus on Iraq. After a brief silence—during which the phrases "PBS—Journalist" and "Dateline: Iraq 1994" do a slow crawl across the screen—the familiar, comforting, vaguely southern American drawl of Jim Lehrer begins with his formulaic phrase that signals the end of the newscast: "Finally, tonight . . ." Usually this signals the transition to an "essay piece" by Roger Rosenblatt or Ann Taylor Fleming, planned to give the viewer a chance to ruminate thoughtfully on the deeper meaning of life. But this time Lehrer continues with ". . . the story of the Shia Muslims of Iraq. They tried to declare their independence from the Saddam Hussein regime in Baghdad." The visuals accompanying this narration are of a desert landscape dotted with crumpled, wrecked military vehicles, tanks and armored personnel carriers, and scattered, slowly burning fires, all surrounding a sleek black plastic television set, perched on a pedestal of similar texture and color, planted incongruously together on the crest of a sand dune. The camera pulls back to show us another perspective of the television set, this time seen through the holes of camouflage netting draped over an empty Bedouin tent. All the while, the soundtrack carries a recording of what seems to be Iraqi folk music that has apparently been distorted to emphasize its resemblance to the sound of the incoherent screams of women in terror. The pictures have likewise apparently been enhanced to heighten the purity and flatness of the colors: the sky is bluer, the sand is yellower or more orange, the fires are redder than our ordinary visual perception of them would be. The narrative voice then shifts to that of the correspondent, who continues "Saddam's republican guard and their tanks had been left intact by the allies. In the end the rebels were hopelessly outgunned. There were no TV cameras there to record what happened. Only this extraordinary amateur videotape taken by two brothers, one of whom was later killed. Most of these people are about to die . . . desperate women and children can only call upon God to help them. . . . This casual brutality has been justified by the Iraqi dictator throughout his career in politics. . . ." The key point here is that, although the report itself seems to have focused on individual Iraqis as human beings, the packaging, or "wrapping,"—to use an important postmodernist term—denies the humanity of these people and makes the centerpiece a barren apocalyptic landscape where Saddam Hussein is the only recognizably human figure to appear on the television screen. This is "doomsday apocalypse" with a vengeance. To put it in other words, and perhaps somewhat crudely, this representation, so glossily packaged as a cultural commodity for the American television viewer's consumption, portrays the "story" of southern Iraq as one that is basically over, finished. There is, the pictures imply, no point in paying further attention to it, because there is nothing left there to save. The irony is that such a reductive visual interpretation of these events directly contradicts the overt message of the advertising campaign—that PBS is the only broadcaster who goes beyond sensationalism to do the in-depth research that will provide the "real story"—and probably violates the humanistic values of those who sponsored it. But such is the power of apocalyptic discourse to shape, perhaps more unconsciously and deterministically than any other, our perceptions of our world.

If the conceptualization of time in Sayyāb's apocalyptic, with its emphasis on the millennial, is able to sidestep provisionally the "ultimate destruction" scenario found in Western apocalyptic readings of the Iraqi landscape, like that found in the PBS announcement, the picture of apocalyptic presented in those lines taken from "Hymn of the Rain" also has a second interesting feature that works against the grain of traditional apocalyptic. In that poem, it is man—not God—who "tears the seal" and unleashes the wind. While this kind of focus on the human may appear, especially when used in conjunction with "atom bomb" scenarios, to heighten the pessimistic prognostications of "doomsday," here, when conjoined with a millennial vision, the privileging of human agency over divine in fact works to lessen the deterministic inexorability of traditional apocalyptic, where man is usually portrayed as the passive victim of another's (in traditional apocalyptic, God's) actions, incapable of mounting any successful resistance to it. Both these features suggest that Sayyāb tends to use apocalyptic imagery in a framework that—beyond its interest in the millennial, postapocalyptic period as a time of idealized redemption—has many features in common with what has been called "prophetic eschatology." This is important because it links this set of tropes to Sayyāb's frequently reiterated concern with the prophetic experience as a model for producing poetry, probably the most stable and lasting framework found in the various conceptions of poetry he sketched out at different points in his career.

An important difference that distinguishes prophetic eschatology from true apocalyptic is what one author has called its "implied 'if-clause,'"—in other words, the destruction only proceeds after and because humanity has failed to heed the prophet's warning.[39] The catastrophe is not posited as inevitable, and the discourse therefore places much more emphasis on humanity as a force that may intervene in history. Attention to the agency of the Iraqi people as an active subject position in the unfolding of the historical process—and more particularly the various strategies, besides armed struggle, that they might use to enact this—is precisely what is missing from Western apocalyptic discourse that purports to construct southern Iraq and its inhabitants as an object of representation. This too should be seen as an element working to simplify the "doomsday" reading and give it a tidy, but false, impression of totality.

Sayyāb's version of apocalyptic, of course, precedes the final formulation of "apocalyptic Iraq" in the American media by several decades. So it cannot be properly considered as a response to the limiting conditions the later formulation the latter imposes. Yet the fact that Sayyāb's version has status as a *discourse*—a construct of words not necessarily bound to remain enmeshed within the modes of power relations in a particular epoch or social body—means that it can be seized upon and redeployed at any time (as, in a sense, I am doing here) to form what might be termed a "*counter*-discourse"[40] designed to critique or resist those discourses encapsulating the epistemes of more dominant centers of power. In fact, it might be difficult for any contemporary reader in the Arab world who is exposed to American attitudes through CNN or other satellite news services to read Sayyāb's apocalyptic poetry now as anything but a discourse that counters—or at least provides an alternative to—the Western media images.

That the exercise of power begets resistance would seem to be a concept rather easily retrievable from any examination of the relationships between social or political groupings. Yet even Foucault, for all his study of the deployments of power within institutional structures and across the levels of social hierarchy, by his own account only slowly came to recognize its importance for his analyses. For a long time, he says, he analyzed power within what he calls a "domination-repression or war-repression schema,"[41] which imposed a reductive, dualistic framework (probably conditioned by the paradigms of binary opposition found in classical structuralist thought) on what was generally a much more complex process. It was only in his later work, from the late 1970s and early 1980s, that he begins to look at power as something that "circulates" and is in constant flux as it moves through the temporal and spatial matrix. As he says in a key passage from this period:

> . . . power is co-extensive with the social body; there are no spaces of primal liberty between the meshes of its network. . . . [yet] one should not assume a massive and primal condition of domination, a binary structure with

> "dominators" on one side and "dominated" on the other, but rather a multiform production of relations of domination which are partially susceptible of integration into overall strategies. . . . there are no relations of power without resistances; the latter are all the more real and effective because they are formed right at the point where relations of power are exercised; resistance to power does not have to come from elsewhere to be real, nor is it inexorably frustrated through being the compatriot of power. It exists all the more by being in the same place as power; hence, like power, resistance is multiple and can be integrated in global strategies.[42]

Such notions of power/knowledge and resistance/counter-knowledge have been immensely helpful as an essential condition of possibility for much of the analysis that has recently been attempted of colonial and postcolonial literatures.[43] What emerges from these examinations is that literature in a colonized society is compelled at least in part to organize itself as a "counter-discourse" to the colonial project, to take that very intrusive "reality" into account. Seen in this way, then, many of its recurrent themes—as we have observed in the case of geographical projections and assertions of control over the land—reveal themselves as not being contingent or accidental (as they are not infrequently portrayed), but possessed of a very real and strategic value. Such strategies are of necessity opportunistic (in the sense of taking advantage of the opportunities for resistance/critique that are made available) and practical, rather than striving for theoretical precision and cohesiveness, which makes them more susceptible to charges of contingency, haphazardness, than might otherwise be the case. But then theoretical precision may be, in fact, the privilege mainly of those whose identity and perhaps even their very existence are not at stake in a given struggle. In the next three chapters I will suggest several ways in which Sayyāb's poetry may be seen as providing examples for such use of opportunistic counter-discourses to directly oppose the colonial discourses of place.

CHAPTER TWO

This Other Eden

So on he fares, and to the border comes
Of Eden, where delicious Paradise,
Now nearer, crowns with her enclosure green,
As with a rural mound, the champaign head
Of a steep wilderness, whose hairy sides
With thicket overgrown, grotesque and wild,
Access denied . . .
. . . Yet higher than their tops
The verdurous wall of Paradise up sprung;
Which to our general sire gave prospect large
Into his nether empire neighboring round.
—Milton, *Paradise Lost*

If Sayyāb's reading of apocalypse is only fortuitously available to be used directly as a counter-discourse to much later Western projections of the eschatological paradigms, he deploys in his work several other significant strategies for reading the landscape of southern Iraq in ways that can be seen as much more specifically responsive to the Western hegemonic discourses of his time. Probably the most ubiquitous—and yet very seldom commented upon—of these strategies is what one might term an "Eden discourse."

I have already drawn attention to the fact that Westerners have consistently used Biblical paradigms as a framework for reading Iraq's landscape and often for justifying their presence there (as the true inheritors of the values of Biblical culture)—that is, when Iraq was not simply for them a "blank spot" waiting to be mapped. An astonishing amount of nineteenth-century archaeology in the Middle East seems to have been driven by the desire to produce restored historical spaces to serve as backdrops where familiar Biblical stories could be re-staged as a kind of theatrical spectacle in the observer's imagination. But of them all, the search for a suitable backdrop in Iraq for the Eden story (constructed for the most part out of the Biblical identification of the Euphrates as one of the four rivers originating in Paradise)[1] was probably the most imaginatively enticing, if one takes as an index the sheer amount of space devoted in traveler's accounts and descriptive sketches of the country to speculations about its location. The following passage from Donald Maxwell's *A Dweller in Mesopotamia* takes as its point of departure the typical intermingling of travel description and allusions to the story of Eden found in such works:

> The backwaters, creeks and sidechannels of both [the Tigris and Euphrates] are exceedingly beautiful, and here one can get a glimpse of the fertility that must have belonged to Mesopotamia when it was a network of streams and when the forests abounded within its borders. Centuries of neglect and the blight of the unspeakable Turk have dealt hardly with this country. It is indeed a Paradise Lost and it will be many a long day before it is Paradise Regained.
>
> A beginning, however, has been made. Our army of occupation includes "irrigation officers," and gradually the work of watering the country is extending. . . . The chief difficulty does not seem to be that of making the desert blossom as the rose, but that of causing the waste places to be inhabited. What the Babylonians with slave labour could do, modern machinery and science can quite easily achieve; but the difficulty of finding sufficient people to live in this resuscitated Eden will be great. Mesopotamia is not a white man's country. India would appear to the direction in which to look for colonists, but it is an unfortunate fact that the Arab does not like the Indian and the Indian does not like the Arab. Sooner or later there would be trouble.[2]

Note how easily the discourse here is deflected from discussion of Eden (activated by allusion to Milton's epic poems, so that the literary connection is made quite specific) to the question of settler colonialism. Maxwell may be slightly unusual in the frankness with which he conflates Eden and the colonial, but the passage's masterful deployment of metonymic slippage is none the less disarming for that. It can hold its own in its persuasive strategy against other such speculative passages that often press their claims by more oblique appeals to what eventually becomes the more well-worn topos of colonial travel writing about Iraq, one based on an antithesis that evokes the magnitude and spectacularly catastrophic effect of the Fall of Adam and Eve through disingenuous comparisons of the poverty and wretched living conditions of the modern Iraqis dwelling outside the writer's window to the supposed grandeurs of the same landscape when it constituted the prelapsarian Paradise.[3]

Although there is no direct evidence Sayyāb ever saw this particular book, it would not have been impossible for him to have done so, especially during the period when he had access to the relatively well-stocked library of the Baghdad Teacher's College where he was majoring in English literature. Nor would he have had much trouble decoding a passage like Maxwell's for, as we saw earlier with apocalyptic, the general outlines of the Edenic narrative are shared by both Bible and Koran. In particular, the key structural elements that attribute the cause of the Fall to Adam and Eve's disobedience to God's command not to eat from one of the trees in the Garden and the proximate cause of this disobedience being a deception on the part of Satan are to be found in both. And even the Miltonic allusions might not have given him too much trouble, for in 1950, he would begin a poem (eventually left abandoned unfinished and only rediscovered after his death) designed to retell Milton's *Paradise Lost* from an Iraqi perspective, which shows he must have had some familiarity with the original work. He gave this epic-length poem the working title of *Al-La'anāt* (*Curses*).

It is difficult to summarize the poem as it stands, for there are many gaps in its development that were obviously intended to be filled in later. The fragments that remain comprise a series of unconnected scenes focusing on the figure of Satan and give us little sense of what the finished whole might have been. What is clear, however, is that Milton is the poet's model. Not only are the telltale elements of the Miltonic grand style with its convoluted syntax, its vertiginous landscapes that marry unsettling ascents to equally dizzying descents, its somber mixing of light and darkness all there, but also the very characters, like Beelzebub and the other devils, as well as the famous type-scenes, such as the descent into hell and the council in the mountains, which are so memorably limned in *Paradise Lost*. The following passage, describing Satan's journey with his minions to gaze upon the earth overlooking Eden and take council upon a mountain in northern Iraq called Mt. Shīrīn, gives some idea of the character of Sayyāb's poem:

170) Shīrīn rose into the darkness—you might have thought it piles of clouds covering the side of the valley.
171) The ice had forged for it a crown, its pearls the shepherds' fire and the reflection of a quiet star.
172) And the wind clattered, wailing in its caverns like the one who cries for succor, having been bound in chains.
173) And phantoms blocked the eastern horizon black, like dead men who have risen before their time.

174) Then they came down, and from them dissolved the gloom of night mixed with them, taking on bodily forms,
175) Until they settled on Shīrīn and stood upon these peaks in Kurdish dress,
176) And Iblīs strutted in a robe, its colors blood red, coveted by every executioner,
177) And said: "O company of Jinn, turn in any direction you would seek to raid, and leave me with my leaders."

***

178) Then he bent down, drawing a picture of the world with his finger upon the ice, erasing it[s lines], smiling,
179) Until it settled in a [particular] form, then he colored it with fire from his eyes, staring as it burst into flame,
180) He did not cease for a moment, with the palm of his hand combing through the dirt, whispering: "I will take revenge!"
181) Once, he touched Greece, alight with rage he stared at Beelzebub, or glowered angrily
182) Then Beelzebub said: "Indeed the stars have gone out behind the mountains and the peaks are almost sparkling with light,
183) So let us anticipate the dawn, before its advent let us carry out the necessary conversation, painful though it be.
184) Look to China, the widening skies are darkened flame and blood fills the deserts and the fields . . ."[4]

Although the argument in this part of the poem is difficult to follow because it is so fragmentary, it appears that here the action of *Paradise Lost* has been projected beyond that earlier poem's completion into the present day, and Satan has decided to take revenge upon Adam's descendants for his earlier humiliating defeat at the hands of God in *Paradise Lost*, since he cannot after his devastating defeat hope to attack God directly. Thus he descends onto Mt. Shirīn to look upon the world from its height (which would conveniently also open the site of Eden in southern Iraq to his gaze) and take counsel with his lieutenants, like the demon Beelzebub, in order to coordinate the forces opposed to the popular revolutions occurring in Greece and China during the late 1940s. He gathers his troops to lead them into battle, and that is where the poem breaks off.

The references to an Iraqi setting for this scene of poem, as well as its valorization of the civil war in Greece and the revolution in China, give an indication of just how much this work is conceived as a counter-discourse to the practices of Western hegemony in general and the anti-Communist rhetoric of the cold war in particular. The uncanny thoroughness with which

Sayyāb surveys the characteristic turns of colonial strategies of containment, like the "mapping" practices I outlined in chapter 1 of this study, can be seen in the lines where he has his Satan perform that identical cartographic gesture as he gazes down upon the earth, drawing in boundaries with his fingertip. This act cannot help but recall to mind Homi Bhabha's description of the disturbing practice he has called "colonial mimicry": a representation "*that is almost the same but not quite*," which exposes to view the ambivalences and uncertainties engendered from the realization that, "in 'normalizing' the colonial state or subject, the dream of post-Enlightenment civility alienates its own language of liberty and produces another knowledge of its norms."[5] The fathering of this gesture upon Sayyāb's/Milton's Satan exposes the seemingly innocent procedure of mapping, or the drawing and redrawing of boundaries, as a practice shot through with illegitimate desires for power and control.

"Curses," in many ways, but most noticeably through its deployment of light/dark imagery to describe a landscape of universal war and destruction, can be seen as having vague links to apocalyptic scenarios. But "Eden discourse" proper also has even more direct links to apocalyptic, especially millennialist versions of apocalyptic, where the portion of humanity judged favorably on the Day of Judgment, it is promised, will be restored to the original Garden of Paradise. Eden can thus stand at both the origin point of the biblical master narrative of human destiny and at the point beyond the End as well. Sayyāb, in some of his best poetry, activates this apocalyptic connection of Eden and does not hesitate to deploy it directly as a counter-discourse to oppose colonialist claims that, with their irrigation projects and agricultural schemes, they were restoring Iraq to its original Edenic condition, as the following lines from "Hymn of the Rain" show:

> And since we were little, the heavens
> Have grown dark with misty clouds in the winter
> And the rain would pour down,
> And every year—when the earth grew green with grass—we hungered
> Not one year passed when there was no hunger in Iraq.
> Rain . . .
> Rain . . .
> Rain . . .
> . . . .
>
> And in Iraq a thousand serpents drink the nectar
> From a flower the Euphrates fed on dew.[6]

Here, in the same poem where he so notably deployed apocalyptic language to project his desire for a remission from the purposeless cyclical temporality dominant in his world, Sayyāb turns to describe the more dismal aspects of life current in that world, using a move belonging to the same kind of disjunctive framework found in Western descriptions of Edenic Iraq such as the one referenced above, but this time asserting a contrastive claim. First, the winter rains are depicted to show that the fertility of the land is not at issue—there is nothing here that needs to be restored. The problem, then, lies elsewhere, and it becomes the poet's job to show us where. Sayyāb does this by having his speaker allude to an element that is generally notable by its absence from those Western accounts he is reacting to: the serpent. The evil intruder into Adam and Eve's original bliss in Paradise is, of course, Satan disguised as a serpent and in these lines—coming as they do just after a passage where the people of Iraq were depicted as being robbed by scavenging "crows and locusts"—Sayyāb seems to be reminding us of that particularly effective form of exploitation, which draws its strength from colonial distortions of social relations, and equating these intrusions of colonial power to this serpent figure. Such reworkings of familiar stories in order to show how their structurings have been manipulated in the interests of power is a well-known strategy in colonial writings—from reversals of Shakespeare's *The Tempest* so that it is presented from the viewpoint of Caliban[7] to retellings of *Heart of Darkness* from a "native" viewpoint such as we find in the Sudanese novelist Al-Ṭayyib Ṣāliḥ's *Season of Migration to the North.* Arab writers have found themselves particularly well-positioned to exploit such strategies of inversion, or the even more dangerous ones—because covert—of supplementation,[8] since the Western and Islamic social worlds share so many of the inherited legitimating cultural narratives on which literary works inevitably draw for their power to move or persuade us, both because of the similarity of their respective scriptures and through their joint reliance on material from the classical heritage of Antiquity, especially the Greek.

Sayyāb's use of the serpent image here, however, appears to be aimed at more than just demonstrating the intruder status of the colonizer. As he presents it in this poem, then, it also exposes the fact that they are there and doing what they are doing in order to gain advantage for themselves, to "suck the dew" and not for the lofty purposes of restoring Paradise or aiding those less fortunate than themselves, as official colonial discourse so often advertised. If Sayyāb's deployment of tropes here seems crude and overly assertive, it should be remembered that it is here enacting a response to a vast body of colonial writing that was equally unsubtle and lacking in nuance. It is also worth recalling that to quote out of context, as I am doing here with these lines, inevitably vitiates the power inherent in the combination of topoi that work together to make up the totality of the poem.[9]

Sayyāb's evocation of Eden discourse in his work from the late 1950s and early 1960s, however, most often and most characteristically focuses on representations of his native village of Jaykūr. In one of his most sweeping attempts to sketch out the parameters of this Edenic Jaykūr, Sayyāb asserts the erasure of all boundaries between himself and the place, even to the point of transgressing the fiction of the division between the real poet and the speaker in the poem, who in this case is quite explicitly labeled as Jesus (the title of the poem is "Christ After the Crucifixion"):

12) Whenever the orange and the mulberry blossom,
13) When Jaykūr stretches out to the limits of the imagination
14) When it turns green as grass, its rich smells singing,
15) With the suns which have nourished it in their splendor,
16) When even its starless night turns green,
17) Warmth touches my heart; my blood runs within its soil.[10]

This unhindered and seemingly unstudied melding of self with landscape, however, is something that Sayyab presents in most of his poetry as at best only a temporary possibility. More often, the Edenic Jaykūr is a place that lies just beyond his reach, as in the 1958 poem "Jaykūr and the City":

63) And Jaykūr is green
64) The first rays of sunset have touched
65) The crests of the palm trees there
66) With sad light.
67) And my path there was like the trail of a lightning bolt in the sky,
68) It appeared and vanished abruptly, then the light returned and set the sky aflame until it lit up the entire city
69) And stripped my hand behind the bandage bare, as though the wounds there were fires.
70) And Jaykūr: before it, ramparts have risen
71) And a great gate
72) And a silence has wrapped it round.
73) Who will breach the wall? Who will open the gate, bloodying his right hand on every bolt?
74) My right hand is no talon [fit] for the struggle, though I strive with it in the city streets
75) Nor a powerful fist [fit] to resurrect life from the clay

76) It is only a piece of clay [itself].
77) And Jaykūr: before it, ramparts have risen
78) And a great gate
79) And a silence has wrapped it round.[11]

Here Jaykūr, for all its beauty, is sundered from the poet by "ramparts" and "a silence" that "has wrapped it round," just as Adam and Eve are barred from entering the original Garden of Eden after the Fall, in both the biblical and the Koranic versions of the story. But even such a provisional and problematic identification of landscape and the generative power of life is only possible, of course, if one proceeds from a very different starting point than the visualization of southern Iraq as barren desert wasteland, the one seemingly now permanently consecrated in the Western media.

One mundane basis for this alternate "truth" about the Iraqi landscape is that, particularly along the rivers, it has always provided the observer with vistas of incredible richness and fertility. The Shaṭṭ al-'Arab area is threaded by a network of small creeks and canals (according to some estimates, more than 600),[12] whose banks are overgrown with fruit trees and groves of date palms growing semiwild (most of the world's date crop comes from southern Iraq, although grapes, oranges, pomegranates, apples, watermelons, vegetables, and rice are also extensively cultivated). Not infrequently we find coupled to this another persistent descriptive trope, whose appearance may seem initially quite surprising, whereby Basra itself was often compared by travelers to the Italian city of Venice, because of its canals and the distinctive high-prowed boats (called bellams) used for local transport. This figure of maritime activity occasionally debouches into reminiscences of the city's most famous citizen: Sindbād the Sailor, that most popular of characters from *A Thousand and One Nights*.

The power of such images to shape perceptions of the landscape before the inscription of apocalyptic on its lineaments obliterated all but the faintest traces of them is perhaps best brought out in the following short paragraph from a report written in the mid-1930s outlining British plans for the development of the port of Basra. In the midst of a discussion about dredging dues, wharfage fees, and the construction of new cranes, warehouses, and a new airfield, the author, who up to this point has consistently demonstrated the prosaic soul of a mid-level colonial bureaucrat, suddenly pauses to say:

> The approaches to the Port of Basrah are very picturesque, the whole course of the river running through dense date palm groves on both banks, the trees and foliage creating a setting difficult to surpass in beauty. These date belts,

> extending well inland from the river, are irrigated by a vast number of canals or creeks.
>
> The frequent references made to Basrah as the "Venice of the East" is attributable to these sylvan creeks, whose still waters reflect the splendor of the beauty that adorns their banks, under the canopy of the bluest skies; likewise to the bellum, or local craft, that navigates these waters, which is very similar in appearance to the Venetian gondola itself.[13]

Such vistas of natural abundance formed the backdrop to Sayyāb's youth, not the deserts and wastes familiar from television footage of military operations during the Gulf war.

There were, however, particular fault lines within the internal discourse of Sayyāb's cultural milieu that tended to push him more decisively in the direction of an "Eden discourse"—rather than, say, a Venetian one, with its echoes of mercantile adventuring and sophisticated cynicism overlaid with a veneer of civilized refinement—when speaking of southern Iraq. First, and probably most mundane, though nevertheless not without a certain providential cogency, is the fact that local tradition holds that the original site of Eden (complete with a withered stump said to be that of the Tree of Knowledge) is located only one hundred miles north of Basra, at the town of Qurna where the Tigris and Euphrates join. But a more irreducible authority is imparted by the Koranic use of Eden discourse. As I noted earlier, the narrative of Adam and Eve—their temptation by Satan, their fall, and their expulsion from Paradise, from which they are then barred—is as much a part of Islamic religious tradition as it is Jewish or Christian. The similarity of the story in all three monotheistic religions guarantees that it comes to represent many of the same tensions and conflicts, no matter which source text is used.

One such tension in Edenic discourse, as we have seen in examining his Miltonic experiment, seems to have found for Sayyāb an early localization in the problem of boundaries, of a separation of Eden from the speaker and the consequently growing awareness of power as a policing and limiting factor, but also—strangely and conversely—as the place where "crossing over" and transcendence becomes possible.[14] If "boundary" has become a privileged term in colonial and postcolonial writing (as well as in the criticism that attempts to chart the course of that writing), it is precisely because of this double nature it possesses, its unusual suitability to deal with questions of self and other, or ambivalent assertions of repetition and difference. And Iraq is a land where numerous projects of conquest, allied or not with colonial designs, have washed up and left traces of their passing, like layers of sediment, so it should perhaps not be unexpected to find that boundary language had become part of the circulating discourse of Iraqi life, long before the transgression of that vital, yet invisible ("a line drawn in the sand") boundary, the one with Kuwait, took place.

For centuries the operative boundary that determined "Iraqiness" for writers, both local and farther afield, arose from the perception that it stood on a map line that divided two empires: the Ottoman Turkish and the Safavi/Qajari Persian. Iraq, after 1516 when it was first conquered by the Ottomans, thus found itself "on the margins," far from the centers of power. There is a sharp contrast between this view of Iraq and the older medieval Islamic ones, where it—and especially its cities of Baghdad and Basra—was portrayed as a center of civilization and culture. Baghdad had been founded by the Abbasid caliphs at the height of their wealth and power to be their capital. It rose upon the river banks as a planned city, perfectly round in shape with the caliphal palace at the center, its buildings all newly constructed but built, many of them, out of bricks salvaged (quite fittingly or so it would seem) from the nearby ruins of the last Sassanian capital at Ctesiphon: a self-conscious proclamation of the power of this rising dynasty over the heartland of the civilized world of antiquity.[15]

Basra, though never an imperial capital on the scale of Baghdad, was nevertheless the first place where an educational style and culture that could legitimately be called "Islamic" in the syncretistic sense appears. Many of the major literary figures attached to the 'Abbasid caliphal court began life and attained most of their education in Basra—poets like Abū Nuwās, prose writers like al-Jāhiẓ. But by the 1500s, Basra had shrunk to the size of a city of probably considerably less than 50,000 in population, at most a regional center of culture and commerce. This reversal was not infrequently contrasted, in both late medieval and contemporary chronicles, with its condition in the first centuries of Islam when it had been, in addition to its status as a center for learning, both an important military hub and a trading entrepôt of considerable significance, having become the new terminus of the ancient spice route with India and points farther east after the Islamic conquests.

This new perception of marginality was reinforced, after the fall of Baghdad in 1258 A.D., by the fact that Iraq underwent a renomadization during the succeeding centuries, with Bedouin tribes moving in successive waves up from the Arabian peninsula to settle in parts of the land that, though they could no longer support agriculture, were certainly better suited than the high deserts of central Arabia for pasturing herds of sheep, goats, and camels. Added to this was the fact that, during the sixteenth century, the province changed hands several times between the two empires. Even after the 1700s, when it was no longer actively pulled into the Persian empire's political orbit, a policy of de facto decentralization pursued by the Ottoman dynasty meant that the real rulers of Iraq were local Mameluk soldiers and the Ottoman governor, if one was even appointed, had only nominal suzerainty. The strong local governments in Iraq during this period, with their dispensation of patronage to literary figures willing to underwrite their rule, ensured that cultural life (which was in the Islamic world as elsewhere in the ages before the spread of the printing press and the rise of the publishing industry, intimately dependent on wealthy patrons) took on a special internally responsive dynamic, one that tended to give it extra support beyond what might otherwise have been the case. It also enhanced, however, a sense of provincialism that grew to be a problem among Iraqis: they saw themselves as only distantly affiliated with the new metropolitan center in Istanbul. This distancing effect was reinforced when, in the late nineteenth and early twentieth centuries, there was a conscious attempt—in conjunction with certain important political changes—to revive Arabic as a literary language suitable for intellectual commerce among the elite in areas outside religion (where it had always reigned supreme), and to install "Arab" (as opposed to "Ottoman" or "Islamic") culture as a primary source of identity for Iraqis, because the first centers of this modern revival movement were in Cairo and Beirut, not Baghdad.

Yet this idea of being on the border or boundary was in the case of Iraq a strangely unstable one that has always participated in a system of endless qualification. Freya Stark, though her writing must always be filtered through an acknowledgment that she was an Orientalist and agent of the British government in Iraq during World War II, seems to have identified strongly enough with her Iraqi acquaintances among the literati to sum up very succinctly and with an inimitable rhetorical skill this not entirely conscious ambivalence, which is reproduced elsewhere in their writings in much the same form, though considerably more diffusely:[16]

> . . . while Egypt lies parallel and peaceful to the routes of human traffic, Iraq is from earliest times a frontier province, right-angle and obnoxious to the predestined paths of man. Wave after wave, from the hills of the East, from the seas of the South, from the sands of the West, meet and break here, struggle, sink, settle and dissolve, subdued to the enduring forces of geography and climate. Sumerian, Elamite and Kassite, Assyrian and Babylonian: we are not concerned with these. But with the wave of Islam,

> which in its early years broke and transcended the Sassanian barrier; which overflowed the Iranian plateau to distant Khorasan and then retreated, mingled and altered forever, so that no definite line can ever now be drawn where the Arabian and Iranian end—with this we are concerned, for it provides the most interesting characteristic of Iraq to-day.
>
> No definite border exists now between the Islam of Arabia and Iran: but the border land is the land of Iraq.[17]

What Stark seems to be reacting to here most strongly is the perception that, if there had been for centuries a political boundary, more or less corresponding to the Shaṭṭ al-'Arab waterway, dividing two empires whose ruling dynasties portrayed themselves and their people as being different in important ways—religiously, as Shī'ī vs. Sunnī, linguistically and culturally, as Persian-speaking vs. Turkish- or Arabic-speaking—the boundaries between these attributes of identity formation did not necessarily correspond well to the political divisions inscribed on the map. To take a relatively simple example, most of the population of southern Iraq, though Arabic-speaking, is Shī'ī, the confessional orientation in Islam most strongly identified with Persian-speaking Iranians ever since the Safavid Shāh Ismā'īl decreed it the state religion of his newly won Iranian empire at the beginning of the sixteenth century. Conversely, the Kurds of northern Iraq speak a language closely related to Persian, but are mostly Sunnīs. Combining these characteristics into a set of stereotypes led to the imposition of another set of coordinates and boundaries on the map of Iraq, the well-known (in the wake of the Gulf war, but conceptually operative long before) division of the land into three regions: the Kurdish north (with Mosul as its regional capitol), the Sunnī middle (centered on Baghdad) and the Shī'ī south (Basra being the metropole, with due respect paid to the Shī'ī religious and educational centers of Najaf and Karbalā'). As we shall see, these divisions tended to simplify and solidify in everyone's imagination networks of relationship that were in actuality much more fluid. A similarly artificial imaginative geography operated as well on the other side of the Shaṭṭ al-'Arab, in Iran, as Sayyāb himself would find when he fled there as a political refugee in the early 1950s. Although he himself did not know Persian, he did not in the end have to rely as much as he thought he would on the English manual *How to Learn Persian in Ten Days* that he packed in his suitcase. He found that the Iranian province immediately abutting the border (appropriately known as Arabistān) was full of Arabic speakers who were only too happy to interpret for him.[18]

When one moves from analysis of groups to the lives of individuals, the fissures that emerge on the apparently smooth surface of this discourse of boundaries become even more striking. A look at the backgrounds of the three greatest poets in the generation preceding Sayyāb's is instructive in this regard.

The oldest of the group was Jamīl Ṣidqī al-Zahāwī (1863–1936). His has been the reputation that has lost the most luster over time, and his poetry is seldom read today for more than historical interest. This is partly because his poems, full of repetitions and with a marked sing-song rhythm, relied on Zahāwī's famed pyrotechnic powers of oral delivery for much of their effectiveness. But another part of his loss in stature has surely been political. Although he wrote many poems on subjects that he perceived as being intellectually and socially progressive, or "liberal"—exposing the plight of the poor, supporting women's rights, even espousing in verse Darwin's theory of evolution—he also collaborated openly with the British after World War I, serving as their panegyrist on official occasions and making extensive contributions to their newspaper, *The Mesopotamian Times*, even serving briefly as its editor.[19] To the younger generation of Iraqi intellectuals, to which Sayyāb belonged, this collaboration was seen as especially self-serving, as al-Zahāwī had been active in Ottoman politics in Istanbul before the war, serving as a member in the Ottoman parliament from 1912,[20] and had often, at least outwardly, supported the reforms of the Young Turks.[21]

This was the Arabized and—to some extent—Europeanized Zahāwī who was a familiar figure on public rostrums and in Baghdad coffeehouses after the turn of the century. But the chronicles of the late nineteenth century reveal a very different Jamīl Sidqī al-Zahāwī: a young man who had been born into a famous family of Sunnī muftis that had come to Baghdad from a village in the north, near Kirkuk, though their family names seem to suggest a Persian origin.[22] This younger version of Zahāwī had been given an exacting and thorough classical Islamic education in Muslim law and theology at the hands of his father, chief muftī of Baghdad for thirty-eight years, and was adept at composing panegyric, congratulatory, and elegiac verse in all three of the Islamic high-culture languages, Arabic, Persian, or Turkish, as the occasion demanded. Thus we see him darting in and out of the events described on the pages of 'Azzāwī's chronicle of the Ottoman period in Iraq, on one occasion inaugurating the construction of a new dam on the river with a poem in "beautiful Arabic,"[23] shortly after having welcomed the new Ottoman governor to Baghdad with "an unequaled panegyric poem in the Turkish language."[24] On the latter occasion he was sharing the rostrum with his brother Sa'īd, who had succeeded their father as chief muftī of Baghdad, "who read the official benediction (*du'ā*') in Arabic." The contrast between these two personae of Zahāwī (before and after the British occupation) is so great that it is sometimes difficult to believe one is reading about the same person. Certainly no trace of the earlier Zahāwī remains in his later incarnation.

The next oldest, and most famous, poet of this generation, Ma'rūf al-Ruṣāfī (1875–1945), came, like al-Zahāwī, from a family that had originally hailed from northern Iraq before moving to Baghdad. But there any similarity in background between the two poets ends. Ruṣāfī's family was extremely poor and his father, who was a policeman working in the rural gendarmerie, was seldom home. The poet's mother was the one who encouraged her son. She saw to it that he was enrolled as a young boy in the traditional elementary school, the *kuttāb*, and later she encouraged him to apply for a place at the new state military school, which offered qualified Iraqi students their only opportunity for a modern education (albeit in Turkish).[25] Al-Ruṣāfī, as the child of lower-class parents who would have spoken only colloquial Iraqi Arabic at home, and a product of the traditional educational system where classical Koranic Arabic reigned supreme, may have had difficulty learning Turkish, and perhaps because of this, he failed the fourth-year entry examination that ended his chances to continue his studies at the military academy. Following this disappoint, however, he reentered the religious educational system and shortly thereafter became a disciple of one of the foremost traditional scholars of the day, Maḥmūd Shukrī al-Ālūsī. Under his sponsor's tutelage, Ruṣāfī pursued studies in Arabic grammar and literature as well as the religious disciplines, the latter leading to a temporary, though intense, interest in the doctrines of Ṣūfism in one of its most demandingly ascetic forms.[26] After he finished his studies with Shaykh al-Ālūsī, he became an Arabic teacher, first in the primary schools and then in the province's single secondary school—the same school, ironically, that he had been unable to attend as a student.

Somehow during these years, Ruṣāfī seems to have also found time to improve his Turkish, if this was actually what had prevented his advancement through the Ottoman state school system in his student days. Now, his facility, newly acquired or not, with the metropolitan language gave him his "big break," for, when the restoration of the Ottoman constitution was announced in 1908, he was able to impress the local dignitaries and government officials with a translation he made into Arabic of the new

Turkish national anthem, composed by the well-known Turkish poet Tawfīq Fikrat. They were so impressed by his translation that they presented it at a special gathering in one of the main squares of Baghdad.[27]

His success with translating the national anthem led to his being offered the editorship of the first private newspaper in Iraq, *Baghdad*,[28] which was to be published in Turkish and Arabic. With this, Ruṣāfī's career as a journalist can fairly be said to have begun. Journalism and politics were to be his major means of earning a living for roughly the next twenty years. He would spend several years editing newspapers in Istanbul, as well as serving as one of the members for the 'Amāra district of Iraq in the Ottoman parliament from 1912 until the beginning of the war. His career in Istanbul was almost certainly furthered by the friendship and patronage of one of the founders of the Young Turk political party, the Committee for Union and Progress (CUP), Ṭal'at Pasha, who studied Arabic with him, and who as Interior Minister at the time had much influence in the capital.[29] Ruṣāfī seems to have found himself caught up in a lively circle of literary men and intellectual ferment during most of the time he spent among the Ottoman reformers.[30] But after World War I, this cosmopolitan life came to an end. There was no place for an Ottomanized Arab like Ruṣāfī in the defeated capital of a much shrunken Turkish state, shorn of its Arab provinces and turning ever more inward upon itself in the search for an elusive, purely "Turkish" past.

But neither was it easy for Ruṣāfī to return to Iraq. The British, still involved in a territorial dispute with Turkey over the northern border of Iraq, were arresting "Turkish sympathizers" of Iraqi origin who sought to return to their native land,[31] and Ruṣāfī could be seen as falling into this category. So he accepted the offer of a teaching job in Jerusalem and did not return to Baghdad until after the end of the traumatic events of 1920, remembered in Iraqi history as "the Great Revolt" against British occupation. When Ruṣāfī did come back to Iraq, it was to edit a newspaper financed by the opposition to the Amīr Fayṣal's British-sponsored candidacy for the Iraqi throne. When Fayṣal[32] won the plebiscite by an overwhelming margin—to the surprise of no one cognizant of the British payments and promises to political and tribal leaders behind the scenes—Ruṣāfī left Iraq for Damascus, vowing never to return. But return he did, the following year, to stand for a seat in the new Parliament. Ruṣāfī had earned the enmity of the new king Fayṣal during World War I, when he satirized the king's father, Ḥusayn, as a lackey of the British eager and willing to open up to their occupation and exploitation the holy shrines of Mecca and Medina. He nevertheless had some success during the 1920s in politics and as a competitor for government appointments, but his opposition to the 1930 "eternal friendship" treaty with Britain (the prelude and price that had to be paid to the British in exchange for their agreement to grant Iraq nominal independence in 1932) cast Ruṣāfī into the political wilderness and in his last years he made ends meet by selling cigarettes at a streetside stand in Baghdad.[33] He died in 1945, intransigent to the last toward both the British themselves and the brand of Arab nationalism they sponsored.

The third of this triumvirate of poets, Muḥammad Mahdī al-Jawāhirī (b. circa 1900),[34] actually belongs to the generation that intervenes between Zahāwī and Ruṣāfī, on the one hand, and Sayyāb and his contemporaries, on the other. Young enough to be the child of either of the two older poets, he is also easily old enough to have been Sayyāb's father. And indeed, at a crucial period he acted as something of a substitute father figure to Sayyāb, helping him with encouragement and some free-lance employment at his newspaper when the latter had been dismissed from his teaching position for Communist activities.[35] Nevertheless, Jawāhirī's writings have generally been viewed as a continuation and a culmination of his predecessors' in their neoclassical style, their traditional form and their concern with mainly political themes. Jawāhirī's poetry may have been stylistically an improvement on Ruṣāfī's and Zahāwī's verse, as many (including Sayyāb himself) have claimed, but it was also an extension of their preoccupations.[36] It does not in any significant way anticipate the new experimental forms of poetry that Sayyāb and his generation would introduce after 1948.

Jawāhirī came from an impoverished branch of an old and distinguished Shi'ī family of *mujtahids* (interpreters of Islamic law), which had lived in the southern Iraqi town of Najaf for a considerable period. Before this, they had long been established in Iran. According to the most generally accepted accounts of his life, Jawāhirī was never particularly religious and early on rebelled against his upbringing, becoming a full-fledged member of the Iraqi Communist Party by the time he was in his thirties. As a member of the Party, he owned and edited a number of leftist newspapers in Iraq, both before and after World War II.

Jawāhirī has been described as a poet who "had no roots in the Ottoman period,"[37] and, by extension, in its traditions of cultural syncretism between Arabic, Persian, and Turkish literatures, which appears so clearly as a factor in the early experiences of al-Ruṣāfī and al-Zahāwī. Although, as a Communist, he did not enthusiastically subscribe to the tenets of Arab nationalism as propounded by the first generation of nationalists, like Nūrī al-Sa'īd, who eventually came to hold supreme power in Iraq under British tutelage, he nevertheless identified very strongly with Iraq as an Arab country and frequently celebrated Iraqi national identity in his poetry. As he himself said in a 1957 poem "I am Iraq, my tongue is its heart, and my blood its Euphrates. . . ,"[38] which would seem to indicate a strong identification with the specifically Iraqī landscape, as strong as that in anything that Sayyāb ever produced. Yet, like al-Ruṣāfī and al-Zahāwī the attribution to al-Jawāhirī of an unproblematically defined identity can be misleading. In what is surely one of the earliest appearances of al-Jawāhirī on the pages of history, in Sāṭi' al-Ḥuṣrī's memoirs of his days as Director of Education in the Iraq of the 1920s, we encounter a very different figure. As Ḥuṣrī tells the story:

> The Minister of Education, Sayyid 'Abd al-Mahdī,[39] said to me: 'In Najaf, [there is a man who is called] Mahdī al-Jawāhirī, a poet and literary figure. Appoint him as a teacher of the Arabic language in one of the schools in Baghdad.'
>
> I said to him: 'I am going on an inspection tour of the schools on the Euphrates in three days. I will get in touch with him in Najaf.'
>
> Sure enough, once I had gone to Najaf, I asked about him first from 'Abd al-Muḥsin al-Shalāshī, in whose house I was staying during the time I was in that city. 'Abd al-Muḥsin told me straight-away: 'He is an Iranian.'
>
> In the evening, al-Jawāhirī came to [visit] me, and he introduced himself, saying: 'His Excellency the Minister [of Education] has ordered me to come meet you.'
>
> I said to him: 'First, I want to know: what is your citizenship (*jinsiyya*)?'
>
> He said without hesitation: 'I hold Iranian citizenship.'
>
> I said: 'In that case, it is not possible to appoint you.'
>
> He said: 'Why? Aren't there Syrian and Lebanese teachers?'
>
> I said: "But these are holders of advanced degrees, in positions where there exist no Iraqis who are capable of filling them. As for you, you would be a teacher of the Arabic language, in one of the primary schools. And there exist a number of Iraqis who would be able to undertake the teaching of Arabic in the primary schools.'
>
> He said: 'Are there no teachers in the primary schools who are not Iraqis?'
>
> I said: 'Not a one.'
>
> He argued insistently, for a period of time, on his appointment, even though he was an Iranian citizen, but when he saw I was determined not to allow this, he said: 'Very well (*khūsh*),[40] I am ready to take Iraqi citizenship. But you know this is a very momentous matter, I have connections, I have

relatives there. Before I give up my Iranian citizenship I must know what salary you will pay me, if I take Iraqi citizenship."[41]

I have reproduced Ḥuṣrī's account of his conversation with Jawāhirī verbatim, not only because of his obvious talents as a storyteller, but also because it is perhaps a unique opportunity to witness in written form one of those transactions redefining identity that were taking place all over Iraq during this period, as well as elsewhere in the Islamic world. Such transactions would end in the redrawing of the boundaries on the maps of identity in ways that would radically change the experience of self, and the way that self was viewed, for Sayyāb's generation. This scene clearly shows al-Jawāhirī, having apparently come to terms not too long before with a new way of framing identities (through the notion of *jinsiyya*, citizenship based on adherence to a "state," itself a new construct based on the drawing of ethnic, rather than religious, boundaries between groups), now suddenly realizing that this new self-definition will require something unforeseen: the exclusion of other possible identities, ones that had not been unavailable to him before. He now finds that taking Iranian citizenship will mean giving up any ties to Iraq and vice versa.

What makes the structuring of the moment even more complex is that Ḥuṣrī, who has positioned himself in the scene so as to seem unproblematically Arab, as well as completely in control of the new discourse of states and citizenship, and is so contemptuous of Jawāhirī's attempts to negotiate his status, had himself not long before been in a similar position. His family was of Syrian origin, from Aleppo, but he had been born in Yemen while his father, a judge in the Ottoman Sharī'a courts, had been stationed there. He grew up and was educated in Istanbul and had already had a long and highly successful career as an educator in the Ottoman Empire, stationed mostly in the Anatolian Peninsula, before attaching himself to Fayṣal's entourage in Syria at the end of World War I, in expectation that the promises made to Fayṣal about establishing an independent "Arab" state in this territory would be kept. Although Ḥuṣrī would be a lifelong ardent supporter of Arab nationalism, and one of its most tireless advocates in print, his contemporaries tell us that he was never as comfortable with Arabic as a medium of expression as he was with Turkish.[42] In all this, one is reminded of Ernest Renan's famous essay on nationalism, where he says "the essence of a nation is that all individuals have many things in common, and also that they have forgotten many things."[43] For Renan, Frenchmen, in order to be *French*men had to forget such inconvenient facts as the St. Bartholomew Day massacre. Similarly Iraqis, in order to become Iraqis after World War I, had to forge a new identity (one that was fictional, but necessary), which said that Iraqis were Arab and nothing else. Zahāwī, Ruṣāfī, Jawāhirī, and Ḥuṣrī all had to reconstitute their old selves in the process of fulfilling this new requirement.

The lives of each of these men, all of whom would have an important influence, either directly or indirectly, on the thinking of the young Sayyāb (for Ḥuṣrī would establish the framework for the educational system and much of the curriculum in use during the time Sayyāb was in school) show just how problematic the drawing of boundaries—whether on a map or in people's minds—became in Iraq between the wars. The master narratives of division, of boundaries, while certainly operative and influential on an intellectual level, do not necessarily correspond well to what we find when we look at the individual narratives of people's lives—as has been exemplified by examining the careers of the three poets described above—and we should be warned to approach such neat categorization with caution, to be aware that, though they may have great power to influence people's thinking, or even the course of political events, their descriptive adequacy will always be at best partial, at worst misleading.

Nevertheless, as Gayatri Spivak once said in an interview, one has first "to posit a [master] narrative in order to be able to critique it."[44] In other words, it is difficult to attack the weak points in a generalization without first outlining the salient features of that generalization. It is unlikely, on the other hand, that anyone now living really needs to be told that at any given moment in a society competing discourses proliferate, circulate, and any attempt to isolate a single idea for examination or designate it a dominant paradigm inevitably cuts it loose with violence from its moorings within the cultural matrix—"reifies" or "flattens" it, as Marxist cultural critics like to say—and distorts its role as a message. So, if I must now resume my examination of Sayyāb's relationship to the question of boundaries by resorting to a certain amount of generalization, I hope it will be clear that such a reifying procedure, while necessary within the context, also elides many things that in other contexts should be, and have been elsewhere, brought out. As long as both parties to the operation are aware of the fictiveness and provisionality of such a gesture, the temporary gain in analytical clarity can often be worth the price.

What becomes relatively clear, however, through reading the literary works, histories, essays, and memoirs of this period in Iraq between World War I and World War II, is that by the time the generation born after the beginning of the British occupation—Sayyāb's generation—had passed through an educational system shaped by the struggles between the not infrequently conflicting imperatives of committed Arab nationalists like Ḥuṣrī and the equally committed (though their commitment was mostly to fiscal conservatism and vocational education) British colonial administrators, these young Iraqi students were aware that they were living with, and were compelled to operate within, a very different set of boundaries than their fathers or older brothers had grown up with. This new set of boundaries created new conditions that could at times be enabling and at times be profoundly disruptive.

For instance, a student in the new state school system, who would likely speak a dialect of Arabic at home,[45] would no longer be expected to learn Persian or Turkish as a second high-culture language. On the other hand, he or (increasingly) she would now be required to study English for as many as ten hours of the school week (by far the largest block of time devoted to any single subject) beginning at one point as early as the third grade.[46] After the school reforms of 1936, a student like Sayyāb who graduated from high school would have been studying English for six or seven hours a week since the fifth grade (more than any other subject except Arabic, which equaled it). This meant that Sayyāb would be far more likely to have read at least some of Shelley or Milton in the original than he would great Persian poets like Ḥāfiẓ or Sa'adī, even though Iran was just across the river from his home and England was thousands of miles away. Similarly he would have been more likely to turn to Edward Fitzgerald's English translation of 'Umar Khayyām's *Ruba'iyyāt* than to have read the poems in their Persian original.[47] Turkish literature, either from the Ottoman or the Republic periods, was virtually unknown to him and his generation. It was not until the Communist poet Nāẓim Ḥikmat achieved fame in the late 1940s and 1950s, and his work became known in Arabic translation (itself a translation from English rather than Turkish), that Sayyāb records any acquaintance with Turkish poetry, either ancient or modern.

After the war, when Iraq suddenly became unquestionably an "Arab" country to the exclusion of anything else, it began to develop even closer ties with other "Arab" countries than it had had before 1914. We have already seen, through Jawāhirī's references to them, how many teachers in the new state school system were Lebanese or Syrian. Egyptian educators and intellectuals were also a presence to be reckoned with; famous figures like Aḥmad Amīn, Zākī Mubārak, and Aḥmad Ḥasan al-Zayyāt all spent shorter or longer periods in Iraq during the 1920s and 1930s. They came mostly as university lecturers or cultural luminaries invited on official visits by the Ministry of Education.

In addition, the textbooks in use in the schools of Sayyāb's day, especially the history/geography books, had been written mostly by Lebanese and Syrian authors on contract with the Ministry of Education. Although such textbooks can be quite difficult to come by now, from the limited opportunities I have had to examine them it would seem that they did not necessarily emphasize events in Arab history from an Iraqi point of view.[48]

The Egyptians, on the other hand, had a virtual lock on the publishing industry in Iraq. By the 1930s, for example, Egyptian printing houses were importing nearly 5,000 Egyptian newspapers into Iraq every week.[49] This is not to speak of the immense quantities of journals, literary and otherwise, and books. Most of these magazines and newspapers did publish the work of Iraqi poets like Zahāwī, Ruṣāfī, and Jawāhirī, but, for the most part, their choice of material and presentation of it were filtered through the point of view of Egyptian preoccupations. This illustrates yet again the highly ambivalent nature of discourses of power and knowledge, especially in a colonial context. Although it may certainly be, as Julia Watson and Sidonie Smith have said in *De/Colonizing the Subject*, that "there have been, as cultural critics point out, colonies within colonies, oppressions with oppressions,"[50] such modeling of the exercise of power as a nested set of concentric circles, each increasingly powerful in its ability to dominate discourse through a totalizing hegemony, is surely inadequate. One needs to be aware that the very same discourses that may be expressing resistance and opposition when considered in juxtaposition to one set of institutional structures, may in another context be just as exclusionary and panoptically figured as any other discourse of dominance. What was, from an Egyptian viewpoint, a gesture of resistance against their own occupation by the British—the assertion that they had a vital and dynamic literature that could produce enough material to fill dozens of magazines, newspapers, and literary journals—was from an Iraqi viewpoint tantamount to an internal colonization, since the flood of cheap and well-produced material coming from Egypt (and also, increasingly as time went on, from the Levant) made it very difficult for an indigenous Iraqi printing industry to establish itself. Even as late as the time Sayyāb sought to publish his first collection of poems (*dīwān*) in 1948, he felt compelled to send it to Egypt, probably because of the better distribution systems and more professional work done there.[51]

Despite the fact that such changes were taking place in the society all around him from his earliest years, the question of boundaries, for Sayyāb, did not emerge in any significant way in his writing until the summer after his first year in college: in 1944. This year was the time when these two problems—boundaries and the retelling of Eden narratives—began that elaborately patterned minuet in Sayyāb's poetry that was to culminate in the figuration of Eden as, at least in part, a colonial narrative about the problem of boundaries, especially the boundaries that both divided Iraq from and linked it to English culture and England as a colonial power, which would be activated so powerfully, as we have seen, in the 1950s in poems like "Curses" and "Hymn of the Rain." In 1944, Sayyāb was not yet at the point of relating the two directly, but both become immanent and surface separately for the first time in texts written during that particular summer.

1944 was an important year in Sayyāb's life for many reasons. It was a year when he would make several important choices about his future, and the ground would be prepared for several others. World War II was winding down. The D-day invasion would begin in June, and after that it was increasingly clear that it was a matter of when, and not if, Germany would be defeated. The implication of this Allied victory for colonial and informally colonialized territories in the Middle East like Iraq was that the British would expect their hegemony in these areas to continue with little change. Thus, the end of World War II in this region would mean the solidifying of old boundaries, drawn by the colonial powers among the victorious Allies, not the redrawing of new ones. In other words, the boundary separating Iraqis from realizing their version of Eden would stay in place.

We know the British colonial presence was already an important issue for Sayyāb because one of his earliest surviving poems is a 1941 elegy for several of the leaders of the Rashīd 'Alī coup, an attempt by the Iraqi army at the beginning of World War II to reduce British influence in Iraq through the ouster of Nūrī al-Sa'īd and his supporters (one of these Nūrī supporters, Ṭaha al-Hāshimī, was actually Prime Minister at the time).[52] In this poem,[53] a very youthful effort, Sayyāb describes the Nūrī al-Sa'īd group as "slaves of the English" who have "poured out the blood of martyrs," and warns them at the end of the poem that "in Berlin a lion is waiting" who would soon take vengeance upon them for the execution of the coup leaders. Thus we may imagine that the realization in 1944 that his earlier wishes for the defeat of the British and an end to their presence in Iraq, so fervently expressed in this early poem, were not to come true in any way must have been a bitter pill to swallow.

This growing awareness that British influence in Iraq would remain strong, coupled with a determination to oppose it in any way he could, may have been what lay behind the two most important decisions Sayyāb would make over the next academic year and into the following summer of 1945. These were choices that would have a determining effect on the course of his life: a decision to change his major at the Teachers College from Arabic language and literature to English language and literature, and his recruitment into the Iraqi Communist Party in May of 1945. On the surface these two decisions may appear contradictory, and neither one particularly closely related to a desire to oppose British colonialism. From the end of World War I, however, with the changed conditions it ushered in for the Middle East, Arab writers and intellectuals had been at pains to stress that a thorough knowledge of Western (particularly British and French) literature and culture was essential to meet their occupiers on their home ground, in order to understand these people who now had so much power over them and to be able to oppose them more effectively.

The Dīwān School in Egypt, under the leadership of the poet 'Abbās Maḥmūd al-'Aqqād,[54] had been particularly vocal during the 1920s and 1930s in its insistence that the failure of the preceding generation of neoclassical writers and poets to effect a revitalization (usually referred to in what has become the commonly adopted terminology as a *nahḍa* or "renaissance"—and the same term is used in referring to the European "Renaissance" as well) of Arabic culture could be attributed to their inward-turning, self-referential attitude toward literature and their inability to assimilate or respond in a meaningful way to Western ideas.[55] The implicit argument ran thus: if one cannot understand Westerners, one cannot be effective either in persuading them to give their colonial subjects more power, or in mobilizing their own strategies of control, both technological and psychological, to force them to do so. Thus Sayyāb's decision to develop what was already more than a passing acquaintance with English can be seen in this context as equivalent to the strategy of "know your enemy" the better to defeat him.

Sayyāb's decision to join the Communist Party may seem even less oriented specifically toward opposing British colonialism than his change of college major, since during the war the Soviet Union, the only major Communist state at the time, had allied itself with Britain, and the official Communist ideology propagated by the Comintern had a distinctly ambivalent position toward anticolonial independence movements, seeing them as essentially of marginal importance in the context of class struggle and world revolution. But the Communist Party in Iraq had become, with the failure of the Rashīd 'Alī coup, the only effectively organized force in a position to offer any opposition to the British.[56] Even before the war, the Iraqi Party seems to have been effective in broadening its appeal by presenting Communist principles as similar enough in their general structure to Islamic ideas of egalitarianism as to be viewed with some sympathy by a surprising number of individuals from fairly traditional backgrounds. Thus we have the interesting episode of the poet Ruṣāfī—hardly a radical anarchist, even though adamantly opposed to British influence—standing up in a 1937 session of Parliament and saying: "I am a Communist . . . but my communism is Islamic for it is written in the Sacred Book: 'And in their wealth there is a right for the beggar and the deprived.'. . . And it was the Prophet that said: 'Take it from their wealthy and return it to their poor.' Was this not communism? Who would then but out of ignorance resist this principle?"[57]

Since, in Iraq at least, the political forces of nationalism, which might otherwise have been expected to lead the anticolonialist opposition, had by Sayyāb's youth become so thoroughly compromised by their collaboration with British interests, the Communists—some of whose leaders, at least, gave the impression that they believed that the British had to be removed first in order to move toward implementing true revolution in Iraq—were able to attract large numbers of young, educated Iraqis like Sayyāb to their ranks. It is significant that, in the early 1950s, at the height of Stalinist cold-war efforts to regain control of third-world communist movements at least in part by ordering them to de-emphasize their role in national independence struggles, Sayyāb made his final and decisive break with the Iraqi Communist Party. Shortly thereafter he wrote in a letter to Suhayl Idrīs, editor of the influential Arab nationalist literary journal *Al-Ādāb*: ". . . the most practical way for nations afflicted by colonialism to [achieve the ideal of universal] peace is for them to struggle for their independence and freedom."[58] Since the Communists were at that time, in Iraq and elsewhere, heavily involved in a "Campaign for World Peace" that advocated the banning of the atomic bomb and an end to war, this passage would seem to indicate that Communism, a commitment to world peace, and anticolonialism had all been at least at one point strongly linked in Sayyāb's thinking, but that now, in 1954, his commitment to anticolonialism had definitely assumed the upper hand. That it continued to grow in strength can be seen in a lecture he delivered barely two years later, at the second Arab Writers' Conference held in Damascus, September 20–27, 1956.

In this lecture he first identifies what are, in his opinion, the six greatest masterpieces of world literature: *The Iliad, The Odyssey, The Divine Comedy, Macbeth*, [Goethe's] *Faust* and *Paradise Lost*. He then goes on to say that one of the things that makes them great is that each of them depicts the struggle between humanity and evil in their time. From this he moves to speak of the themes contemporary writers should deal with that will allow them, like their illustrious predecessors, to discuss and analyze the problem of evil:

> I am saying nothing new when I say that evil is represented today—in its most repugnant and dangerous form—in colonialism, along with its forces and those groups that it depends on. And so that these words of mine appear true in relation to all those whose opinions differ about the source of evil, let me revise the form of this expression and say: the most repugnant powers of evil and its most dangerous troops are embodied in the figures of colonialism and colonizer, and in social oppression and the oppressors, and the misery and death both have spread so widely.[59]

One of the things that makes this speech interesting is how it seems to function as an index of Sayyāb's ambivalent view of Western culture in these years. On the one hand, the great masterpieces of world literature are all Western or had been appropriated by the West (as in the case of *The Iliad* and *The Odyssey*) as part of their canon. And they are identified as representations of the struggle against evil. Yet, at the same time, it is the West and its various forms of colonialism—which we realize now were very much underwritten by the discourses propagated through the literary canon—that he points to as the most present danger for the rest of the world to combat. The two ideas are incommensurate and Sayyāb leaves them here at an unresolved point of tension. But what has become clear by this point (the year of the Suez Crisis), is that the question of colonialism had assumed dimensions in his mind that made it "larger than life," and ensured that apocalyptic and other highly patterned symbolic discourses would seem most appropriate as the grids on which to map such a protean phenomenon.

All this, however, was far in the future in the summer of 1944. Then, the available evidence seemed to suggest that Sayyāb was preoccupied by a deepening interest in poetry as a vocation. We know that he had begun to compose poetry much earlier: by the poet's own recollection, he composed his first poem "in Iraqi colloquial" in 1932, and his first poem in Modern Standard Arabic in 1936 or 1937, while he was "in the fifth grade."[60] But the first poems he kept were from 1941, and until 1944 they were relatively few in number. In 1944, however, there was nearly a fourfold increase in the number of poems Sayyāb wrote from the previous year (from nine to thirty-five), a number that would not be exceeded or even approached until 1963, at a time when the poet knew he was dying and he wrote feverishly to accumulate enough material for the publication of poetry collections that would help offset his medical expenses and support his family when he was gone.

Moreover, these poems of 1944 differed from his previous work, reflecting a much more serious and systematic program of reading in both Arabic and European literature. From his earliest attempts at verse, Sayyāb had indulged in what is called *mu'āraḍa*, or contrafaction, of popular Arab romantic poets, especially the work of the Egyptian poet 'Alī Maḥmūd Ṭaha.[61] But now one can recognize in the poems allusions to and transpositions of the works of a much larger range of poets: not only classical as well as modern Arab poets, but a wide variety of Western poets ranging from Catallus[62] to Renaissance poets like Christopher Marlowe to almost all of the English romantics. Especially interesting in this regard are a series of five poems discovered by the poet's biographer 'Īsā Bullāṭa in his effects after his death. All are "landscape poems," and all were apparently composed in the summer of 1944. Four of them bear the epigraph "To the spirit of Wordsworth" and one "To the spirit of the Poet of Nature, Wordsworth."[63] These poems are distinguished by two characteristics that had not been particularly noticeable in Sayyāb's verse before this year: their minute attention to descriptive details of nature and the countryside, and their concern with particularizing this landscape, making it recognizably the landscape of the village of Jaykūr and the Shaṭṭ al-'Arab, not a generalized "world of nature."

Perhaps the best representative of this is the poem "Aṣīl Shaṭṭ al-'Arab" (Late Afternoon on the Shaṭṭ al-'Arab):[64]

"To the spirit of Wordsworth"

1) The setting sun shifts from side to side on the Shaṭṭ but it goes on, slowly, flowing.
2) An ebbing tide has come to it after the flood, so it is weakened, spent.
3) The water has drawn away from its two banks and [the need for] departure has begun to urge it on.[65]
4) The two banks have been divested of a blue swath[66] decorated with palm trees.
5) O eye, rove and rejoice for the place where you rove is the beautiful Shaṭṭ.

6) Travel over the crests of the water's [waves] just as the moisture-laden breeze has traveled.
7) Here [you see] a sail, with fluttering edges, gilded by the setting sun.
8) And there is a mast, appearing, and then an oar, rotating.
9) And covering the heavens there is a red diaphanous gown, spread out by the sunset,
10) A red that kindles in the body[67] of the waves a fire that will not fade.
11) And the palm trees on the other bank appear, set swaying by the east wind.
12) There are many places to stop beneath them where a sojourner can find no rest
13) Fronds and a trunk have risen—but beside them, he is [standing] weary, preoccupied.
14) A calmness surrounded by green *yarā'*,[68] and a stunted lotus tree.
15) And in front of it there is a *balam*[69] tied up, which has sunk low, having been tied up for so long.
16) And there, in the forest of the palm trees, wrapped in dappling shadows,
17) Is an ox lowing, and a ewe bleating, and song flowing.
18) And hear you a tiny child, answered by a noble patriarch,
19) And a gladsome maiden, a youth sharing her words with her.
20) And before my eyes there is a brook, sweet is the place to kiss it, [but] tiny,[70]
21) Embracing the Shaṭṭ, it is its friend bountiful, chaste.
22) It complains to it of the passion for water jars, but its thirst is never quenched.
23) O Shaṭṭ, if only you would hear me or if only your heart would incline toward me.
24) O waves, O sailor, O white ships, O palm trees,
25) O wind, O white flock of birds, guided in the right direction by a pathfinder.
26) Share with my heart in th[is] joy: there is no spy, no censurer.[71]

The poem begins with an apparently neutral descriptive strategy in which figurative language is at first allowed only the smallest of openings into the scene. We may initially only be aware that the speaker is highly focused on the minutiae of the scene before him, enough so as to register that the sun is moving back and forth on the river's surface. This is the first hint of figuration: the sun's movement registers a restlessness that is almost humanlike[72] and, moreover, is contrasted with the slow, steady movement of the river. But the speaker does not at this point move further in the rhetorical direction opened up by his use of personification and antithesis; rather, he turns aside quickly to reinforce the particularity of his descriptive system—already established in the first line through the naming of this river as "the Shaṭṭ"—by, in the second line, foregrounding what may be the most unusual characteristic of this stretch of the Tigris–Euphrates river system: because of its proximity to the Persian Gulf, its water level is affected by the ocean tides. The changes wrought in the river landscape by this regular rising and falling of the waters was a source of fascination for Sayyāb, and this is only one of the first instances out of many where he mentions the phenomenon in his poetry.

Yet, even though the focus of this and the next few lines is on particularizing and localizing the landscape description, we can observe in them a subdued but insistent move toward personification of the river, so subtle that the reader may not even be consciously aware of it at first. It initially becomes noticeable in the patterning of adjectives. In the second line, the effect is not particularly strong, but the attribution to the river of being "weakened" and "spent" implies at least an animate subject, if not a human one. On its own, the reference in the fifth line to the "beautiful" Shaṭṭ could not be expected to evoke a humanized image, but placed in a context where personification has already been established (albeit weakly) there is a noticeable pull in this direction. The same is true of the use of *thabaj*, which I have translated as "crests," in the next line. It can simply mean generally "the highest or middle portion" of something, and is frequently coupled in this sense with "waves" in poetry, as it is here. But in a medical or anatomical context it refers to a specific portion of the human body, roughly equivalent to the area described by the English term "clavicle." Similarly, in line ten the waves are described as having "ribs."

These ambivalent usages, then, prepare the way for the more insistent personification that begins in line 9, where the "heavens" are clothed in a "diaphanous gown," and reaches full force in lines 20 through 22, where the Shaṭṭ and its tributary become lovers, "embracing" and "complaining." This reach beyond personification to feminization is then followed up in the next lines, where it becomes possible for the speaker to address the river now as a beloved, one that he hopes will "hear" him, whose "heart" will "incline toward" him. Thus what began as a simple, neutral descriptive cataloging of a landscape scene has turned at the end into what is quite overtly a discourse of love and desire.

Now it may be true that love, as a subject, dominated the repertoire of most Arab poets in the mid-1940s and Sayyāb was no exception to this rule. So in this sense, one could say that it is quite "natural" to find him writing his relationship to the landscape in the form of a love poem. Yet "Late Afternoon," while it incorporates the lexicon of love in ways that are quite suggestive if we think of it in terms of the colonial context of 1944, (loving a land that is not fully your own must always be problematic) also possesses other significant features that are worthy of consideration in this respect, ones that clearly distinguish it from both the generality of love poetry in this period and Sayyāb's own previous work.

Most immediately noticeable is its concern with language. By framing the poem in a Wordsworthian discourse, both through the dedication and through his notes that highlight an awareness of breaking with the conventions of poetic language, Sayyāb is demonstrating, first, his knowledge of Wordsworth's famous dictum about poetry and language found in the preface to *The Lyrical Ballads*: that he, Wordsworth had sought to "choose incidents and situations from common life, and . . . relate or describe them, throughout, as far as was possible, in a selection of language really used by men."[73]

But here this principle for writing is being repositioned in a colonial context that inevitably changes its terms. Sayyāb is not writing Wordsworth's English; instead, he must find or invent a set of collocations, a language, within the very different field of Arabic that will allow him to respond to the idea of deploying "a selection of language really used by" a very different set of "men" than the ones that Wordsworth had in mind. He must do this while at the same time finding a way to let that language allow him to describe this southern Iraqi landscape in such a way as to repossess it and reclaim as it his own. That a search for a descriptive language adequate to the poet's purposes seems to be going on throughout the poem would go far in helping to explain what would otherwise be an anomalous feature within the poem's framing by Wordsworth discourse: the "poeticity" of its language.

To be sure, on the one hand, Sayyāb uses a work like *balām*, which is Iraqi colloquial for the specific type of watercraft used for transport on the southern reaches of the Shaṭṭ, and ostentatiously eschews the Modern Standard Arabic, and more poetically "correct," word for small boat, *zawraq*. But, on the other hand, he resorts to language that is "poetic" in the sense that is seldom used as part of modern speech and writing in Arabic even more frequently than he dips into the reservoir of colloquial. For instance, in the second line, he describes the ebbing river water as being "urged on by departure"—not only a rather noticeable use of metonymic figuring that is very poetic in its local texturing but also producing an image strongly tied to conventional topoi from the classical three-part poem, the *qaṣīda*, where either the poet's camel, or his beloved's, is frequently depicted as being driven away from their meeting place by the departing tribe's camel-driver, who thus emerge as the nemesis of the lovers, seeking to drive them apart. Or there is the reference in line six to the "crests (*thabaj*)" of the waves, a word that is virtually nonexistent outside of poetic usage. Why, in a poem dedicated to the English poet most closely associated with the romantic "revolution in poetic diction," whereby "plain-speaking" was elevated to a poetic touchstone, do we find such disparate levels of language yoked together? Is it simply that the youthful Sayyāb is as yet unable to control his linguistic resources to the point where he can adequately shape them to his purposes?

Inexperience, of course, should always be considered as playing a role in circumstances such as these. But ineptitude does not have to be the *only* reason for this disturbing inconsistency—in fact its very pervasiveness and the way Sayyāb calls attention to his strategies here would suggest that there might be something more to it. Here, again, the structuring of the question within a framework of discourse/counter-discourse may prove helpful in providing a point of purchase for opening up this aspect of the poem to interpretation. Wordsworth's statements on language in his Preface, of course, manifestly point to his having conceived them as a counter-discourse; in his case, they are a challenge to those critical arbiters whose limitations on the lexicon that would be allowed into any given poem made it impossible to speak of certain things within the constraints of the poetic discourse of the time. The exclusion of "language really used by men" thus suddenly became a problem, a "source of cultural disquiet," for romantic writers.

For Sayyāb, on the other hand, the problem is rather different. To use a "language really used by men" would entail adopting a colloquial version of Arabic, and to do so would mean acquiescing to a subaltern role in a linguistic power dialectic that had been provoking struggles in Arabic-speaking countries ever since Britain and France had begun to consolidate control over the educational systems in their respective territories (roughly since the 1880s). The British, especially, had floated numerous proposals in Egypt before World War I to adopt Egyptian colloquial in the schools and they would do much the same in Iraq after the war.[74] To many Arab intellectuals, especially but not only nationalist ones, such proposals savored of a policy of "divide and conquer." In other words, for them to allow without resistance the division of the inhabitants in the Arab world into separate linguistic groups would underwrite a set of current state boundaries that were obnoxious to some, burdensome to all who had to live within their limits. Further, to acquiesce in any such project of implementing the colloquials as standard languages would have the direct effect of making it more difficult for Arab leaders to cooperate in presenting a united front opposing colonial policies, as well as denying to the inhabitants of these lands direct access to their common cultural heritage—written in classical Arabic—which had been a source of identification for them at least since the appearance of Islam. To be sure, the maintenance of a single standard form of Arabic (authorized by Koranic usage) as the written language meant that any literature produced in the colloquials would be marginalized, but to most intellectuals of Sayyāb's generation, confronted as they were with the need to resist the divisive strategies for control that they saw as being devised by colonialism as a paramount imperative, the benefits of having a single, standardized language for communication purposes far outweighed any negative factors.

If Sayyāb cannot strictly pursue the fulfillment of Wordsworth's dictum through valorization of the "selection of language really used by men" because, in the Arabic colonial context, such a project would raise more problems than it solved, then what can he do to render his world local, particular, and thus reclaim it as his own in the face of a colonial discourse of Eden? One solution to this problem may have been to experiment with the use of a language that is recognizably allied with one's own poetic heritage, thus producing an early example of what is a relatively common phenomenon in Sayyāb's work as it is in so many other colonial writers: a "hybrid" text,[75] what Bakhtin has called the "perception of one language by another language, its illumination by another linguistic consciousness"[76]—in this case Sayyāb would seem to be choosing to illuminate his home landscape, not through the refocalization of colonial Eden in an "Islamic" retelling of it, nor yet through a totally committed adherence to Wordsworth's notion of common or natural language as the one that allows the poet to describe what "poetic language" must not notice, but instead dominantly through an appeal to his own traditions of reading the landscape as found in Arabic poetry. The fact that he sees the two landscapes, the colonial and the traditional, as intersecting can perhaps be seen best in the last line of the poem, where he asserts that "there is no spy, no censurer." "Spy" and "censurer" are privileged signifiers in the descriptive system of Arabic love poetry, to be sure, where they represent stock characters whom the lovers seek to evade so that they can meet and express their love, but they would also easily be naturalized within colonial discourse, where the colonizer fixes the sovereign gaze of administrative surveillance on the newly colonized territory and, based on the knowledge (in the form of censuses, ethnographic reports, etc., as well as intelligence assessments by its secret agents) thus obtained, proceeds to critique the colonized subject for the social and moral inadequacies that "require" the colonizer's disciplinary presence in the territory and elide the issues of strategic, material, and, above all, economic interest that drive the colonial impulse in the first place. It is the opening allowed through the absence of this disciplinary figure in the conventional discourse of poetic love which allows the love poet to show his feelings for the woman, and, in "Aṣīl" it is a similar absence that allows this poet to speak to, and ultimately, to "love" the land.

The landscape in "Aṣīl" can be said, indirectly at least, to evoke Eden in its idyllic splendor, and there is a further similarity between the two places in that the poet, like Adam and Eve, finds himself shut out of his paradise. He is only able to reenter its precincts through the imaginative transformation captured by the process of making the poem itself. But the Shaṭṭ and its environs would also seem to draw some of their poetic power from their *not* being Eden (or at least colonial Eden), so that they may be retrieved as well, and perhaps more fully, through an alternative discourse of place, the *locus amoenus* or lover's idyll, at least in the version found in the Arabic poetic tradition.

In another poem, however, from this year and probably from this same summer, Sayyāb moves to confront that Edenic discourse more directly. This is the poem "Ḍalāl al-Ḥubb"(Love Gone Astray), whose text runs as follows:

1) By the sunset hour with hennaed fingers and the lovely wild flowers,
2) By the morning filling the dew, a [liquid] perfume, with baskets of daisies,
3) By the full moon (*badr*), arching over the night like a palanquin capturing my senses,
4) Indeed the heart wanders astray and subservient, because of passion.
5) Once love enters into the heart, it (=the heart) becomes a house for longings,
6) Or should it spend the night in a meadow, and enter the morning smiling, ripe for plucking,
7) It will fall upon bliss,[77] and its dwellers, it will transform it into empty bowers.
8) Ask the wildflowers about it (=love) as they bend over their brooks,

9) Ask the apple blossom, with laughing features and expression:
10) O apple blossom, why don't you tell us about the garden?
11) Where passion one day inflamed two hearts that [then] spent the night beating [as one].
12) Tell us the story of the One Who Was Cast Out, for you are time's storyteller.
13) Eve tempted him, then he stretched his hand toward the snake.
14) There was a fruit, God had forbidden the two of them [to touch] it, and they declared it lawful.
15) They tasted it; they became two tyrants,[78] and how are tyrants to be requited?
16) Then they decided to conceal it, thus there were two wrongs [done].
17) They began to sew [garments] upon themselves made from the leaves hanging down [around them].
18) What misfortune to him who shames God, he will get nothing but humiliation.
19) The shade tree did not know autumn, and the loss of its lovely leaves,
20) Until the two sinful lovers stripped off its leaves.[79]

This poem, like most of Sayyāb's early works, has usually been used mainly as a source for biographical information, and interpreted as referring to one or another of his fleeting adolescent love affairs at the Teacher's College. But this begs the question of certain unusual features that set it off from the general run of his other love poems.

First is the question of why he chooses to incorporate narrative—and a relatively lengthy narrative at that, taking up more than half its total length—into the poem. Although narrative poetry had been popularized in the previous generation through the pioneering efforts of Khalīl Muṭrān, it was not a genre that was traditional in Arabic literature, and this is virtually the first instance of Sayyāb using a narrated incident in his poetry (although he would later try to make it his main style of writing—see chapter 8 of this study). That this first narrative is one of the Garden and the Fall from Eden makes it doubly important in the context of examining the characteristic preoccupations of Sayyāb's work.

The narrative style adopted here underscores one particularly noticeable thing about this poem. Narrative, by its very nature as a succession of incidents, must thematize at least potentially issues of temporality and this is a poem haunted by time, in particularly seasonality or cyclical time, which is clearly viewed as being destructive (it causes the trees to lose their leaves and the vegetation to die). This preoccupation with time very noticeably differentiates this poem from "Aṣīl." There, the idyll is timeless, or, to be more precise, it is oriented toward the notion of recovering the "fullness of the moment" and thus has its own temporal rhythm divorced from outside considerations. In "Ḍalāl," on the other hand, an implicit thematization of time passing is established even in the first three lines where the reader is invited to view a series of tableaus set in as many different time frames—sunset, morning, night—before the speaker reveals in lines 3 and 4 the causes of his restlessness: the promptings of desire and love. In line 6, morning and evening are reintroduced in the form of verbs that now are usually employed as synonyms for, respectively, "to remain" and "to become" but often contain at least an echo of their original senses "to spend the night" and "to enter upon the morning," and can be interpreted as being used in their full original senses here. But now, in addition, a seasonal marker is introduced obliquely through the comparison of passion to "[fruit] ripe for the plucking," evoking autumnal associations that are then reinforced by the reference to "empty bowers," a poetic phrase conventionally associated with a wasteland or a winter landscape. All this, of course, leads up to the reference to the falling leaves of autumn at the end of the poem, where autumn becomes an annual reminder of Adam and Eve's attempt to conceal their sin, thus bringing death into the world not only for themselves and their descendants but for all nature as well.

Then suddenly the time frame shifts to spring with mention of the "flowers of the fields" and especially of the "apple blossoms," but the awareness on the speaker's part that this moment is contaminated by mutability, subject to temporality, is made clear by his reference to the "apple blossom" as the "one who narrates time" or "on behalf of time"; that is, if nothing else, it reinscribes in the brevity of its existence the dominance of temporality over the experienced world. But here, in the poem, it also tells a specific story. Because of its traditional associations with the Eden narrative, the apple blossom can tell, like no other, the story of the Fall of Adam and Eve, which becomes in the end of the poem a "fall" also into temporality for both human beings and the natural world. This temporality is enacted in the story through human agency, as Adam and Eve strip the leaves from the trees in order to cover their nakedness—and this becomes the seemingly permanent "death" of vegetation in winter.

Although this poem provides many fewer obvious points of purchase for colonial readings than "Aṣīl," there is one such moment in the text that is worth pausing at, since it can easily be seen as a harbinger of those much more overtly political/colonial allegories we see in later poems incorporating Eden discourse, like *Al-La'anāt* (*Curses*). This occurs in line 15: here the key word is *ẓālim* (tyrant). Today this word has associations that are primarily political. To be a *ẓālim* is to embody all the qualities of a ruler that are directly opposed to those of the ideal, or just, ruler. Even in the medieval Islamic world, the political valences of this word might be said to be primary. But its use here would appear to go back much more specifically to a slightly different context: the first time the Eden narrative is invoked in the Koran (2: 30–39).There, when God brings Adam and Eve into the Garden for the first time, he warns them not to eat from one of its trees, lest they become "among the tyrants." The political connotations of this word were apparently even then so strong as to make the word usage seem strange enough to cause the medieval commentators some pause—for they, virtually to a man, are at pains to point out that what is meant here is the older, more general meaning of the word: "someone who puts something somewhere other than its [proper] place."[80] Now, one way to put something outside of its proper place is to take it beyond some boundary that is set up around it, and this is what seems to lie behind both the application of the word in a political context (i.e., a "tyrant" is someone who exceeds the boundaries of proper behavior) and the frequent rendering of the word in English translations of the Koran as "transgressor," someone who crosses boundaries that should not be crossed.[81] Thus, the use of this particular word, so strongly linked with the Koranic narrative of Eden, could be seen as at least obliquely bringing up the question of boundaries.

Yet oddly enough, Sayyāb here does not accept the invitation he proffers himself to speak of boundaries. Instead, he evinces a kind of fascination for the political connotations of the term, even reactivating its jarring uncanniness in the original Koranic usage by saying "and how are tyrants to be requited?" "Requited" implies a legalistic mechanism of rewards and punishments and is thus equally naturalizable in political or religious contexts. However, unlike "Aṣīl" where the same appeal to overdetermination is used as a concluding device that forces the reader to go back and reinterpret all that has gone before, thus opening up new vistas of complexity in the work itself, here the ambiguity is awkwardly dropped almost as soon as it is raised, and the reader's attention is diverted to be refocused on other, entirely different issues.

Sayyab's strategy for focusing on questions of colonial discursive formations about temporality, though perhaps less direct, is also perhaps more successfully sustained throughout the course of "Ḍalāl." After all, Adam and Eve show themselves *in this poem*[82] to be tyrants or transgressors through their introduction of time (and death) into Eden, thus turning it into the fallen "nature" that we, as human beings, know. This recalls, certainly, the debilitating effects of various colonial discourses of *time* that are introduced no less often than discourses of *space* to legitimate the initial conquest and occupation, as well as to elide important elements of those same events.

Particularly important for the Islamic world in this temporal sphere was the colonialist appropriation of the historical discourse of progress. To get some sense of the issues at stake here, it would seem expedient at this point to review briefly some of the relevant ways that "progress" has been used in epistemic discourses taken from both cultures. It is clear from even the most casual perusal of histories written in the West of the development of "progress" as a concept, such as J.R. Bury's classic *The Idea of Progress*, that how one charts this development depends very much on the meaning with which one endows the term. Certainly, if one chooses a sufficiently high level of abstraction, concentrating for instance on the element of a valorization of a linear—as opposed to a cyclical—framework for containing temporality, one could pick and choose examples showing an interest in, or a nascent formulation of, the idea of historical progress, going as far back as the ancient Greek Epicurean philosophers, with illuminating excursions into the works of Seneca, the Franciscan friar Roger Bacon, the late Renaissance French historian Jean Bodin, and probably most importantly the philosophers Francis Bacon and René Descartes. But if one were to search for a period when the idea of "progress" becomes a problem, a "source of cultural disquiet," then the time known as the "Enlightenment" in the West would best fit the requirements. This is when a historical view begins to congeal that says if one were to reflect the dominant discourse of institutional power in the Middle Ages and Renaissance, one would tend to stress the greatness of "the Ancients" and the inability of later figures to measure up to their example, while Enlightenment thinkers (and post-Enlightenment ones as well) would have characterized their own hegemonic narrative in quite the opposite terms: that modern humanity's ability and knowledge has far outstripped the Ancients and things will only continue to improve for succeeding generations. The fact that any diligent reader can find plenty of voices from the Enlightenment onward prepared to contest such a view only shows the validity of framing the discussion in terms of when progress becomes a "problem" as a guide for charting its trajectory.

Before the Enlightenment, seeing human history as a narration of progress seems to have been consistently an interesting, if marginal, alternative to the two dominant senses of history and time as either cyclical or (although the two do not have to be mutually exclusive) the present as a degeneration from some "golden age" existing in the past. After the Enlightenment, "progress" (or its lack) becomes central to almost any serious discussion of the course of human history or the development of society.

Islamic thinking on the subject has tended to incorporate a similar set of contrasting and potentially incommensurate discursive frames. The dominant trend of thought, however, has been disposed to see the "golden age" scenario as the most valid one for organizing discussions of human history. Thus one finds even such an early writer as Ibn al-Muqaffa' (d. 756 A.D.) beginning his important and influential prose work *Al-Adab al-Kabīr* with an introduction that praises "those who came before us" as being incomparably better in all ways: physically, intellectually, morally, and spiritually. From this, he draws the somewhat discouraging conclusion that "[n]othing remains, great or small, for anyone who has come after them to say."[83] In his own work, he says, he will content himself with simply synthesizing the choicest parts of the knowledge they have already discovered. This, of course, is uncannily similar to a historical instantiation of the "affected modesty topos" found so frequently in classical rhetoric,[84] and Ibn al-Muqaffa', who was educated in the highly Hellenized atmosphere of the late Sassanian intellectual establishment as it made the slow transition to Islam, may have drawn upon the same sources as his European counterparts.

There were, to be sure, discourses within medieval Islamic thought that made the idea of progress more recuperable. Most notable of these would be the theological paradigm that made Islam "the last and best of the three monotheistic religions." This underwrote a teleological reading of history in which Islam stood as the potentially morally and spiritually perfect ideal at the end of a progression leading from Judaism through Christianity. A slowly crystallizing expectation among Muslims that periodically (once every Islamic century according to most versions) a *mujaddid*, or renewer, would appear to reform the institutional structures of Islam could also be seen as allied to this former idea. At best, however, this renewer was expected to restore the corrupt present to a closer approximation of the ideal Islamic golden age, when the Prophet Muhammad personally ruled the nascent Muslim community in the city of Medina, where the individual believer could both practice his or her religion freely and consult the Prophet directly, receiving through him the guidance of God in meeting the problems of life.

Nevertheless, the fact that there were certain views within traditional Islamic thought that could be seen as favorable to the idea of progress certainly must have made Enlightenment notions of progress more easily assimilable when Muslims began to journey to various European countries for educational purposes. This was a route that became increasingly well traveled as the nineteenth century progressed as various Middle Eastern rulers, like Muḥammad ʻAlī in Egypt, sought to assimilate Western technological advances into their own societies for both military and industrial purposes. A developing linkage between the mindset based on the notion of progress and the need for technical appropriation is clearly visible even in the first narrative about such a journey, the Egyptian Rifāʻa Ṭahṭāwī's *Takhlīṣ al-Ibrīz fī Talkhīṣ Bārīz (The Extraction of Pure Gold in the Summary of [My Trip to] Paris)*, published for the first time in 1834 and reissued in slightly different versions in 1849, 1905, and 1958.

In setting up the background for his journey to France, Ṭahṭāwī first seeks to justify to his Egyptian audience the decision to seek for knowledge among the Europeans, whose learning had traditionally been held in low esteem as far less advanced than that of the Islamic lands. He does this by appealing to the concept of historical progression—that all societies move from savagery to barbarism to civilization.[85] Thus, even a non-Muslim people, like the French, can become civilized and eventually develop forms of "civilized" knowledge worthy of the attention of other "civilized" peoples.

As he endeavors to explain ideas that are radically different from the authoritative views of his predecessors like Ibn al-Muqaffaʻ we can see Ṭahṭāwī choosing, whether deliberately or not, language that highlights the incommensurability of the two master narratives of progress and the golden age. He says: "The farther back I followed time in its ascent,[86] the more I have found the people to be backward in human arts and crafts and civilized knowledge, and the further I have gone forward and looked at time in its descent,[87] the more I found—for the most part—that people had progressed and advanced in these same things." Here, in the use of upward motion to describe movement into the past and downward motion to describe movement toward the present, we hear echoes of the more traditional view valorizing the Ancients, which is, of course, diametrically opposite to the stated view of the passage itself in its assignment of advancement to later humanity and backwardness to their ancestors. Nevertheless, what is clearly coalescing here are the beginnings of a discourse of progress that would place all those peoples fortunate enough to receive the label "civilized" on a more or less equal footing and legitimate their interrelationships, their borrowings from one another. This accords very well with the essentially optimistic attitude operative in Egyptian government and intellectual circles at the time (the late 1820s) about their ability to acquire Western knowledge in the form of technology and use it to create their own strong apparatuses of power, occasioned by the initial successes (both military and commercial) of the reform initiatives being promulgated by Muḥammad 'Ali in these years.

Despite the earliness of his sojourn in France, however, Ṭahṭāwī apparently had already been exposed to the use Europeans would increasingly make of the discourse of progress in justifying their colonial ambitions: the characterization of the West as the civilization that has advanced the most, progressed the farthest, and therefore superseded all other world civilizations and consigned them and their achievements to subordinate status. The Enlightenment revaluation of the Ancients is thus extended to contemporary "others" as well, and priority becomes the instrument through which they are repositioned as subaltern in the new hierarchy that will henceforth rule their lives. A textual allusion to precisely this kind of epistemic framing occurs in *Talkhīṣ* in the same chapter where Ṭahṭāwī outlines his reasons for going to the West to study. He concludes his narrative of humanity's progression from savagery to civilization with a paean to French ingenuity and skill in the practical sciences, and he compliments them judiciously on the wide-ranging curiosity they exhibit, noting that they have even begun to study seriously the Islamic religious sciences, like those that inform the *sharī'a* legal system, even though they are not believers (and would thus seem to have no practical need to understand this system in the discharge of their daily social or religious obligations).

This leads him to comment with regret that these Islamic disciplines are the only areas left where the Europeans still concede Muslim intellectual superiority. Then he goes on to say: "Nevertheless, they do acknowledge that we were once their teachers in the rest of the sciences, by virtue of our coming before them. It is well known that merit on account of coming first—or at least not coming after—is acknowledged to be among God's special gifts."[88] Muslims, in other words, must settle for the recognition of having been first because they are no longer best. And, although Ṭahṭāwī will go on in his work to assert that the superior position, that priority, is recuperable for Muslims not just in a temporal but also in a hierarchical sense, this is not the way that the colonizing West will read the narrative. The Western, especially the British, reading of the Muslim Middle East in this sense accords very well with their reading of India and the equally venerable

Indian civilization, which has been very nicely captured by Sara Suleri in the following passage from her book *The Rhetoric of English India*:

> Since India is too old to be rational, it follows that the colonial need waste as little time as possible on attempting to read the social structures that are in place on the colonized territory. In the rhetoric of English India, as a consequence, the ancient cannot command respect but instead represents a malevolent entropy, a choric reminder that on the stage of imperialism the British arrival at the possession of India has indeed been premature. . . .
>
> India is old, and to be old is evil; only the litmus test of British colonialism will usher the subcontinent into rationalism and modernity. On the obverse of this belief, however, lies the hidden fear that the colonizer is young, too young to understand the addictive functioning of a power so phantasmagoric that it may amount to nothing but its own dismantling.[89]

To prevent the dismantling of colonial power by its own self-doubts, then, the colonizer must demonstrate the efficacy of youth, and especially the colonizer's own youthfulness, to act as a necessary precondition for the successful regeneration of the colonized society to the benefit of both colonizer and colonized. Suleri and others have traced with great care and precision the permutations of this youth/old age paradigm through the literature of European colonial powers, especially the genre of the adventure tale as represented by works like Rudyard Kipling's *Kim*, the Tarzan stories, H. Rider Haggard's adventure novels, and even in a sense *Huckleberry Finn*. The symbolic importance in colonial narratives of the attributions of youth and age can be imputed to a number of poems from Sayyāb's mature writings where children figure prominently as personifications of hopeful optimism for the future, such as the poem "Madīna Bi-lā Maṭar" (City Without Rain) already discussed in chapter 1.

Although the reappropriation of the figures of childhood and adolescence provide one possible counter-discourse to a colonial reading of Islamic civilization and the Arab world as hopelessly "past" and retrograde, Eden discourse also can be seen as countering this Western totalizing reading in a sense that may be even more directly aimed at its temporal bias. Eden discourse, especially as presented by Sayyāb in "Ḍalāl al-Ḥubb" acknowledges a "fall," a "decline," but it also asserts that there will be a return, that the land will eventually be retrieved by those who were banished from it, and/or their descendants, and thus harmony will be restored.

If the two poems, "Aṣīl" and "Ḍalāl," act as oblique yet powerful indices of certain preoccupations that would later "flower" in Sayyāb's mature poetry, there is a third text from this period with equal claims to consideration because of its illustrative power to figure what will come. This text does not occur in the form of a poem, but as a paragraph in one of the three letters Sayyāb sent to his school friend Khālid al-Shawwāf during the summer of 1944:

> I am writing this letter of mine to you after having returned from a journey—exhausting but beautiful—to the other side of the Shaṭṭ al-'Arab. If only you could have seen me once the boat had cast me forth onto a swampland, overgrown with reeds and water grass, a land of which I knew nothing save the names of a few of its inhabitants. I stood there on the empty shore, with bloody feet and hands decorated with wounds. I looked all around me, but saw no one. . . . I listened carefully, but I heard only the sighs of the wind. Imagination had spun a tale whose title is "The Poet's Death," . . . and if I were to tell it, the telling would be long.[90]

It would be easy to dismiss this, as others have done, as evidence of an exuberant youthful taste for self-dramatization. But it takes on a rather different coloring in the light of Sayyāb's already documented interest in Eden discourse and what it will eventually lead to in the matter of boundaries. He has crossed the Shaṭṭ into an unmapped landscape, one that should offer him tantalizing possibilities for interpretation. But this river/boundary is not the Shaṭṭ we saw located in the idyllic landscape of "Aṣīl." Nor does it exist simply to separate the poet from Eden. It actively threatens him. Once he has crossed the boundary, the very vegetation, the lineaments of the landscape wound him, make him think of dying, of the extinction of the self and most especially the self who is "poet."

It is in this context—of the recognition that attempting to reread and remap the landscape with an eye toward reappropriating it may involve death or at least a threat to the autonomy of one's self-conception—positing it in this sense as a heroic and dangerous act—that we can see emerging in Sayyāb's later poetry a set of tropes for reading the landscape, which are presented as an alternative discourse to Eden but can be seen as forming just as directly a counter-discursive strategy aimed against Western hegemony as expressed in its literary works. These tropes are to be found in the primitive myths of death and rebirth as they were classified by James Frazer in *The Golden Bough* and were taken over by T.S. Eliot for his poem *The Waste Land*.

CHAPTER THREE

Jaykur Stretches Out to Meet Margate Sands

Reclaiming the Land Laid Waste

> "On Margate Sands.
> I can connect
> Nothing with nothing.
> The broken fingernails of dirty hands.
> My people humble people who expect
> Nothing."
>   la la
> To Carthage then I came.
>   —T.S. Eliot, "The Fire Sermon," *The Waste Land*

Like almost every other poet of his generation who lived in a current or former English colony, Sayyāb was well acquainted with the writings of T.S. Eliot, and especially *The Waste Land*,[1] a work that he said on more than one occasion, "provided the most damning critique of modern Western civilization [imaginable]."[2] This, of course, was also how many young English and American intellectuals in the 1920s and 1930s had seen the poem when they first encountered it. For them, in an oft-repeated formulation, it "expressed the disillusionment of a generation."[3] But such an insistent characterization of his poem as the record of a contingent historicity so irritated the normally imperturbable and reticent Eliot that he felt compelled to make a response to it—a latitude he seldom allowed himself in reference to his own work[4]—saying in 1931: "I may have expressed for them their own illusion of being disillusioned, but that did not form part of my intention."[5] This statement, combined with the emphasis by the New Criticism (the literary critical school Eliot allied himself most closely with) on closely studying "the text itself" and divorcing poetry from the incidental circumstances in which it was produced in order to isolate the qualities that made it "a great work of art," eventually touched off a revaluation of *The Waste Land* in which its relationship to the times that produced it was minimized or even denied. The impact of this can be seen in the fact that an author writing recently about the French Symbolist movement felt compelled to say upon mentioning *The Waste Land*, "Present-day critics, . . . no longer take *The Waste Land* as primarily a lament for European civilization or the direct result of the First World War. We now see that the poem is about personal relations and only incidentally a *Blick ins Chaos*."[6] More recently, the pendulum has swung back in the other direction as a greater awareness has grown that modernist disavowals of political concern should perhaps not be taken at face value, but seen instead as discourse strategies intended, among other things, to control the reception of their works.[7] The story of the reception of *The Waste Land* inside its own milieu, then, has been a complex one, one that, like so much of the evaluation modernist legacy in general, is still very much in a state of flux.

This lack of consensus about the legacy of *The Waste Land* becomes even clearer when we look at it through the lens of how it utilizes the myths of death and rebirth for which it is so famous, and how the various speaking voices in the poem avail themselves of these myths to articulate a relationship to the space they inhabit, to the land. In a sense, the question of the land could be seen to frame the poem's quest, as it begins with the observation "April is the cruellest month, breeding / Lilacs out of the *dead land*, mixing / Memory and desire . . ." and the last verse paragraph—just before the jumble of quotations that formally ends the poem—starts with the Fisher King's question: "I sat upon the shore / Fishing, with the arid plain behind me / Shall I at least set my *lands* in order?" [emphasis mine]. But what is this land that needs to be rejuvenated, "set . . . in order"? Is it simply a periphrasis for nature in the abstract, the countryside overrun by the sterility of the modern city, or is it some more specific location: America? England? Europe after the War? Should it be seen solely as an interiorized landscape, an "objective correlative" for the sexually traumatized psyche? Or as history spread out in spatialized form? Or some fluctuating combination of these? Land, for Eliot as an American "returned" to England, the country his Puritan ancestors had left generations before, choosing to stay in London in defiance of his family's wishes after long sojourns in France and Germany before the War, must have been problematized in ways that would be closely related to the questions of history and tradition much more directly thematized in his poetry. How to project a shape upon the space that he inhabited certainly seems to have been a troubling aspect of the subject position Eliot sought to construct for himself in both *The Waste Land* and *The Four Quartets*, calling forth discourse strategies as complex as those of any colonial writer relating to a metropolitan tradition, yet this "land question" is not a topic that has seemed to attract any sustained interest in the major readings of Eliot's poetry to date.[8] Perhaps the difficulties attendant on sketching out the differences between modernism and postmodernism (a process, as was suggested in chapter 1 of this book, that is only just beginning) have contributed to this neglect of the question of Eliot's relationship to the practices of mapping and territorialization. Once this critical project—the contouring of modernism and postmodernism for the purposes of writing literary history—has been carried out, it may then be possible to return to *The Waste Land* (as well as other icons of modernism) in order to examine them afresh from a perspective that would emphasize their links with (rather than their differences from) the postmodern spatialization of discourse.

Even if we return now, however, to the seemingly more straightforward question of how the death–rebirth myths are treated in *The Waste Land* and whether or not they should be seen as representing there a failure or a success for rebirth, we do not find unanimity by any means. Among the critics that Sayyāb might have read (and we know that he did read English literary criticism, including Eliot's own "Tradition and the Individual Talent"[9]) or whose work might have influenced him indirectly through the synthesizing of literary critics writing about Eliot in Arabic, F.R. Leavis comes closest to providing a categorical statement on the matter. "The thunder," he says, "brings no rain to revive the Waste Land, and the poem ends where it began."[10] But writers like F.O Matthiessen[11] and, later, Hugh Kenner[12] were less certain, and both of them try to recuperate from the text some message of hope for resolution on a different and less despairing plane by noting that the very last words of the poem are the voice of the thunder speaking in Sanskrit (the language of origin, of beginning for Indo-Europeans): "Give. Sympathize. Control. Peace. Peace. Peace." More recent writers, with more privileged access to material that illuminates the "personal conflicts" that seem to have underlain the genesis of the poem, have even less certain answers and more complex interpretations about how to read the conclusion.[13]

If it is the case that one must tread cautiously when looking at efforts to interpret *The Waste Land* inside Anglo-American criticism itself, then the operative assumptions of postcolonial literary theory would suggest that even greater care be taken when we look at how the poem was received within a conceptual framework, like that of modern Arabic poetry, where very different discourse dynamics obtained. Sayyāb's announced reading of the poem as a critique of modern Western civilization, for example, may not be most productively approached as simply his unreflective mimicry of a supposedly mistaken interpretation made by certain youthful Western critics and intellectuals, but instead might be better seen as a choice to "misread" Eliot in a particular way that initially empowers him to construct *The Waste Land* in his imagination as a counter-discourse to be deployed in testing and weighing, if not breaking open the monolithic façade comprising the canonical texts of Western civilization: that nearly invisible, yet silently pervasive force behind the political assertions of colonialism as he experienced them during his years in the Iraqi educational system. Added to this necessity for contextualization is the fact that Sayyāb's relationship to T.S. Eliot, mediated both through *The Waste Land* and a number of his other poems, was an enormously intricate one, lasting nearly twenty years, one that went through several distinct phases of development that in their emphases may be viewed as quite heterogeneous. Probably no other poet, European/Western or Arab, modern or classical, had a more profound and many-sided series of influences, both in terms of technique and of themes, on Sayyāb's work. Here I wish to focus mainly on how Eliot's precedent inscribed itself upon Sayyāb's depiction of landscape—and his relationship to that landscape—but it would seem impossible to appreciate the contours of that particular aspect of their relationship without briefly sketching in the broader outlines.

Sayyāb's introduction to Eliot's work was probably effected by Lewis 'Awaḍ's pioneering article on the Anglo-American poet published in the May 1946 issue of *Al-Kātib al-Miṣrī*. 'Awaḍ—who went on to become one of the most influential literary and cultural critics of the 1950s and 1960s in Egypt—had been at Cambridge from 1937 to 1940, reading for a M. Litt. degree at King's College. A few years after he returned to Egypt, the dean of Egyptian letters, Ṭaha Ḥusayn (at that time editor of *Al-Kātib al-Miṣrī*) asked 'Awaḍ to do a series of articles on various recent English writers who had made a mark in their respective fields. Eventually the series stretched to include nearly a half dozen figures, ranging from Oscar Wilde to George Bernard Shaw to James Joyce to H.G. Wells. The article about Eliot, however, was probably the most influential of this group in that it introduced modernist ideas about poetry and T.S. Eliot's poems in particular to an audience in the Arab world that had hitherto only heard the vaguest rumors about this movement and its members.[14]

'Awaḍ's article draws heavily on English critical studies of Eliot from the 1930s and 1940s, especially C. Day Lewis's chapter on Eliot in his 1934 book *A Hope for Poetry*.[15] The essay also translates a considerable quantity of Eliot's poetry[16] but only one complete poem: "The Hollow Men" from 1925. It uses these extracts to illustrate the three issues the article explores in some depth: (1) the problem of obscurity in Eliot's poetry; (2) the trajectory of development in the characteristic concerns of the poetry, with emphasis on Eliot's changing religious/philosophical views; and (3) the reasons for the characterization of Eliot as a conservative, even reactionary, poet.

Sayyāb could certainly have read the article shortly after it came out in January 1946.[17] Just after this date, he was suspended from school for the remainder of the academic year because of his leadership of a student strike protesting the lengthening of the teacher training program from four to five years. From January to September of 1946, then, Sayyāb was back home in Basra with plenty of time on his hands to read and compose poetry.[18] Like 1944, this year would be an important year in Sayyāb's poetic development. If it was indeed the case that Sayyāb read the article around this time, then 'Awaḍ's emphasis on the "obscurity" of Eliot's work would help to explain an otherwise very puzzling passage that appears in a letter Sayyāb wrote to his literary confidant Khālid al-Shawwāf, which is probably from midsummer of 1946:

> On many occasions you have criticized me for the obscurity in my poetry. But I realize now that this obscurity is the magic knot tied by the hand of emotion. If it unravels in the hour of madness, the talisman will lose the spell of genius that has been cast over it . . . and here I stay my reed, because I imagine that you will have identified in my thoughts a Baudelairean direction . . . absolutely not . . . there is nothing of that![19]

Something had clearly happened around this time, then, which gave Sayyāb new confidence in his experiments with pushing language to its limits (as we find him doing not infrequently during this period), in allowing his poetry to become "difficult," a keynote of modernist poetics. It would not be surprising to find this was triggered by an encounter with Eliot's poetry, for Eliot was certainly one of the most "difficult" of the Anglo-American moderns. 'Awaḍ, following C. Day Lewis, had stressed this, saying in his essay that Eliot's obscurity was due to the fact that modernist poetry in general relies on something Day Lewis calls "emotional association," which is expressed through techniques that recall the "free association" of psychoanalysis and the cross-cutting styles found in modern cinema. Sayyāb may have found this relevant to his own practice in poetry and, in general, to the tradition of Arabic poetry that stretches back to Imru' al-Qays, where very similar associational techniques of ordering are often used.

But Sayyāb seems to have been even more clearly impressed by the conclusions drawn by Awaḍ about Eliot's political convictions, because in a poem also very likely written in the summer of 1946, he makes his first unequivocal reference to Eliot's poetry in such a way as to suggest that he is drawing on material from 'Awaḍ's article. In a footnote appended to a line in the text of a poem where he uses the phrase "waste land," he says: "This is the title of a poem by the reactionary (*raj'ī*) English poet T.S. Eliot."[20] This labeling of Eliot as "reactionary" echoes exactly the judgment pronounced by 'Awaḍ at the end of his article. This use of the term "reactionary" has always drawn the largest part of critical attention[21] because it gives a fairly specific point of reference for establishing the date at which Sayyāb became acquainted with Eliot's work, but the actual allusion, to the "waste *land*," should probably have received more attention than it has. It is interesting, given the fact that only a relatively small portion of *The Waste Land* was translated in 'Awaḍ's article in comparison with some of Eliot's other poetry, that Sayyāb should have singled out this poem for mention and evoked it precisely through its title, with its powerful figuration of landscape imagery. Clearly the reference to a "land" laid waste has a great deal of resonance given his earlier—and later—concerns with Eden discourse. In fact, it is worthwhile to consider in more detail the local texture of the lines where the phrase occurs:

92) And art will bear fruit and be transformed to arms that will not bend,
93) Angry, they will rise in waves, to seek rest on the necks of the tyrants.
94) They are the tear of the mother who has lost her child, the shivering of
the naked and the hungry,
95) The writhing of the wounded man in his blood, the dreams of the
prisoner,
96) They are the smiles of the victims, and the rising up of the
revolutionaries.
97) Then, by the light of the sad star, let the waste land grow
98) Its cacti—we will fill the world of tomorrow with jasmine![22]

Here Sayyāb's speaker attributes to Eliot and his poem a view of the modern world as an unredeemable location where inequality, injustice, and oppression are the accepted norm. This is, of course, a simplistic reading of such a complex poem as *The Waste Land*, but it is not done gratuitously: it allows the speaker to sharpen the opposition between a pessimistic, essentially defeatist vision of the future, which he imputes to the Western poet as reflecting where Western capitalist[23] civilization leads, and his own optimistic hopeful vision, which, if he can share it with others, make it real to them, will allow the creation of a better world for all.

Here we can see posed very sharply the essential difficulty for Arab poets of this period in appropriating the basic tenets of the Western modernist *weltanschaaung*. Modernism valued *representations* of the social disarray and lack of reliable economic, political, or cultural structures that modernist writers perceived as characteristic of their world. It did not see a value in *exhortations* to transform that world, with their close links to the idea of resistance, probably because of the view held by some of these modernists that earlier calls of this sort (by romantic poets in particular) had failed to result in beneficial change. Arab poets of Sayyāb's generation, as poets who had become spokesmen articulating the discourse of those intellectual forces in their society committed to resisting the apparatus of colonialism, could not afford to adopt such a viewpoint as long as there was even the faintest possibility that their own experience did not inevitably have to parallel that of their counterparts in the West. To mobilize art in the service of the extirpation of colonialism and effecting social change could not make the already unacceptable situation worse and it might possibly make it better, whereas to adopt the modernist vision would be to concede victory to the other side—Sayyāb's "forces of evil"—before the struggle had even begun. Eden cannot be realized if a wasteland is your only model for representing reality.

It is precisely in its neat and easily containable opposition to Eden discourse that we can see here an element of Sayyāb's fascination with the title to Eliot's signature poem over and above any other aspect of his work. Using the "waste land" to create a binary opposition to "paradise" (the "world of tomorrow" filled with "jasmine") not only allows Sayyāb to invert and undermine the Western master narrative of colonialism, which says that the European colonial powers were merely *re*claiming the biblical *space* of Eden that had been theirs in the beginning, but it also allows him to contest the Western colonial appropriation of the *temporal* discourse of progress and to lay claim to it for his own society where the "jasmine will bloom" while London becomes "the unreal City." It is not so much, then, that

Sayyāb at this point sees Eliot producing a "critique" of Western civilization which he could parallel with a critique of his own society (this will be the overriding characteristic of Sayyāb's later poetry that appropriates elements of Eliot's work), but that he considers the representation of Western civilization found in what he has read of Eliot's poetry to be inadequate as a vision of civilization and therefore subject to critique.

That this direct confrontation and reinterpretation of *The Waste Land* is seen only briefly at this point in Sayyāb's career and is confined in the main to this single poem does not mean that Sayyāb would not continue to be keenly interested in Eliot's work. For a long period, however, his interest would be less oriented toward Eliot's worldview than toward his technique, in particular his incorporation of multiple voices into the framework of the lyric poem using strategies derived ultimately from the dramatic monologue form, as invented by Robert Browning and refined by him and Tennyson.[24] As we shall see in chapter 7 of this study, Eliot's model, especially in some of his early poems like "The Love Song of J. Alfred Prufrock" or "Portrait of a Lady," would be of great importance to Sayyāb in his experiments with the metrical form and generic allegiance of the modern Arab lyric poem that began in 1948. But even as late as the early 1950s, Sayyāb would tell one of his literary friends that Eliot had been more influential on his style than on the thematics of his poetry "because I am his complete antithesis with respect to his ideas and with respect to my view of life."[25]

It was only in 1954 that Sayyāb would be in a position to re-evaluate Eliot's cultural stance and move toward an accommodation with the other author to the point that he would see himself as conducting a parallel project, critiquing Arab/Islamic civilization—especially insofar as it could be made representative of civilization as a general phenomenon—in much the same way as he believed Eliot had conducted a critique and demystification of the sources of Western civilization after World War I in *The Waste Land*. In extending Eliot's method beyond the limits of Western civilization to show how it could be used to "read" another cultural world, Sayyāb could in a way be seen as practicing "supplementation" in the Derridean sense: offering an additive reading that would tend to supplant its precursor because it was more comprehensive and inclusive than the original.

This shift in perspective on Sayyāb's part seems to have been occasioned by his first reading of Eliot's source-text for much of the symbolic–allusional structure and rhetorical strategies found in *The Waste Land*: James Frazer's *The Golden Bough*. Sayyāb came to this work in 1954 through the mediation of a new friend, the Palestinian poet, novelist, and critic, Jabrā Ibrāhīm Jabrā, who had by this time taken up residence in Baghdad after a two-year stay in the United States on a research fellowship at Harvard University.[26] The poet Buland al-Ḥaydarī, also a friend of Sayyāb, was trying to start a new literary magazine to be called *Al-Fuṣūl al-Arba'a* (*The Four Seasons*) and he had commissioned Jabrā to translate the first two sections of part 4 of *The Golden Bough*—the part dealing with the myth of Adonis[27]—so that they could be published in the inaugural issue of his magazine.[28] While Jabrā was translating from the English, Sayyāb—as Jabrā tells us himself—was reading along with him in the Frazer volume:

> It so happened that Badr was informed about this myth [of Tammuz] in two sections of a volume I was translating from *The Golden Bough* by Sir James Frazer (the two sections were published in a Baghdad magazine at the end of 1954). When Badr read them, he found in them a tremendous poetic instrument which he later used as a source for ideas for more than six years, writing during that period his most beautiful and deepest poetry.
>
> After 1954, all the lines of his poetry meet in the myth of Tammuz and branch out from it. It is the wellspring from which most of his poetic images drink. He tried once, in "Min Ru'yā Fūkāy (From Fukai's Vision)," to imitate the quotations that T.S. Eliot uses in his poem *The Waste Land*. However, for some reason, he ignored the myth of Tammuz quoted in Eliot's poem—despite his [own] allusions to Christ, whose "blood made roses grow in the stones." Nevertheless, the poems he composed after "Fukai" began to explode with images from the myth which he had adopted as his own.[29]

What Jabrā says here about Sayyāb not immediately adopting the language of the death/rebirth myths into his poetic lexicon is important because it highlights the fact that Sayyāb was more interested in something else about Frazer's work, something that was represented by the use of "poetic quotation" (note how Jabrā conflates the influence of Frazer here with that of Eliot). Now, poetic quotation in *The Waste Land* is used primarily to contrast the (idealized) past with the (denatured) present—in other words it works, through a process of comparison, which is usually unfavorable to the contemporary, to critique the present state of society.[30] An example would be the "Sweet Thames, run softly till I end my song . . ." scene in "The Fire Sermon" section of *The Waste Land*, where quotations from Edmund Spenser's "Prothalamium" and Andrew Marvell's "To His Coy Mistress" are used in an altered form to underline the speaker's contention that "the nymphs are departed" and what has replaced them is "the rattle of the bones, and chuckles spread from ear to ear."

Such "poetic quotation" is one of many techniques of comparison that Eliot had found in Frazer's *The Golden Bough*, where it formed an essential element of the rhetorical structure of a work that aimed for encyclopedic completeness through the use of analogy and comparison. Frazer not infrequently found the apt quotation drawn from English poetry or folk song an appropriate way to signal the closure of one of his segments examining the permutations and reincarnations of some mythic figure or element of a ritual. An example from the section that Jabrā translated, which we know particularly piqued Sayyāb's interest,[31] is the following, where an Arabic source is cited as the authority in the chapter where the wide diffusion of the rituals of mourning for the vegetation god Adonis is being documented:

> The character of Tammuz or Adonis as a corn-spirit comes out plainly in an account of this festival given by an Arabic writer of the tenth century. In describing the rites and sacrifices observed he says: "Tammuz[32] (July). In the middle of this month is the festival of el-Bugat [sic], that is, of the weeping women, and this is the Tā-uz festival, which is celebrated in honour of the god Tā-uz. The women bewail him, because his lord slew him so cruelly, ground his bones in a mill, and then scattered them to the wind. The women (during this festival) eat nothing which has been ground in a mill, but limit their diet to steeped wheat, sweet vetches, dates, raisins and the like." Tā-uz, who is none other than Tammuz, is here like Burns's John Barleycorn—
>
> *"They wasted o'er a scorching flame*
> *The marrow of his bones;*
> *But a miller used him worst of all—*
> *For he crush'd him between two stones."*
>
> This concentration, so to say, of the nature of Adonis upon the cereal crops is characteristic of the stage of culture reached by his worshippers in historical times . . . [33]

Here, lines by the Scottish poet Robert Burns imitating folk songs concerning the milling of the grain at harvest festivals are positioned in such a way in Frazer's text so as to suggest they represent the culminating proof of his argument that the survival of nearly forgotten fertility rituals in the artifacts of modern culture can often, especially in what was then commonly seen as a deliberately atavistic art like poetry, explain what might otherwise would have to be dismissed or at least passed over as unmotivated and irrational nonsense.

Poetic quotation, however, was only a small component within Frazer's larger strategy for presenting his material in *The Golden Bough*. This was what had become known in the nascent field of anthropology in the late nineteenth century as "the comparative method." The comparative method relies on the assembling of information about as many different cultures as possible, ransacking not only the records made of contemporary societies but also the archives of the historical past for material on cultures and peoples that had ceased to exist, in order to search for patterns of significant similarity under a welter of seeming differences.[34] Frazer's adaptation of this method to the study of the myths of death and rebirth purported to show that many modern customs in different parts of the world, composed of seemingly unique elements that appeared to have no precedent and thus no history, as well as no connection to one another (appearing therefore, in those privileged modernist signifiers, as "discontinuous" and "fragmented") could in fact be traced back to a common origin in that extremely widespread set of myths where the seasonal "death" of nature and its "rebirth" in the spring is figured through the story of a the death of a young man or woman, "a beloved of the gods"—whose subsequent mourning over the corpse leads to some provisional form of his or her resurrection. Over the years, as *The Golden Bough* went through edition after revised edition, it became increasingly clear to his readers that the keystone of Frazer's purpose was to apply this "comparative method" to various elements of Christian belief and thus show, as John Vickery has noted, "how the uniqueness of Christianity is dissolved in its emergence from primitive fertility rituals."[35] As a confirmed rationalist, Frazer wanted to demonstrate that much of what the popular imagination of the nineteenth century saw as spiritually uplifting and morally unique, such as the celebration of Christ's resurrection at Easter, in fact had its source in what were quite often bloody and violent rites and rituals intended to ensure the fertility of the earth. In this he joined a number of voices belonging to nineteenth-century intellectuals who were, for one reason or another, critical of the role of religion in society and wished to demystify its origins, including figures like Robert Strauss (author of *The Life of Jesus*), Julius Wellhausen, William Robertson Smith, and Ernest Renan (whose notorious anti-Semitism can be seen as arising, at least in part, out of his desire to undermine Christianity through the discrediting of its Jewish matrix). They all opposed any supernatural element in religion, on the one hand, yet equally for many of them, the central linchpin of establishment society in their age, the bourgeois version of Christianity being spread across the globe by increasingly zealous and self-righteous missionary activity, was an extremely questionable formation, and in a sense Frazer crowned their achievements by persuasively demonstrating—at least to many of his contemporaries—that Christianity was nothing but a degeneration of the same pagan rituals it had supposedly come to supplant as a genuine alternative (and superior because more spiritual) vision of life: that of course could mean in its turn that those pagan rituals might actually embody a superior, or at the very least equally valid, approach to the problems of living. In terms of the narratives of cultural history, then, it was the return of the repressed temporal narrative of the golden age to lay its claims to the laurels so recently awarded to "progress."

That the techniques developed by Frazer to critique Christianity through comparing it with elements of pagan myth could be applied to other elements of modern culture was one thing that Eliot—and later Sayyāb—drew from *The Golden Bough*. Sayyāb quickly applied these lessons about using the apparent survivals of ancient myths in present practices as a means to critique his own contemporary culture and show its inadequacies in his experimental poems of 1954 and 1955, most notably the "Fukai"[36] poems and "Song in the Month of August." These poems rely heavily on Sayyāb's new insights into how Eliot had adapted Frazer in *The Waste Land*, and they are ultimately best read as cultural critiques, as representations, not exhortations immediately concerned with questions of how the land could be reclaimed by the colonized. That this was Sayyāb's intention can be seen in how he uses references to Tammuz in the final section of "From the Vision of Fukai," where the clerk reports the ravings of a patient suffering from the last stages of syphilis as he lies dying in the Red Cross Hospital in Hiroshima:

60) What do those black eyes want from a man who has gathered the flowers of sin wherever he met them?
61) Flowers [like venereal spots] on my fevered body which I pluck [and gather] into a bouquet from wounds whose heat I have spent the night enduring.
62) This is the spring whose anemones will be guided by the winds of doom to my heart with their rain-filled scent,
63) The flowers of Tammuz, what I tended: shall I hand them over to him in the underworld twilight?
64) Or Eve's snake: with apples would he repay me, when not long ago he tempted her with apples?
65) What do those black eyes want? They have something of her about them I have not been able to forget in forgetting her.[37]

Here, the delirious man is haunted by the unwavering gaze of two black eyes that seem to stare out at him, disembodied, from the shadows. Certainly there is an element in these lines that attempts both to evoke and to undercut the fleeting ideal of sexuality represented by the Hyacinth Girl in *The Waste Land*: "—Yet when we came back, late, from the hyacinth garden, / Your arms full, and your hair wet, I could not / Speak, and *my eyes failed*, I was neither / Living nor dead, and I knew nothing, / *Looking into the heart of light*, the silence"[emphasis mine].[38] But what is far more interesting for our purposes is the way in which the sick man's outburst links the narratives of Eden and Tammuz. Having compared the lesions on his body to anemone flowers, the sick man imagines himself in the role of the fertility god, handing them over as tribute to Hades, Lord of the Underworld, upon arrival for a six-month sojourn in the dark land (as Adonis does every year in one variant of these myths).But this causes him to wonder if perhaps it would not instead be more appropriate to give the gifts signifying fertility and therefore sexuality to Satan, since the latter had used a similar gift of a fertility symbol, the apple, to lead Eve down the garden path to the guilty knowledge of her own sexuality. Thus, what links the Eden and Tammuz narratives in this poem is not a concern with rejuvenating or restoring the land, as it turns out. Instead there is a linkage through sexuality: the quest for fertility on the one hand and a seduction/temptation leading to the labeling of desire as evil on the other. The impasse created by the collision of these worldviews (the quest for love, the denial of love as a positive value) leads to death. Both on a personal level, as the syphilitic dies in the hospital, having been condemned by his society to seek love illicitly, and on a cultural level, as nations pledged to destruction rather than love fill the earth "with a fierce storm of iron and lead" culminating in the carefully described horrors of the bombing of Hiroshima, which in the course of the last poem in the sequence merges imperceptibly into Jaykūr:

51) Hear the wind! Fill the wind, Jaykūr, with laughter and rose petals!
52) Silence frowns where once you sang, those perfumes now are stinking pus.
53) A century has come and gone, and the cities are in chaos, [but] still they count their change,
54) The voice of the weak, the prophets' groans, the entreaties of those pursued have all vanished there,
55) And even space has been transformed (by machines that roar and slaves gasping out their labored breath)
56) This space has changed to something not for men—perhaps for apes

57) Perhaps for wolves and worms, and those lower than worms in the witless swamps.
58) The noise remains, like a corpse pregnant with what can only be a sterile birth
59) There it winds itself into balls of fire and the silence of the tomb has fallen upon you!

With this, seemingly, we have arrived back at the unplaced and dehumanizing discourse of nonmillennial apocalyptic. Space is mentioned, to be sure; at first the specific place of Jaykūr is dwelt upon, but it then becomes the abstract and homogeneous emptiness of *al-faḍā'*, the Arabic word that is used most often to render the vast reaches of airless outer space, that realm where human beings are not welcome. "Places are all the same, evil is everywhere and we are all equally implicated" seems to be the message of these poems, and the last of them ("Marthiyat Jaykūr") ends with a bleak vision of the world as "a marketplace where the flesh of men is sold without stripping off the skin." A fitting home, in the speaker's view, for those infected by the Western worship of reification and the cash nexus. In an appropriate tribute to Eliot's precedent for the technique of poetic quotation and its importance to the "Fukai" poems, Sayyāb makes the final line of this section a reworking of a famous verse by the medieval philosopher poet al-Ma'arrī, whose heterodox views and disdain for the role of courtier-poet has made him a special favorite of modern Arab poets. Sayyāb changes al-Ma'arrī's line "And what should leave all creation confounded there is an animal generated from an inanimate substance"[39] to his own version, "And what should leave all creation confounded there is how to explain a creature with cash,"[40] which again underlines how, for the speaker, the language of life, organicism, and tradition has been recast for the modern world as a whole into a denatured language of monetary exchange. That the colonial aspect of this commodification of the world has been de-emphasized (though not totally abandoned) in the poem is accentuated by the placing of its setting in wartime Japan—a neutral location, not strictly within the colonial domain as unequivocally either colonizer or colonized. Thus, unlike the 1946 poem, there is no hint of the positing of a world outside the reach of this particular power nexus. This change would suggest that Sayyāb has begun the shift to position himself more within the Eliotian world as he conceived it, where the poet advertises himself as critic of the entire panorama of modern civilization laid before him and takes no sides. Where he strives for his particular "originality," then, would be in his comprehensiveness. Unlike Eliot, whose dissections were confined mainly to Western European civilization, Sayyāb's critique would attempt to encompass all.

The three installments of "The Vision of Fukai" were published in the most innovative and influential literary periodical of the day, the Lebanese magazine *Al-Ādāb*, edited by the Francophile, yet passionately Arab nationalist, intellectual Suhayl Idrīs who is best known for introducing the latest postwar French intellectual fashions to the Arab world and especially the existentialism of Jean-Paul Sartre and Albert Camus, along with its attendant ideological positions espousing the "commitment" of art and literature. Idrīs had befriended Sayyāb a couple of years earlier—as he had done and would do with many other promising young writers—and encouraged him, giving him a place to publish his work at a time when Sayyāb was perhaps at the lowest point of his fortunes.

One of the more attractive features of *Al-Ādāb* for these young intellectuals was the immediate feedback it provided for their literary and critical efforts, in the form of a regularly published review article in each month's issue critiquing the previous issue's poetry, stories, and essays, entitled "Qara'tu Al-'Adad al-Māḍī (I Read the Last Issue)." These review articles were written by a rotating (more or less) group of well-known intellectuals, as well as rising young literary critics and writers. The reviews would often stimulate a lively exchange of views in the magazine's letters column that could go on for several months. Thus, an aspiring writer could, if he or she were published in *Al-Ādāb*, reasonably be assured, for better or worse, of finding out very quickly how experimental techniques or provocative subject matter had been received.

Sayyāb's experiments with Eliot's techniques of allusion and quotation in the three "Fukai" poems were greeted in this forum with almost universal rejection—not only from the reviewers, but in the letters as well. Their reactions were remarkably uniform. They saw the poems as "lacking in coherence,"[41] "obscure and discordant,"[42] and "an unwieldy mass of myths, unconnected images and undigested ideas."[43] In what was perhaps the unkindest cut of all, the Egyptian critic Maḥmūd Amīn al-'Ālim described "Marthiyat al-Āliha (Elegy for the Gods)," the second installment of the series, as reminding him of the techniques used by Ezra Pound and later T.S. Eliot. These poets, he says, used to quote multiple literary allusions in their poetry in order to evoke different sorts of atmospheric effects. But, he goes on

> There is a huge difference between the attempts of Pound and Eliot, and the attempt of the Iraqi poet. We are able to follow along with Eliot's symbols and

> appreciate his artistic work without having to look up his historical and anthropological allusions and his literary quotations. That is because these additions constitute a tightly knit, organic content in the poem, and our knowledge of their sources deepens our appreciation of the poem and our grasp of what it signifies, but it is possible for us to appreciate the poem in ignorance of these researches and allusions . . . in the Iraqi poet's poem the notes and allusions are added on as an afterthought and not knit into [the structure], standing at a distance from the organic unity despite the fact that they are connected to it. It is a connection of addition, not a connection of organicism.[44]

Sayyāb clearly felt that he had tried—as Eliot had done before him—to represent the sense of fragmentation and disjunctiveness that consciousness experienced when faced with the multiplicity of the modern world. He said as much in a series of angry letters written to each reviewer as a new installment of the "Fukai" poems appeared. But to no avail. The representation of modern consciousness as fragmented and disordered was not a discourse strategy that received a high valuation in the Arab world at that time—and given the political situation (which demanded that all contribute to a cohesive united opposition to the continuation of colonialism), probably for very good reasons.

June 1955 saw the publication of the last of Sayyāb's letters of outrage over what he saw as the misinterpretations of his poem. After this no more was heard of the project to fashion a long poem from the installments of "Fukai." In 1956, Sayyāb turned his attention instead to writing a series of much shorter lyrics, all of which—though in some respects quite different from each other—refocused attention on the question of land and its connection to the myths of death and rebirth in a quite new and different way from both his confident prediction in 1946 of being able to fill "our land with jasmine" and his bitter vision of the world as a floating signifier, empty of all associations except those of a mobile, interchangeable marketplace for human commodities in the "Fukai" poems.

Although Jabrā, as we have seen, was incorrect in saying that Tammuz does not appear in the "Fukai" poems, he was quite right to emphasize the importance of the myths of death and rebirth themselves—taken directly from Frazer rather than through the mediation of Eliot—as an element in Sayyāb's later poetry and how the use of these mythic allusions renders these poems qualitatively different from those composed prior to 1956. This difference relates very closely to their new emphasis on the theme of restoring the *land* to its inhabitants and ensuring its fertility for their benefit, which in turn underscores even more urgently their relevance to the adjacent discourse of Eden. But coupled with this was an equally noticeable tendency, especially at first, to de-emphasize the more overt markers that would signal to the reader that he or she was dealing with a poem resting on the basis of this particular mythic discourse.

Typical of most of these poems in its deployment of the death–rebirth myths as an underlying pattern for experience that will relate them directly to questions of land is the poem "Fī al-Maghrib al-'Arabī (In Arab North Africa)," published in the March number of *Al-Ādāb*. The French colonization of North Africa, and especially of Algeria, begun in the mid-nineteenth century, had long been the most egregious example of settler colonialism (the most deracinating kind) in the Arab world. In 1955 and 1956, the Arabs's struggle in North Africa for the return of their land had seen major gains in that Morocco and Tunisia were being granted their independence by France. On the other hand, in August of 1955 the Algerian picture had turned far bleaker with the incident known as the Philippeville massacres, where FLN freedom fighters had savagely attacked and murdered a large number of French colonials in and near the town of Philippeville and the *colons* had, with the support of the French Army, taken their vengeance on the local Arab inhabitants with equal ferocity. With Philippeville, then, the Algerian conflict entered a new and much bloodier phase that would not end until seven years later when the French would be forced to leave the colony they had once sworn would remain forever an irrevocable part of France.

The speaker in Sayyāb's poem is an Algerian freedom fighter and as the poem opens[45] Sayyāb pictures him standing in front of a grave where the headstone has his name written on it. This unnerving sight leaves him unsure: is he dead or alive? Not even the sight of his own shadow stretching across the sand can reassure him that he is among the living,[46] for its shape reminds him of other shadows he is seeing, cast by "a dusty minaret" and "a graveyard"—perhaps visible off in the distance, perhaps only in his mind's eye—which are for him dead things: "a vanished glory." The minaret, however, refuses to release its hold on his imagination and draws his eye back to its green, glazed-tile decorations, with their interlacing calligraphic motifs incorporating the Arabic words for "God" and for his Prophet, "Muḥammad." But the sight of these tiles, which were once "proudly ensconced on the heights," only serves to spark a recollection of having seen one of them on a more recent occasion, lying on the ground:

15) Its meaning is now faded, eaten away by dust
16) And bombardments,
17) The invaders kicking it, without shoes,
18) Without feet,
19) And without blood, a wound bled
20) From it/him, without pain—
21) So it/he died,
22) And we have died in it/him, both the dead and the living.
23) We are all dead:
24) I and Muḥammad and God.
25) And this is our grave: the debris [left] of a minaret covered with whitish dust
26) Where the names of Muḥammad and God have been written,
27) Upon a broken fragment of tile and fired clay.[47]

Here, by exploiting the ambiguity of the third-person masculine pronoun in lines 20–22 (the referent can be either "he" or "it") in a move that suggests the breaking down of boundaries between past and present, animate and inanimate (creating the "motivated" sign) the tile with the name "Muḥammad" written on it becomes its signified, Muḥammad the Prophet, who in turn becomes his signified, his namesake, the modern-day individual Arab called Muḥammad, lying on the street being kicked and trampled by young French Army conscripts or excited *colons* (perhaps one can see in the mention that the invaders are "shoeless" an allusion to "*pied noir* [black foot]," the somewhat derogatory nickname for the North African French colonists—'Abbās says only that the invaders lack of shoes means they lack culture, but this would seem to vitiate Sayyāb's very precise visual imagery in his best poetry), which was a staple of newsreel footage of the period. But this linkage of past to present remains purely assertive at this point. Having made the connection, the speaker finds himself forced to say the "we" are all dead—where he was uncertain before, now he is sure, and the resolution of that uncertainty will not be to his advantage. Not only has it forced death upon him and his past but the only memory he can summon up from that past is one of peril: the attack led by the Ethiopian king Abraha that very nearly destroyed the Kaaba, the sacred shrine of the pre-Islamic Arabs as it would become later for Muslims, in the year of Muḥammad's birth. Even though the traditional version of the Abraha narrative has the Ethiopians defeated through divine intervention before they can carry out their plans of conquest, this is not what our speaker remembers: it is rather the time of danger prior to that miraculous rescue.

But the speaker glances at the headstone again, and this time he sees that it actually lies between two graves: his own and his grandfather's (for whom he is presumably named). So perhaps there is hope: perhaps the headstone is for his grandfather's grave and not yet for him. Perhaps he is still alive. And, even though the speaker knows that his grandfather's body is nothing now but dry black scraps of flesh and bone mixed in with the sand of his final resting place, he seems to hear his ancestor's voice rising up from the grave: calling out first to the valley—to the land itself—to rise up in rebellion, and then exhorting the generations of his descendants living in that valley to "throw off their yoke." This time, with the echo of his grandfather's words still ringing in the air, the speaker has a second, much more reassuring vision from history: of a great battle during pre-Islamic times where the outnumbered Bedouin Arabs nevertheless won a decisive victory against their foreign foes. This is followed by a more recent battle: the successful fight of the Moroccan freedom fighters in the Rif mountains against the French. All of this, we may surmise, comes about because the speaker now has a personal connection to this past: it happened to those whose blood flows now in his veins. It is not "mere" history.

This potent retrospective epiphany, however, is immediately followed by a less sanguine sight: of God, having descended from the heavens to the Palestinian city of Jaffa, now occupied by the Israeli army, walking among the crowds of inhabitants in the beleaguered city who offer him a quick meal but do nothing to "bandage his wounds," nor do they seem willing to sacrifice anything they hold precious to help him. The only response of most of them to his subsequent death is to recite elegies for him and perform the appropriate prayers in his honor. But another group would do something else:

66) [Those words] will cure our fear by our knowledge that we will make him live
67) If the revolutionaries among us cry out jubilantly: "We will sacrifice ourselves for him!"[48]

This unselfish pledge by the rebels to give their lives in order to save another then leads to yet another historical vision for the speaker: this time of the Crusaders, ancestors of the modern French soldiers, invading Syria eventually to suffer defeat at Muslim hands; but not before they have shod their horses with iron crescents torn from the minarets they left behind in ruins there (thus bringing us back to the destroyed minaret image used at the beginning of the poem) and they have fed "Jesus to the hungry lions." This propensity to violence, and willingness to destroy their God for material gain (After all, do the whores in Paris not attend church—a place where they drink Christ's blood in the form of wine and eat his body in the form of the Eucharist—and then return to ply their trade in beds where the image of the martyred Jesus hangs above their pillows?) is the true nature of these people, the speaker realizes. But the depiction of their innate destructiveness also registers a converse implication: they are shown to be sterile, their victories only temporary, military ones. They cannot renew or make fertile the lands they occupy.

So, one final time as the poem ends, the speaker returns to gaze upon his headstone:

98) I read my name upon a stone
99) In the space between two names in the desert
100) The world of the living drew breath
101) Like blood in your veins flows between heartbeats,
102) And from a red tile standing upright above a sunken grave
103) Blood has illuminated the features of the land
104) Without a flash of lightning
105) Then gave it a name
106) So that it could take from this blood its meaning.
107) So that I could know that it is my land,
108) So that I could know that it is part of me,
109) So that I could know that it is my past, that I cannot live without it
110) And that I would have died without it, as I walked amongst its dead.
111) Is this concourse choked with banners our valley?
112) Is this the color of our past
113) Given light by the windows of Al-Ḥamrā'[49]
114) And by green tiles
115) On which the name of God is written with the last drops of our blood?
116) Are those the rising tones of the call to dawn prayer? Or the cries of
the revolutionaries, "God is great,"
117) Rising from our fortresses?
118) The graves have gone into labor, to give birth, so that the dead will
rise in their millions,
119) And Muḥammad, and his Arab God, and Al-Anṣār have all risen up:
120) Indeed our God is within us.[50]

It is worth noting that generically this poem, like many of Sayyāb's later works, evokes the paradigms of what has been called the "greater romantic ode,"[51] in its focus on the representation of the mind in the *process* of thinking or meditation about "the change in aspect" of a landscape detail described at the beginning of the poem. Although there were Arabic models for structuring poems as a (fictively) organic representation of the thinking process in this teleological way, they had not dominated the tradition, which relied more on associational patterns of representation where the poem brought together syntactically independent lines—like the (apparently) isolated thoughts that might occur to a consciousness in a state of dreamlike reverie rather than focused meditation—and allowed the quasi-independent observations to play off one another in ways that could give rise to an exciting sense of new connections made, new perspectives on the world glimpsed, but only provided the reader was willing and able to make the effort to supply the necessary connections. The "meditative" models of Western poetry, especially those that became popular with the rise of Western romanticism, tended to draw on more structured models of mental practice, like confession, dialectic, philosophical speculation, religious devotions, or prayer for their inspiration.

Sayyāb's generation, with its new, though often not entirely voluntary, access to Western models of the meditative (as opposed to the reverie) poem—which was, after all, not entirely foreign to their own literary heritage—via the Western-influenced educational system, seems to have found this kind of "descriptive-meditative poem" an especially engaging and dramatically useful structure on which to build poetic compositions. It was certainly one that Sayyāb would find particularly congenial and would become an accomplished master of by the end of his life.[52] In this poem, as in other such "greater odes" Sayyāb wrote in the mid- to late 1950s, the thinking mind that is placed before us is engaged in working out the solution to a problem. In this case it is the question posed by the speaker upon being confronted by the sight of a headstone standing before him with his own name upon it: Am I alive or am I dead? This in turn leads to a more philosophical question whose resolution takes up the bulk of the speaker's meditation: How can I—in my cultural identity as an Arab—*tell* whether I am alive or dead? What do these two words—life and death—really *mean* for me?

The resolution seems to occur through a combination of the practices of meditation (focused thought processes mimetic of the logical sequencing of argumentation) and of reverie (the representation of thought processes as associational). Thus, although we can say with confidence that the speaker's attitude toward the headstone has changed by the end of the poem—from one of ontological confusion and uncertainty to absolute certainty in the "triumph of life"—we readers are not necessarily led by the hand and carefully shown every step along the path of the speaker's thinking process. There are some elements we must supply ourselves through an active engagement in the dynamics of the poem as we read it.

Those of us already aware—directly through Frazer or whatever intermediary source—of the underlying pattern of death/rebirth that the comparative method of anthropology had imbued the fertility myths with, have been supplied with a valuable clue for organizing this heuristic journey. Clearly the chain of events described in the poem follows the pattern of death/rebirth, where the sacrificial death of a youth, the "beloved of the gods" (in this case the speaker), leads directly to the regeneration of the land—repossession by the colonized of the space they inhabit—and, in some versions at least (like the Christian one, where Christ's death on the cross is an expiation of Adam's sin that will only bear its fullest fruit on the Day of Resurrection) to an eventual rebirth of all who were dead. All that is missing are the outward trappings that would tie the representation to a specific myth: the gods' names, the pagan settings, the symbolic objects and actors (like the anemones and the wild boar in the myth of Adonis). Therefore, unlike the Fukai poems, which advertise their mythical connections through incorporation of just such specific markers, this narrative offers us the vital linkage through making its endpoint the rejuvenation of the land, with all its powerful suggestiveness for a discourse of postcolonial reappropriation. Thus in one sense Sayyāb is once more asserting, this time through a much more thorough exploitation of the medium of the fertility myths than his brief 1946 evocation of "the wasteland," his unnerving counter-claim to the colonizer's discourse of Eden. In effect, when he says "So that I could know that it is my land / So that I could know that it is part of me," he is also addressing the representatives of colonial power, saying: you the colonizer do not have the power to make the land revive because it will only respond to us, who have the power/knowledge derived from living with it for many generations as though with another living thing,[53] something you cannot duplicate. Your only achievement has been to make us forget that knowledge, but we will soon be able to retrieve it through imaginative reconstructions such as the one this poem enacts.

Thus far, this discourse would seem to be articulated through a relatively uncomplicated redeployment of the Frazerean material as given, showing that it can be in and of itself an alternative discourse used to read this situation of colonial violence in such a way as to obtain very different results from the colonizer's characteristic discursive interpretations of the same events. But Sayyāb moves beyond that here to problematize the Frazerean corpus itself in such a way as to present it as being strategically contained within a larger discursive formation, one that is "truer" because it contains the signifier that was absent from *The Golden Bough*: Islam.[54]

Frazer, as we have seen, found in the fertility myths an opportunity to deconstruct Christianity, among other things, to show that there were many survivals of these so-called "primitive" beliefs and practices in their supposedly more sophisticated successor. Like Christianity—as Sayyāb and his contemporary poets would begin to suggest in their poetry of the 1950s—Islam contained elements that could be seen as survivals from the earlier fertility religions. But in a move quite different from Frazer's use of them to deflate Christianity, Sayyāb seems to be endeavoring to show in this poem—as well as in later ones—that this residue in his view works to enhance the spiritual validity of Islam rather than call it into question. An example from "In Arab North Africa" would be the deployment of symbolism associated with the color green.

Green is, of course, the dominant color of young vegetation and was thus associated with new life, ensuring its central role in the symbolism of the fertility cults. In Islam, green has also had an important symbolic role, becoming the color most closely associated with Muḥammad in particular and prophets in general.[55] Muḥammad, for example, often used a green flag as a standard in battle, and green is the usual color of the turbans traditionally worn to indicate that the wearer is a descendent of the Prophet. Although possible connections between this symbolism and the older fertility religions are never explicitly discussed in official Islamic discourse, that there might be such connections between these Islamic usages and more ancient symbolic structures well understood throughout the area would not be difficult for someone like Sayyāb, with his knowledge of Frazer's comparative method, to make, nor do they seem particularly strange or automatically subversive if one considers them in the context of that widespread metanarrative found in modern versions of Arab nationalism, that Muḥammad's message was instrumental in giving life and a new cultural vitality to the Bedouin Arabs, inhabitants of a vast desert "wasteland" on the fringes of ancient civilization. Such overdetermined symbolic valences would, for example, help to explain why it is so important for the speaker of "In Arab North Africa" to describe the tiles with Muḥammad's name on them as being green. But this does not vitiate in any way their status as objects independently imbued, through the tracery of the names appearing on them, with the numinousness of Islam.

A similar case can be made for the poem's use of the color red. Red in the fertility myths is associated with the dying youth's blood—with death—which must therefore be transformed symbolically into an association with life. In one version of the Adonis myth, as an example, this is done by having bright red anemone flowers, which normally appear in the fields of Mediterranean countries in the spring, grow from the drops of Adonis's blood as they fall onto the ground. At the beginning of "In Arab North Africa" red is also associated with death, in that the headstone of the speaker's grave is explicitly described as being "red." But at the end of the poem, in consequence of the speaker's new perspective, red becomes associated with a new object: the Alhambra palace in Granada, whose name in Arabic means "the red one." The Alhambra, of course, was the last Arab Muslim stronghold in Europe and fell to the Christians in 1492. But, despite falling into the possession of hostile European rulers the palace itself has endured in much the same shape and configuration as when it belonged to the Amir of Granada. Thus it can function, and does seem to do so in Sayyāb's poem, as a symbol of life and survival, as a continuing and ineradicable Arab presence in a land that, like colonial North Africa, had been subject to appropriation by hostile European armies.

Sayyāb uses in his poem, then, both these colors (with their links to fertility symbolism as well as significance in Arab Islamic discourse) in ways that work to enhance our valuation of both discursive formations, and this is of utmost importance in differentiating his deployment of the myths from Frazer's. One needs only to look at the first time Frazer mentions Christianity in Volume Five of *The Golden Bough* to register a sense of the dissimilarity. Frazer has been speaking of a group of demi-gods and heroes with links to the Adonis cult, who have all been begotten by the union of human women with snakes. Then he mentions that the classical author Aelian has an anecdote about a similar thing happening in the time of Herod, when "a serpent . . . made love to a Judean maid." Then he adds, as an afterthought. "Can the story be a distorted rumour of the parentage of Christ?"[56] Since there is nothing to motivate a connection between the two events other than the fact that they both took place "in the time of Herod," the observation would seem to be a mischievous thrust intrusively inserted at this point in order to place Christian dogma on the level of "mythology" and perhaps to suggest a conflation of the divine and the demonic in first-century Palestine, since in biblical narrative it is Satan and not God who is usually associated with the serpent form. Although it by no means has to be the case, it is certainly possible that it was reading such passages as this that gave Sayyāb the initial idea for the way he represents the survival of the fertility myths in Christian ritual in his poem. There, the point of purchase for deconstruction of Christian ideology is not in the first instance sexual but alimentary, but the effect is much the same:

86) . . . they sold
87) Their god which they made from gold we toiled for,
88) Just as they ate him when they were hungry,
89) Their god whom we shaped from our blood-soaked bread.
90) And in Paris the whores take
91) Christ's torment for a place to rest their heads,
92) And all night long sterility sows in their entrails
93) [The teeth from] the dragon's mouth, as it draws breath to hiss
94) And hurl into our homes, soulless
95) Iron legions [that look] like warriors.[57]

The French Christians, when they participate in communion "eat" their god; thus they are no different from cannibals.

As numerous authors have shown, cannibalism is a word to conjure with on both sides of the colonial divide. By the time the great age of exploration and colonization began in the sixteenth and seventeenth centuries, Christians of both Catholic and Protestant allegiance had already become sensitized to the issue of claims of resemblance between the rites of the Eucharist and cannibalism, because one of the dogmatic issues around which definitions of difference between the two sects had crystallized was over whether the drinking of the wine and the eating of the wafer were to be considered actual consumption of Christ's blood and flesh (the Catholic position) or merely symbolic (the position of most Protestants). It is in the context of this debate, as Stephen Greenblatt points out, that one should read that momentous event when Cortez's men are escorted into the Aztec temples (where human sacrifice was practiced) and see all around them religious paraphernalia that remind of them of Christian churches.[58] Usually, however, the label "cannibal" was used—quite literally from the time of Columbus—to set the natives of the New World apart from their Christian conquerors and, because it renders them inhuman/unhuman, to justify their enslavement. The beginnings of this Western obsession with, or fetishization of, the figure of the cannibal even leaves its trace on Shakespeare's plays: elements of *The Tempest* are based on narratives of New World exploration, and even the name of the grotesque slave who is the villain of the piece, Caliban, is an anagram for "cannibal."[59] The historian Hayden White has suggested a psychological explanation for this symptomatic cultural anxiety that may be relevant as well to Sayyāb's decision to include it as part of his indictment of colonial exploitation in "In Arab North Africa": that it is a sublimation "of an idyll of unrestricted *consumption*, oral and genital, and its alternative, the need to destroy that which cannot be consumed."[60]

Islamic discourse, too, exhibits a profound revulsion/fascination for the notion of eating human flesh. Cannibalism is used as a metaphor several times in the Koran. Perhaps the manifestation of this that is most memorable occurs in Sūrat al-Ḥujurāt (49:12) where slander and dissension among the believers is being condemned: ". . . so do not spy upon one another and speak critically of each other—would any one of you want to eat the flesh of his brother, dead? Surely you would find this disgusting." The vividness and detail of this comparison between undeserved reproof and cannibalism suggests that the latter was a strongly tabooed practice among the Bedouin Arabs who were the initial audience for these revelations.[61] More relevant, however, to the present discussion would be the Koranic verses (Sūrat al-Nisā', 4:2, 6, 10), which compare cheating orphans of their possessions to "eating" their wealth. That the consumption of human flesh and the consumption of wealth illicitly gotten are both characterized by the Koran as "eating" makes it easy for Sayyāb to use the figure of cannibalism in his poem and apply it to the French whose activities, from taking communion to expropriating the wealth of their colonial territories can be seen, then, as forming a seamless continuity: Hayden White's "idyll of unrestricted consumption." But seeing this as an "idyll" depends, of course, on the vantage point from which it is viewed. From the viewpoint of the poet caught up in the dynamics of resistance, Frazer's consistent coupling of Christianity with the primitive fertility cults might have seemed just too good an opportunity to miss: to use the colonizer's own authoritative text to undermine one of the pillars upon which they assert their superiority. So Frazer can be seen as the vehicle through which Sayyāb has deconstructed the colonizer's Christianity, showing it to be inferior to Islam because it cannot create symbols that are *symbolic* enough—they remain too closely tied to the pagan, to the literal, to real eating, just as the French *colons* lack the transformative power of the imagination that would allow them to become one with the land.[62] Thus the symbols given potency in the poem that have an Islamic valencing are the green tile and the Alhambra (both inanimate objects that project stability and permanence) while the Christian ones are the Eucharist and the

Greek myth of Cadmus who sowed the dragon's teeth to raise a soulless army that would slaughter all in its path.

It is worth noting that Sayyāb would later be criticized on the pages of *Al-Ādāb* for his reading of Christianity in this poem. It would be suggested that the view he expresses is too reductive, too condemnatory of the whole religion, rather than its French practitioners. This was important because there were, of course, Christian Arabs, many of whom fully shared in the beliefs of Arab nationalism. Although Arab nationalism laid special importance on the role of Islam as a formative force in the development of the civilization, it posited a cultural identity based more on a common language and a common history than on any religious beliefs beyond those general ones shared by both Muslims and Christians. Thus a reading of Christianity, as such, as exploitative or even cannibalistic would be highly problematic. Although Sayyāb often reacted angrily to criticism, he usually seems to have taken it to heart, and we find in later poems like "Al-Masīḥ Ba'da al-Ṣalb" (Christ After the Crucifixion) and others, a markedly different attitude toward Christianity, based on its very powerful valorization of self-sacrifice.[63]

Even as early as Sayyāb's "In Arab North Africa," the transformative power of the imagination is localized in this image of self-sacrifice. The colonized peoples will sacrifice themselves—thus enacting the life-renewing death of Adonis and the other fertility figures—which differentiates them from the colonizers, who will only eat the sacrificed flesh of others. It is precisely this element of self-sacrifice possessed by the fertility myths that is lacking in Eden discourse. After all, from the standpoint of traditional Christian theology it is only with the death of Jesus on the cross that the sin of Adam and Eve, which causes their expulsion from Paradise, is finally expiated. In most of the *pagan* fertility myths (as opposed to the Christ story), however, the youth's death is pictured as accidental. In the myth of Venus and Adonis, for example, Adonis is fatally wounded by a wild boar while hunting; he does not choose to die for a purpose, then: it simply happens. Thus the fertility myths, while containing the important idea of sacrifice, can also be seen as lacking a vital element, if they are to be construed as a model for and parallel to the discourse of resistance among the colonized: these latter should choose to sacrifice themselves for a greater goal, on behalf of others; just to die—without being aware of why one is dying or what one is dying for—is not enough. This is where the death of Jesus is so valuable: he stands out among the ranks of the dying gods and heroes because his sacrifice was consciously planned, as a selfless act of atonement for the sins of mankind.

In "In Arab North Africa" what seems to motivate the speaker to be willing to sacrifice himself is precedent. First his grandfather, and then more universal culture heroes, show him the value of self-sacrifice. Thus Sayyāb's concern with self-sacrifice as a way to retrieve the contested colonial space reveals itself to have a temporal dimension as well. In other words, one knows the validity of this strategy through history, not just myth. In fact, "In Arab North Africa" shows us that the appropriation of the temporal is not only integral to, but necessarily prior to, the reclamation of the land. This is because one must have an identity (know *who* you are) before you can choose how and in what way to make a meaningful sacrifice of self that will allow you or those who remain behind after you are gone to reclaim the land. Such a strong sense of identity has always been most easily obtained through a process of recollecting/constructing a common history for oneself and those one wishes to identify with. In addition, as we have seen, for the colonized to construct an effective counter-discourse they must reappropriate the colonizer's time narratives just as thoroughly as they reappropriate and seize control of his spatial narratives.

A sense of historical continuity is what gives the idea of self-sacrifice meaning for the colonized in a colonial context. The history of the colonizer tends to fall into a series of "timeless moments" where tableaux celebrating imperial achievement are publicly displayed. This allows the elision of the fact that the colonizing power has generally created its presence in those moments through violent usurpation, and that it has no real history on the land.[64] To force the presentation of historical continuity, then, would expose the discontinuities in the colonizer's rhetoric and through such a strategy the one who is being asked to sacrifice in the cause of decolonization will see the efficacy such actions have had in the past and will develop a teleological awareness, will come to believe that the future will also be better because of what the individual does. One can see ample illustration of this in the second half of "In Arab North Africa." If further evidence is needed, however, one of a handful of statements Sayyāb made on the subject of myth in his poetry demonstrates the very great importance he attached to temporalizing and historicizing the mythic narratives:

> You will observe in my poem an attempt to return to the past, to the heritage (*al-turāth*). . . . As for the Babylonian symbols, my use of them is not only because of their [artistic] richness and signification. They are yet close to me: not because they arose in a land we inhabit today, and not because the Babylonians were cousins of our ancestors the Arabs, not for just these [reasons] alone . . . but rather because the Arabs themselves had adopted these

symbols. The Ka'aba, between [the time of] Abraham and the appearance of the great Arab prophet [Muḥammad], knew all these Babylonian gods. . . . When Islam came—and it was the greatest victory ever achieved by Arab nationalism (*al-qawmiyya al-'arabiyya*)—it came to extirpate . . . the . . . idols the Arabs had known. So to call them today by their Arab names when we are using them as symbols, would constitute a kind of challenge to Islam, and hence to Arab nationalism.

And this is what makes us return to the distant roots (*uṣūl*) of these symbols. I do not deny that there are those who would use these symbols solely because they are Babylonian (or Phoenician—especially—), but there is no one among the Iraqis who feels that the Babylonians are closer to him than the Arabs. I would even venture to say that there is no one who feels that there is any link—other than the link of place—between him and the Babylonians.

Nevertheless, there is no condition which says that we must use symbols and myths that are connected to us by environment (*muḥīṭ*) or history or religion, to the exclusion of symbols and myths that are not linked to us by any of these close ties. Anyone who refers to Eliot's great poem *The Waste Land* will find that he uses Eastern pagan myths to express Christian ideas and Western cultural values.[65]

This passage makes two important points. First, we can see here Sayyāb's ambivalent attitude toward the use of the Babylonian versions of the fertility gods. He disassociates himself from those groups who used pagan religious symbolism from the area to express nationalistic ideological positions that were hostile to Arab nationalism (like Pharaonism in Egypt, or Phoenicianism in Lebanon). He uses these names, he says, because he does not want to mention directly the names of the pagan Arab deities who were equivalent in their pantheon to the Babylonian gods. But he also valorizes Islam—in the name of Arab nationalism, to be sure, but nevertheless quite forcefully—and clearly expresses the idea that Islam was a superior religious form to the earlier paganism. This gives us some important clues for the interpretation of Sayyāb's increasingly frequent use of the Babylonian gods, especially Tammūz and Ishtar, after 1956. It is true that, as Jabra says, these mythic figures were important, but the implication he makes—that Tammūz was a positive symbol of life and renewal for Sayyāb—is considerably more suspect. In fact, when one looks at the way Tammūz and 'Ishtār are portrayed in poems like "Madīna Bilā Maṭar" (City Without Rain), and "Madīnat Sindibād" (City of Sindbad), from the late 1950s and early 1960s, these gods inhabit a sterile wasteland where there is no rebirth.

It is only with the insertion into the poems of symbols that are functional within the monotheistic religious tradition shared by Judaism, Christianity and Islam, or by an appeal to Arab history, that these figures take on positive, regenerative functions in a given poem. An example would be the use of Babylon as a symbol in "City Without Rain" (see chapter 1 of this study). Babylon is double valenced, functional in both the fertility religions and in the millennial apocalyptic of the Book of Revelation in the New Testament. But it is only when the latter, Biblical, associations are activated through the phrase "and Babylon will be cleansed of its sins," that rebirth becomes possible. So it is very important to examine how these symbols are used and how their use develops in the course of Sayyāb's career in order to understand how they function in his work.

The second significant piece of information that can be gleaned from the above-quoted passage is how very important Eliot's example was to Sayyāb in regard to his use of myth by 1958. Although the passage itself is vague and perhaps even misleading on exactly what it was that Sayyāb found so inspiring in Eliot's work (as what Sayyāb has been discussing—about the importance of historicizing myth—is not just related to Eliot's transvaluation of symbols from other cultural contexts, but also to the latter's way of putting the atemporal myth into a historical situation—like the Stetson passage of *The Waste Land*—in order to put it into a new light), it is clear that Eliot has become by this time—and with relation to the issue of temporalization—a much less problematic figure than he was even in 1956. It should be remembered, however, that Eliot's historicizing consciousness was related primarily to the temporal anxieties of high modernism, which means that it is possible to study his use of temporal symbolism in myth apart from issues of spatialization and reclaiming land (although the two may be more related than critics have hitherto been willing to grant). For Sayyāb and the poets of decolonization, on the other hand, while offering counter-narratives aimed at dismantling the hegemony of imperial time were extremely important strategies, they were almost always conducted in conjunction with similar strategies whose ultimate goal was the reappropriation of the colonial space.

We have already seen the importance attached to the concept of self-sacrifice in Sayyāb's poetry and how this led to a concern with giving that self the tools to make such a sacrifice meaningful. As time went on, and the revolutionary promise of the mid-1950s faded, it seems to have become increasingly important to Sayyāb to devote attention to the development of "technologies of the self,"—to use Foucault's memorable phrase[66]—that would make it possible, in his view, to integrate the subject of colonialism sufficiently to allow him or her to create effective modes of resistance to the increasingly complex phenomenon that colonialism (especially neocolonialism) had turned out to be. To mark this shift in his interests, he abandoned—or at least modified his focus on—the discourses of Eden and the fertility myths, choosing instead a new set of narratives with which to chart his relationship to the land, narratives that focused on reintegration after exile: the stories of Odysseus and of Sindbad.

CHAPTER FOUR

Odysseus Returns as Sindbad

The Quest for an Inner Landscape

> And Sindbad said: 'Then my soul became desirous of travel and diversion, and I longed for commerce and gain and profits; the soul being prone to evil.'
>
> —*A Thousand and One Nights*

There is one final discourse of the land to consider in reading Sayyāb's poetry—though it, like the apocalyptic, may initially not seem to fit very comfortably within such an epistemological framework and will require us to take a detour by way of the mythic in order to arrive back at the place and "know it for the first time." "I have almost stopped using any myths in my poetry now," Sayyāb told an interviewer in 1963, shortly before his death, "except for the mention of two mythical personages . . . the Arab Sindbad and the Greek Odysseus."[1] This announcement of his abandonment of mythic references in his poetry was a startling admission from the writer whom many saw as the preeminent popularizer if not the founder of Arabic mythopoesis, who had led the way in implementing this technique during the postwar period.[2]

Since myth—and especially the myths adumbrating paradigms of self-sacrifice—had become associated in Sayyāb's work with the dramatization of the increasingly insistent imperatives of political involvement in the decade of the 1950s, this shift in focus could be—and has been—seen as indicative of a growing introspection in his poetry,[3] which has not infrequently been characterized as a return to his youthful allegiance to romanticism,[4] and the texts for the most part bear this out. Sayyāb at the end of his life seems to have found what many had found before him: that the figure of the aging quester makes an ideal vehicle for exploring the twists and turns of the human mind in meditation and, not the least, meditation on the final mystery of death.[5]

Once one looks more closely at the poems from this period, however, it becomes clear that Sayyāb's move away from the landscapes associated with the discourses of Eden, of apocalyptic, and of the wasteland does not mean that he had necessarily abandoned all interest in the question of reappropriating place, especially in the contextuality of the decolonization struggle convulsing Iraq (like the rest of the Arab world) throughout the 1950s. It was only that the mapping coordinates had changed. Both Odysseus and Sindbad may be seafarers, exiles, and questers, but their journeys (and especially that of Odysseus), however far they may seem to deviate from this course, always seem to focus in the end on a desire to return to a definite place, a home, be it Ithaca or Basra or somewhere else entirely. In this sense, they undergo an alienation from their "home" land—an exile—that is more literally physical than the colonized subject's internalized, psychologized displacement from the natal territory. Yet the experience in the ways of the world, the acquisition of knowledge about how to avoid the dangers of Sirens or giant rocs, which will translate the quester's desire for home into a real movement in space, seems to require also an interior journey through the landscape of the mind—a move that would align these wanderers more closely with the figure of the colonial subject. As Charles Segal reminds us, the ancient Greeks regarded exile from home as one of the most terrible fates that could befall a man precisely because it divorced him from his "self." For them, "the man out of touch with family and country, cut off from his roots in the known and familiar that will tell him what he is," was quintessentially the man for whom "nothing is quite 'real'," whose ratiocinative capacity to discriminate between right and wrong, good and evil, worthy and base was under the severest stress. To escape, he had to either rediscover his original "firm clear point of reference" or find some substitute for it. It is particularly in this last respect—the need for an effort of will directed at reclaiming or reinterpreting what can no longer be taken for granted because it is no longer self-evidently there—that Segal calls "Odysseus' return, as for any voyager, . . . a reclaiming of self."[6]

Sayyāb's interest in the mythic figures of Odysseus and Sindbad took on a new prominence in the poetry he wrote in the bloody aftermath of the 1958 Iraqi revolution, when it became increasingly clear that simple repossession of the territory would not automatically obliterate the effects of forty years of de facto colonial rule. The struggle to dis-place the colonizer had required in Iraq, as in so many other places, the discursive installation of an idealized version of untroubled national unity—however fictive it might be—in the precolonial past. The failure of that imagined unity to reappear, to manifest itself spontaneously once colonialism no longer threatened, had forced the intellectuals of Sayyāb's generation into a mode of self-reappraisal in the early 1960s that focused on inward change rather than outer-directed activism. To transform the land, to really reclaim it as one's own, they recognized, required *first* that the *mind* perceiving that land be transformed. The same glass may be either half-empty or half full—only the point of view has changed.

It was here, then, that the quester figure, however named, becomes a point of purchase upon which one can begin to build a scaffolding designed to reclaim identity. What Sayyāb discovered notably and early among his contemporaries, then, was that to *sacrifice* the self simply could not be enough, one had to emerge from that alienating nihilation armed with the patterns for constructing a re-formed self. Odysseus and Sindbad, for him, became particularly useful in this project because they had not only functioned for centuries as well-defined identity prototypes, but they also had a respectable history as figures for exploring the difficulties to be encountered in trying established such "strong" subject positions in the first place.

Sayyāb, however, had begun his encounter with Odysseus, at least, long before 1958. The earliest instance where this definitely registers in his poetry can be found in the 1947 poem "Ahwā'" (Passions). Composed in his junior year at the Baghdad Teachers College, this poem is notable mainly for its length (192 *bayts* [verses]) and the high frequency of literary allusions—mostly to European works—including, as a "high point" of sorts, an entire stanza (lines 161–168) translated practically verbatim from the lyric "Cupid and Campaspe" by the minor English Elizabethan poet John Lylye, whose work Sayyāb had most likely read in Francis Palgrave's widely disseminated anthology *The Golden Treasury*.[7]

The speaker begins "Passions" with an address to his beloved and complains to her of the sorrow in his heart at losing her. Then he imagines a future rendezvous where, he declares, he will tell her stories (*aḥādīth*) to which he has given the collective name "passion." The first of these stories ends with an allusion to the famous episode in *The Odyssey* where Odysseus's wife, Penelope, promises the importunate suitors for her hand that she will decide among them once she has finished weaving a tapestry begun during her husband's absence at the war against Troy. Each day she weaves, and each night she unravels the stitches woven during the day:

25) This is the countryside, do you see the palm trees?
and these are its songs, do you hear?[8]
26) And that young man is a poet in his youth,
And that girl, she is the one who taught him yearning.
27) She is art—from its delectable fountainhead,
she is love, from its sad place where one drinks.
28) He saw her singing behind the flock,
like Penelope asking the lovers to wait.[9]

While this could simply be read as the kind of automatized allusion used by an apprentice poet to signal his familiarity with a given poetic tradition, it has several features that suggest something slightly more idiosyncratic and disturbing at work here. First, and most important, the speaker seems to identify with the suitors, not with Odysseus, in framing his relationship to this countryside Penelope: he sees himself, like them, longing for a woman who is "out of his class" and therefore unattainable. Such positioning foreshadows the basically ambivalent attitude he will later, in more substantial and mature poems, evince toward the figure of Odysseus as a structural model for his own behavioral paradigms. The other noteworthy element in this stanza is its juxtaposition of the Odysseus story with lines that focus on setting or, more precisely, the evocation of an idealized pastoral place. This too is a foreshadowing of later concerns, but this time ironically—for in later poems Odysseus will be represented almost invariably as exiled or at least alienated from the ideal place of origin, from "home."

After "Ahwā'," it was not until the early 1950s that Odysseus stages an oblique reappearance in Sayyāb's poetry. In the never-completed and unpublished Miltonic epic "Al-La'anāt" (Curses), Sayyāb briefly alludes to Homer and Socrates as models for the revolutionary masses in their struggle against tyranny. He depicts a Chinese peasant as "transferring" (*anqala*) a "red song" directly from the "mouth of Homer" to the waiting ears of his audience while at the same time another revolutionary "worker" snatches the cup of hemlock from Socrates' dying hand in order to make "the tyrant drink from it."[10] Then, a few years later, in one of the "Fukai" poems, "Marthiyat Jaykūr" (Elegy for Jaykūr), Sayyāb gives a rather different picture of the man he calls, in an accompanying footnote, "the blind Greek storyteller":

61) Now is the time of lumps of coal where worms gnaw feverishly before
it flames anew:
62) That legendary creature in Jaykūr, Homer—his people, the
downtrodden—

63) He sits, squatting, in the March sun, his eyes on the court of Rashīd,[11]
64) Chewing tobacco, histories, dreams with his toothless jaws and impassive imagination.[12]

Here, and in subsequent lines, the speaker pictures Homer, not as the defining model for those who would fashion the grand new narratives needed to create a new reality suitable for the age of decolonization, but as a subordinated yet exceptionally serviceable ally of the dominant order, a figure whose stories he likens in a vivid metaphor to spider webs issuing direct from the poet's lips, snaking out to close round and strangle struggling revolutionary energies in a falsely soothing cocoon of traditions and homilies, just as a spider uses its web to smother its helpless prey:

68) He clenches a fist and launches the spinning shuttle, directing it on a new course!
69) And he ends his portentous story with a portentous [amount] of yarn, and he ends his sitting,
70) Half-naked, dragging a heavy-lidded glance from a chest uncovered and a shirt that is missing,
71) Except for a few threads [hanging] from his lips, too fine even for a spider's mouth, on the head of a stick:
72) A spindle that undoes what the loom has woven, an energy that destroys [the fruit] of other energies,
73) He toils but it is not [honest] toil: he has destroyed two before him, and he claims even more,
74) A present that is not a present, by him the past is destroyed and also the promised future![13]

The phrase "a spindle that undoes what the loom has woven" in line 72 would seem to be, again, an allusion to the story of Penelope from a perspective that asserts the discursively marginalized and largely unarticulated point of view of the suitors rather than the one more frequently encountered in the legitimized and legitimating versions of the story based on Homer, which validates the ruse as a supremely justifiable tactic for the desperate, actively threatened Penelope. In point of fact, furthermore, it must be noted that the rhetorical strategy here is doubly disturbing in the sense that the relationship between the spindle and the loom is not spelled out in the text. Clearly, the spindle is Homer's. It is the tool that gathers up the story-threads that issue from his mouth. But is the loom also his? The most immediate reaction would be to see spindle and loom as opposites, to posit Homer the unraveler/destroyer and Penelope the weaver/maker as dialectical terms.

But one should remember that in *The Odyssey* Penelope is both the weaver and the unraveler, which would make it more plausible to read the tools as both belonging to Homer, who would then be seen performing a discursive act analogous to Penelope's. He creates a seeming order—the weaving—on the visible surface (the daytime), which is then undone by secret (nighttime) strategies that have been selected for their ability to undermine the coherence of the elements found in the original text (in this case, the grand narrative of progress). Thus the use of Homer in these two poems would seem to dramatize the same ambivalence toward the signification of the Odysseus story we first encountered in "Passions."

It is just before the composition of "Elegy for Jaykūr" that Sayyāb first evokes the figure of Sindbad, in his long poem called "Al-Asliḥa wa-al-Aṭfāl" (Arms and the Children). The allusion is brief (only three lines), but it is enough to show that his attitude toward Sindbad seems to differ in significant ways from the attitude displayed toward Odysseus and his creator, Homer:

1) Birds? Or young boys laughing
2) As light plays upon their [faces]?
3) And their bare feet
4) Seashells chiming within a waterwheel,
5) The hems of their dishdashas like the northern breeze
6) Traveling [at night] across a field of ripe wheat
7) Or the hissing of bread [baking] on a holiday,
8) Or a mother murmuring her newborn's name,
9) Cuddling him on his first day.
10) As though I hear sails flapping
11) And the tumult as Sindbad puts out to sea.
12) He saw his vast treasure between the ribs
13) He chose no other as his treasure—then he returned![14]

The scene in the poem depicting Sindbad is placed so as to seem the final member of a series of scenes culled from the speaker's childhood. These preceding scenes could probably best be characterized as exercises in the portrayal of idyllic harmony, and Sindbad's scene thus acts as a kind of summative culmination for the discursive taxonomy enacted by the others. It functions, then, as more than just the closure of the series; it is their hyperbolization. Given that the importance of "return" as a keyword is nearly always highlighted in critical discussions concerning Homer's version of Odysseus's story, it is not without significance that we find

Sayyāb aligning his abbreviated recounting of Sindbad's tale with the same thematic by placing the word "return" at the end of the recitation in this section. This would seem to link the story of Sindbad more strongly with the positive reading of Odysseus's story (as a narrative of return to the harmony of home) than the actual allusions made to that latter story in Sayyāb's earlier poems, thus opening up an operative distinction between the two where Sindbad's quest is portrayed as achieving wholly positive results, while Odysseus' journey incarnates the dangers that attend this experiential paradigm. The valorization of Sindbad here is reinforced by the fact that the rest of the poem is concerned with representing—in what resembles in some respects an eerie reenactment of Adam's and Eve's expulsion from Eden—humanity's falling away from the idyllic world pictured in this first stanza. Of all the scenes depicted there, however, only the scene of Sindbad is not repeated within the fallen reality in debased form, so the sailor/quester from the fairy tale is the only element in the poem that remains whole and uncontaminated by the operations of mutability.

A similar pattern can be observed in the 1960 poem "Madīnat Sindibād" (City of Sindbad), where the Arab mariner's name appears only in the title. He is not mentioned at all in the text, which is a stinging denunciation of the failures of the leaders of the 1958 revolution. Thus Sindbad is projected into an idyllic, irretrievable past (just as the title is positioned *before* the beginning of the poem), and effectively delinked from the poet's horrifying vision of the present, one that oscillates between the apocalyptic and an inversion/perversion of the fertility cults. At the end of the poem we are, tellingly, given to see the city named in the title as Babylon, "come again": a referent whose valences can be linked to either the discursive universe of the Bible or the fertility myths, but not that of *A Thousand and One Nights*.

This clear separation between the two figures lasts until 1961 (the year in which Sayyāb first became aware that he was seriously ill). In that year Sayyāb begins to pay new attention to both, and his ambivalence toward Odysseus as the protagonist of a successful narrative of return begins to carry over into his attitude toward Sindbad, or so it would seem from casual perusal. In an otherwise unremarkable dramatic monologue written in October of 1961, entitled "Al-Umm wa-al-Ṭifla al-Ḍā'i'a" (The Mother and the Lost Girl-Child), Sayyāb briefly describes a scene where a storyteller "stares deep within a fire / To catch a glimpse of the tattered mast of Sindbad's ship." The depiction of the paradigmatic quester now shipwrecked, where previously he was so strongly associated with images of reintegration and return, reminds the poem's speaker, the bereaved mother, of her lost daughter who has disappeared, victim of some unknown fate. The now metaphorically linked pair, then, become emblematic in the poem's discursive framework for the wrecked and destroyed hopes for a better future, which Sayyāb sees as unsalvageable after the failures of the 1958 revolution.

Nevertheless, Sindbad in these later poems does still retain certain links to that scene of primal integrated harmony between subject and landscape that Sayyāb comes increasingly to locate in the past and specifically in his childhood. We can find its traces, for example, in a poem, "Dār Jaddī" (My Grandfather's House)—probably composed shortly before or after "Al-Umm wa-al-Ṭifla al-Ḍā'i'a"—where he recollects the time spent in his youth at his grandparents':

58) And in the evening I used to bathe in the stars,
59) My eyes harvesting them one by one, riding the crescent
60) Like a ship, like Sindbad on his travels
61) My sail the clouds
62) My [destined] harbor impossibility,
63) And I would see God in the form of a palm tree, like the crown of a palm tree [glowing] white
64) In the darkness.[15]

In the past the speaker sees himself as having been more than able to overcome the boundaries between himself and the exteriorized world, a skill whose loss he laments in the rest of this poem. We, in turn, can see this figuration of Sindbad as a nostalgic attempt to overcome the absence of such harmony in the present, so that the evocation of the quester with links to the Arab cultural tradition never seems to quite lose, for Sayyāb, the power to recall at least the *desire* for unity and identity. This remains true even in Sayyāb's very last efforts, before the progressive paralysis of his disease made the work of composition impossible for him. In two of his best poems from the period, "Shināshīl Ibnat al-Jalabī" (The Enclosed Balcony of the Nobleman's Daughter)[16] and "Iram Dhāt 'Imād" (Many-Pillared Iram),[17] allusions to Sindbad call up, become a kind of Eliotian "objective correlative" for, an idyll of childhood that has very strong overtones of Wordsworth's "Ode: Intimations of Immortality." In this sense then, the figure of Sindbad continues right up until the very end of Sayyāb's life to be a signal for recourse to the privileged arena of childhood, where in the process of recollecting and reconstructing that childhood Sayyāb carries out the work of fashioning a poetic self that is capable of confronting and overcoming the problems attendant upon the commencement of the new realities brought about by the processes of decolonization.

Such attempts, however, never seem quite able to transcend the nostalgic. If one considers only the present, then Sindbad joins Odysseus among the ranks of the unforgiven exiles, as in the April 1962 poem, "Al-Waṣīya" (The Testament), where the two are deployed in parallel fashion. First Odysseus is depicted as having been "pursued by the vengeance of the gods" even after his return to Ithaca, a vendetta that forces him

> 12) To spread [again] the sail, to wander lost upon the ocean,
> 13) Not knowing whether he would return some other day to his home.[18]

And, a few lines later, Sindbad is also presented as one who cannot return home:

> 29) I am afraid that I will slide out of the painkiller's haze
> 30) Into oceans that have no harbors
> 31) Where Sindbad, once he sets out,
> 32) Cannot return to lutes, to wine and flowers.

What differentiates the two here is that Sindbad is more strongly tied to the individual experience of the speaker, while Odysseus is noticeably more distanced from the speaking voice in the poem, a public and abstracted figure with whom there is less possibility of personal identification.

The element of "otherness" and alienation in the portrayal of Odysseus (in contrast to that of Sindbad) presents itself as a consistent feature of Sayyāb's poetry after 1960. In this connection, it is perhaps worth noting that there is a strong "alternative" reading of Odysseus the wanderer in Western literature, one that does not descend directly from Homer's hero, but from other mythical legends and tales of his exploits. This "alternate Odysseus" (whom I shall for convenience refer to hereinafter as "Ulysses") is a highly unsympathetic character, a master trickster and deceiver whose Trojan horse stratagem is indicative of a chronic pathological willingness to sacrifice honesty and heroic principle for the expediency of the moment. The poet Pindar and the dramatists Sophocles and Euripedes are notable exploiters of this Ulysses figure in their works.[19]

This "guileful Ulysses" was actually better known to European authors in the Middle Ages than the Homeric Odysseus, and it is this tradition that Dante draws upon for his—probably the most famous medieval—version of the legend, as told in Canto 26 of *The Inferno*. Here Ulysses is represented as being condemned to the eighth circle of Hell, among those known as the "Fraudulent" (or "Crafty") Counselors. Dante, through the medium of his guide Virgil, adjures the ghost of Ulysses, imprisoned within a flame, to speak and tell his story. The wanderer then relates that, after his return to Penelope and Ithaca, he was unable to remain content at home, because of his "zeal (*ardore*) to gain experience with the world and with human vices and virtues,"[20] but sets out for the open sea with those members of his crew still willing to travel with him, voyaging westward beyond the Pillars of Hercules, the limits of the known world to the ancient Greeks. They traveled onward for five days, then came in sight of a towering mountain, "dark because so far away." This "mountain" was in fact Purgatory (which in *The Divine Comedy* is represented as being originally the site of Eden) and, as punishment for their impiety in daring to approach this sacred territory, the ship was overturned and Ulysses and all his men were drowned.

This story of Ulysses's final voyage, one that "supplements" the events of *The Odyssey* in many ways, has been rightly celebrated as medieval Western Europe's most lasting contribution to the Odysseus legend. What is particularly interesting about it, for our purposes, is that this version of Ulysses as restless explorer of the unknown has also been persistently linked in subsequent Western critical accounts with the figure of Christopher Columbus. This linkage is perhaps most aptly summarized by a noted Dante scholar, Dino Bigongiari, at the conclusion of a lecture on Canto 26 he gave in the 1950s:

> In the depths of hell, Dante gives us the sensations of airborne flight and an experience of geographic "discovery" on the scale of Columbus; and on the heights of heaven, he gives us a spiritual equivalent of inertial motion in orbit. The last thing we should perhaps say, with respect to the Ulysses canto, is that it has probably discouraged Italian poets from attempting to celebrate Columbus properly, in an epic fashion. It isn't likely that Columbus will ever be more fittingly celebrated in Italian poetry than he has been, by anticipation, in Dante.[21]

Thus Dante's Ulysses becomes a kind of instantiation for the general type of the colonial adventurer to at least one way of thinking, and it is not impossible for Sayyāb, given the fact that he admired Dante greatly and probably therefore read at least parts of *The Divine Comedy* through the medium of English translation,[22] to have assimilated in some sense this way of looking at Odysseus, especially since his depiction of the figure in his poetry is closer to Dante's Ulysses than it is to Homer's Odysseus.

There is also another source that Sayyāb could have easily have come in contact with, that would have also given him this alternative way for reading Odysseus as Ulysses: Alfred, Lord Tennyson's dramatic monologue, first published in 1833, entitled simply "Ulysses."[23] Tennyson's debt to Dante's Ulysses has been well established;[24] what has been less well examined is how Tennyson's version might relate to the theme of rereading Columbus's voyages in particular[25] and the project of colonial exploration in more general terms. Oddly enough, given the fact that Tennyson lived through the height of the age of British overseas expansion, and that he often wrote on public themes, very little attention has been paid to his work as a discourse on imperialism and the little that has been done has tended to give a much too simplistic reading of his attitudes. Put another way, for Tennyson and his generation, colonialism was a "problem" and they seem to have approached it as such. Part of the difficulty that critics seem to have had is in locating the central voice in Tennyson's poetry, probably because of his extensive use of the dramatic monologue as a form.[26] In the dramatic monologue, one of the main points of interest in the poem's development is the reader's growing awareness of the gap between the speaker's words and the set of controlling norms validated by the author, a silent auditor introduced into the poem's framework, or even the poem's audience, insofar as they may be conceived as subscribing to the values of "society" at large. Generally, it seems all too common for critics reading Tennyson's poetry to forget that a given poem has begun as a clearly demarcated dramatic monologue, and they end by attributing the speaking voice's often quite idiosyncratic views to Tennyson himself. Such is the case, for example, when the otherwise astute analysis of Patrick Brantlinger attributes to Tennyson himself the endorsement, in "Locksley Hall" and "Locksley Hall Sixty Years After," of "progress" as an unproblematic value, when it is in fact the pronouncement of a speaker whose every reported word throughout the poem declares him to be an "unreliable narrator," one whose judgments should be accepted only with the greatest caution.[27]

"Ulysses" is a similar case of a dramatic monologue with an unreliable narrator in charge. This is evident from the very first lines of the poem:

> It little profits that an idle king,
> By this still hearth, among these barren crags,
> Matched with an aged wife, I mete and dole
> Unequal laws unto a savage race,
> That hoard, and sleep, and feed, and know not me.[28]

This is a person whose allegiance to the bourgeois virtues of duty, honor, and country and to the responsibility and respect for the institution of family—all of which might fairly be imputed to Tennyson's projected audience—is signally lacking. Moreover, he registers his boredom with the very code of values that would later form the backbone of the colonial ideology as summed up in the phrase "white man's burden": to believe in a particular system of laws as "just," capable of being administered evenhandedly and fairly, so that those governed by them will become "civilized" through their appreciation of the benefits to be derived from submitting to such apparatuses of control.

This Ulysses, from the outset, seems determined to outrage every one of these conventions by telling us that the laws he enforces are "unequal"; he himself "mete[s] and dole[s]" these laws, verbs that suggest not the operation of impartial justice but the world of commerce where the rules of buying and selling (in administrative terms: bribery) ensure that monetary values reign supreme; finally, he suggests that the "savage race" that constitutes his subjects are unregenerately savage. They and he have nothing in common. They only seek to satisfy physical wants ("hoard, and sleep, and feed"), no different from animals—there is nothing there to "civilize."

Ulysses' last complaint, "they know not me," is a kind of crowning irony in this context, since his coming to be known, to exhibit his inner self to all and sundry, would undermine his authority and render him unfit to rule (here one might cite the Foucauldian precept that to *be known* and *not* to *know* is to surrender power, and Ulysses has expressed no inclination thus far in the poem to know anything about these "others"). Nor would it be possible to say that these misgivings are mitigated by what we, as readers, have already come to *know* about him from his own words. If this is not sufficient evidence that Ulysses as a character inverts all the elements of the bourgeois ideal, we are directly given in the poem the example of his son Telemachus:

> This is my son, mine own Telemachus,
> To whom I leave the scepter and the isle—
> Well-loved of me, discerning to fulfill
> This labor, by slow prudence to make mild
> A rugged people, and through soft degrees
> Subdue them to the useful and the good.
> Most blameless is he, centered in the sphere
> Of common duties, decent not to fail
> In offices of tenderness, and pay

> Meet adoration to my household gods,
> When I am gone. He works his work, I mine.

Here we have Ulysses himself thematizing the difference between his own set of values and the early Victorian audience of the poem by presenting to us his son Telemachus as the very embodiment of the dutiful bourgeois, who adores the "household gods." And again, the basic linkage between the bourgeois and colonial virtues can be seen in the fact that this introduction could also be interpreted as applying to the ideal type of "civilizing" official in the Empire, as is registered by a remark from the Tennyson scholar Matthew Rowlinson that Ulysses here "sounds, in fact, like a colonial administrator turning over the reins to a successor just before stepping on the boat to go home."[29]

Yet, on the other hand, it is possible to argue that the virtues of Telemachus are undermined, even as they are enumerated, by his father's scorn, registered in the adjectives used to describe Telemachus's activities: adjectives like "slow, soft, common, decent," culminating (in a sense) in the most unheroic and even unmanly noun, "tenderness," which sums up Ulysses' estimate of his son's character. While the wary reader has already been led not to suppose Ulysses' value system as a normative one, it is still true that to allow him, as the speaking voice in the poem, to present his son (rather than some other voice—that of a narrator, or implied author, say) immediately opens up the latter's character qualities to critique because the audience does not see them as universally lauded even at the moment of instantiation. Nor should we forget that Tennyson's Ulysses, even though he is realized in the poem as an unreliable and limited character, is also given certain heroic characteristics that lend to his discourse a certain authority in that arena at least.

What does Ulysses here counterpose to the bourgeois/colonial paradigm? The answer would seem to be, as for Dante's Ulysses, the romance of exploration:

> . . . Come my friends,
> 'Tis not too late to seek a newer world.
> Push off, and sitting well in order smite
> The sounding furrows; for my purpose holds
> To sail beyond the sunset, and the baths
> Of all the western stars, until I die.

Earlier in the poem, he has echoed the Dantean Ulysses even more firmly in identifying "knowledge" as his real purpose in seeking "a newer world." His goal, he says, is:

To follow knowledge like a sinking star
Beyond the utmost bound of human thought.

A noble ambition, surely—at least in a post-Renaissance context. But the rhetorical ground in which it is embedded should give us pause for thought. Death, after all, is the only thing pictured as waiting beyond "the baths of all the western stars." Even more disturbing is the characterization of knowledge as a "sinking star," which somehow cannot be contained in "human thought." What renders these images of decay and incapacity even more problematic is that they are being formulated by an intelligence that has already demonstrated in the poem its own lack of self-knowledge. If Ulysses does not recognize his own deficiencies, is apparently not interested in even minimal "knowing" of those around him, how can further knowledge—which it is likely he will not be able to use in any functional way—avail him?

It is precisely this question of "self-knowing"—and its potential crystallization in a colonial context—that seems to have preoccupied Sayyāb when he began to reexamine the figure of Odysseus/Ulysses in 1961. Although we may never know whether or exactly how much he drew from Dante and/or Tennyson, his poetry registers remarkably similar concerns to theirs with respect to the potential problematics of Homer's Odysseus. The passages from poems of this period quoted earlier in this chapter will have already given some hint of this, but to see it fully at work one needs to examine two poems where Ulysses plays a key role.

The first of these poems is in fact the poem in which Ulysses is "resurrected" for the first time after his long hiatus: the March 1961 composition entitled "Shubbāk Wafīqa" (Wafīqa's Window). This poem marks a decisive shift in Sayyāb's poetic strategies in that it weaves together three different discourses (all of which had played only minor roles in his earlier poetry)—Greek myth, Sufism, and what one might call "personal" myth[30]—together with biblical references (which had since "Christ After the Crucifixion" been central to his vision) in an attempt to chart a path back to the primal unity of self with land/nation/other, which is the speaker's implicit goal. The poem begins with the "personal" myth: an allusion to Sayyāb's early beloved, a girl named Wafīqa, who died young.[31] The speaker is looking at the empty window of her house:

1) Wafīqa's window in the village
2) Is radiant,[32] looking out over the courtyard
3) (Like Galilee, it awaits the walking

4) And Jesus) and it spreads open its panes
5) Icarus anointing the eagle's feathers
6) With the sun, and setting forth,
7) Icarus, caught by the horizon [like a ball]
8) And thrown into the grave-like deep
9) Wafīqa's window, O tree—
10) Eyes upon you, expectant,
11) Take deep breaths in the wakeful twilight,

12) Watching for the apple blossoms,
13) And Buwayb is a hymn
14) And the wind sends back
15) The water melodies over the palm fronds.[33]

The first four lines of the poem anchor us in a landscape of primal unity valenced to the past. The "waiting" window is personified, teased from the world of things into the world of the animate through Wafīqa's energizing presence that works even from beyond the grave. Although we do not yet know that she is dead, the comparison of the transformed window to the shiny, reflective water surface of the Sea of Galilee seeming to wait expectantly for Jesus to perform one of his most compelling miracles, walking on water, tends to place her in the same category of unearthly, inspiring celestial figures, especially those who have died and been resurrected.

This vision, however, is immediately countered by the appearance of another figure, Icarus, whose advent is less auspicious. Icarus, of course, was the son of the master inventor Dædalus. He and his father fashioned wings of wax on which they could fly, but Icarus flew too near the sun, which melted the wax and caused him to fall into the Aegean sea. This is the source of the reference in the poem to Icarus being caught by the horizon and thrown into the "tomb-like deep." The two tableaus are linked by their common incorporation of sun imagery but are otherwise very different. Probably the most significant difference at this point in the poem is that the Icarus story (the pessimistic tale of human limitation and failure) comes from the Greek tradition while the Wafīqa story is drawn from the poet's personal mythology and is reinforced by allusions to biblical–Koranic material, thus associating that discourse with the valorized imagery of untroubled unity.

This unity is revealed in the next lines, however, to have been dissolved, or at least threatened with dissolution, by death, for the speaker turns from his ecstatic vision to contemplate Wafīqa's grave. He imagines her staring out from beneath ground with wistful longing for the world of living but unable to reach out to it. He is thus led to visualize her headstone as forming a kind of gateway through which he can cross to that other world and rescue her from death. In his desire to restore that idyll of the past, he addresses the stone directly in a kind of invocation whose mystical overtones (and mysticism characteristically valorizes a very cohesive discourse of unity, since its stated goal is *union* with the divine) are probably more marked than anywhere else in his poetry:

29) O stone [where] the *mi'raj*[34] of the heart [begins]
30) O Forms of concord and love
31) O pathway ascending to the Lord
32) If not for you, the village would not have laughed for the breezes,
33) There is a perfume in the wind
34) [Coming] from the garlands of the river, as it rocks us [in its cradle] and sings to us,
35) (Ulysses travels with the waves
36) While the wind reminds him of forgotten islands:
37) "Our hair has gone gray, O wind, so leave us alone").[35]

In the midst of the speaker's paean to oneness, we find the intrusion of Ulysses. Here we see him not as the Homeric castaway, desperately seeking to return home, but as the ambivalent Dantean/Tennysonian figure of arrogance and hubris in his individually oriented, never-satisfied quest for knowledge that leads him to reject a return to his past. And, like Icarus in the first part of the poem, he is a figure taken from Greek mythology that acts to interrupt and short-circuit the speaker's invocation of the process that will integrate him with his environment. Thus we are invited to see him, along with Icarus, as peculiarly "Western" in his valencing, a presupposition that is reinforced by the succeeding lines, where the speaker seeks to counter the disruption of their presence by invoking counterparts of Wafīqa and her window:

38) The world opens its window
39) From that blue window,
40) It becomes one, making its thorns
41) Into flowers in a repose that breaths perfume.
42) There is a window like you in Lebanon,
43) There is a window like you in India,
44) And a maiden dreams in Japan
45) As Wafīqa dreams in the sepulcher
46) Of thunder and green lightning.

Notably absent from this catalog of windows and maidens is a "Western" Wafīqa. She can only arise, it would seem, outside the orbit of European hegemony, where the colonial Ulysses is a foreign intruder without power to determine the parameters of the cultural discourse.

If in "Shubbāk Wafīqa" the colonialist dimension of Ulysses is implicit, allowing such a reading but not requiring it, Sayyāb wrote a poem shortly thereafter where the referencing is much more overt and inescapable. This is the poem "Al-Ma'bad al-Gharīq" (The Sunken Temple), which became the title poem of a collection published late in 1962, though the poem itself had already been completed in mid-February of that year. Thus it comes about a year after "Shubbāk Wafīqa."

As the poem opens we are taken, through a short description of the surroundings, into the frenetic nighttime activity of an anonymous port and led through its streets to one tavern in particular where an old man is animatedly recounting the story of an ancient legend he has heard about a Buddhist temple that was destroyed in a volcanic eruption. As the old man tells it, the temple was located above the waters of a volcanic lake deep within the Malaysian jungle, and when the eruption began it quickly slid into the depths of the lake with all its treasures intact. He describes in some detail the sea creatures, the crocodiles and octopuses, who now stand guard over the hidden temple's wealth. Finally he reveals his resolution—to retrieve those "thousand treasures from that sunken world / Which will fill the stomachs of a thousand hungry children and stay a thousand diseases / And rescue a thousand people from the executioner's hand. . . ." To aid him on his perilous journey, he moves to summon the company of a perhaps unexpected companion: Ulysses.

44) Accordingly, Ulysses has not returned to his family from his journey
45) Accordingly, his wind-filled sails sow the riotous waves
46) With the months he counted and numbered until he was struck down by
despair.
47) Ulysses, your boy's hair has gone gray, your wife's radiant smile
48) Has become firewood, why now should you return to your family,
cleaving the arms of the waves?
49) Forward! for the water of the Chine[36] waits for you with bated breath.
50) As yet no bird's beak has wounded it, nor breeze's fingers disturbed its
depths.

51) Forward! Indeed, a wild beast [awaits you] there, dreaming of you
above all others,

52) And he fears that you will make his red eyes explode into the darkness
53) And that his virgin treasure will ask about your sail blowing in the breeze.
54) Did not the cries of the wounded and the dying
55) Cause you pain in Troy?
56) Oh! the blood that has been shed, dirtying the walls
57) Turning their thirsty earthen surface into soft clay, turning it into one
58) Huge wound, a wound opening in the entrails of humankind
59) To cry out to the heavens.
60) Oh! that voice echoed by the windows and the walls:

61) "Because of female debauchery and the fire kindled by vengeance within a crowned male
62) Even the stair steps of stupidity are dyed with heart's blood;
63) And our day has stepped outside of time, and all lifetimes are the same
64) Like a field is all the same to a scythe,
65) And there in the twilight
66) Our widowed women mourn, the children at the stair steps of heaven wail continuously."[37]

Clearly, this is the restless Ulysses and not the noble Odysseus, for his interlocutor notes that he has not returned to stay with his aging wife and son—though the reference to his "despair" suggests that the separation was not entirely one of his own choice. Thus we are again faced with the kind of indeterminate ambivalence that Sayyāb seems to make a trademark of his treatment of the Odysseus theme in this period. The ambivalence carries over into the next section of the poem, where the speaker reminds Ulysses of the violence and suffering of the Trojans—for which one tradition suggests Ulysses is at least partly responsible, since it is his stratagem of the wooden horse that causes the city finally to fall—but he fosters the assumption, through making his inquiry into a rhetorical question, that this slaughter of innocents caused Ulysses pain and that he regretted it. Thus, he intimates, Ulysses should now be eager to join in the quest for the sunken temple.

After an extended interlude where the speaker makes a comparison between the extermination of the Trojans and the butchery occurring in modern-day Iraq, he returns to his hortatory enterprise:

88) Forward! In Pahang[38] we will plow a field of water with our oars,
89) And scatter [over it] the stars of darkness, dropping them into the depths,
90) Pebbles among which the eye cannot distinguish shimmering turquoise

91) From pearls speckled with dark spots.
92) We will frighten the shepherd
93) Who will scurry with his lambs to the fold, fearing that they will drown in the depths.

94) Forward! For the night of Asia, stretching to the farthest horizon, calls us
95) In a voice [filled with] sleepiness, with death, with the rhymes of priests.
96) Forward! Fate is still in our hands,
97) Let us traverse its darkness before a colorless sunrise
98) Scatters the world of dreams, silencing—as beaten gold tolls within it—the rhymes of the priests![39]

At first this appears to be a fairly conventional piece of anticolonialist rhetoric, designed to encourage the masses to arise. This point of view would tend to be reinforced by the speaker's use of such conventionalized referents as the "night of Asia," which speaks "the rhymes of priests" (the hyperbole of religious discourse, in Marxist rhetoric at least, whose purpose is to lull the oppressed into acceptance of their lot) in a sleepy and deathlike voice. The symbolic code of revolutionary ideology is further evoked by use of the phrase "Fate is still in our hands," implying that resistance is not only possible but likely to succeed. Interspersed with these expressions, however, are others that do not belong to this particular discursive apparatus, and, in fact, inject a sense of disquieting discontinuity into structures normally marked by an almost impregnable cohesiveness. First, when the speaker predicts that the arrival of the adventurers will cause the "stars of darkness" to scatter, "dropping . . . into the depths," he mentions almost as an afterthought that they will "frighten the shepherd." It should seem somewhat odd to the reader that the actions of the supposed liberators alarm those that they are seeking to free from tyranny—that perhaps their activities are difficult to distinguish from those they seek to supplant. The reference to "the colorless sunrise," and the context in which it appears, at the end of the quoted passage is equally disturbing. This sunlight will not "scatter" the darkness, but rather the "world of dreams" which is a more ambiguous phrase altogether, since dreams can be worthy aspirations as much or more than vain illusions.

This ambivalence carries over into the reference to "beaten gold," for it is the clanking echo of this metal that will drown out the religious discourse of the priests chanting. And this gold is, of course, what the speaker and

Ulysses have come to retrieve from the treasury of the sunken temple. The gold takes on an even more sinister cast in the final lines of the poem:

99) The beaten gold within it will rove like a wild beast, eating the dead
100) And drinking the blood of the living, stealing the children's food
101) To feed the flames in its eyes, to lend it a voice
102) Which will destroy all the voices of the prophets there.
103) Hear the chains rattle!
104) Hear the echo of the hours! It has touched the children's heads with shrouds
105) And disrupted the embrace of all the lovers, and plunged a knife made of
106) Dying cries into a kiss, the fingers on men's hands have reappeared
107) As bones without flesh, and chiffon veils
108) Have become sheets beneath which lie bodies without skin.
109) Forward! As yet the Magi have not seen the new star in the heavens toward which fingers will stretch,
110) And Ḥirā'[40] and its morning are not yet filled with sūras and āyas.
111) Forward! Zeus still stains the mountain summit
112) With his wine, and looses a thousand eagles whose eyes drip sparks
113) To kidnap one who will serve the wine,[41] bearing cups of honey and ambrosia.[42]
114) Forward! We will visit the gods of the lake, then we will raise them to dwell on the mountain summit![43]

Here the gold is personified, turned into a ravening wild animal that destroys all in its path. It does not bring aid to the oppressed, but rather worsens their situation. Where before they suffered, now they die.

This passage is also notable for the way the religious discourse deployed previously has been recast. Before, religious words were "the chanting of priests." Now they have become the authentic "voice of the prophets"—a religious group that has been consistently valorized as a model for the poet in modern Arab poetry. So, to "silence the voice of a prophet" is a very different thing from silencing "the chanting of priests." The difference is further underscored by the assertion in lines 109 and 110 that in this debased world, the most significant events in Christianity and Islam, the birth of Jesus, and the revelation of the Koran to Muḥammad on Mount Hira, have not yet taken place. This is, instead, a world of Greek mythology where Zeus reigns supreme. And Ulysses is part of that world, inevitably associated with its values. So, when the speaker predicts in the last line of the poem, that "we" (presumably Ulysses and himself) will go to the gods of the temple in the lake and "raise them to dwell on the mountain summit," the careful reader will be reminded that these gods are the "gods of gold"—not the monotheistic God of egalitarianism—and will be forced to ask him/herself whether the effect of raising them up will not be the very carnage so memorably depicted in the previous line.

Thus, despite the equivocacy of "Shubbāk Wafīqa," "Al-Ma'bad al-Gharīq" should be seen as an even more disturbing portrayal of the "questing" Ulysses. While Sayyāb here allows his speaker full play to acknowledge the attractions of the glorious quest, he also calls upon us to attend to its terrible price for other human beings. In this sense, then, we can see that the person of Ulysses should be treated as being even more relevant to the critique of colonialism as a disruption of relation to the land than that of Odysseus or Sindbad, who seem to figure more singly the meditations of the poet as individual on the questions of the role land plays in the actualization of "self."

My hope is that this examination of the dimension of place in Sayyāb's poetry has shown the utility of a heuristic strategy that draws upon the theorization of colonialism in highlighting aspects of his work that might otherwise remain obscure or at least disconnected to its context. In the second half of this study I will turn my attention to several other features of his verse (his relationship to the question of self, his experiments in poetic form, and his flirtation with epic narrative poetry) whose contours may also be better—or at least differently—illuminated through recourse to the perspectives generated by developments in postcolonial literary theory.

CHAPTER FIVE

This Boy's Life

A well-written life is almost as rare as a well-spent one.
—Thomas Carlyle

In even so pedestrian a writing project as literary criticism, there are moments that partake of what one might term "epiphany." Such moments are precious—otherwise, one might not be moved to either undertake such a daunting task, or continue it once begun. Sometimes these moments are only incidentally related to the work at hand, but on a few occasions they become central to one's understanding of the subject. Even then, they are often not immediately recognizable for what they are. They may only slowly open themselves to reveal new perspectives, new vistas about the subject that may very well cause one to catch one's breath in admiration later at the symmetry and perfection of the pattern suddenly visible—even if, in the end, the pattern does not turn out to "fit" so well as it did at first sight.

For me, in the process of doing research about Sayyāb, one such epiphanic moment came in discovering the story of the winged horse of Basra. In the late 1960s, an Iraqi historian by the name of Ḥāmid al-Bāzī published a short history of Basra province from the Islamic conquest to the end of Ottoman rule at the conclusion of World War I. He had access to a number of unpublished historical chronicles belonging to local notable families, and in the last chapter of the book, he provides a selection from those works. There, in the midst of short annotations about floods, natural disasters, the appearance of Halley's Comet, and other noteworthy incidents that occurred in the late Middle Ages, you will find a story whose lack of contextuality is startling and truly "epiphanic":

> In 868 A.H./1463 A.D. a horse with two wings with which he could fly approximately 75 meters appeared in Basra.

> This animal came out one day from the sea and entered the outlying areas of Basra. The people chased after it, mounted on the backs of purebred Arabian steeds, for which Basra is famous, and which are traded to all parts of the world and especially to India.
>
> This sea animal was faster than all the horses; nay he was as swift as lightning. When the men on their horses cornered him, he would fly away using his wings.
>
> It is said that this flying ocean horse used to go back to the ocean at night. Then, when morning came, he would [re]appear before everyone's eyes, prancing and galloping with his head raised high, and his wings open at one moment and folded the next.
>
> And it is said that more than 500 riders tried to capture him, and chased him, but to no avail, since he used flight to escape from them.
>
> His body was like that of a purebred horse, and his conformation was beautiful. No one could be sure whether he ate food or perhaps some grass, only that he sometimes drank from the water in pools and the rivers.
>
> He stayed in the area for about ten days, then he disappeared, but the stories of him were on everyone's tongue for nearly half a century. It was remembered that his coat was golden in color, and that his neck was long, covered with a thick coat of hair. When the sun rose, the sun rays would strike his coat and shine on them so that some called him Buraq.[1]

That the "strangeness" of this story is accentuated by its being sandwiched in between two dry factual reports about events in Basra (an earthquake that was felt as far away as Baghdad and Kufa, and an account of the taking of the city by a minor outlaw chieftain) cannot be doubted. Added to this is its own rather bizarre mingling of the quotidian with the fantastic. And that was at first enough to make it intriguing for me, to give it the flavor of the epiphanic. But it was only later, as it continued to haunt me, that I began to be aware that this flying horse was becoming in my mind inextricably linked to the figure of Sayyāb, that it was in some sense becoming emblematic for me of his experience.

At first, I had no idea why this should be the case. It seemed that there might be any number of reasons. I thought, for example, that the connection in my mind may have formed because this was the sort of story that Sayyāb himself would have found attractive, for his poetry is full of references to the magical folk tales of Arabic tradition, like *A Thousand and One Nights* or the adventures of popular epic heroes like Abū Zayd and 'Antara. Then again I thought it might be the connection of both to the river and the sea, for as the last chapter suggested, Sayyāb frequently drew upon sea imagery in his work. And there was at least one reason not to posit a similarity between them: the flying horse was beautiful—as only a fairy-tale animal can be—and Sayyāb's most notable physical quality according to all the sources who have written of him was his ungainly and almost cadaverous appearance.

It was only after a considerable period of time that I realized what that nagging hidden resemblance most likely was: both the winged horse and Sayyāb were anomalies in their environments. They were misfits whose ontology could not be convincingly explained by the phylogenetic rules operative in their formation, beings who tarried briefly and then disappeared as suddenly as they had come, leaving behind an army of baffled interpreters in their wake vainly seeking to assign a "meaning" to their presence.

One immediately corroborative element supporting this equation would be Sayyāb's early and—in a sense—unexpected death, when he succumbed to amyotrophic lateral sclerosis (ALS) at the age of only 38. Although this probably made it easier for biographers and scholarly interpreters to collect material about him before it became subject to the inevitable losses of time, it also made it much more difficult for them to use that material at the time it was collected as a means to assess the impact he had made upon modern Arabic literature during his all-too-brief career as a poet, with his innovations in form and theme and his unique style. In 1964, the year of his death, it was still impossible to tell how permanent the effect of something like free verse would be, as it had come to the attention of the literary public only slightly over a decade earlier.

But there were other things as well that would make him seem an inexplicable anomaly in his time and place. For instance, he grew up a Sunnī Muslim in an area where Shi'ism was a fundamental marker of identity, which has sometimes generated an automatic assumption among students of his career that he would be heavily influenced by either opposition to or acceptance of the attitudes peculiar to such an environment.[2] Yet the religious situation of his milieu seems to have had very little effect on him. Although he did go through a phase in his youth when he wrote some poetry on the death of Ḥusayn at Karbalā'[3]—probably under the influence of his liking for a popular Shi'ī teacher at his school—when he chose later in life to dramatize the issues surrounding the act of self-sacrifice, it was to the death of Christ he turned, not the murder of the Prophet's grandson.

Similarly, his educational background was anomalous. Simply by virtue of having gone beyond primary school, he would have to be considered unexpectedly well-educated in a land where illiteracy was the norm. His having advanced to secondary school and then to college certainly placed him within the elite, among the intelligentsia, but conversely his position within this group was never very secure. Unlike most of his intellectual friends and acquaintances who would have an impact similar to his on Arabic arts and letters—the poetess Nāzik al-Malā'ika; the novelist, poet, and critic Jabrā Ibrāhīm Jabrā; or Suhayl Idrīs, the editor of *Al-Ādāb*—Sayyāb had neither the wealth nor the influence to enable him to travel abroad for any part of his education. He spent his entire university career at the Teachers College in Baghdad, and it was not until 1961 that he visited Europe even briefly, for a four-day conference in Rome.[4] Only in the last year of his life did he spend any extensive amount of time in the West, when he went to England and France for medical treatment, but by this time his paralysis had become so bad that he was rarely able to leave his hospital bed. In contrast, many of his contemporaries had been to school, especially for advanced studies, in the United States or England or France, and this meant that there was a gap between his experience and theirs that must have been at times difficult if not impossible to bridge. Equally, he was isolated from many of his childhood playmates as well as his associates in the Communist Party by the fact that he had had the opportunity for any post–elementary education at all. He was painfully reminded of this by his Communist housemates during the crucial period of his exile in Kuwait in 1952, when they dismissed his contributions to their discussions as being those of a petit bourgeois, incapable by virtue of his background and education of participating in their revolutionary struggle.[5]

His family's social status was probably just as crucial as his education in isolating him from his fellows, if not more so, since the manner of his education was due to his middle-class background, which gave him an incentive to go beyond primary school but not enough money to pursue expensive study options abroad. There were only a tiny number of people in Iraq during this period who could be said to cling to a precarious middle ground between the great landowners whose estates covered vast areas of the countryside and who had a corresponding influence on the machinery of government, and the immense numbers of the poor who had no property whatsoever. These latter either eked out a living as sharecroppers on the great estates or, increasingly after the end of World War II, crowded into the city slums where only a few could find work at even subsistence wages.[6] Sayyāb's grandfather, 'Abd al-Jabbār Marzūq al-Sayyāb, was one of this handful of middle-tier landowners. Prior to the 1930s, 'Abd al-Jabbār and his father Marzūq (who died in 1936)[7] had owned enough date palm groves to earn a comfortable living and cultivate a reputation as local notables with considerable standing in the community.[8] They lived in a palatial—in the villagers' eyes—house in Baqī', a hamlet (or perhaps suburb might be a better term) adjacent to Jaykūr, in which Sayyāb spent much of his childhood, especially after his mother died when he was six and his grandparents stepped in to take care of him and his two younger brothers.

All this began to change in the late 1930s, and continued to do so throughout the 1940s, as Sayyāb's grandfather became increasingly hard pressed financially. This decline in the family's fortunes may have been due at least in part to the general worsening of world, as well as Iraqi, economic conditions during the Great Depression, but it was also exacerbated by the risky political associations of his two younger sons.[9] His eldest son, Shākir (Badr's father), was apparently relatively uninvolved in politics. After the War, in 1945 or 46, he would join the People's Party, but it is unclear how active he was in this organization—one that at first opposed, then made common cause with the Communists. In general, Shākir helped his father with the cultivation of the family's lands and, because he had had some education in the Ottoman schools, he found occasional outside supervisory work during the date harvesting, as well as acting as an agent for some of the local landowners.

The next brother, 'Abd al-Qādir, was another case entirely. He was deeply involved in the nationalist politics of the day and worked with various partisan newspapers in the Basra area, most notably *Al-Nās*, on the publishing license of which he was listed as the owner.[10] This newspaper was often in financial as well as political trouble because of its frequent suspensions and the fines it incurred, much of the burden for which no doubt fell upon Badr's grandfather. Also, as Īsā Bullāṭa makes clear, the paper was known for its attacks on the oppressive practices of local landowners, which could only have made the whole family's financial situation more precarious.[11] 'Abd al-Qādir seems to have spent much of the Second World War in a concentration camp at Amara, for his support of the Rashīd 'Alī coup as well as his anti-British and allegedly pro-Nazi activities.[12]

The youngest brother, 'Abd al-Majīd (who was not much older than his nephew Badr), became involved in the Iraq Communist Party during and after the War. He was the one who recruited Badr into the Party in 1945, and like his nephew he was put in prison following the Iraqi government's purge of the Communist leadership in 1949.

The conflicting political allegiances of the family seem, in a sense, to have mirrored their turbulent personal relationships. In this, they tellingly contravened the cultural ideal in Iraqi society, which, like traditional communities throughout the Arab world, gives family ties a paramount importance. Badr himself, indeed, seems to have been particularly unfortunate in this regard, and this may have engendered or enhanced in him a sense of anomalousness, of standing apart from those around him and their experiences. The event that he mentions most often as triggering this sense of traumatic alienation was his mother's death in childbirth in 1932, when he was six, after which he went with his brothers to live with his grandparents. Even when their father remarried, the boys did not leave the big house in Baqī' for long, because their new stepmother disliked having them around, and they ended up quarreling with their father whenever they stayed with him. All their lives, Badr and his father never seem to have gotten on well and their relations often deteriorated into outright hostility.

Sayyāb was moreover forced to relive the traumatic loss of his mother only ten years later, when his paternal grandmother died in 1942. By this time he was living in Basra with his maternal grandmother while he finished secondary school, but he seems to have felt the loss keenly. One of the earliest poems he preserved was the elegy he wrote for his grandmother on this occasion. That we should come to know the intensity of his emotions only once they have been filtered through literary conventions as structured as those found in elegy is in itself suggestive of the role poetry and literature had already come to play, and would continue to play, in the process of "self"-mastery embodied in the projection of himself as a thinking, sovereign subject. We have already seen an example of this in his letter quoted in the second chapter of this study, where he turns an excursion across the river into a kind of "internalized quest-romance" (to use Harold Bloom's apt formulation about the structuring of romantic poetry that has proven to have such enduring suggestiveness and applicability in a variety of situations) that seeks to delineate the boundaries of self in relation to both time and space.

It should be noted, however, that this notion of Sayyāb as a self-"represented" and constructed personality—rather than a "natural," unmediated and spontaneous one—runs directly counter to the many descriptive sketches of him left by his contemporaries, nearly all of which exhibit a remarkable consistency in structure and impression. As a group, these portraits tend to emphasize his enthusiasm, impulsiveness, lack of reserve and sincerity, painting him as a naïf without intellectual pretensions, an untutored genius brushed by a touch of the vulgar. Typical are the reminiscences of the poet Buland al-Ḥaydarī, who befriended him in his college days:

> In the Baghdad of those yesterdays [after World War II] there was one among us who tried to find for the anxiety, the dismay and the fear accumulating in his soul an outlet in literature, establishing new values in it that were in accordance with his feelings and his empathic understanding of the world's problems. The world was talking then in a hoarse voice about the horrible crime of murder which had occurred in Hiroshima, and about the suicide of a German writer in Brazil, and about a student who had sent a letter to the American president, asking him whether he ought to finish his studies after the invention of the atomic bomb. Meanwhile, the newspapers of Baghdad were talking about a merchant who had mixed sawdust with flour and made this mixture into bread for the people.
>
> During the passing of this whole dark panorama [before us] there was a wizened little hand that used to fasten itself onto ours with overflowing sincerity. This was Badr's hand, as he talked to us about all these things as though he were a part of them and he had no importance outside of them. Then suddenly, with the same intensity he would express his admiration for the laughter of a pretty girl as she crossed the street, or the lisp of one his female classmates who sat next to him in composition. And there were those snippets of paper that used to carry us through many evenings from one café to another, so that we could listen to this new experiment and criticize that poem as we tried to create a philosophy for the world around us. Some of us kept trying desperately to reconcile Marx and Nietzsche so that we could extricate ourselves from that bitter impasse. For Badr, on the other hand, it appeared to us as though each one of those two lived in a separate corner of his soul, in a life that never developed.[13]

Note how poetry here is not seen as something that gives structure to Sayyāb's personality but rather the opposite: his anxieties and uncertainties are freed and given a place to flow outward there, without structure and constraint, to be dissipated and drained away through his writing. If Marx and Nietzsche can be seen as standing in, respectively, for the poet as spokesman for social reform and the poet as hedonistic individualist, then Ḥaydarī clearly sees Sayyāb as oscillating unpredictably and unselfconsciously between both, giving himself over entirely to the surface allure of each alternately, without ever imposing upon himself the discipline of at least trying to reconcile their subject positions in a construction of self. Since this heroic, though inevitably futile, attempt to integrate one's personality is a strategy that Ḥaydarī privileges through self-identification, we are forced to posit Sayyāb, then, as something like an idiot savant, the perfect exemplar of Keats's negative capability in human form, where poetic genius goes hand in hand with naiveté, artless behavior, directionless enthusiasm, and perhaps even buffoonery. Allied to this latter observation, his life as presented to us often incorporates a kind of theatricality, a "spectacle-ness," that tends to pull the reader out of the poem and into the life.

In descriptions by those who knew Sayyāb less well than did Ḥaydarī, such judgments are, if anything, even more strongly salient. Thus we have Yūsuf Ghassūb, who met Sayyāb for the first time at a poetry reading in Beirut, saying he was "a voice exploding from deep within, just as he exploded from the depths of his country," a voice whose "authenticity" exposed the insincerities and affectations of "counterfeit poets" for what they were.[14] The Lebanese poet Unsī al-Ḥājj, probably on the same occasion, recalls his initial apprehension at his first meeting with the by-then famous Iraqi:

> I was expecting a "professor" of poetic philosophy, or a metaphysical Don Juan, or a revolutionary who would cut off your head, wrapping himself in a mantle of alienation and obscurantism, or a respected intellectual, or at least a complicated personality who would hint at secrets within secrets.
>
> But here I was, face to face with a broken reed that loved to laugh, with an open heart, hands brimming over with generosity, and a half-paralyzed tongue spouting psalms and pithy stories.
>
> I had come there in a hostile mood, a defensive mood, ready to attack. Then I found myself, once this man had enfolded me with his liberality, a prisoner of his love, confused and guilty like a boy or a fool.[15]

In this passage, Ḥājj seems to be most amazed—and no doubt relieved—at Sayyāb's apparent lack of interest in adhering to the conventions of behavior expected of intellectuals and his unconcern with whether or not he is identified as a member of the intelligentsia. Interestingly, both Sa'dī Yūsuf, an Iraqi poet slightly junior to Sayyāb,[16] and the critic Jalīl Kamāl al-Dīn have independently chosen in their writings to call him a peasant (fallāḥ). "An educated (*muthaqqaf*) peasant," Kamāl al-Dīn goes on to say, "if such an expression would be correct and possible," but nevertheless a peasant.[17] Even more suggestively, Kamāl al-Dīn notes that Sayyāb labeled *himself* in this way, saying to him once "I am a peasant; I take pride in the peasants. There is nothing like the peasants for purity (*naqā'*) and revolutionary spirit (*thawriyya*)."

Taken as a whole, such characterizations appeal to a comforting version of the master narrative of art as something that cannot be consciously sought after or acquired by those seeking to practice it, but rather something mystified, that simply "appears." Their very consistency, the way they seem to blend into a seamless whole, would furthermore argue that to convey the impression of being an untutored genius was something that Sayyāb himself strove after and actively embraced. It was, after all, as the testimony supports, a supremely disarming strategy, one designed to defuse tension and place others at their ease without necessarily leaving oneself vulnerable to criticism. So it is not surprising to find that this reading of the poet's personality has been installed as canonical in both Iḥsan 'Abbās's and Īlīyā Ḥāwī's bio-critical evaluations of his work.[18] They both read Sayyāb's life into his work as if it were all surface, one where interpretation is univalent and unproblematic because there is such a high degree of correlation between what the poet writes and external reality, the "facts" of his life.

The only problem with this as a way of containing and describing the phenomenology of Sayyāb's writing is that it requires us to ignore the "literariness" that seems to inhere in the poetry at a very basic level. For, in truth, if one were to seek to capture Sayyāb's poetry by reference to a single characteristic, the chosen descriptor would have to be its obvious, foregrounded intertextuality. In other words, when one begins to pay attention to this stratum of "literariness" that informs in some way virtually all the instantiations of Sayyāb's discourse—whether poems or letters or lectures—some new and rather unexpected points of purchase become available for hermeneutic use. Instead of seeing his poetry as solely the raw material for biographical speculation one can begin to see instead how literary paradigms and conventions may have become for Sayyāb the indispensable matrix in which the unformed flux of biographical fact could be shaped and given meaning. Here, Edward Said's distinction between filiation, a largely unconscious bonding with "one's natal culture" through the "natural" relationships established by the family structures of biology and genealogy, and affiliation, a conscious identification with pasts, traditions, and ancestors that are chosen by the individual, may be useful.[19] Said documents how, throughout the period conventionally designated as "modernist," there is a shift toward the valorization of affiliation at the expense of filiation, which is represented in the work of such writers as T.S. Eliot, Joyce, Proust, Conrad, Hardy, and Thomas Mann—not to speak of Freud himself—as rendered problematic, if not impossible, by the various alienating pressures of modernity.

The relevance of such a model for Sayyāb's writing is obvious. Coupled with the focus in modernist works on affiliation, his own background and experiences would powerfully underwrite its presuppositions. To choose one's own genealogy, through literary models, must have seemed powerfully attractive to someone whose filiative bonds had been so badly frayed in childhood. This may explain why Sayyāb's identification with his chosen poetic predecessors could sometimes seem even to extend beyond the realm of the written word into the lived details of their experience. For instance, at the height of his enthrallment to the poetry of John Keats, he imagines himself coming down with the symptoms of tuberculosis, the disease that had killed the English poet more than a century earlier, and then proceeds to write a poem on the subject.[20]

Notwithstanding such evidence of willed empathy with other poet's *lives*, it is within the engagement of his poetry with other *poems* that we find the most compelling evidence of Sayyāb's fascination with literary models for "self-fashioning" (to use Stephen Greenblatt's apt phrase). The variable nature of these models offered him a range of strategies that he could employ in his dialectic encounters with their ideological presuppositions, but in his maturer poetry he tended to remain within the horizons of certain favored maneuvers that had served him well in the past, where particular groups of affiliative predecessors habitually occupied niches in his discourse specific to themselves.

It was with the canonical poets of Arabic literary tradition that Sayyāb presents to us his blandest face, one that effaces "self" most fully within the governing rules of filiation. In the short autobiographical asides he makes throughout his career, Sayyāb gives us a genealogy of his relationship to these poets that is nothing if not conventional. He tells us that he first read and was influenced by the poets (mainly pre-Islamic and early Islamic) found in Ibn Qutayba's *Kitāb al-Shi'r wa-al-Shu'arā'*.[21] Elsewhere, he goes on to list the "golden age" poets al-Buḥturī, Abū Tammām, and al-Mutanabbī as favorites.[22] To this, one should probably add the names of Ibn al-Rūmī and Mihyār al-Daylamī, who are mentioned with admiration in early letters,[23] as well as al-Ma'arrī, a line of whose poetry we have already seen quoted at the end of the Fukai poems.[24] Taken together, these names form an absolutely unexceptionable list of canonically classical Arab poets covering the entire chronological spectrum with admirable thoroughness.

To evoke these poets' work, the strategy Sayyāb most often used was one of quotation. Such a maneuver is telling, because quotation is precisely the case of intertextual citation that gives the greatest dialogic power to the evoked text and its characteristic voice. And, although Sayyāb frequently "misquotes" or alters the substance of the original quotation in the process of placing it within his own work, he does not appear to do this primarily in order to challenge or contest the ideological underpinnings of the original, but rather to show how short his own world has fallen in terms of realizing this ideology.[25] The general tenor is therefore a nostalgic one.

Thus, as Ḥasan Tawfīq has argued,[26] when Sayyāb chooses to quote a line from the classical poet ʻAlī ibn al-Jahm in his 1960 poem "Al-Mabghā" (The Whorehouse), the purpose would seem to be to "elicit in the mind of his target audience the image of Baghdad in the ʻAbbāsid period" when it was at the height of its glory and contrast it with the debased Baghdad of contemporary times. The original line runs as follows: "ʻuyūn al-mahā bayna l-ruṣāfati wa-l-jisri // jalabna l-hawā min ḥaythu adrī wa-lā adrī" (The eyes of the wild cows between al-Ruṣāfa and al-Jisr // draw forth desire from whence I know and do not know). Sayyāb leaves the first hemistich of this line unchanged, but alters the second half completely to "thuqūb raṣāṣin raqqashat ṣafḥati l-badri" (. . . are bullet holes that have pockmarked the surface of the full moon). In so doing he changes the world from one where desire is the metonymic result of looking at the wide, dark eyes of the young women who are likened to gazelles, or "wild cows," into a world where the same sight metaphorically recalls black, empty sockets reminiscent of the craters found on the airless surface of the moon. One moves, in other words, from the generative power of love as a dominant in medieval Baghdad to death as the authenticating value of the modern city. This would seem to parallel the problematization of the "natural," biologically based links of filiation by modernist writers described by Edward Said, in that love and desire, which lead to children, to generation, exist only in the past, in the quotation's original text, and have been ostentatiously eliminated from the reworked version in Sayyāb's poem. And, in that it introduces an element of unresolved temporal instability into the poem, no opportunity offers itself to bring up the modernists' redemptive counter-discourse of affiliation.

Interestingly, the line of al-Maʻarrī, which Sayyāb quotes and alters at the conclusion of "Elegy for Jaykur"[27] appears to thematize even more directly the notion of a contrast between filiation and affiliation as proposed by Said. In al-Maʻarrī's line, "And what should leave all creation confounded there is an animal generated from an inanimate substance," the problematic concern is spontaneous generation, that is, producing a creature without antecedents, without a filiative genealogy. Sayyāb then changes this line to: "And what should leave all creation confounded there is how to explain a creature with cash." In so doing, he problematizes the question of choice in much the same way that the practice of affiliation does. To affiliate oneself is to *choose* one's antecedents, and money, as representing exchange value in the economy becomes the dominant instrument allocating *choice* in modern capitalist society. Only those with "cash" can choose. Said himself would seem to point to this close connection between the loss of filiative power and the rise of capitalism when he notes that the Marxist concept of "reification is the alienation of men from what they have produced, and it is the starkly uncompromising severity of [its] vision that [it] means by this all the products of human labor, children included, which are so completely separated from each other, atomized, and hence frozen into the category of ontological objects as to make even natural relationships virtually impossible."[28] Thus a major element in the way Sayyāb uses quotations of canonical poets would seem to be as instancing nostalgic desire: the attempt to summon up an idealized version of the past when reification and alienation from one's surroundings was not operative, when it was still possible to see the loss of filiative bonds as a threat—something to be resisted—rather than a simple statement of fact.

One encounters a similar nostalgic strategy governing even Sayyāb's appropriation of modern Arab neoclassical poets like Shawqī or al-Jawāhirī.[29] Thus, in the 1957 poem "Jaykūr wa-al-Madīna" (Jaykūr and the City) he includes the following lines:

70) And Jaykūr: before it, ramparts have risen
71) And a great gate
72) And a silence has wrapped it round.
73) Who will breach the wall? Who will open the gate, bloodying his right hand on every bolt?
74) My right hand is no talon [fit] for the struggle, so that I could strive with it in the city streets,
75) Nor a powerful fist [fit] to resurrect life from the clay
76) It is only a piece of clay [itself].[30]

The imagery here draws upon a famous line from a poem composed by Shawqī deploring the French bombing of Damascus in 1925 and calling upon the Arabs to fight for their freedom against the invaders:

And freedom colored red has a gate
where every hand dyed with blood shall knock.[31]

Although the rearrangement of wording is more radical than in previous examples, the goal of the strategy is similar: to demonstrate the way the present has not lived up to ideals pictured as operative in the past, not to question the validity of those ideals themselves.

Sayyāb also tells us, however, when he gives an account of the development of his poetic style, that at least one postneoclassical Arab poet had an important influence on it: this is the Egyptian romantic poet 'Alī Maḥmūd Ṭaha. Ḥasan Tawfīq has suggested additional names from the ranks of Arab romantics to add to this list and makes a convincing case for doing so.[32] That we should find Sayyāb somewhat evasive in constructing his genealogy at this particular point should not perhaps be surprising in a poet seeking to lay claim, as Sayyāb clearly was, to a canonically impeccable set of antecedents on which to base the construction of a cohesive poetic self. We ought to expect him to be more hesitant in claiming affiliation with poets whose place in the pantheon was not yet as secure as those of their illustrious predecessors. The fact that today 'Alī Maḥmūd Ṭaha is a much less well known and less highly regarded figure than he was in Sayyāb's youth should be lesson enough in this regard.

Yet, when we look carefully at the poetry itself, we find evidence that would clearly suggest that, not only was Sayyāb less willing to acknowledge a relationship between his poetry and that of his immediate predecessors, he also interacted with their works in ways that were quite different from his use of material taken from earlier poets. Gone are the accommodating quotations that were used primarily to contrast valorized past with degenerate present. In their place we find practices installed that are much less respectful of the authority of their voices, practices that in fact invite subversion, contestation, and even direct challenge to their hegemonic power.

Probably the most elastically assimilative and assertive of these strategies is one that has no parallel in Western literatures: *mu'āraḍa*. According to the criteria most widely accepted among modern critics, the definition of a *mu'āraḍa* is quite uncomplicated and straightforward: it is a poem composed in the same rhyme and meter as a previously written poem.[33] The assumption is generally made in the definitions that this resemblance between the two poems is conscious and intended by the author of the second poem, but this is nowhere explicitly made a prerequisite for the poem to be labeled a *mu'āraḍa*. Thus, the question of intention—so important when dealing with practices that thematize influence, as *mu'āraḍa* does—is (perhaps deliberately) left obscure, and the arguments for its applicability in any given case would thus seem to rest at first glance on the reinforcing power of any biological metaphors used in the supporting critical discourse, the Arabic equivalents of Said's theories of filiation/affiliation, and perhaps even more appositely, the "family romance" of strong father-poets and anxiety-ridden son-poets so powerfully argued in Harold Bloom's *Anxiety of Influence*.

On the basis of the meaning of the word *mu'āraḍa* alone, Bloom's framework might seem to be the most promising, for the usual signification of *mu'āraḍa* in modern Arabic writing is "opposition" or "protest." Yet no critic, to my knowledge, medieval or modern, has ever directly explored *mu'āraḍa* as a technique implying any kind of consistent literary *confrontation* specifically between the two poets involved on a personal basis.[34] Any suggestion of a dialectical exchange between the two parties involved in the *mu'āraḍa* is consistently disregarded in favor of subsuming and containing the relationship within a model of impersonal restructuring or reordering of the instantiated words (*lafẓ*). The closest approach to a more direct treatment of the subject by a rhetorician/critic in the classical period may have been the fourth/tenth century authority al-Āmidī, who began his book on the comparison of the merits of the two Abbasid poets Abū Tammām and al-Buḥturī with the following promise:

> I do not wish to clearly state an absolute preference for one of them [i.e., Abū Tammām and al-Buḥturī] over the other. But I will weigh in the balance one poem against another, *if the two agree in meter (wazn), rhyme (qāfiya) and the case endings of the rhyme (i'rāb al-qāfiya)*, and [I will weigh in the balance] theme (*ma'nā*) against theme. Then I will say which of them is more poetic in that poem and on that theme.[35]

Although he does not mention the word *mu'āraḍa* outright, the restrictions al-Āmidī places on his procedure of comparison, limiting it to poems that are in the same meter and rhyme, surely suggests that this is what he had in mind. Yet, by the time he came to the second part of his book, the one that contains his promised comparison of individual poems by the two poets, al-Āmidī appears to have forgotten this earlier statement, for he does not explicitly compare entire poems "head-to-head." Instead, he chooses to organize his comparisons more conventionally on the basis of theme, quoting at most a few lines of the poems. Further, he rarely juxtaposes lines in the same meter and rhyme, and when he does, he does not call attention to it.

If one might think it prudent to question the applicability, then, of Bloom's theories to classical Arabic literature (or any preromantic literary period in any literature), when one scans the anecdotal literature about the actual poetic practice of *mu'āraḍa* what is most striking about these anecdotes is that they represent *mu'āraḍa* as being both ubiquitous throughout the entire history of classical Arabic literature and thoroughly grounded in relationships of tension and conflict.

Probably the best evidence for a Bloomian reading of Arabic *mu'āraḍa* can be found in a place that might at first seem notably unpromising: those treatises that deal with attempts to demonstrate the sacred status of the Koran as a scriptural miracle, one containing the verbatim words of God as they were revealed to the Prophet Muḥammad, and thus confirming his claims to be a truly inspired prophetic messenger to mankind. One of the proofs that these treatises repeatedly point to as a demonstration of their contention is the fact that the Koran itself challenges "both men and jinn" to compose something similar to its words, yet no one who took up that challenge was ever able to convince a significant proportion of the available audience that what he had produced truly equaled or surpassed the Koran's characteristic brand of eloquence. These works on the inimitability (*i'jāz*) of the Koran—and there are many—consistently refer to the unsuccessful imitations of the scripture as *mu'āraḍa*s. Thus they are led to discuss the dynamics of the production of *mu'āraḍa*s among poets—in order to give a context for their discussion of the relationship between the Koran and its *mu'āraḍa*s—and in the process the anecdotes they use reveal more about the presuppositions their contemporaries had about what constitutes *mu'āraḍa* than all the rhetorical handbooks put together.[36] One of the most frequently quoted of these anecdotes, about the poet Imru' al-Qais, his wife Umm Jundab, and the poet 'Alqama is paradigmatic in this respect.[37]

According to the story, one day Imru' al-Qais and 'Alqama (considered to be two of the earliest pre-Islamic poets) got into an argument about which of them was the greater poet. So they went to Umm Jundab to ask her to judge between them. She told them each to compose a poem, using the same meter and rhyme, describing his horse. Imru' al-Qais went first, incorporating the following line in his poem:

> On account of the whip is [his] brisk running, and on account of the leg is [his] swiftness
> and on account of the urging cry is [his] light, prancing step.

Then 'Alqama recited his poem, also including a line boasting of the swiftness of his mount:

Then I overtake them, with his rein [still] slack,
he passes by like a streaming wind.

After hearing both poems, Umm Jundab said to Imru' al-Qais: "'Alqama is a greater poet than you." When Imru' al-Qais asked her how she had come to this decision, Umm Jundab replied: "Because you had to urge your horse on with your whip and your heels, while 'Alqama, once he had sighted his quarry, only used the reins to urge his horse and did not hit him with a whip." At this, Imru' al-Qais angrily exploded: "He is not a better poet than I am, but you are in love with him." Then he divorced her and left her with 'Alqama.[38]

Whether or not it is historically factual, this anecdote is rich with information on the social presuppositions surrounding the reception of poetry in the classical period of Arab/Islamic civilization. It indicates, first, that contemporary audiences did not find it unreasonable to expect even the earliest (and most famous) poets to be engaging in *mu'āraḍa*. Further, it shows us that thematic engagement was emphatically a possible, if not necessary, element of the rhetorical strategy. Finally, it foregrounds and makes quite clear the competitive dimension inherent in the form.

As was mentioned earlier, most definitions of *mu'āraḍa* in modern Arabic literary criticism are even more evasive than those found in classical handbooks, seldom venturing beyond situating its defining parameters securely on the grounds of form. Discussions of *mu'āraḍa* in Arabic literary criticism before the early 1980s are rare; when they do occur, they almost invariably demonstrate this formalist bias.[39] The more recent theorists, however, have begun to examine with greater seriousness the possibility of a relationship between the two pieces in terms of content as well.[40] One critic has even gone so far as to say that only when the later poem contrafacts[41] the theme (*mawḍū'*) of the original is it a complete, full *mu'āraḍa*, thus reversing the trend of earlier times.

Upon first examination, it might seem likely that this apparent relaxation from the stricter formalist criteria of earlier days had resulted from the recognition of a change that had taken place in modern poetic practice that would require a rethinking of approaches to this topic. Since the beginning of its romantic period, in the 1930s, Arabic poetry has increasingly been written without monorhyme. This change has made it more difficult to contrafact the *form* of a precursor poem in its entirety, since it is much more difficult to reproduce complex multiple rhyme schemes in a new poem than it is to adhere to a particular monorhyme. Thus, it would seem a natural development in modern poetry and literary criticism to find more emphasis placed on *mu'āraḍa* as the contrafaction of themes, and a turn away from strict formalistic criteria: in short, such a definition might be supposed to mark a greater receptivity to *mu'āraḍa* as a literary practice, if only by widening the definition to encompass a broader range of poems.

This notion, however, is not borne out by further statements made by the critics themselves. Contemporary critics have coupled their new willingness to revalue the definition of *mu'āraḍa* as it has appeared in the history of Arabic literature with a firm determination to treat it as a purely historical phenomenon, of little or no relevance to modern poetry or (perhaps more importantly) modern poets. For these critics, the golden age of *mu'āraḍa* was the last half of the nineteenth century. Then poets labeled their poems as *mu'āraḍa*s, with an openness that was relatively rare even in the classical period. And, as part of a poetics, now known as "neoclassical," that emphasized revival of the past glories of Arabic literature through imitation of models taken from that past, primarily from the Abbasid and earlier periods, *mu'āraḍa* was well integrated into the dominant aesthetic.

Such an aesthetic, however, would have no place in the Western-influenced, twentieth-century romantic and modernist schools that followed the nineteenth-century neoclassical Arab poets. Contemporary critics, affected themselves by the same romantic and modernist literary doctrines as the poets, were not likely, either, to respond to any indications that *mu'āraḍa*, a literary form that flaunts the fact that its author has been influenced, had survived into a period when, as in the West, "influence" has become a very problematic term. One should not forget that one of the earliest important defenses of modernist Arabic poetry begins by saying that "from the first modern poetry has appeared as a revolt against the ancient poetic forms and models [found in Arabic literature], and a total rejection of its attitudes and styles, whose purposes have been exhausted."[42] Thus, it is not surprising to find even one of the least dismissive and most discriminating evaluations of *mu'āraḍa* by a modern critic concluding, albeit regretfully, with the following:

> By their very nature, however, the intentional *mu'āraḍat* represent an activity that is hardly open to innovation; and in the poems written by the neoclassicists in this fashion, the traditional elements are preserved without significant functional transformations.[43]

The terms "innovative" and "original" have been situated as central touchstones of quality in the evaluative vocabulary of Arabic literary criticism ever since the Dīwān school attacked the neoclassical poet Aḥmad Shawqī for his imitativeness in the early twentieth century.[44] Therefore, to label a literary practice as not "open to innovation" is implicitly to deny it any relevance to the modern modes of literary production. In the context of this discursive practice, even if *mu'āraḍa*s did occur, they would have to be tagged as curiosities, aberrations from the norm—at best the products of a lesser poetic talent, one unable to innovate on its own.

This is why it is so surprising to find the practice of *mu'āraḍa* crucially relevant to understanding the work of Sayyāb, whom—as we have seen—is most often pictured by his contemporaries as the paradigmatic "unstudied" and "original" poetic talent. Interestingly, the poems he most often chose to contrafact were by romantic poets—Ibrāhīm Nājī, Mikhā'īl Nu'ayma, and especially 'Alī Maḥmūd Ṭaha—who had themselves rejected the aesthetics behind the practice of neoclassic *mu'āraḍa*.[45] In this way his choice of method for engaging their discourses could be seen as doubly open to contestatory maneuvers.

One thing that all of Sayyāb's *mu'āraḍa*s share, whatever the circumstances of their composition, is an unusual sense of active engagement with the *themes* of the work being imitated. Often this is expressed by the use of shared imagery to present a lively argument with, or even a complete reversal of, the thematic structure of the original. This phenomenon is certainly observable from Sayyāb's earliest experiments with the technique; in fact, it is eminently clear in his second surviving poem, entitled "Yawm al-Safar" (Day of Departure). This poem has been identified by one of Sayyāb's biographers[46] as being in the same meter and rhyme as—and therefore is, at least technically, a *mu'āraḍa* of—a famous poem by the Egyptian romantic poet 'Alī Maḥmūd Ṭaha, "Buḥayrat Kūmū" (Lake Como)

The earliness of "Day of Departure" makes it a particularly valuable specimen for forming a "baseline" picture of Sayyāb's *mu'āraḍa*s, with which we can compare later developments. In addition, we are fortunate to have two versions of the poem: one from the time of the poem's original composition, sent in a letter to his childhood friend, Khālid al-Shawwāf, the other a revised version that was published in Sayyāb's *Dīwān* after his death. When the two are compared, the later version of the poem shows a sharpening focus on the denial of Ṭaha's basic argument in *his* poem: an invitation to a young American woman he has met at Lake Como to experience the sensual pleasures of life in his company, because they must store up memories in anticipation of their inevitable separation and death.

In its turn, "Lake Como" seems to represent an engagement (since it cannot technically be called a *mu'āraḍa*) with a precursor poem from French romantic literature, Alphonse de Lamartine's "Le Lac." This poem was particularly popular among the Arab romantics and was translated several times in the 1920s and 1930s, most notably by Ibrāhīm al-Nājī; Aḥmad Ḥasan al-Zayyāt, editor of the Egyptian literary magazine *Risāla*; Niqūla Fayyāḍ; and by Ṭaha himself.

As is clear from their respective titles, both poems use as a central, focusing symbol a body of water, and in both cases this lake has become a place of rendezvous for a pair of lovers. Lamartine's body of water was the Lac du Borget in Aix-les-Bains, where, in 1816, he met Julie Charles, the wife of a well-known physicist. She became the "love of his life," and a year later they made arrangements to meet again at the lakeside. But when the time came for the appointed rendezvous, Madame Charles had fallen ill (an illness that would result in her death), and Lamartine found himself alone at their former lovers' haunt. The poem begins with a series of scenes representing the lovers' trysts, remembered from the year before, when they walked together on the same shore where the speaker now stands alone. At the end of these reminiscences, the poet recalls his beloved's voice as she apostrophized time, asking it to "Suspends ton vol (Suspend your flight). . . ." She argued then that only those who are suffering and unhappy should be subjected to the effects of time's passage. For them it is a mercy; whereas for those who are happy, like the lovers, the passage of time is a hardship, leading as it does to change and loss. Acknowledging, ultimately, that time cannot be stopped, the woman turns to her lover, urging him ". . . de l'heure fugitive, / Hatons-nous jouissons! (. . .let us hasten to enjoy the fleeting hour!)."

This act of remembering his beloved's words a year later, of making her present through them, far from being cathartic, transfixes the poet and offers him no solace because he realizes that his powers of memory are themselves subject to the destructive effects of time. Thus, he seeks to depersonalize and detemporalize this process of remembrance by apostrophizing the elements of the landscape around him—the trees, the rocks, the cave in which they once sheltered, the lake itself—calling upon them to "remember," because they are not subject to the ravages of time as he is. Thus he suggests that they are far better qualified than he to perpetuate the record of the passion of the lovers.

This involvement of the natural landscape in the human activity of remembering would naturally strike a responsive chord in someone like

Ṭaha, brought up in the Arabic literary tradition, which was similarly steeped in the conventions of using a natural setting, the "abandoned campsite" of the *aṭlāl* and *nasīb*, as a locus for the poet's meditation on the joys of love past and the agonies of love present. So it is perhaps not surprising that Ṭaha was moved to translate Lamartine's poem early in his career and included it in his first collection of poems, *Al-Mallāḥ al-Tā'ih* (The Lost Sailor) (1934).

In his translation of "Le Lac," Ṭaha remains unusually faithful to the imagery of Lamartine, given that he produced this translation within an environment and in an atmosphere where translators were allowed a great deal of latitude in their renderings. He does not attempt to replace or supplement the highly specialized language of French romantic elegy and European climatology with the Bedouin language conventional to the *nasīb*, the type of "landscape poem" more familiar to his readers. For example, he keeps the water/lake imagery of the original, within whose bounds love and time are treated metaphorically, intact. He does not succumb to a temptation to supplement it by use of the rain imagery with which Arabic poetry is so liberally endowed and that often serves the same purpose of dramatizing the contrast between plenitude and lack. As a specific instance of this faithfulness to the original, he translates the phrase "when love pours us happiness in long draughts" almost word for word, when it might have been very easy to invoke the imagery of rain showers.

Structurally, Ṭaha observes the same rigor of fidelity to the original, except at the end of the poem, where Lamartine had asked nature "to remember." This had been something quite new in French poetry: always before *man-made* ruins, particularly those of classical Greece and Rome, had performed the function of "memorializing," of preserving and evoking the past.[47] Nature had, at most, performed a supporting role in this process, providing a picturesque backdrop against which the ruin could perform its unique function. The *aṭlāl* in the *nasīb*, however, had never been so functionally separated from the natural world. The two interpenetrated from the earliest times, as in Imru' al-Qays's *mu'allaqa*, where the lines in the sand drawn by the winds cannot be told from the fading traces of the dwellings, or Labīd's *mu'allaqa*, where the spectacle of the gazelles reproducing and nursing their young and the renewal of nature itself, both take place inside the boundaries of the abandoned camp site. Thus, when Ṭaha comes to reproduce Lamartine's text here, he does not dwell upon the notion of nature becoming the memorializer—for this must have seemed so routine to him as to scarcely need pointing out—but on two other elements: the apostrophe to nature and the figure of prosopoeia (personification): of humanizing nature and thus endowing it with a voice capable of answering the poet's, which delivers the final statement of the poem: "They have loved."

When, a few years later, Ṭaha came to write "Lake Como," it would appear that this experience of translating Lamartine's "Le Lac" was still quite fresh in his mind. The tone of active engagement with the precursor is very much set by the fourth line of the poem, where the speaker says: "We were sent there for an unanticipated rendezvous," directly inverting Lamartine's image (as well as the *nasīb*'s) where the destructiveness of time is dramatized by the lover's return to a place of *anticipated* rendezvous, where he might naturally have expected to find his lady, but did not. This signals that the operative assumptions upon which the world of Ṭaha's "Lake Como" is built are very different from either Lamartine's, or, interestingly enough, from the *nasīb*'s.

Ṭaha appears to reinforce this distance from the text he had previously translated with such exactitude by constantly resorting to what one might call a "Bedouin" discourse or idiolect in his own poem to emphasize the strangeness of what he observes. This is most noticeable at the beginning of the poem as he describes the Bergamasque Alps (which he calls the "Brunat") that surround the lake:

8) The Brunat are young beauties, wearing evening gowns,
9) Atop them houses lie scattered like flowers.
10) We crossed their glades, then they beckoned to those who crossed—
11) Take [from] them a kiss! He who desires, let him do it with a whole heart!
12) So we have soared to their hidden chambers, group after group,
13) In glass [carriages] circling through the air, without smoke or fire,
14) Which crosses the empty sky with us, on flower bright silks,
15) Stairs which resemble the *ṣirāṭ*, soaring out of sight,
16) To the stars rising, to the clouds descending.[48]

In addition to describing the mountains in language customarily reserved for maidens in pre-Islamic poetry, Ṭaha employs the same periphrastic technique in picturing the funicular car that takes him to the mountaintop (lines 12–16). Here, he resorts, rather surprisingly, to a convention that had become very much discredited early in the neoclassic period and was the source of much amusement to later generations. The neoclassic poets used to introduce Western technological devices into a poem and then compare them descriptively with elements traditionally found in the *qaṣīda*. For instance, Al-Bārūdī compares the whistle of a locomotive to crows cawing, traditional harbingers of the beloved's departure in the *nasīb*.[49] Ruṣāfī, after riding in an automobile for the first time, compares its hardiness and endurance to the camel of the pre-Islamic poet Ṭarafa.[50]

Why should Ṭaha employ a technique that had been so completely rejected, long before he began writing, here in this poem? The answer that suggests itself is twofold. First, it is consistent with his insistence throughout the poem on the fact that the speaker is a stranger to this place. Although the point is made at several points in the poem, it is made especially explicit toward the end, when he turns to address his American companion directly:

42) O daughter of the New World, join a world gone by,
43) In my blood, from its heritage, lies the scent of Bedouins and great civilizations,
44) Songs for one who sings, and themes for one who would boast.
45) What is it you whisper? Speak clearly! There is knowledge in your eyes.
46) The two strangers here, caution will avail them nothing,
47) We are two rebellious souls, and two bodies from some hell.

Here, the notion of being a stranger is linked quite openly to being from a "Bedouin" background. This emphasis on strangeness inverts another element of the Lamartinian/*nasīb* world: its insistence on the familiarity of the site where the poet finds himself when he engages in his meditation on love lost. Everything he sees there reminds him of the past and is an occasion for memorializing it. For Ṭaha, in contrast, Lake Como is totally unfamiliar and this unfamiliarity, as he implies in lines 34–40, is precisely what gives the landscape the power to "feel and inspire the one who composes poetry" (line 36).

The second important element introduced in the description of the Brunat and the funicular car is the use of religious language. Here, it is no more than a brief allusion. The cable supporting the funicular car as it crosses space to reach the top of the mountain reminds the speaker of the *ṣirāṭ*, the narrow bridge of Islamic eschatology, "sharper than a sword, thinner than a hair," which everyone must cross in order to reach Paradise. Those who have sinned fall from the *ṣirāṭ* into the pits of Hell, which lie below it. This comparison—though it may seem at this point to be incongruous, suggesting a seriousness that the context does not support—reinforces an identification between the Lake Como region and paradise already made in the second line, where the poet calls it "the paradise of desires." These seemingly casual and offhand references, however, are not simply throwaways. They are taken up again at the end of the poem, where the seriousness latent in the imagery is allowed to develop fully:

59) For whom do the smiles flutter, for whom is the hair loosened?
60) A fruit ripe for picking, and how can a fruit not be plucked?
61) Adam did not refuse eternal life, or go astray in it, or stumble,[51]
62) A slip which made him inherit reason, and showed God who disbelieved!
63) Our cup laughs with its bubbles, free of stain,
64) So pour out the wine and sip it to [the rhythm of] the strings
65) And if you want, make me drink to the tunes of the rain
66) For tomorrow youth will go and memories [will be all] that remain for us.

The innocent sensuality that the poet had been celebrating up to this point, having been previously shorn of its potential connection to memory and death via Lamartine and the *nasīb*, is now framed within the bounds of another sort of discourse, scriptural language, in which this sort of behavior is no less problematic. More precisely, Ṭaha now frames it with the story of Adam and Eve, where temptation, once succumbed to, leads to all sorts of dire consequences, including the expulsion from the Garden of Eden and the subjection of humankind to pain, misery, and death.

Why does the poet choose to acknowledge the power of this discourse, when he could just as easily have excluded it from his poetic world? The speaker himself makes one justification explicit (in line 62) by arguing that the Fall led to certain positive consequences: humanity was given the power of reason, and thus God would be given henceforward an enhanced opportunity to judge mankind on the basis of their behavior, because of their awareness of the difference between right and wrong. However, since the behavior the speaker is proposing has been declared "wrong" according to the religious precepts he is here invoking, this justification does not entirely stand up.

Much more powerful is the argument he implies but does not make explicit. Islam, just as Christianity had done to Classical literature, introduced the concept of eternal life into the world of pre-Islamic poetry, which before this had seen nothing existing after death but a meaningless oblivion. The lack of a concept of an afterworld impels the pre-Islamic poet to tell himself to "leave off" memory and seek new experience,[52] because it was necessary for him to fill up this life as fully as possible; it was the only one he had. The Islamic poet, like Ṭaha, on the other hand, was promised eternal life—either a very pleasant one in heaven or a miserable one in hell, but eternal life nevertheless. A lifelong uncertainty, however, hovers about whether the believer's fate will be heaven or hell. He may, for example, repent sincerely after a life of evil deeds and be allowed to enter Paradise. Or he may, after a life of pious and saintly works, be condemned by major sin committed just before he dies. As long as this uncertainty exists, the believer's behavior is rendered problematic: no matter what he does at each specific moment of choice, he may go to heaven or he may go to hell. The final determination will only be made at the very moment of death itself.

Based on this framework of belief, Ṭaha's argument seems to be as follows. If his fate is to be hell, memory will develop a new significance for him: pleasant memories may well be a solace to him amid his torments. The storing up of such memories will certainly do him no harm, as long as he takes care to repent before death claims him. Thus another, far more problematic, set of issues appear to lie hidden beneath the superficial "eat, drink, and be merry" frivolity of lines 63–66.

Ṭaha, in his construction of an earthly garden world where the narrative of expulsion from a garden world (Eden) is made exemplary, does not in the end completely resolve the tensions present in "Buḥayrat Kūmū," thus showing that he is no less vulnerable than any other poet to the deconstructive project. Sayyāb, in his *mu'āraḍa* of Ṭaha's poem, will put his finger on several instances where his predecessor seems to him to stumble into a *mise en abîme*. Sayyāb's poem, of course, especially in its first version, is much less accomplished than Ṭaha's, but its engagement with its precursor is nonetheless very complex and subtle, especially given the fact that its author was only a seventeen-year-old high school student.

"Day of Departure" opens with seven lines that evoke the *nasīb* and the tableau of parting lovers, in very specific contrast to Ṭaha's poem, which began with the happy arrival of the traveler at Lake Como:

1) Who will protect my heart from Fate,
   who has cast the die for departure?
2) Oh, if only he had passed by
   with them, following the track,
3) I wonder, if it had been he who was turning away from
   his loved ones, would he have been equal to it?

4) Who will be my helper with passion,
   when it clamors or blusters?
5) Its [passion's] waves swamp [my] heart
   then the heart is unsettled and defeated.
6) It [passion] is victorious over the stones—
   my heart is not made of stone.
7) Regretfully, the ship of desires
   has been engulfed amid its waves.[53]

In addition to the evocation of the *nasīb*, Sayyāb also evokes the Lamartinian world where lakes and water form the substratum of the figurative language in his reference to passion's "waves," which wear away the stones (one of the images in Ṭaha's translation of Lamartine's poem is of the contrast between the waves of the lake, in the past, breaking gently over the beloved's feet, and the waves of time, in the present, which have completely obliterated any "land," any refuge from their power).[54] In fact, line 7 becomes a locus where "Lake Como" and the Arabic translation of "Le Lac" meet and are both evoked. The influence of "Le Lac" in this line is seen in the continuation of the boat image, since a central image in both the original and the translation is the boat that can find no harbor on the shores of time. The poetic code of "Lake Como" is summoned up by the phrase "ship of desired things (*zawraq al-munā*)," which echoes the phrase "paradise of desired things (*jannat al-munā*)" applied by Ṭaha in Line 3 of his poem to describe the landscape surrounding Lake Como. The importance of Ṭaha's phrase in Sayyāb's poem is underscored by the fact that he will allude to it again, in a line even more central to the poem's argument: "I will never see the paradise of desire (*jannat al-hawā*), / no, nor will I pluck its fruit." This can be seen by his splitting of the original phrase, "paradise of desired things" into two: "ship of desired things," and "paradise of desire." The significance of this split can be seen most clearly in the second phrase, where Sayyāb has replaced *munā* ("things desired/wished for") with *hawā* ("desire, passion"), because *hawā*, as a synonym for *munā*, has a more negative moral implication. Often it has the sense of "physical, sensual passion," or even "(religiously) blamable inclination,"[55] while *munā* is more neutral, implying nothing about the acceptability from a religious point of view of what is being wished for. Thus, Sayyāb's characterization of the "paradise" he has drawn from Ṭaha's poem is as a place where one finds pleasures that have a sinful moral connotation, thus implying a negative evaluation of Ṭaha's paradise on Sayyāb's part. Likewise, siting these "desired things" in a ship in the first phrase—rather than a paradise—

emphasizes their instability and vulnerability to the caprices of *gharām* ("unreasoned love"), itself a synonym for *hawā*, which has the same negative connotations within the Islamic religious vocabulary.

Thus the reference to "picking fruit" draws upon the imagery of the Garden of Eden in "Lake Como," while at the same time denying the validity of Ṭaha's vision in the context of Sayyāb's poem. Perhaps Ṭaha's speaker, in the "strange" landscape of Lake Como, can overcome the religious and literary conventions, but Sayyāb's speaker sees the weight of these conventions as exerting an influence too powerful for him to overcome in their shaping of his reality. Given Sayyāb's later sensitivity to the power of an Eden discourse to underwrite colonial claims to control the biblical landscape, what we may have here is an early instance of him responding in a similar way to the opportunities and dangers inherent in Ṭaha's assertions of a power to construct a European Eden, outside the reach of conventional social laws.

In the first version of the poem Sayyāb reverts in the lines following 7 to the language of the *nasīb*, which he established in the first lines of his poem as the proper discourse for contradicting Ṭaha's motifs in "Lake Como":

8) You, O one whom I loved,
were generous with lover's trysts or with abandonment.
9) You, who acted as camel driver for the caravan of my
happiness, to you belongs the one led astray.
10) He came to you complaining of injury,
he had been sleepless as long as he could endure.
11) How many hearts did you kill
before [their] aim was attained?
12) You did not allow him to achieve what he desired,
no matter that he spent many sleepless nights.
13) Show your pity to me with a kiss—
he has won, who has obtained it.
14) Indeed a people whom we have loved
have forbidden it [the kiss] to mankind.
15) And a meeting, even though short,
is far from being achieved.

Here we see a highly conventional complaint (focalized within a *nasīb* discourse through the "camel driver" reference) by the lover to the absent or haughty beloved. The main purpose seems to be to establish that Sayyāb's speaker suffers from unrequited love and that he lives in a world where time and loss reign supreme. The only direct reference to Ṭaha's poem comes in line 13, which alludes to line 41 of "Lake Como": "He has won, who has seen [this] / he has lived, who has attained [this]." This allusion serves to reinforce the basic contrast between the two poets: Sayyāb does *not* win his kiss, while Ṭaha has "won," because he has arrived at the enchanted landscape of Lake Como. In the revised version Sayyāb will omit all these lines and will replace them with an entirely different set of images:

8) Then the seductress of the heart approached
with knowledge in her eyes,
9) Tears hurl themselves down
upon the ground in vexation,
10) Truly, they [the tears] are the wine of passion,
that we gave to the stones to drink
11) When it appeared that it [i.e., the wine]
was forbidden to mankind.
12) Indeed, that has become our last day,
it has revealed [our] separation.
13) Immortalize it [the day] with a kiss
which will dismiss worry and pain.
14) A pleasure vanishing, and a memory
which will endure for a lifetime.

These lines are notably different from the others in that they employ the same Nuwasian discursive structures that Ṭaha had used throughout "Lake Como." But here that discourse is used to portray the failure of passion to endure, not a successful conquest. It is contaminated with temporality.
The section begins with a line (8) that comes the closest, in all of Sayyāb's poem, to direct quotation from Ṭaha. It echoes line 45 of "Lake Como" where the poet has turned to address his American companion: "What is it you whisper? Speak clearly! *There is knowledge in your eyes*" (emphasis added). But, where Ṭaha's poem goes on to put the poet and the woman on equal terms, calling them "two strangers" and "two rebellious souls," in Sayyāb's poem the woman is portrayed in much more conventional terms as "the seductress of the heart." The implication seems to be that, for Sayyāb, once the woman begins to play a more active role in the lovers' drama (as she does here by becoming the subject of the active verb: she "approaches," while Ṭaha's beloved does nothing, remaining a totally empty vessel into which the poet pours his own imaginings), she automatically reverts to the conventional role of unattainable "cruel beloved," the character with the upper hand in the hierarchy of love.

Nevertheless, even in this version of the poem, Sayyāb delays until the last two lines to directly engage Ṭaha's use of religious imagery and characterize it as being an inadequate rendering of the lover's situation. He tells the beloved to "immortalize" their last day by giving him a kiss, but he immediately undercuts this reference to eternity and transcendence of time by saying that the pleasure that the act itself brings will not last and that even the memory of it will only last for "a lifetime," not forever. This abjuration and recantation of the original command, then, becomes a very effective transition to the poet's statement in line 15 that he "will never see the paradise of passion," where he engages Ṭaha's religious imagery even more directly.

Sayyāb produced two versions of the end of "Day of Departure." The published version is much shorter and more allusive:

18) The hour of parting has revealed
 fragments of images:
19) Tears, then two smiles,
 then despair, and patient endurance.

The letter, however, contains a longer version that makes clearer the source of these "fragments of images":

18) The hour of parting has revealed
 fragments of images:
19) The heart has carried its desire like an eye
 which has been decorated by the strong contrast of black and white.
20) Hair stroked a cheek—from the aroma
 of its [the cheek's] perfume, it [the hair] got drunk.
21) And an eyebrow giving warning
 was revealed, bidding farewell,
22) [It was like] a scythe harvesting hearts
 nothing remained standing.

These "images" are all drawn from the standard inventory of conventional description in the medieval Arabic love lyric. The characterization of them here as being "fragmented," indicates that the speaker in "Day of Departure" is acknowledging his inability to bind these images together into a coherent whole, which would withstand mutability and create an enduring monument to his love. Since this same inventory of conventional images also forms the basis of the idiolect in "Lake Como"—especially in the description of the mountains and the lake at the beginning of the poem—this would seem to be a negative judgment on the functioning of the framework in Ṭaha's poem, or at least a denial of its workability outside the context of the original work. This is further underscored by the fact that Ṭaha had previously used the word *ṣuwar* ("images") himself in "Lake Como," where he implies an analogy between the landscape around the lake, created—as he reminds us—by God, and the imagery used in his own poetry (lines 29–33), thus suggesting the latently blasphemous equation between God and the poet as creators.[56] And, if Sayyāb's poem does not deny the absolute validity of Ṭaha's claim to the Creator's powers, at least he denies that Ṭaha has achieved the right to make such a claim through his writing of "Lake Como."

"Day of Departure" is usually said by Sayyāb's biographers to be a response to his grandmother's death[57] or to the period of his love for a young Bedouin girl, named Hāla, whose family was allowed by Sayyāb's grandfather to settle temporarily on his land during a period of drought.[58] Yet this focus on the poem's real-life background has led his biographers to neglect almost completely the poem's *literary* importance. It was the first of many poems where Sayyāb appears to have been moved to imitate one of 'Alī Maḥmūd Ṭaha's works because he wanted to grapple directly with the literary and philosophical issues it raised.

This poem, and its successors, clearly show that for Sayyāb, as a poet, the concept of *mu'āraḍa* could still retain a high degree of usefulness in practice even though it could not be easily accommodated within his generation's overtly romantic poetics. It should not be surprising, then, to find that poems using this strategy of engagement with predecessors do not seem to have been explicitly identified as such during Sayyāb's lifetime. In the years following his death, however, several who have chronicled his career have placed a number of these poems in the category of *mu'āraḍa*, although they have not been quick to discuss the implications of such an identification. The list of poems identified as *mu'āraḍa*s in Sayyāb's *oeuvre* has nevertheless grown steadily over the years and will perhaps continue to grow further.

'Alī Maḥmūd Ṭaha's poems comprised Sayyāb's favorite archive upon which to draw for *mu'āraḍa* material, and he would continue to contrafact Ṭaha quite openly in a number of poems right up to 1948. In 1948, Sayyāb's invention of free verse seems to have opened new possibilities for poetic composition up to him, and contrafaction as such abruptly disappears (instead, in an ironic twist of fate, he will become the contrafacted one). During the 1940s as whole, while his work never ceases to engage with the Arabic literary tradition, he grows increasingly aware of, and appropriative of, Western literature, especially English (his interest in other Western literatures is strong, but his acquisition of knowledge concerning them is always approached via English translations). This new source of textual models is at first mediated through the famous nineteenth-century anthology of English verse, Francis Palgrave's *The Golden Treasury*.[59] The authors Sayyāb relies on are drawn from all periods, ranging from the canonically irreproachable like Shakespeare[60] and Wordsworth to the more obscure poets known mainly for a single lyric, like Christopher Marlowe[61] or John Lylye.[62] Such eclectic appropriation of source material would seem to argue for a positive potential latent within the educational practices used by the colonizer for imposing cultural hegemony on the colonized subject. It suggests the availability of a resistance strategy that is seldom acknowledged but seems to have been an entirely characteristic reaction among Arab authors to the impositions of a Western literary discursive apparatus: to revalue the colonizer's canon in terms that would make it more responsive to one's own preoccupations and interests. Sayyāb seems to have selected among his authors with little regard for how they were ranked on a Western scale of values or what their allegiance was in a literary historical sense. Thus we see him saying: "My regard for Keats was not less than my regard for Eliot" during his last year at the Teachers College.[63] Shortly afterward, he would begin to place the now-canonically-decertified poetry of Edith Sitwell on level equal to or perhaps even higher than Eliot's.[64]

In his active rewriting of the Western canon, Sayyāb was merely following a path other Arab writers had trod before him. 'Abbās Maḥmūd al-'Aqqād, for example, together with fellow members of the Dīwān school, had loudly pronounced their high regard for the English man of letters William Hazlitt and claimed that, in so doing, they were giving the English a valuable lesson in understanding their own literature since they did not appreciate this genius sufficiently. Equally, we have Kahlil Gibran in the United States visiting the famous Armory Show of modern art and dismissing it in favor of the painting and writing of William Blake. Or consider the example of 'Alī Maḥmūd Ṭaha that we have so recently examined. In the 1920s, the height of modernism in England and France, he chose instead to focus his attention on the work of the French romantic poet Lamartine whose reputation was at that time probably at its lowest ebb. Instead of condemning these writers for their lack of discrimination and taste, as is so often done, perhaps it would be more useful to consider (as I will do within the framework of the next chapter) why they made these judgments, and to see them as a salutary reflection on "the contingency of value" in the making of literary history.

In a sense, it was almost as though the lack of personal investment by these poets in the various instrumentalities grounding the Western literary establishment opened up to them a possibility for the kind of "colonial mimicry" that thrives, following Homi Bhabha's arguments,[65] on slippage or ambivalence, the "almost the same but not quite." But we may have to depart slightly from Bhabha's path here, in order to suggest that this in turn nurtures an internally focused discourse of power—at least in Arabic—that has been quite successful in offering new avenues for expression (or self-construction) to its practitioners virtually in direct proportion to its ability to confound the expectations inherent in the narcissistic gaze of the colonizing other.

Thus, there would seem to be a descriptive adequacy worth invoking in the metaphor implicit in the term "hybrid text" and applying to Sayyāb's writing. A hybrid enriches the gene pool on a general level, while making available to individual organisms new potentials, which, if they are actualized, may render the offspring radically different from either parent. And, as we shall see in chapter 7 of this study, Sayyāb's hybrid texts—his post-1948 poems in free verse—were the result of just such a creative mixture that developed out of his attempts at radical "self-(re-)fashioning." But, before proceeding to the momentous days of 1948, it is first necessary to contextualize Sayyāb's experience more firmly within the characteristic structural patterns we find in modern Arabic literary history.

CHAPTER SIX

Resisting Otherness

Colonialism and the Writing of Modern Arabic Literary History

> 'One fate attends the altar and the throne.' So sings Mr. Southey. I say, that one fate attends the people and the assertor of the people's rights against those who say they have no rights, that they are their property . . . the livestock on the estate of [royal] Legitimacy. This is what kings at present tell us with their swords, and poets with their pens. He who tells me this deprives me not only of the right, but of the very heart and will to be free, takes the breath out of the body of liberty, and leaves it a dead and helpless corse, . . .
>
> —William Hazlitt

Given the fact that individual authors like Sayyāb appear to be able to appropriate the colonizers' canonical texts and enter into active, creative, and productive associations with them that may eventually produce new and stronger hybrid texts, when it comes to the broader questions of describing this association—of literary history as it is written by authors and literary critics in the colonized culture—one might expect a similar "sly mimicry" or even a defiant disregard of the periodization constructs used to channel and shape the experience of literary works in the West. But such is generally not the case. Modern Arabic literature, for example, is today normally divided into three periods: neoclassic, romantic, and modern. All of these periods are portrayed as part of a broader phenomenon: the *nahḍa*, or "renaissance," of Arabic culture that is conventionally held to have begun in 1798, with the invasion of Egypt by Napoleon. By means of this taxonomy, then, all the typical period divisions mobilized by Western literatures for structuring their own master narratives of literary development following the Middle Ages are redeployed to serve as a scaffolding for developing a discursive episteme centered on a collection of texts whose differences from Western literary texts risk being lost in a litany of similarities.[1] Nor is this superficially unproblematized affiliative gesture unique to Arabic literature. Similar categorical borrowings of paradigms from Western literary history can be found, for instance, in Indian, Caribbean, and Malaysian literary histories, and—with slightly different overtones—in the settler colonial literatures of Australia, Canada, South Africa, and the United States.

This is not to say that this particular temporal taxonomy has not, in many ways, functioned admirably as a descriptive tool for coming to an understanding of the particular patterns of production found in each of the periods of modern Arabic literature. Further, as a heuristic framework for charting hierarchical relationships and clarifying connections between seemingly diverse practices, no one should doubt its discursive efficiency and ability to create a satisfying explanation for many developments in the trajectory of modern Arabic literary history.

Using this model, we find, for example, in roughly the period from 1860 to just beyond the turn of the century that there is a revival of interest in Arabic poetry from the pre-Islamic to early Abbasid times, which for the Arab poets of the late nineteenth century becomes the "golden age" of Arabic literature. Such claims of close affiliation with a past period of the literary heritage would normally comprise the single most distinctive marker indicating any literature's entry into a "neoclassical" period. A poet like Maḥmūd Sāmī al-Bārūdī—generally considered the founder of this school—will do two very characteristic things vis-a-vis this tradition in defining himself as a neoclassical writer : he will from the beginning of his career use *mu'āraḍa* as a means for engaging with the work of those golden age poets, a practice that he will make explicitly clear through the use of headings inserted at the beginning of these poems identifying the precursor being contrafacted. Equally characteristically for a neoclassical author, he will spend his last years compiling an anthology selected from the work of these great past poets, thus creating his personal archive of canonical texts, through which he seems to have hoped to claim a stake in creating a "classical" literary heritage for his successors. His own poems emphasize the connection between reworking of this past tradition and the task of creating an active poetic self so that the two come to dovetail with remarkable fidelity. Because he is himself an aristocrat, politician, and soldier, it is particularly easy for him to appropriate the vocabulary of a poetry devoted to praising, and therefore delineating, a body of similar figures from the classical period, and apply that vocabulary to himself.

Then, in the years immediately preceding and following World War I, several separate literary schools emerge whose members set themselves up in opposition—either covert or overt—to the school of Bārūdī and his successors, most especially to the Egyptian poet Aḥmad Shawqī. They all espouse similar poetic values, at least to certain degree, championing such key terms as "freedom, liberty, the individual, imagination, originality, sincerity," and selecting as their most important poetic goal the achievement of "organic unity" in their compositions. The similarity of such evaluative touchstones to the ones found generally in European romantic writings scarcely needs to be pointed out. We can see very clearly, for example, an echo of Coleridge's definition of poetic genius as the ability "to represent familiar objects [so] as to awaken in the minds of others a kindred feeling concerning them"[2] in the statement of the Dīwān[3] poet and essayist 'Abbās Maḥmūd al-'Aqqād that poems that interest their readers are those that "excite their sympathy and . . . embody their own feelings and place their imprint on the souls of their brethren."[4] This emphasis in both definitions on how the poem should reproduce its maker's feelings and emotions and on achieving a transparency of communication between one mind and another may profitably serve us as a reminder that "psychological" as a technical term was first popularized by the romantics as part of their advocacy of the notion that "the self was not found but made."[5]

As a final point of congruence, it should be noted that these Arab authors as a group ally themselves quite consistently with various figures from European romanticism. These elective ancestors are mostly English or French. There is, however, a strong minority Russian influence that is injected into the mix primarily because some of the most influential of these poets were educated in Russian Orthodox–sponsored missionary schools founded in Lebanon during the late nineteenth century.

The first such literary school to emerge chronologically was the Mahjar, or "emigrant," school in North and South America. This group was composed mostly of poets of Lebanese or Syrian origin[6] who had left their homeland late in the nineteenth century in search of better opportunities in the countries of the New World. All of them were, to a greater or lesser degree, bilingual and bicultural, educated both in Arabic and either English or Spanish. Probably the most famous of the group was Gibran Kahlil Gibran,[7] whose family emigrated to Boston while he was still a young boy.

He attended school in the United States but returned to Lebanon as a teenager for further education in Arabic. This mixed education resulted in a typically hybrid choice of literary forebears. He claimed as formative influences William Blake and Nietzsche, on the one hand, but also the Arab Sufi poets Ibn al-'Arabī and Ibn al-Fāriḍ.[8] Like Sayyāb, Gibran often chose to revalue the canonical judgments of Western critical discourse, as can be seen in his response to the famous Armory Show that introduced modern art to the New York intellectual world in 1913:

> It is a revolt, a protest, a *declaration of independence*. . . . The pictures, individually are not great: in fact very few of them are beautiful. But the Spirit of the Exhibition as a whole is both beautiful and great. Cubism, Impressionism, Post Impressionism and Futurism will pass away. The world will forget them because the world is always forgetting minor details but the spirit of the movement will never pass away, for it is real—as real as the human hunger for freedom.[9]

Although he acknowledges this exhibition's importance, he does so in a way that is quite differently valenced than the responses among contemporary as well as later Western art critics. He dismisses the modernist schools and their aesthetic programs as "minor details" and chooses instead to focus on the artists as avatars of a "hunger for freedom," freedom being perhaps the single most frequently cited catch phrase in the discourse of Arab intellectuals of this period.[10] This subversion of conventional reactions carries over into his evaluations of the individual artists, where he valorizes today unknown figures like Davies and Redon over Matisse and Marcel Duchamp (creator of "Nude Descending a Staircase," the single most famous painting in the exhibition). In a certain sense, Gibran could be said to be even more subversive in his affiliative practice than Sayyāb, because in neither the Arabic nor the European traditions did he select precursors who were, at the time he was writing at least, regarded with particular favor as canonical authors.

It should also be noted—in view of the demonstrable influence his work had on later poets like Sayyāb—that that quintessentially cross-cultural text, the Bible, left a discernible impact on Gibran's writing, an impact no doubt encouraged by his family's Christian background.[11] The hybridizing impulse in his work can further be seen in the fact that after his return to the United States upon finishing his schooling in Lebanon, he wrote at first in Arabic but later switched to English—a choice that meant his writings were eventually available to a much wider audience[12] than those of most of his fellow Syrian American compatriots, like Amīn al-Rīḥānī or Nasīb 'Arīḍa, who continued to compose their creative offerings predominantly in Arabic. All of these factors underscore the presence of a new sort of openness to hybridity in the Arabic poetry of this school, one that orients itself in new ways toward Western literature.

An interesting counterpoint to Gibran in terms of educational formation and affiliative preferences was the Mahjar school's most influential literary critic: Mikhā'īl Nu'ayma.[13] Like his friend Nasīb 'Arīḍa, Nu'ayma was educated in Russian Orthodox schools in Lebanon and Palestine. Because of his exemplary academic achievements, he was eventually sent by the mission to Russia itself, in order to complete his education and study for the priesthood. Through his teachers at the seminary in Poltava where he was sent, he was introduced to a wide range of Russian authors, including such quintessentially romantic figures as Pushkin, Lermontov, Gogol, and (slightly later than the others) Turgenev.[14] In 1911, however, he was expelled from the seminary for having helped to lead a student protest (though he was allowed to sit for his final exams), so he was forced to make plans to return to Lebanon. While he was in Russia, he had already been thinking of attending the Sorbonne to study law, but his expulsion ended those expectations. November of 1911 found him leaving for the United States and the home of his two older brothers in Walla Walla, a small farming community in eastern Washington State, where he learned English and soon after entered the law school at the University of Washington in Seattle. Despite the lateness with which he learned English, he seems to have made a vigorous and largely successful effort to assimilate the English literary canon, for we find him making wide-ranging use of it in several reviews and articles that appeared in literary papers published by members of the Arab community in New York, when he went to that city following his graduation from law school in 1916. A number of these articles were collected and published in Egypt following World War I, in a volume entitled *Al-Ghirbāl* (The Sieve), which had an enormous impact on intellectuals in Egypt and elsewhere in the Arab world.

The introduction to *Al-Ghirbāl* was written by an Egyptian poet, essayist, and literary critic named 'Abbās Maḥmūd al-'Aqqād. 'Aqqād had been one of the founding members of an Egyptian literary group called the Dīwān school. Two years before *Al-Ghirbāl* appeared in print, in 1921, he and another founding member of the group, Ibrāhīm al-Māzinī, had published a selection of articles in two volumes, intended to serve as a preface to a collection (*dīwān*) of their combined poetic output (hence the name "Dīwān" later given to their school). These articles expressed many of the same ideas about the reformation of Arabic literature found in the work of Nu'ayma and the other Mahjar writers. The members of the Dīwān group had all learned English during their schooling in the by-now thoroughly British-dominated educational system of Egypt, and it was to English romantic poets and writers, especially Hazlitt, Wordsworth, and Coleridge[15] that they turned. From Hazlitt, they imbibed a revolutionary, antimonarchical political philosophy and from Wordsworth and Coleridge they were to appropriate certain key ideas about the nature of the poet, seeing him as a figure centrally concerned with the process of individual "self-making," whose carefully crafted creation of a unified sensibility would eventually make it possible for him to incorporate as part of his own consciousness the thoughts and feelings of others in a doubling that would ensure perfect understanding between all the minds involved. Although the Dīwān further claimed inspiration from the works of romantics whom they saw primarily as poets, like Shelley, Keats, and Byron, they have been generally considered less successful in making a transition from revolutionary critical ideas to poetic practice than the Mahjar poets.

By the early 1930s the influence of both the Mahjar and the Dīwān schools among younger Arab intellectuals had begun to wane in its turn in favor of a group of poets who were regular contributors to a literary journal called *Abūllū* (Apollo) after the Greek god of poetry, music, and medicine. Certainly the selection of a classical Greek deity as the affiliative eponym for this group was no accident, because one of the themes constantly emphasized in articles and editorials appearing in the journal during its short period of publication (1932–34) was that the Western and Arab/Islamic civilizations owed a shared debt to the legacy of ancient Greece as a source of cultural inspiration, a point of contact between the two cultures that *Abūllū* had been founded, at least in part, to draw attention to, revive, and make a part of modern Arab experience.[16] Although this Hellenistic element, with its potential for linkage to the Hellenism of the European romantics, was probably more important theoretically than it was in the actual practice of the poets as represented in the journal, nevertheless the orientation of their writing to Europe was at least as pronounced as that of the Mahjar poets and discernibly greater than that of the Dīwān school.

Perhaps part of the explanation for the choice of *Abūllū* as title may also lie in the fact that the founder of the journal, Aḥmad Zākī Abū Shādī, was both a poet and a doctor who had studied medicine in England before returning to Egypt in 1932.[17] Although Abū Shādī was the sponsor and chief mover of the journal (he owned the printing press on which it was typeset, for instance) he was not generally seen as the best of the poets published on its pages. This distinction has probably been most frequently accorded to two Egyptian poets who became very famous and influential throughout the Arab world in the 1930s and 1940s: Ibrāhīm Nājī and 'Alī Maḥmūd Ṭaha (the poet whose work would so attract the youthful Sayyāb). Several others, like the Tunisian poet Abū al-Qāsim al-Shabbī, the Sudanese poet al-Tījānī Yūsuf Bashīr, and another Egyptian poet, Muḥammad 'Abd al-Mu'ṭī al-Hamsharī, were also frequent contributors of important work and deserve mention. Al-Shabbī's and al-Tījānī's works are of special interest because, unlike the others, they did not know any European languages. Yet they were very much aware of intellectual debates among Arab intellectuals fostered by contact with Europe and they knew many European authors through translations, which points to the greatly increased flow of information about the West into the Arab world, largely as a result of colonial pressures, so much so that it would be difficult to point to any sector or segment of society by this time that remained untouched by its influence or wholly traditional in its orientation.

Another observation worth recording about the Apollo group is the greatly enhanced value they placed on French romanticism, as opposed to its English counterpart.[18] For all these poets, although English romanticism continued to be highly influential, it was accompanied now by a new and pronounced regard for the work of French romantics like Lamartine, Victor Hugo, Alfred de Musset, and Alfred de Vigny—whose work was often assimilated, however, through the mediation of Arabic or English translations. Not only were they constructing new literary genealogies, then, that drew on a wider range of European, as well as Arab, literary ancestors than their predecessors in the Mahjar and Dīwān schools, but they were also beginning to valorize the notion of translation as a practice for assimilating influences that could, and to a large extent during this period did, displace *mu'āraḍa*. This would seem to highlight even more clearly the oppositional nature, then, of Sayyāb's use of *mu'āraḍa* in his own strategies for engaging with 'Alī Maḥmūd Ṭaha's poetry discussed in the previous chapter.

It was only after World War II and the first attempts by literary critics to map the emergence of these three schools—the Mahjar, the Dīwān, and especially the Apollo—that the period division of neoclassic, romantic, and modern actually came to the fore. Although none of the poets belonging to these groups seems to have ever explicitly labeled himself a "romantic," their frequent assertions of affiliation with various European romantic poets certainly invited such a comparison, and thus it is not surprising to find the eminent Egyptian literary critic of the 1950s and 1960s, Muḥammad Mandūr, calling them so in the influential lectures he delivered at Cairo University and elsewhere in the years immediately following World War II. In a characteristically well-nuanced passage from one of these lectures he makes a notable early attempt to relate the characteristics of the Apollo group, as a romantic school of literature, to their lived environment:

> . . . in our return to the history of our country in the period when the Apollo movement appeared, it will soon become clear to us that it was natural for a personal (*dhātī*), emotional (*'āṭifī*), romantic (*rūmānsī*) current to dominate in this period, for our country was then being ruled by a man who believed in himself more than he believed in his people. The people were aware of that and refused to respond to him, which led to a violent confrontation between him and the people, pushing him to seek help from King Fu'ād, and then from the English, [in order to move] against this people so that he could degrade and humiliate them. This man was Ismā'īl Ṣidqī Pasha, who distorted parliamentary life in such a way that it could never be set right . . . and in such an atmosphere it was impossible for any kind of literature to appear but the literature of complaint and personal (*dhātī*) anguish. The poet could not speak of anything but himself, his dreams, his infatuations and his spiritual desires, or [to seek] to escape from the hell surrounding him into the world of nature, and its scenes and places of amusement, by which he could make himself forget his pain and the pain of the people, since he was not able to articulate the sources of these pains.[19]

Once the connection between an indigenous school of literature, on the one hand, and romanticism, on the other, is authorized by so respected a figure as Mandūr, then the flanking elements of the taxonomy, modernism and neoclassicism, seem to fall into place without further ado and, by the 1960s and 1970s, this periodization for modern Arabic literary history has become a critical commonplace whose presuppositions are rarely, if ever, seriously questioned.[20]

The legitimating and self-validating function of this schemata for contemporary poets and critics should not be underestimated as a factor in its success. As eminent and careful a scholar as M.M. Badawi (who had a foot in both camps, as a modernist poet and professor of Arabic literature at Oxford University) would allude to the anxiety that this model of literary history allayed when he spoke at the conclusion of his history of modern

Arabic literature of the perception that "until quite recently Arabic poetry turned to western fashions or styles after these fashions or styles seemed to have run their course in the West. Perhaps the case of romanticism is the most striking. By the end of the nineteenth century when Arabic poetry was beginning to enter into its romantic phase, European romanticism which had set in more than a century earlier had already given place to other movements."[21] Here, Arabic literature is represented as irremediably *belated*, caught up in an inexorable sequencing not of its own making, but with the saving grace that following the sequence will eventually allow the literature to become truly "modern." Only with the advent of Sayyāb's generation of modernist poets—and perhaps not even then[22]—can Arabic literature, in Badawi's opinion, be said to have overcome this problem of belatedness vis-à-vis the West.

Here we can see demonstrated the greatest danger of this otherwise quite useful period scheme: the notion that Arab romanticism, as well as Arab neoclassicism, were simply repetitions of their Western counterparts—and thus, in a very significant sense, a waste of time, that had to be "gotten through" so that one could arrive at the teleologically determined endpoint of modernism, which alone had value because it represented the arrival of Arabic literature at a point where it was fully integrated with "modernity" and could unproblematically assume a leading role on the stage of world literary activity. Such a set of syllogisms may be empowering for Arab modernist writers and those who identify with them, but the opposite obtains for the study of earlier writers and their works, which are rendered simply superfluous and without functional importance.

A further danger of this scheme's presuppositions is illustrated even by the earlier Mandūr quotation. This is the tendency to equate the Arab literary school with its Western namesake on a point by point basis. Thus, Western—especially English—romanticism was understood by Western critics (largely under the influence of T.S. Eliot's and F.R Leavis's negative evaluations of the movement) at the time Mandūr was delivering his lectures in Cairo as being an essentially "escapist" school of literature without connection to the "real" world. This judgment is transferred wholesale by Mandūr to the Apollo school and their predecessors, thus eliding and mystifying some very important aspects of these poets' work. We saw an example of this in the preceding chapter in how 'Alī Maḥmūd Ṭaha, for example, contends with—and seeks to qualify—the "otherness" of the West through his representation of a love affair with an American woman in his poem "Buḥayrat Kūmū." Although this form of strategic engagement may be indirect, to gloss its presence in the work in question, and others like it, as mere "escapism" becomes a serious omission in the work of evaluating its impact as a strategy for containing and limiting the threat of colonialism as a discursive structure, both on Ṭaha's contemporary audience and those who followed them, like Sayyāb.

Here, perhaps even more clearly than in the case of an individual poet like Sayyāb, postcolonial literary theory may supply us with some important conceptual tools that will allow us to see the course of modern Arabic literary history from a different perspective, one that will have greater (or at least a differently oriented) explanatory power than the familiar determinate progression of neoclassic, romantic, and modern. The two most relevant of these conceptual tools for the matter at hand would seem to be (1) the activity of resistance, and (2) (to conflate Greenblatt and Foucault) the "technologies of self-fashioning," or identity formation, as they oscillate in a dialectic of power-seeking or hegemony between colonizer and colonized.

"Resistance" was early on articulated by Foucault[23] as a possible and indeed likely response to any attempt to impose an apparatus of control by a dominant power or, more precisely, a power *seeking* dominance. In terms of discourses, then—where control is sought through the medium of words—"resistance" to the dominant would be expressed through the equivalents of what Richard Terdiman has called "counter-discourses." In her seminal book *Resistance Literature*, Barbara Harlow took these provisional hypotheses articulated by Foucault, combined with certain largely parallel but more limited formulations presented by Fredric Jameson in *The Political Unconscious*, which posit the use of "interpretive codes," like those deployed in the discourse of literary history, as "strategies of containment,"[24] and applied these formulations about power and resistance to the theories and practices of writing actually encountered in a variety of world literatures now emerging from the experiences of colonization and decolonization into a condition that might legitimately be called "postcolonial."[25] Although Harlow used the work of recent and contemporary Arab writers and academics, like Samir Amin, Ghassan Kanafani, and Elias Khouri, very effectively as a ground for her presentation of how centrally the experience of colonialism, and the resistance strategies that emerged from it, still determine choices and emphases found in the discourses of formerly colonized cultures, she does not attempt to give her treatment of Arabic literature a historical dimension, and thus attenuates the ability of readers to grasp the complex set of contending matrices out of which those modern literary concerns emerged.[26]

What my main interest here will be, then, is to sketch out a set of provisional parameters that will allow us to appreciate more fully just how pervasively the work of resistance to colonialism has helped to determine the discursive structures and presuppositions utilized by Arab poets and other literary figures in creating their works and yet, at the same time, to acknowledge how its particular forms, strategies, and goals have varied over the course of the struggle. This notion of resistance to colonialism as a determining factor in the process of literary choice has been largely ignored as an important element in the formulation of the "interpretive codes" grouped together under the rubric of the discourse commonly known as "modern Arabic literary history."[27]

There is one major exception to this rule, however, that should be noted at the outset of any discussion of this discursive formation, for it concerns the point of origin usually chosen for beginning modern Arabic literary history: the year 1798.[28] Now, 1798 is not a year in which a seminal work of modern Arabic literature is composed or a great modern author is born. It is not even a year in which an important or decisive historical event wholly interior to the Arab world takes place. It is the year in which a young French general named Napoleon invades Egypt with at least some notion in his mind of making this territory subordinate to the political power of France. As Edward Said has shown in *Orientalism* with such devastating accuracy and detail, this "expedition" incorporates a whole array of new techniques like the careful rhetorical control of public proclamations, mapping, archaeological excavation, and public displays of scientific knowledge as strategies designed in part to disguise the aggressive nature of the enterprise, in part to make its control more pervasive and effective—techniques that would later be revived and redeployed over and over again in the nineteenth-century empire building of Britain and France.[29]

This nearly unanimous choice of date for the beginning of modern Arabic literary history would seem to suggest that literary historians were not entirely unaware, and may even have wished to foreground the possibility in their audience's mind, of a relation between the "rise" of modern Arabic literature and the Western colonial enterprise. Such a hypothesis is reinforced by the often explicit connections that are drawn between the content of modern Arabic literature and Western literature, as when Jabrā Ibrāhīm Jabrā says "what is occurring now in the world of Arabic poetry has no equal in our literary past" and further asserts that the only "models" and "parallels" for "the concerns of modern Arabic poetry" are to be found "in Western literature and art, not in Arabic."[30] Yet, on the other hand, it is virtually impossible to find a sustained analysis in works dealing with modern Arabic literary history that postulates this interchange with any degree of precision as a structure whose framework is determined in large part by strategies of resistance to colonialism.[31]

If we look, however, at the first works that have been consistently identified as part of "modern" Arabic literature and not just holdovers from the classical period, the element of resistance to colonialism in them becomes increasingly more salient as time goes on. Rifā'a Ṭahṭāwī's *Takhlīṣ al-Ibrīz fī Talkhīṣ Bārīz*, already mentioned briefly in chapters 2 and 3, is usually conceded to be the first such "modern" work. Its basic premise, of course, was to present Western knowledge to the Arab reader—and to show the conditions of possibility that would make appropriation of this epistemic apparatus possible. Written as it was in a period (the 1830s) and in a country (Egypt) where direct and successful competition with the West still seemed to be a viable option, Ṭahṭāwī's work was not so much oriented toward resistance to Western hegemonic structures as it was to articulating a similar and parallel system that could be developed for the use of his own fellow countrymen. This parallel system of dominance that Ṭahṭāwī was seeking to delineate would seem to have been open, perhaps not surprisingly, to strategies of colonial control comparable to those being developed at that time in Europe. Thus we find Ṭahṭāwī saying, in his description of the discovery of the New World and its subsequent colonization by Europe, that it would have been far better had Muslims explored and conquered this territory, because then the people inhabiting it would have been converted to Islam rather than Christianity, "and Islam is more deserving of this distinction."[32] One matter of interest here is that Ṭahṭāwī relates colonizing activities quite closely to the notion of proselytizing for a religious faith, thus suggesting that he saw the activity as possessing a religious base that informed its structures. But what is of more immediate moment for our purposes is that, clearly, Ṭahṭāwī does not find the notion of colonial empire-building inherently repugnant or inhuman. He has already, earlier in the book, congratulated the Egyptian Khedive Muḥammad 'Alī for his successful conquest of the Funj kingdom in the Sudan, an enterprise that had obvious parallels with Western colonial projects in Africa.[33] Indeed, his only regret would seem to be that the Egyptians did not "get there first," that they had not been more successful in anticipating the potential benefits to themselves of joining the colonial enterprise.

When we move, however, to the 1860s and the second set of literary works with an undeniable claim to a "modern" pedigree—the poems of Maḥmūd Sāmī al-Bārūdī—we find a very changed situation. In al-Bārūdī's own lifetime Egypt had gone from being a relatively autonomous power to one drawn increasingly into the "new world order" of colonial domination. He was born in 1839 into a family of Circassian origin, whose earliest traceable ancestor had been imported as a Mameluk into Egypt in the Ottoman period. His descendants had served as soldiers and ministers under the rule of various Mameluk leaders until the time of Muḥammad 'Alī. Both al-Bārūdī's paternal and maternal grandfathers perished in Muḥammad 'Alī's massacre of the Mameluks at the Citadel in 1811. Al-Bārūdī's father had nevertheless been enrolled at Muḥammad 'Alī's new military college and had graduated from it to serve in several campaigns as a relatively high-ranking officer before he was killed while his son was still a young boy. Al-Bārūdī was raised by his mother to follow in the family's military tradition, but by the time he himself had graduated from the military college, Muḥammad 'Alī had died, the Egyptian army had been drastically reduced in size, and there were no commissions available in the officer corps either for himself or most of his classmates . Therefore, in 1857 al-Bārūdī left Egypt to seek employment in Istanbul, as he was fluent in Turkish and Persian as well as Arabic.[34]

In 1863, al-Bārūdī would return with the new Egyptian Khedive Ismā'īl from Istanbul, where he had spent the previous six years working in the Ottoman foreign ministry in a junior secretarial post. At this time, Egypt was riding high on a tide of wealth generated from greatly increased revenues for one of its major cash crops, cotton. The American Civil War had created a shortage of this raw material needed in large quantities by the English cloth mills, and it was to the Khedival estates in Egypt that the English merchants had turned to make up the shortfall. Ismā'īl, son of Muḥammad 'Alī's oldest son Ibrāhīm, had decided to revive the reformist, modernizing policies of his father and grandfather, which must be seen as a move designed at least in part as resistance to the increasingly intrusive colonial and commercial activities by the European powers in the areas immediately surrounding Egypt as well as in Egypt itself. France, for example, had been extending its control over Algeria, which it had annexed in 1830, and the neighboring territories in North Africa. Britain, meanwhile, had moved into the areas east of Egypt and begun to establish control over selected strongholds on the Arabian Peninsula, which safeguarded its route to India and gave it greater control over trade in the Red Sea and the Persian Gulf. Of particular importance to all three parties—France, Britain, and Egypt—was the imminent completion of the Suez Canal (begun in 1854, finished in 1869), which would greatly facilitate the movement of goods and people in the area and whose control would be a vital point of contention between Britain and Egypt (as well France) for more than a century, right into Sayyāb's lifetime.[35]

In such a highly unstable atmosphere, it is perhaps not surprising that Ismā'īl saw an advantage in attaching someone like al-Bārūdī, with his noble lineage, extensive government experience, and evident poetic talent, to his entourage.[36] In this regard, it should be noted that the avenue that al-Bārūdī used to bring himself to the new Khedive's attention was the composition and recitation of a traditional panegyric poem in praise of the latter's accession to the throne and encouraging his proposed reforms.[37] And surely al-Bārūdī saw similar advantages in such an association. But it would also appear that the mutual regard the pair had for each other was short-lived.[38] By 1868, when al-Bārūdī was twenty-nine years old, he was disenchanted enough with his patron to write a poem looking forward to the celebration of his thirtieth birthday, which has been generally taken as critical of Ismā'īl's policies in general and of his extravagant spending in particular, because this put him more and more under the thumb of British and French bankers, who were loaning him money secured against Egypt's shares in the Suez Canal project. Al-Bārūdī seems to have feared by this time, and correctly as it turned out, that this would put Ismā'īl and the Egyptian government under the control of Britain and France, as a colony in all but name.[39]

The poem begins innocuously enough, with the speaker reproaching himself for having wasted his youth in the pursuit of pleasure and amusement. Now, however, that he sees "the sign of doom" written upon his brow—in the form of white hair heralding the approach of old age—he resolves to reform and lead a more sober life. These reflections on the brevity of human life and the ubiquity of mortality cause him to ask himself the following question:

22) Where are the ancient kings who mounted up to the very heights? The land is devoid of them.
23) They have gone away, and time (*dahr*) has come to stay, and after them many kings have come and gone and [other] rising stars have taken their places.
24) I see every living thing going hand in hand with death and how could anyone who has made that journey ever return?
25) I cry out at the top of my voice, I ask about them, but do you hear, O time of wonders?

26) If you will not hear a cry, nor return an answer, then what kind of thing are you, that I contend with?
27) A phantom, by my life, whose seekers find no benefit, and a cause for grief from which fingers are made to bleed.[40]

Although these lines stop short of direct *lèse-majesté*, they do seem to question the ability of the current king, Ismā'īl, to take his place among the pantheon of great sovereigns through the speaker's question, "where are the ancient kings?" and his even more telling answer "The land is devoid of them."—i.e., no representative of their noble tradition is left. This, at least, was the way the lines were interpreted by contemporary audiences and later commentators,[41] and this is borne out in significant ways—though indirectly—by the text itself. To evoke the discourse of kingship only to declare it an empty place holder whose occupant is constantly changing is certainly disquieting, to say the least, in a tradition with such an elaborate coding for panegyric as Arabic possesses. The uneasiness is underscored by the "time of wonders" apostrophized in line 25. This "time of wonders" can only be interpreted here as the present. The personification initiated here through the use of vocative then conflates this "time of wonders" with the sovereign in line 27 (since a ruler would also be the object of "seekers") and thus, by reverse application of this metonymic contiguity, the sovereign, like the time, becomes a "thing" the speaker "contends with" and "a cause for grief."

The speaker's dissatisfaction, however, is not limited to the ruler figure. When, near the end of the poem, he exhorts his fellow citizens to rebel, he does not incite them against a single individual:

39) O people (*qawm*)! Rise up! Life is but an opportunity and in time (*dahr*) there are many paths abounding and chances to secure advantage,
40) Will there be forbearance (*ṣabr*) despite humiliation's touch, when you are too many to count? Indeed to God is my returning.[42]
41) And how can you see abasement as a place of residence when the bounty of God is widespread?
42) I see heads ripe red there for harvesting—but where, oh where, are the swords that will cut?

This is resistance with a vengeance. Line 42 here alludes to a famous speech by the early Umayyad governor of Kufa, al-Ḥajjāj ibn Yūsuf. The people of Kufa had been near to rebellion against the Umayyad caliph Mu'āwiya in the period following the death of the fourth caliph, 'Alī. Al-Ḥajjāj, partly because of his reputation for severity, was sent to compel them to remain obedient. Upon his arrival, he delivered a speech to the assembled residents of the city that included the following chilling image: "I see [before me] heads that have become red-ripe and harvest time for them draws near. They belong to me, and it is as though I gaze upon [masses of] blood between the turbans and the beards."[43] This ferocious threat of mass bloodshed so frightened the people of Kufa that they abandoned all plans for rebellion. Since al-Bārūdī has previously called upon the people to "rise up," the context would seem to make the comparison apply, not to the rebels themselves but to the object of their rebellion. But his referent in line 42 remains equally clearly not a single individual, but rather a group. It is not one head "ripe for harvesting" but many. Simplicity would seem to dictate that this group could be naturalized either as the servants (courtiers, ministers, etc.) of the ruler or some collective of true outsiders, such as the foreign colonial representatives. A choice is never explicitly rendered through textual cues.

There is, however, an interesting return to the definition of this group in the concluding lines of the poem, where discourse in the form of poetry is also thematized as a resistance strategy, metaphorically equal to the arms of war:

47) Take thou this [poem], for it is a straight spear shaft with a speaking tongue that will shatter the tips of spears that are pointed directly at it.
48) The riders (*rukbān*) will carry it to every dwelling and crowds will collect out of a longing for it,
49) For one people (*qawm*), it shall be made into embroidered belts and necklaces, for another people it shall be iron collars to which their hands are shackled.
50) This [poem] is one which, if it were made to settle upon a mountain, would cause it to fall down and be humbled.

Lane tells us that "riders" (*rukbān*) can be rendered more specifically as "riders of camels"—i.e., Bedouin Arabs—and this reading of the word would seem to anticipate the very strongly "Bedouinized" embroidered belts (*awshuḥ*) to which the poem itself is transformed in the following lines. This metaphoric strategy anchors the poem's world very strongly within the *Arab* literary tradition and would seem to push the reader in the direction of interpreting the "other people" as a *non-Arab* people, which would make them fit more comfortably within an identification with colonizers than with the ruler's native henchmen.

Later al-Bārūdī would eschew such delicately indirect resistance strategies and become much more open about his opposition to Ismā'īl, both through discourse and through action, as the debt crisis worsened and representatives of the French and British governments were brought into the Egyptian cabinet to ensure that Egyptian tax revenues were used to pay off the debt to the British and French banks. Eventually, al-Bārūdī would be caught up in the 'Urabi rebellion in 1882 against this foreign interference and, like the rest of the leaders of that uprising, would be sent off to exile on the island of Ceylon, from whence he would only be allowed to return in 1901 as a figure of pathos, an emaciated and ailing old man who had lost his eyesight while in exile. He would die in 1904.

One of the notable characteristics of al-Bārūdī's later poems is the equal attention they give to the idea of resisting both the depredations of the Khedive and his foreign masters, on the one hand, and the glorification of the poet himself as a hero in the ancient Arab tradition, on the other. Typical is a poem he composed, probably in the late 1870s, which contrafacts one of the last panegyric poems written to the Egyptian ruler Kāfūr by the dean of medieval Arabic poets, al-Mutanabbī, before the latter began a series of devastating satires belittling this patron who had proved less than generous.

Al-Bārūdī's poem begins with a very conventional opening drawn directly from the inventory of the *nasīb* section of the traditional Arabic *qaṣīda* poem, where the speaker in the guise of an abandoned lover laments his beloved's unwillingness to meet with him. But the imagery quickly moves into a political register, so that by line 7, "Love" has been personified and is compared to "an unjust ruler; if he desires something, he will find no one to oppose him."[44] The emphasis on this metaphoric equivalence between love and the capricious sovereign is carried through to the end of the section as a dominant motif, intensifying as it goes. By the last line, line 13, love is being characterized as "Extremely tyrannical, in every quarter it has [committed some] outrage on account of which [both] the lowland and highlands of an empty country cry out."[45]

As Julie Meisami has convincingly argued, in the traditional *qaṣīda* poem the relationship between lover and beloved as represented in the *nasīb* is often exploited by the poet as an adumbration of his relationship to the patron, and frequently explores aspects of that relationship whose open expression could not necessarily be accommodated within the conventions of the panegyric section proper.[46] Here al-Bārūdī, while maintaining that basic framework, uses the *nasīb* more straightforwardly as a simple anticipation and foreshadowing of his main theme, which like the 1868 poem explores the connection between the idea of leaving youth behind, taking upon an adult role in society, and demanding political accountability from the ruler. In this poem, as in the earlier one, the speaker sees the passage of time as incorporating an experience of decline and the dashing of his youthful hopes for progress. All this disappointment is crystallized in his attitude toward the ruler figure, who as before becomes conflated with "time" (*dahr*):

33) Time has refused [all] except that its menial become lord and its servant exercise dominion over the necks of [our] demands.
34) Its foxes have summoned one another to wreak vengeance upon us and its lions have slept during the whole procedure.[47]
35) How long must we travel in the darkness of an ordeal in which the scabbard is too narrow [to hold] its sword?[48]
36) If a man does not cast back the hand of a tyrant when it falls upon him, then let him not regret when his glory is lost.
37) One who is humbled by fear of death, his life will be more hurtful to him than any dying which might seek him out.
38) The most deadly disease is for an eye to see a tyrant doing evil, while his praise is recited among the multitudes.

This delegitimation of the ruler is succeeded in the poem by a set-piece of *fakhr*, or self-praise, that would on the surface appear as though it has only a tenuous connection with the immediately preceding passage:

43) It is shameful for a youth to resign himself to humiliation when in the sword is what will suffice a matter he is preparing.
44) I am a man who does not quail in the face of an attack even though my leg be tied by a cord which stops me short in my endeavors.
45) A proud soul prevents me from bearing oppression and a heart whose fire leaps up if it is seared by injury.
46) A branch which has flowered long has raised me to the heights, its root is in glory and its good fortune has smiled.
47) It suffices a youth in glory, if he seeks the heights with that which his father and grandfather have bequeathed to him.
48) When a boy is born among us, his mother's milk is the blood of the hunt, and his cradle is [the back] of a thoroughbred steed.
49) If he lives, the unending deserts are his dwelling place and if he dies then the birds flocking [to the battlefield carnage] are his tombstone.

Here the movement is from a general statement of gnomic universality in line 43 to a more personal boast of the speaker's virtues in lines 44 and 45—a transitional concentration on the creation of a strong "self"—and then finally to an ascription of these heroic traits to the speaker's ancestors (lines 46–49), in whose care male children are represented as being brought up very much to live the life of desert warriors we find described in pre-Islamic and early Islamic poems.[49] Of particular interest for our purposes is line 45, where the speaker makes his inability to "bear oppression" an innate part of his definition of self. Thus tyranny and a strong sense of self are explicitly made incompatible in this line and, through its role as the transitional line to the next topos (that of the speaker's noble lineage), the development of a strong identity is indirectly linked to one's traditions and heritage, which are very specifically labeled as "Arab" in this case.

Such attention to the figuration of self in these lines, if approached as a counter-discursive strategy being used to oppose and reveal the unnatural bases of the authority claimed by a tyrant whose power lacks—unlike the speaker's—a true, culturally sanctioned legitimacy, will begin to appear far more adroitly motivated in its juxtaposition with the preceding section of the poem. Put more directly, al-Bārūdī seems to be asserting here the importance of his own practice of constructing a strong identity (completely and securely grounded in the traditions of an Arab heroic past) as an example that others in his audience may follow in constructing their own "selves" in similar circumstances. There would seem to have been a particular, virtually unreproducible value for modern Arabic literature, then, in seeking to recover through neoclassicizing strategies the heroic tradition of classical Arabic poetry.

This heroic tradition, once recovered, would in its turn possess a very specific utility insofar as it underwrites a tactical program of resistance—based on the strengthening of individual identity—to what the author perceives as discourses (whether internally or externally generated) of illegitimate hegemony in his contemporary society. This may even explain in part why al-Bārūdī's choice of classical poets to valorize, like al-Mutanabbī, so often settles on figures whose own relationship to political power was problematized and at the forefront of their concerns as these were encoded in their poems.

While this initial foray into the study of relationships between literature and resistance in modern Arab poetry can hardly be said to have exhausted the potential for further investigation of responses in the works of writers whose lives were so drastically affected by the impact of new technologies of power, manipulated from so many different sources, it would seem to show the potential such analyses can have for extending and enhancing the applicability of the traditional triadic division of modern Arabic literature into neoclassic, romantic, and modern. The power of such modeling can only be increased by investigating how the twin practices of resistance and identity construction entered into the process of the transition in Arabic literature from neoclassic to romantic, and how the appropriation of romantic values served the poets' desires to resist elements of their contemporary milieu they had come to regard as inimical.

Here, as before, the regulation of resistance seems deeply implicated in the construction of a notion of individual identity as a sovereign self, capable of exercising power. Al-Bārūdī could be seen as fashioning his own image of self as strongly *Arab*—and therefore *different* from outsiders like the Western colonizing powers—partly as a response to the threat potential of a colonizing discourse that said the conquerors were simply moving onto "empty" lands, inhabited by less advanced peoples who needed the benefits conferred by contact with more "civilized" people. Al-Bārūdī's rejoinder to this would be his assertion that Egyptians already have their own ancient and highly civilized traditions,[50] which deserve respect. If the colonizer accepts this argument as valid, then there might be less tendency to interfere with the internal functioning of institutional structures within the country, even if an invasion should take place. In this sense, the difference of approach al-Bārūdī uses in contrast to Rifā'a Ṭahṭāwī—who was constrained, by his own goal of introducing Western knowledge to his fellow countrymen, to assert a similarity between the Westerner and the Egyptian—begins to make sense. Although the strategy of winning over the colonizer to the belief that Egypt possessed an ancient and vital civilization must have surely taken second place to the more urgent one in al-Bārūdī's poetry of strengthening the internal will of the Egyptians to resist, the two could be seen as quite compatible, strengthening and supporting one another. The presence of one does not obviate the presence of the other within the same discourse.

By the turn of the century, however, the flaws in the neoclassic strategy were becoming more apparent to the younger generation of writers. While the assertion of an Arab identity and a relationship to the Arab heritage had been the centerpiece of the *nahḍa* and had had important successes in strengthening the social bonds of the poet's primary audience, a perception that the internal features of that identity were less than well-differentiated and were not cohesively related to one another was becoming an increasing liability. In the early years of the twentieth century, colonial practices in Egypt and elsewhere in the Arab world were becoming more regularized and institutionalized, thus suggesting to colonial subjects in these areas that the colonial powers saw themselves as permanent rather than temporary occupiers. Similarly, especially after World War I and the awarding of mandates over the former Ottoman provinces of Syria and Iraq to France and Britain respectively, colonialism as a set of institutional practices was being significantly extended to new Arab territories as well. This extension and tightening of colonial control was accompanied by a significant shift in the nature of that control to emphasize more strongly the use of *discursive* (rather than military) maneuvers as its underwriting ground. In other words, educational systems were becoming the arenas of choice for the struggle, rather than actual battlefields where armies meet.[51] Another example of such discursive constructs is the increasing use of a set of well-defined stereotypes as "strategies of containment." A classic example would be the passage in Lord Cromer's study of *Modern Egypt* where he says:

> Want of accuracy, which easily degenerates into untruthfulness, is, in fact, the main characteristic of the Oriental mind.
>
> The European is a close reasoner; his statements of fact are devoid of ambiguity; he is a natural logician, albeit he may not have studied logic; he loves symmetry in all things; he is by nature skeptical and requires proof before he can accept the truth of any proposition; his trained intelligence works like a piece of mechanism. The mind of the Oriental, on the other hand, like his picturesque streets, is eminently wanting in symmetry. His reason is of the most slipshod description.[52]

This is part of a longer quotation Edward Said used from Cromer's book in his own *Orientalism* as evidence for the totalizing nature of the Orientalist's use of stereotype.[53] And he was quite right there to emphasize its broad nature, the very large number of negative qualities Cromer manages to pack into a relatively constricted space. But there is, upon closer examination of this section, one characteristic that stands out in particularly high relief as the focus of the passage. That is the "Oriental's" inability to think logically, to exhibit a cohesion in his mental processes that would qualify him for the status of "sovereign subject," equal to the European.

In this judgment Cromer was hardly alone, although he was, as the Consul-General and British Agent in Egypt from 1883–1907, in a unique position to put his prejudices into practice. One can find numerous examples of similar statements, both in the decade before *Modern Egypt* appeared (it was published in 1908) and in the two decades after, which coincided with Britain's move to establish its colonial control in the region more securely as its view of this area shifted from the value it possessed as a transportation corridor to India to its value as a major supplier of the precious resource that made British sea power and industrial might possible: oil.

The fragmentation and disunity of the "Oriental" or "Arab" mind is the theme that dominates this process of estranging the colonized subject and conditions its rhetorical shaping wherever one looks. It grounds, for instance, practically the entire evaluation of the 1919 uprising in Egypt as covered by the British press. As the *Spectator*, mouthpiece of conservative thought in the period, tells us in reporting the British restoration of order:

> The futility of challenging the victorious [English] Army which had just shattered the Turkish Empire would have been obvious to the [Egyptian] Nationalists had they been in a rational mood. But they had slowly worked themselves into a childish passion and would not be restrained. That is the Eastern way.[54]

Here, the twin stereotypes of the Egyptian/Arab/Easterner as (1) irrational, and (2) the bad child are combined so that each reinforces the other while leaving open a rhetorical hiatus out of which the reader may conveniently extract the opposite, positive characteristics of the European: rationality coupled with a youthful energy usefully directed and channeled by the exercise of reason.

For the purpose of understanding how these attitudes affected the production of discourse—and especially literary discourse—in Egypt and the rest of the Arab world, it is most instructive to begin by returning to an earlier period (1905) and an anonymous article from one of Cromer's (and the British establishment's) favorite venues: *The Edinburgh Review*. It is tempting to read this article, entitled simply "The Arab," as being an early and especially clever parody of the totalizing stereotypes that dominated colonial discourse of this and later periods, but there are no markers within the text, unfortunately, that would authorize such a reading. One is compelled, therefore, to take it seriously—as a sort of hyperbolized form of the kind of colonial apologetic endlessly reproduced elsewhere. Thus we find at the very beginning a brilliantly detailed version of the conventional comparison between "winding, tortuous alleys" of the Arab city (in this case Algiers) that "meander aimlessly in all directions" and the equally labyrinthine, confused, and unintelligible wanderings of Arab thought processes.[55] The article then moves forward to anticipate Cromer's discovery of the irrationality of the "Oriental mind" by several years, identifying the "fatal flaw" in the Arab character—which has precipitated the decline of Arab civilization from its formerly lofty position—as the inability to think logically, or "consecutively," to construct a "reasoned" argument. The author then invites us to contemplate the "crumbling ruins" of Arab civilization as being essentially akin to the "sandy wastes" of the Arab's ancestral home, the desert. "We have but to ask ourselves," he concludes, "what it is that this landscape of shifting sand lacks to be brought face with the deficiency in Arab character and the Arab civilization. It lacks that principle of cohesion with is the first condition of all progressive development."[56]

What is most interesting about this article, however—apart from the perfection with which it reifies the constituent elements of the overall stereotype while appearing to contextualize them—is its somewhat unusual focus on literature. The author makes frequent reference to, and clearly had more than a passing acquaintance with, Sir Charles Lyall's *Translations of Ancient Arabic Poetry*, published in 1885—a then-standard collection of Arabic verse that is dominated by Lyall's renderings of pre-Islamic poems taken from Abū Tammām's famous medieval anthology, *The Ḥamāsa*. He exploits the connection between this poetry, the desert environment, and his own generalizations about the Arab character in the conclusion to his article:

> For if there is one thing more remarkable than another about the extraordinary Arab character, with its mingled fierceness and cruelty, generosity and courtesy, it is the tenacity with which it has maintained itself unchanged through ages. The desert Arab of to-day is the desert Arab of twelve hundred years ago. What he was in those days we know from the salient portrait of him in Arab ballad poetry. We have referred already to Sir Charles Lyall's translations of these ballads. There is no mistaking for a moment the man there depicted. One after another these poems are as like as two peas in a pod. They are all perfectly agreed as to the kind of man they admire and what those qualities are which form an ideal character. And the man they paint is a man strongly marked with the aggressive and virile virtues; full of pride and valor, fiercely militant, keen and wary in mind, lean, hard and tireless in body, vengeful to a high degree, yet courteous and generous; the pride of his own tribe and the terror of all others— . . .
>
> Not an ignoble ideal certainly, and yet with what terrible limitations! In describing what the Arab is, we have already described what he is not. The active and virile virtues he undoubtedly possesses and always has possessed; but the reader may search through every one of these poems, and of such qualities as humility, self-sacrifice, long-suffering, forgiveness of injuries and the like, he will not find a trace. . . . And—alas, for the Arab's claim to a personal as apart from a collective estimate—not only are these qualities the cement of society, they are also the qualities that give richness and depth to character itself. All races have their ballad-poetry stage. But with most races this passes. The poetry of thought succeeds to the poetry of action. The

> Shakespeares and Wordsworths come in their season. But the Arab has remained always in the stage of ballad poetry.[57]

There is nothing in this passage that is any more severe than the judgment that had been rendered nearly half a century earlier by the French philologist Ernest Renan, who had similarly emphasized the unchanging nature of the Semitic literatures (both Hebrew and Arabic), and had concluded that the cultures producing these literatures were unique in "constituting themselves" by "negations": they had "neither mythology, nor epic, nor science, nor philosophy, nor fiction, nor plastic arts, nor a civic life."[58] In fact, one could argue with at least some justice that the *Edinburgh Review* essay sees a great deal more of value in Arabic poetry than had Renan's eccentric, sweepingly opinionated, and unabashedly bigoted mind. But during the time since Renan had written, Arabic literature had been undergoing its neoclassic phase—a literary movement that had been, above all, dedicated to reviving the very kind of writing that was here being held up to ridicule, or at least being judged as vastly defective in comparison to European literature.

Nor should it be forgotten that the political situation had changed as well. Now it mattered much more than in Barūdī's time what Englishmen and Frenchmen thought about the "Arab mind." For Arab intellectuals and political leaders no longer had only to be concerned with uniting their own people in order to ensure their participation in activities designed to prevent colonial assumptions of power. They also had to construct strategies to persuade or compel the colonizer to give up control of territories and institutions they already possessed. The British and French had become the decision makers and agents of change in the region. And groups among the power apparatus in London and Paris who supported colonial policies would use these stereotypes about the incoherence of the Arab mind to undergird their arguments, especially after World War I, that the Egyptians and their new Arab subjects in the Mandated territories were "not ready for," or were even inherently incapable of, governing themselves and managing their own affairs as independent states.

As an additional element in the mix, Arab intellectuals had by the early twentieth century much more ready access to the discourse of the European metropolitan culture than had their neoclassic predecessors. Nearly all the younger generation of Arab intellectuals were educated at least partly in English or French. Some, like the Mahjar poets, actually lived in the West. Others had studied there for longer or shorter periods. With the growing number of colonial officials living in the Arab world (by the end of World War I, 77 percent of the senior Egyptian civil service employees were English),[59] access to books and periodicals imported from Europe became much easier. And, given the pervasive similarity of these stereotypes that I have been discussing, it would have been difficult for anyone in the Arab world who thought himself a progressive intellectual to remain unaware of their nature. So, it is not surprising to find, when we look at the early poetry of these younger voices, passages that seem directly aimed at resistance to these negative characterizations by European writers. From one of the earliest surviving poems by the Dīwān poet ʻAbd al-Raḥmān Shukrī come the following verses:

> Stand firm; for shame is harder to bear than humiliation. Let humiliation not
>   lead us to shame.
> You think we followed a frivolous path; but indeed we are resolute people,
>   who do not condone the tyranny of a despot.
>
> ******
>
> They [the foreign rulers] will be defeated by the zeal of the illustrious
>   the ambition of the valiant, and the determination of the mighty.[60]

Here, the keywords are *ṭaysh*, "unsteadiness, frivolity," and *ʻazm*, "determination, resolve." An otherwise unspecified "you" has said that "we" are "frivolous" but this "you" is wrong: "we" are in fact "resolute" in achieving our goals. By deploying this antithesis in conjunction with the inherently dialogic pronouns "we" and "you" (thus foregrounding the potential of apostrophe to create intimacy), Shukrī vastly increases the sense of direct engagement with the other and threat to the self arising out of the discursive incompatibility. In the context of the relative disengagement between self and other we find in al-Bārūdī, where the oppressor is notable mainly as an absence, a negation of the qualities that should characterize a king, while the focus is directed toward the self authorized by its link to the tradition, it is almost shocking to see the shift toward the other as the controller of the discursive terrain in Shukrī's poem. To negate the reified and flattened stereotype projected upon the colonized and objectified self by the counter-construction of a selfhood directly antithetical to the stereotype (but to that same extent dependent on it) may be empowering in a sense for Shukrī's speaker, but it limits the arena of his struggle to the objectified colonized identity and directs the spotlight onto it to the exclusion of that belonging to the colonizer, which would tend to uncouple any sense of a dialectical movement of negotiation between the two.

Although it would probably be over-interpreting the data to suggest that Shukrī's poem should be seen as inaugurating some kind of inexorable, irreversible trend in the presentation of the self in the Arabic poem, it is suggestive to see that, by the 1920s, one can find an abundance of examples of *'azm* and its synonyms being used to subsume a set of fairly common practices that were becoming available to the native inhabitants as means to oppose unjust rule and/or colonial initiatives. A passage from a poem commemorating the return of Sa'd Zaghlūl from his second exile in the spring of 1923 is especially instructive because it deals with a key episode in the ongoing struggle between Britain and Egypt, but also because it is by 'Abbās Maḥmūd al-'Aqqād, whose critical writings had already had (and would continue to have) a disproportionate impact in publicizing the dissatisfactions of the generation represented by the Dīwān school:

28) What the people seek cannot be prevented by a powerful tyrant nor denied by a brutal one,
29) So seek your deserved portion, people of the Nile, and climb upwards to it, and look with your own eyes at what perseverance will do.
30) There is nothing [that stands] between [your decision] to seek the glory prepared for you, and your obtaining it—except for determination (*'azm*) and the seeking.[61]

This poem focuses even more exclusively on the objectified, colonized self than Shukrī's poem, so much so that it is difficult to be sure whether the "tyrants" really refer to the colonial power or simply to a kind of undifferentiated oppressive ruler. In his criticism from this period, 'Aqqād is less self-referential, however, and this provides us with the means to more precisely build up a picture of his attitudes toward the colonized self as manipulated by the discursive strategies of the colonizer and how he supposed it might be possible to overcome their power.

Instrumental in this regard would be an article 'Aqqād published in the *Dīwān* volume attacking a poem composed by the neoclassical poet Aḥmad Shawqī, which had been recited at a reception welcoming Sa'd Zaghlūl and his Wafdist comrades back to Egypt on the occasion of their first encounter with British intransigence, when they sought in 1919 to place the case for Egyptian independence before the victorious Allied Powers assembled at the Versailles Peace Conference. The Wafdists were exiled to Malta before they could get to Paris and were not allowed to return to Egypt until after the Conference had concluded, but the train of events their action put in motion ended in Egypt being granted nominal independence in 1922.[62]

Zaghlūl and the Wafd clearly, then, had exhibited a determination that could only have been guided by the kind of integrated, cohesive personality that 'Aqqād and his fellows had been advocating for many years (Shukrī's poem was written in 1907) and would continue to advocate for many more. Thus, when Shawqī chose to greet these national heroes with a poem conceived in the best tradition of the archaizing, Bedouinizing style of neoclassicism (it even began with a *nasīb*), 'Aqqād responded with a critique that focused on showing the incommensurabilities between this technique and the occasion it was celebrating.[63] He asks the reader to imagine that a Western poet comes to Egypt, having heard that a *nahḍa* (renaissance) in Arabic is currently under way, in the desire to learn more of these new developments. He makes friends with a member of the local literati and asks to be supplied with some samples (suitably translated) of poems that are currently making the rounds. The Egyptian connoisseur obliges by reciting and translating Shawqī's poem honoring the Wafd. The Western poet declares himself puzzled by its opening lines:

> Double the reins of the heart in your hand, and keep it safe
> from the herds of gazelles in the sand, from their flocks.

As 'Aqqād tells it, the Western poet decides that the tautology of "from the herds . . . from the flocks" indicates that this line is intended to be understood as a kind of warning of danger, just as one uses repetition in English phrases like "Fire! Fire!" or "To horse! To horse!" On this basis of this, the Westerner:

> imagines that these bands of gazelles or goats or deer attack people and frighten them in this corner of the earth, so that they are wary of them and run away from them on account of their ferocity and their violent nature. He decides that he would like to see these African beasts, so what can he do but ask his friend about it? Then comes the answer, delivered with the smile a professor bestows on his ignorant pupil: "No, no, there are no gazelles in our country that frighten people, nor even any tame ones—that was not what the poet had in mind; he meant, rather, women."
>
> "Women? and what do women have to do with this animal?" the man asks in surprise. But the smile of his friend the translator does not waver, and he replies to him: "Yes, women. We compare women with gazelles, following the precedent of the [Bedouin] Arabs. They so admired the eyes of gazelles, ringed as they are with a dark outline like a woman draws around her eyes with cosmetics, that they began to compare them to women's eyes, and thenceforth women became gazelles."

The Western poet does not understand the explanation, and allows himself a mildly derisive observation about the oddity of a convention that would have the author of the work pretend that the city he lives in is a desert and the people he meets are animals, but then, he remarks, love poetry in any culture is generally full of odd conventions. The response to this sally is not what he expects:

> How great his astonishment will be when his interlocutor says to him, with lips pursed and neck stretched out like someone who sees no call for such a supposition: "And why not?? The poet is singing according to a hallowed custom, one established by the greatest of the ancient poets."...
>
> Nevertheless, he takes refuge in good will and imagines that he begins to understand somewhat and he says to his translator: "It seems to me I understand. Perhaps your poet has intentionally written this poem in this manner as an imitation, as some of our poets do." But the translator does not grasp his point, so he says to him by way of explanation: "Westerners likewise amuse themselves sometimes by dressing in the clothes of Romans and ancient Greeks or by putting on the costumes of Persians and Indians, and it occurs as well to the poets among them to amuse themselves by emulating the style of poets from distant nations or from generations that have vanished—as an exercise or an amusement without serious intent or commitment. This emulation is not considered among them to be the highest thing one can aspire to, nor part of the essence of poetry. Its sole purpose is as a harmless pastime."
>
> The poor translator's mouth gapes open in astonishment at the puzzling and grotesque images these words conjure up in his mind. . . . He informs the foreign poet of the reasons for which this poem was composed, and that its author did not compose it as an imitation or an exercise, but in order to greet a nation in the midst of revival . . . and welcome home its leaders . . .

'Aqqād's major objective here would surely seem to be the generic belittlement of Shawqī's poetic ability, as he goes on to censure him directly for being imitative, for failing to produce poems that are "consistent with his lived experience," and for not at least being innovative in his presentation of the *nasīb* imagery, once he had chosen to begin his poem with it. But the subtext, driven home by the framing of the critique in an elaborate anecdote describing how Shawqī's poem would be seen through a Westerner's eyes, seems also to want to raise the issue of the inadequacies—for the purposes of creating a cohesive identity that can withstand the Westerner's gaze of dominance—to be found in the neoclassic practice of creating a wholly Arab identity through ransacking the archives of the literary heritage. This essay would seem to be readable, perhaps even demand reading, not so much as an attack on Shawqī as a call to rework the Arab subjectivity in order to anchor it on new grounds more in tune with the times.

There must have been several possible discursive constructs that offered themselves up for consideration to 'Aqqād, or Shukrī, or Gibrān, or Nu'ayma as candidates to provide a framework for this project. But European romanticism would have been an overwhelmingly attractive possibility, no matter how wide the field. This is primarily because so much of romantic poetry hinges on precisely the question of how it might be possible to make a "self," a coherent and cohesive identity.[64] In addition, as we have already seen in Coleridge's statement mentioned at the beginning of this chapter, the romantic goal is to construct a self that can, then, in its turn communicate with other "selves" in a totally transparent and unambiguous way. The importance of this for colonized peoples who must somehow find a way to communicate convincingly across cultural boundaries that are constantly being widened by the colonizer cannot be overemphasized. It is in this context that we should probably seek to interpret the frequent references in Arab writers of this period to "*insāniyya*" (humanism). It is a term that carries none of the vagueness of its English equivalent—it means quite precisely, from the evidence of usage, to work under the operating assumption that there are a set of universal "human" values that can be communicated unequivocally among human beings with no slippage of meaning. The fact that this is not a vague term to its Arab users may perhaps be attributable to its value as a survival tool in their situation. "The crisis in the subject," the subtle attractions of *différance*, may be a luxury affordable in its purest form only to that tiny elite, found mainly in the West, who feel no need for improving their communicative strategies, because the power of their discourses are already so dominant.

To return momentarily to the question of how this "self" that Arab poets like 'Aqqād will end up constructing on models found in the works of Western romantic poets relates to the "nation" will perhaps help us to understand the particular dynamics of this transition a bit more clearly. 'Aqqād almost certainly chose Shawqī's poem welcoming the Wafd delegation for analysis at least in part because it dealt with an event of great magnitude for the Egyptian "nation" at what was clearly a turning point in its history, and the critique of the poem as lacking originality speaks to the issue of how well an identity grounded in a tradition that no longer relates directly to the lives of most members of the "nation" can be said to have value for encoding this flux of experience. Because 'Aqqād so consistently practiced what was primarily advocacy criticism, however, we should be aware that he has chosen here to ignore the potential alternative reading of Shawqī's poem (one that would have been well-grounded, of course, in the responses of the educated audience at the time) as an absolutely typical exemplar of the neoclassic presupposition that the heroism of modern-day nationalist groups like the Wafd was able to come into existence and be effective because it was a continuation of the same deeply rooted heroic values enshrined in pre-Islamic and early Islamic verse. It was thus a system of correspondences, of metaphoric analogy, then, that was being denied validity.

Although 'Aqqād here draws attention to the fragility of literary conventions as ideological presuppositions, he is not above creating analogical presuppositions of equal vulnerability in the service of his own literary movement. They are simply differently valenced. Hence, in a slightly later article that was incorporated in his 1927 book *Shu'arā' Miṣr wa-Bī'ātuhum fī al-Jīl al-Māḍī* he defends his own generation against the countercharge that was brought against them by the defenders of neoclassicism: that they were escapist and unwilling or unable to confront the problems of the larger society in their environment, most particularly the problems of political or social oppression that nationalism as an ideology had been appropriated in part to oppose:

> The school of Egyptian poetry after Shawqi was concerned with the [individual] human being, and did not understand [how one could speak about] "nationalism" (*al-qawmiyya*) in poetry except on the basis that it is a humanism (*insāniyya*) characterized by [loyalty] to one particular homeland. It turned its attention entirely to [the representation of] the feelings of the human being (*insān*) in all classes, not confining itself to those who must work for a living or the economically enslaved. Yet, despite this, it was a school embracing all [human] nature (*al-ṭabī'a*) and all humanity (*insāniyya*). It would not be feasible for it to exist in isolation from nationalism because "nationalism" is a part of the make-up of a natural (*maṭbū'*) human being, even if it should be oriented toward the north pole or the pole star in the heavens.[65]

For 'Aqqād, then, individual experience—and the representation of it—is analogous to the experience of the nation. The individual is the nation in microcosm. This accords well with how the focus on individual emotions was understood in the writings of his contemporaries: not as an escape from social problems but a necessary prelude to their solution. This solution could not be achieved without developing a fully coherent and cohesive model for the individual "self" that could be deployed to oppose directly the set of stereotypes clustered around Cromer's "oriental mind."

When one reads the poetry produced by the Arab romantic poets with this paradigm of "self-fashioning" in mind, an entirely new terrain begins to emerge from within the topography of the textual surface. For example, to read Mīkhā'īl Nu'ayma's "Al-Ṭuma'nīna" (Peace of Mind)[66]—where the architectural discourse, used in a seemingly literal way in the first stanza ("The roof of my house is iron; the pillar of my house is stone") is revealed by the third stanza to be figuring the speaker's assertion of a strong structure and cohesion to his inner emotional life ("The door to my heart is a bulwark against all manner of distress")—as being occasioned by this urgent imperative to reconstruct the self on a new basis after the confidence-shattering events following World War I, will allow the reader to get a firmer purchase on the reasons for the author's choice of imagery in the first place and for the direction in which he develops it during the course of the poem.

Despite the perception that the later Arab romantics were "escaping" from commitment to the world even more than their immediate predecessors, their poetry in fact shows evidence that they saw themselves as continuing the same trend of concentrating on "self" development and refinement of the patterns available for the construction of a new individual identity because this project was still being seen as a necessary precursor, on which work was not yet complete, to the construction of an effective national identity.

This is quite apparent, for instance, if we take a look at the poems of Ibrāhīm Nājī, probably the most famous love poet among these later romantics. Like his friend Ṭaha, Nājī appears to have been haunted by the idiolect of the traditional poem, particularly that of the first section, the *nasīb*, at the same time the critical world was calling upon him to reject it.[67] Two of his most famous love poems, "Al-'Awda" (The Return) and "Aṭlāl" (Encampment Traces), for example, evoke the language of the *nasīb* for the purpose of describing contemporary love affairs. As M.M. Badawi has astutely observed,[68] the governing conceit of "Al-'Awda" transposes the constituent elements of the *nasīb* situation (the poet stopping at an abandoned encampment in the desert, reminiscing about a past love affair conducted within its boundaries, and then resuming his journey) into the modern urban environment. The speaker returns to a ruined house where he once lived and recalls trysting with his beloved there. He then has an eerie vision of death spinning its webs around the still-living bodies of his memories, like those spiders who preserve some of their prey in a state of suspended animation to serve as a food store for their young. This vision so unsettles the speaker that he resolves at once to retreat from his former home. He cannot summon up an alternative vision that would give him the confidence that would allow him to stay, and at the end of the poem he addresses the memory of his beloved, saying "You are my homeland (*waṭanī*) but I am a fugitive (*ṭarīd*) // eternally exiled in this cruel world." Here it would seem that the speaker is neither able to control the power of the tradition or to overcome it, but finds himself its object, forced to enact an unalterable sequence of events against his will.

In contrast, for "Aṭlāl" the speaker seems to have found within the romantic archive of self-making two subsidiary discursive formations with a potential to counter the discourse of the poetic tradition. These are the literary reproductions of the discourses of Sufism[69] and music. Before this appropriation can be enacted, however, the legacy of the ancient poetic tradition is thematized, encoded in the very title of the poem, since "Aṭlāl" in *nasīb* discourse are the faded traces of the abandoned campsite where the lover/poet stops to weep. To use this word in such a prominent position in the poem is to summon up that entire heritage with extreme verbal economy and simultaneously to point out its relevance for any interpretive work that is undertaken by the reader.

The first stanza continues the thematization of the tradition through the repetition of, first, the word *aṭlāl* itself, and then through references to conventional phraseology from *nasīb* language, such as the description of "desire" as "fallen"[70] or disintegrating (like the *aṭlāl* of the encampment would be), the image of tears watering the ground[71] and the observation in the final line that the lovers and those who knew their story are "departed":

1) My heart, pray God's mercy on a desire (*hawā*), once a castle in the imagination—fallen (*hawā*) now.
2) Let us drink to its aṭlāl, and tell (*rawā*) of me, as long as tears water (*rawā*) [the ground].
3) Tell how that love became a tale (*khabar*), a true story (*ḥadīth*) of passion,
4) Spread far and wide by those who regret a dream. gone are they, and it, too, is hidden deep away.[72]

Clearly, all the references here to the poetic tradition also link it to a state of disintegration and dissolution—the castle is fallen, the tears are spilling out onto the ground, the story of the love, like the lovers, is scattered far and wide—which would be in keeping with a view of it as symptomatic of a disordered, incoherent mentality. Thus it is interesting to see it also linked with the idea of narratives (*khabar, ḥadīth*), which should instead be models of coherence and structuring. But not only does it seem a troubling move with a potential for undercutting the dominant tenor of the passage, which associates the past with the unraveling of formerly cohesive structures—like the "castle in the imagination"—but it is even more troubling in that it does not seem to be (at least at first glance) an adequate description of what occurs in the rest of the poem, where very little narration occurs, each stanza standing on its own as an independent scene, a sort of tableau with minimal action, with relatively few links to what comes before and after. Thus the reference to "stories" here would seem unmotivated, unless one were to posit that the word "story" here does not refer to the reproduction of a narrative chain recounting external events but to the development of the emotional states in the lover's soul. Perhaps a passage from a section of *Al-Ghirbāl* where Mikhā'īl Nu'ayma criticizes Shawqī for yet another poem in which he employs a *nasīb* section would serve to better place what Nājī seems to be doing here:

> . . . an eye which has not seen these phantoms, these traces, and these remnants of the encampment will not pour out any tears for them, unless these images in the imagination are given physical form before it through the descriptions of a teller of tales or the picture of an artist or the statues of a sculptor or the movements of an actor on the stage. *The poet is nothing but a teller of tales (rāwī) who narrates* in a beautiful form *the story of the emotions in his soul* as they move in waves, along with his hopes and the rise and fall of his ideas in everything he hears, sees, and feels.[73]

One could scarcely find a description that dovetailed more precisely with Nājī's opening stanza in "Aṭlāl," and it is invaluable in helping us understand why Nājī speaks of "stories" and then proceeds to show us tableaux of internal "states."

Probably the most significant of these tableaux is the fifth stanza, because it forms in many ways a crucial turning point in the poem:

> I cannot forget you—you have seduced me
> on the highest summits, and I have given myself up to ambition.
> You are an angel (*rūḥ*)[74] in my heavens
> ever higher I reach to you, becoming like unto pure spirit (*rūḥ*).
> Yea, we were once high upon mountain fastnesses
> there we met, and our secret hearts revealed.
> The Beyond we descried from those towers,
> looking down upon men: mere shadows on the foothills.

Here we have a vision of the Beloved—the desired "other"—as a spiritual unity (*rūḥ*) that gives the poet through his love for her[75] temporary access to a model upon which he feels he could create his own cohesive vision of the world (symbolized by the sweeping panorama of the human landscape as dwarfed by "the Beyond," which the two witness from the heights). But in the next stanza, the speaker finds that, once he turns his thoughts inward, away from the unity of the Beloved, his own inner self appears very different:

I see the world with the eye of discontent,
 glimpse all around me the ghosts of my distress
Dancing over the severed limbs of passion (*hawā*),
 howling over the carcasses of hope.

His inability to sustain the vision here is very significant, since up to this point in the poem he had been steadily developing a set of discursive structures based on the terminology of Sufism—that discourse of unity *par excellence* for the Islamic world—which he had used to displace the *nasīb* code prevailing at the beginning of the poem. Although in the rest of the poem, the speaker will try a number of strategies to revive the power of this Sufi discourse (which had succeeded insofar as it was through employing that language he was able to craft the vision represented in the fifth stanza), and when this fails, he will try to substitute others. It is only when he turns to address a being he calls "the singer of eternity," however, that he is gradually able to rebuild a cohesive self that seems capable of responding to the invitation of this being, which is offered to him in the last two stanzas of the poem:

The night is still, though it has no heart
 O sleepless one, it knows your dismay.
O poet, take up your lyre
 sing of your sorrows and pour out your tears.
How often there have been melodies that the stars have danced to,
 until they attacked the clouds and slew the stars,
Sing until we see the dawn rising
 above the curtains of darkness, to ravish them.

Whenever blossoms hide in panic
 and you see terror wrap their hearts,
Then take pity, relent and play for them
 delicate melodies to dissolve their fear.
Perhaps they have slept in the cradle of sorrow
 and wept, calling out to their lord for help.

> O poet, how often a flower has endured punishment,
> not knowing for what sin.

Music, of course, has long been used in Islamic civilization, mediated through the classical music theory they inherited from the Greeks (note the exhortation to the poet to take up his "lyre"), as one prototype—through its base in harmony—of cohesion and the "strong discourse" whose model would seem very beneficial to someone whose "discourse of self" was under siege. Through the "music" of his verse, then, the speaker will be able to rescue the flowers (in a broad sense, other human souls) around him, and this will give purpose and meaning to his life. Given the fact that Nājī, like nearly every other Arab romantic poet, did not hesitate to mix political imagery with the language of love (and in this sense, at least, they were following in the footsteps of their predecessors like al-Bārūdī), as we saw in "Al-'Awda," it would not have been unlikely that his readers would have seen in final tableau a perfect adumbration of the imperative that the romantic poet could only sing to himself for so long: once he had reinstituted a satisfactory "technology of self" within himself, he would have to be willing to impart it to others (whether in the form of the "nation" or in some other guise), lest all his efforts should be considered to have been in vain. In the Arab world, however, that task of reintegration would become the work of Sayyāb's generation—though in very changed form, because in their lifetimes de-colonization would begin and the hegemony of the colonial sovereign subject would appear to vanish as suddenly and swiftly as it had come. As we shall see in the next chapter, that appearance was misleading: traces of that colonial experience would be left, as stubbornly persistent as the traces of the Bedouin's *aṭlāl*.

CHAPTER SEVEN

1948

Seeking Brave New Worlds

> *Miranda*: O wonder!
> How many goodly creatures are there here!
> How beautous mankind is! O brave new world,
> That has such people in't!
>
> —*The Tempest*

If we were to succumb to the lure of casting Sayyāb's life in the familiar form of a melodramatic plot, 1948 would be the year of triumph and tragedy, that cliché scene where the hero seems to have all his ambitions within his grasp, like ripe fruit, only to have them snatched from his hands at the last moment. In the best tradition of the melodramatic master narrative—of imposing an exclusionary, totalizing pattern on events in order to maximize their pathos, knowing that this will gratify our need for catharsis—many commentators have indeed interpreted Sayyāb's frustrations in this period as the heralds of a slow decline, leading straight to his early death.[1]

Although Sayyab's real life, of course, did not follow such a satisfyingly deterministic pattern, it is nevertheless unlikely that he ever again experienced the same emotional intensity and sense of optimism about all aspects of his life as he did in 1948. By the beginning of the next year, he would be in jail, unsure of when he would be released—if ever—and jobless, barred for at least the next ten years from his chosen career of teaching, eventually to be thrown back upon the charity of an indifferent father and brothers who were just as destitute as he was.

January of 1948 found Sayyāb in Baghdad, about to begin his last semester of study at the Teachers College. Studying, however, was probably the last thing on his mind as he found himself fully caught up in a hectic series of committee meetings, strikes, and marches leading up to the first popular uprising in Iraq since the Rashīd ʻAlī coup in 1941, a mass insurrection that would later become known popularly as the Wathba.[2] By the end of the month the streets of Baghdad would be filled with crowds of demonstrators from virtually every class of Iraqi society: students, industrial workers, the day laborers and unemployed, middle-class members of the liberal political parties.[3] All of them would be united—temporarily at least—in one desire: to get the British out of Iraq.

What had precipitated this new commitment among Iraqis to united action directed toward opposition to the colonial presence on their soil was a meeting then being held in Portsmouth, England, between the British and Ṣāliḥ Jabr, the current Iraqi prime minister (accompanied by Nūrī al-Saʻīd, leader of the Free Officers and *éminence grise* behind the monarchy), to conclude a new treaty of long-term alliance with the British government.[4] This treaty (including many provisions considered highly unfavorable to Iraq) was signed on January 16. On January 21, before Nūrī and Ṣāliḥ Jabr could return to Iraq, what began as a small incident between activist students and the police at the Royal Hospital sparked a massive protest in which two students were killed and seventeen others were wounded. When news of the killings spread through the city, as Hanna Batatu puts it, "resentment mounted to a fever heat. Tempestuous protests pervaded the streets. Crowds, thick with Communists, and armed with huge canes, clashed with the police, who became much like aidless flotsam in a wrathful sea."[5] ʻAbd al-Ilāh, regent for the young king and the highest voice of authority then in the country, panicked when he saw the spreading disorder and publicly repudiated the Portsmouth Treaty. This action temporarily split the opposition and brought a brief lull in the protests. Demonstrations still occurred sporadically over the next few days, but they mostly passed off peacefully.

On the 26th of January, Nūrī and Ṣāliḥ Jabr arrived back in Baghdad. Not having witnessed the mass demonstrations of a few days before, they underestimated the seriousness of the situation and were able to persuade the regent to reverse his position. That evening, Jabr made a radio broadcast "in which he appealed for calm, and affirmed that the nation would shortly have a detailed explanation of the clauses of the treaty and could then say its final word on it."[6] They hoped by this minor concession to salvage the new agreement. Instead, public outrage was renewed, and the next morning crowds—many organized by the Communists and student groups—began to collect in both the eastern and western halves of the city around the approaches to one of the principal bridges crossing the Tigris River (the Ma'mūn Bridge, later renamed Martyrs Bridge). The crowds tried to cross the bridge and were raked by machine-gun fire from police armored-car detachments. By the time the shooting ceased, three to four hundred demonstrators were dead. It was difficult to estimate the exact number of casualties because so many bodies had fallen into the Tigris and floated downriver before they could be retrieved. In the aftermath of these bloody events, Jabr's government fell and he fled the country. The Treaty of Portsmouth became a dead letter. A caretaker government (with Nūrī, as usual, pulling the strings behind the scenes) precariously held on to power, until a new election could be held in June.

Even in the Arab world, where poetry has never suffered that artificial divorce from the realm of events so rigorously enforced for the last two centuries in the West, the Wathba is notable among modern popular uprisings for the extent of the poets' participation in it. They, especially Communist poets like Muḥammad Baḥr al-'Ulūm and Muḥammad Mahdī al-Jawāhirī[7]—along with a full complement of more conventional political leaders—played an important role in keeping the demonstrations going, whipping up and maintaining the anger of the crowds by reciting their verses and making speeches. The dynamics of this process have been frozen and captured for posterity in a striking photograph of al-Jawāhirī taken during the demonstrations leading up to the massacre at Ma'mūn Bridge. He is clinging precariously to what seems to be a ladder set up in the center of one of Baghdad's public squares, a bullhorn in his left hand, surrounded by an unbroken sea of human bodies, which comes right up to the foot of his perch. He is obviously the center of attention for this entire enormous crowd, one that probably reaches into the thousands. His audience appears as a true cross-section of the (male) Iraqi citizenry of that period: of all ages and sizes, dressed in all manner of clothes from immaculate Western business suits to ragged tribal dishdashas and kuffiyahs, many with arms raised in fists—they completely fill the vast public square and trail away into the side streets.[8]

Jawāhirī himself would be personally touched by the tragedy about to happen. His brother Ja'far would be one of the first to be killed in the gunfire on Ma'mūn Bridge. Jawāhirī's elegy for his murdered brother, recited before a crowd of thousands during a commemorative ceremony held at Ḥaydar Khāna(h) mosque forty days after the funeral, became a rallying cry against the British among the Iraqi people, one of the most famous and often-quoted literary works of twentieth-century Iraqi poetry.

Although on a less exalted scale than Jawāhirī, Sayyāb, too, played an active role during these demonstrations. He was invited to deliver a poem at the ceremony honoring Jawāhirī's brother, and he spoke to the same huge crowd of mourners as did his mentor. But even before this Sayyāb had seen the power of his poetry to move and focus the emotions of a mass gathering. We have an eyewitness account of his participation in a demonstration on January 23 at the Mu'aẓẓam Gate in the northeastern part of the city, near the Royal Hospital and the Ministry of Defense. According to Khāliṣ 'Azmī, then a young man of literary bent, the clock above the gate was striking one o'clock when he joined with the crowd of demonstrators streaming into the square. Just in front of him, he saw a student being carried on the shoulders of a newly arrived group of protesters:

> His index finger, fixed defiantly in the base of his other [bunched] fingers, rose up clearly [into the air]. It writhed and moved in circles, then came to rest [for a moment] only to rise up again. At first, it appeared that this young man was giving a speech, but then I realized that he was [in fact] reciting poetry, when the throats [of the crowd] rose in unison to a fever pitch: "Again, give us . . . 'Qarṣa Ḥamrā' (A Red Lever)!" Here all obscurity fled away in different directions and the picture became clearer as we approached Mu'aẓẓam Gate. That was when I learned from the late nationalist poet Maḥmūd al-Ḥubūbī that the young man was the poet of whom we had read so much: Badr Shākir al-Sayyāb.[9]

Sayyāb would continue to be much in demand during the succeeding weeks of those first months of 1948. He was invited to recite his political poetry on many occasions in March and April, as the Communists worked behind the scenes to organize opposition to the June elections, which many feared would be engineered by Nūrī and the Free Officers as a rubber-stamp endorsement of the treaty. A number of the poems Sayyāb declaimed at these gatherings were subsequently published in the Baghdad newspapers.[10] Also in April, he would be elected by the students at the Teachers College as their official representative to an important National Student Congress (secretly organized by the Communists), which was attended by about 5,000 students from all over Iraq.[11] Thus, in both a discursive and activist context, Sayyāb found himself during these months directly exercising the power of agency, influencing the events occurring around him to at least some small degree.

While all this was taking place more or less on the public stage, Sayyāb's private life was in a similar state of ferment. He had fallen in love. This new affair was far more serious than the series of largely one-sided infatuations that had marked his first two years at the Teachers College. This time, as well, the attraction seems to have been a mutual one, based on a shared interest in poetry and politics. Sayyāb had met the new recipient of his affections, Lamī'a 'Abbās al-'Amāra,[12] at the beginning of the school year, and his feelings for her had grown slowly but progressively more intense, until by February 1948 he was sure that this was no passing fascination.[13] By summer, she would be visiting his family in Baṣra and Jaykūr, and they were, some speculate, seriously considering marriage. But there was a problem—she was a Sabean,[14] and her family objected to the idea of her marrying a Muslim. So eventually, sometime near the end of 1948, they parted—though whether it was only for religious reasons is not entirely clear.

But perhaps even more important than his new love—though it may not have seemed so to Sayyāb at the time—was his initial taste of literary fame. His first collection of poetry, *Azhār Dhābila* (Withered Flowers) had been published in Egypt at the end of 1947. Now it was attracting interest among the literati of Baghdad, including Jawāhirī, and had been favorably reviewed in the Egyptian press as well as the local papers.[15]

What marked this collection as being of more than ordinary importance was the fact that it contained a poem—otherwise unremarkable—in an unusual form of the Arabic meter *ramal,* one which used a variable number of feet in each hemistich. This was clearly a conscious attempt at something new, as Sayyāb appended to the poem a note saying that this was an experiment in writing poetry "like most Western poetry (and especially English), [in that] it combines a meter with its shortened form."[16] It was this poem, entitled "Hal Kāna Ḥubban?" (Was It Love?), which Sayyāb would later claim as his first poem in *al-shi'r al-ḥurr* (a term usually translated as "free verse").[17]

By what is probably the most extraordinary coincidence in modern Arabic literary history,[18] another aspiring Baghdadi poet, Nāzik al-Malā'ika,[19] a young woman a few years older than Sayyāb who had also graduated from the Teachers College, would write a poem in October 1947 using the identical innovative change in Arabic metrics. Her poem would be published in a Beirut literary magazine early in December, a couple of weeks before Sayyāb's *Withered Flowers* appeared in Baghdad bookshops. This coincidence later led to much inconclusive arguing over who was first to write in this form, arguments that have perhaps unduly absorbed the attention of those who have written about free verse and the literary movement that grew up around it. On the other hand, the publicity that surrounded these arguments indelibly associated both Sayyāb's and Malā'ika's names with *al-shi'r al-ḥurr*. If one were to ask someone in a university lecture room today in the Arab world what Sayyāb is best known for, the answer would almost surely come back "his invention of free verse."

What cannot be argued, however, is the tremendous popularity that the form has enjoyed since it was introduced by Sayyāb and al-Malā'ika. From a "degree zero" in 1948, by 1952 poems in free verse by some of the most prominent young poets (from all regions of the Arab world, not just Iraq) then writing had become a regular fixture of the avant-garde literary magazines. *Al-shi'r al-ḥurr* has impressed many contemporary intellectuals and literary critics as the most visible, if not necessarily the most consequential, innovation in Arabic poetry since pre-Islamic times.[20] Certainly, it radically changed the form of Arabic poetry and constituted a direct and uncompromising challenge to the rules that had formed the traditional poetic canon. This rupture perhaps would have been most immediately recognizable to the contemporary audience in the visual impact of the free verse poem rather than any aural differences, since these difference were more subtle. As M.M. Badawi has put it, "a printed page of the 'new' poetry looks different from Arabic verses written before the late 1940s: what is known in Arabic as *bait*, the line that consisted of two hemistichs of equal length or metrical value, has disappeared and has been replaced by lines of unequal length."[21] By the same token, this could be seen as appropriately marking a shift that was occurring in the Arab world, as elsewhere, with poetry being received more and more as a written product and less and less as a heard or recited one.

In the traditional prosodic system, the number of feet in each line had been fixed at a certain number, dependent on the meter chosen by the poet. For example, the most highly respected meter was *ṭawīl*, considered ideal for "serious" subjects like panegyric and elegy. *Ṭawīl* has four feet in each hemistich of line. These feet are made up of patterns of alternating long and short syllables. In *ṭawīl*, two different "foot" patterns are used: a short foot made up of three syllables (˘ - -) and a long foot made up of four syllables (˘ - - -). These feet are used in *ṭawīl* in an alternating pattern: (short foot) (long foot) (short foot) (long foot). This alternation, and the number of feet used, cannot vary at all.

Other meters have variant forms. *Kāmil* meter, for instance, Sayyāb's favorite meter in the early period of his life, has two forms: dimeter or trimeter. *Kāmil* is based on repetitions of only one foot pattern (˘ ˘ - ˘ -) throughout the line. If the poet chooses *kāmil* dimeter, this foot will be repeated twice in each hemistich. If trimeter is chosen, then the foot will be repeated three times in each hemistich. However, once a particular variant of *kāmil* has been chosen, then the poet is committed to it throughout the poem. In contrast, in an Arabic "free verse" poem, the poet may have anywhere from one foot to nine feet in a given line, depending entirely on the poet's own choice of where to begin a new line.[22]

In a rhetorical sense, adoption of free verse by its practitioners was seen as having specific implications for the shaping of the individual poem. One of the most important effects of making the number of feet variable and insisting on the use of meters that had uniform feet (like the foot pattern in *kāmil*) was that the power of the old convention in Arabic poetry of the end-stopped line was broken. Each line of the poem was no longer necessarily an independent unit. As Salma Jayyusi has pointed out, this convention, stretching back to the pre-Islamic period, had had an enormous influence on the syntactic structure of the poem, creating a strong presupposition that there would be a balancing of statements in each hemistich of the line.[23] With the breaking of this convention, enjambment, for one thing, became possible. Many poets of this period, still influenced by the Arab romantic imperative to present the poem as the mimetic product of a unified, autonomous subjectivity, found the openness of free verse to enjambment particularly attractive. As they saw it, the poet now had a choice of expanding or contracting the line to fit the natural flow of thought, or s/he could even allow the thought to cross the line break, in order to create specific poetic effects. This greatly increased flexibility made poets and their audiences perceive *al-shi'r al-ḥurr* as a "freer" form when compared to the traditional form.

Although enjambment and the creation of syntactic units that might encompass several lines have always been most frequently mentioned by poets and critics as salient features of the form, free verse also apparently made it easier to present mimetically the speech of conversation in such a way as to dramatize its sharp breaks and discontinuities. This may have been because brief spoken propositions—affirmations, denials, questions, rejoinders—could not fill up the necessary complement of syllables to make up a full line of verse in the traditional poem. Such short propositions would then have to be "run on" with statements from another speaker, thus working at cross-purposes to the convention of the independence of a single line. In free verse, however, the line could accommodate disjunctive syntactic rhythms of this kind because it could contract to the length of a single foot (three to four syllables) if necessary. Such potential for a differentiated mimesis of speech could be—and was—deployed effectively both to represent the dialogue of multiple voices within a single poem or the contrast between a single speaker's thought processes and his/her actual spoken words. This is in fact one way that Sayyāb would initially adopt free verse in his own poetry—to explore the possibilities of representing the shifting perspective of more than one voice in a lyric context—and it is also seen in a number of early successful free verse poems by other poets, like Nizār Qabbānī's "Ḥublā" (Pregnant),[24] and 'Abd al-Wahhāb al-Bayyātī's "Fī Sūq al-Qarya" (In the Village Market).[25]

A final element that made *al-shi'r al-ḥurr* appear "freer" to many poets was its association with variable rhyme schemes. The traditional poem was monorhymed; that is, it uses the same rhyme sound at the end of each line of the poem. The free verse poem almost never uses monorhyme. Its rhyme schemes are based on variable rhymes, very similar to the practice common in European literatures. However, variable rhyme is not an integral part of the definition of Arabic free verse. In fact, we find the introduction of variable rhymes even in the classical period, in the strophic forms that originated in Arab Spain: the *zajal* and *muwashshaḥ*. One of the features of the Nahḍa was a revival of the strophic poems, and they became the particular province of the Arab romantics, who pushed the use of variable rhyme schemes to new limits, even imitating the European sonnet.[26] However, it seems to have required the break in convention that was engendered by the advent of free verse to really establish the use of variable rhyme, on the European pattern, as the dominant form over monorhyme in Arabic poetry.

The utility of these new tools for the modern Arabic poem in terms of representing consciousness, the processes of thinking and self-formation, should be immediately apparent. It certainly seems to have been so to a number of young poets who, like Sayyāb, were growing dissatisfied with the old paradigms of Arab romanticism, and its valorization (or so it seemed to them) of the individual at the expense of the collective. In a sense, as we saw in the last chapter, this dissatisfaction was the result as much of the successes of Arab romanticism as its failures: it had concentrated on the projection of the individual mind of a speaker as a unified and coherent construct—in part at least because colonial discourse had so monolithically presented the "Arab subjectivity" as an inherently disassociated and fragmented one. Arab romanticism had thus become, through the work of poets like Ṭaha and Nājī, so adept at dramatizing this subjectivity and projecting it as organically unified (as well as depicting the successful overcoming of any challenges to that unity) that this was no longer perceived by the younger generation as a significant problem. For them, the problem had instead become—in an era when "the nation" was being challenged, as it was in the Iraqi Wathba, to act as a single unit—how to relate this unified individual consciousness to the outer world: in short, how to successfully mediate between self and other.

It was rapidly becoming clear that simply to assert the identity of the two (the "poet" and the "nation") was insufficient. This is what the old style of political poetry from the generation of al-Bārūdī, Shawqī, Ruṣāfī, and even Jawāhirī had done (and was still, to a very great degree, doing). Experience had shown—as it was even then showing in the fragmentation of Iraqi solidarity occurring subsequent to the Wathba—that such assertions were only temporary, however, in their effect. In other words, Jawāhirī's poetry could move a crowd to act in the heat of the moment, but it seemingly could not provide a structure capable of informing sustained resistance to the threat of colonial discourses of power. New ways had to be found to represent, explore, and negotiate the manifest differences contained within that construct labeled "the Iraqi people" (or, in broader context, "the Arab people") so that more effective strategies of resistance could be devised.

The new flexibility that free verse brought to those who were interested in this problem made it an undoubtedly convenient tool for opening up new counter-discursive strategies. This may perhaps explain why so many of them were so adamant in asserting that free verse reflected not only a change in form but also a change in content of Arabic poetry, even in the nation's way of thinking. After he had been writing free verse for a number of years, Sayyāb himself would quite unequivocally express this viewpoint in an interview

> Free verse is more than using a different number of similar feet between one line and another, it is a new artistic structure, a new, realistic tone, which has come to crush the soft flaccidity of romanticism, the literature of the ivory towers, and the rigidity of Classicism. Likewise, it has come to crush the platform poetry that politicians and social reformers have been accustomed to write.[27]

Even Nāzik al-Malā'ika, although she focused in her critical writings and her poetic practice on the unifying potential of free verse to represent the historically conditioned fiction of a sovereign subject, nevertheless speaks in the same terms as many who would much more radically reject the paradigms of their romantic forebears when she says:

> The truth is that it should be well within our capacity to consider the free verse movement as a purely social phenomenon, by which the Arab nation (*umma*) is seeking to rebuild its mentality (*dhihn*) upon a new (*ḥadīth*) foundation, in those deep and capacious recesses where so many treasures lie hidden.[28]

Here, she specifically calls our attention to the capacity for free verse to represent the restructuring of mental processes and expresses the need, in her view, for a singleness of this mental activity in all the different individual subjectivities that comprise the construct of "the nation." Thus, we should never lose sight, when reading and interpreting these free verse poems, of the fact that they were being produced in the context of the political struggles of the decolonization period and that they were ultimately seen by their makers as having important resonances within the context of those struggles, whether or not those resonances leave traces that are immediately apparent on the surface structures of the poems themselves.

Although free verse eventually came to be identified with a rejection of the values of Arab romanticism and became a magnet for controversy about this issue, it does not appear to have been the case that either Sayyāb or Malā'ika initially saw it as a particularly important innovative gesture, either formally or historically—until, that is, they witnessed the unexpectedly strong, often vehement and generally antithetical reactions to it among their friends and colleagues. People either loved the new poetry or they hated it. A major piece of evidence for this initial underestimation by both Malā'ika and Sayyāb of the significance of their discovery would be the gap between the first experimental poems and the time when they begin to write extensively in free verse. The grounds here are stronger for Sayyāb than they are for Malā'ika, because there was a longer interval between the time he wrote his first poem in free verse and the time it was published. If, as he says, he wrote "Hal Kāna Ḥubban?" in November of 1946,[29] then over a year elapsed before he wrote another free verse poem: in late February or early March of 1948. And even though we know that Malā'ika did not write her first free verse poem until October of 1947, it was still only after the beginning of 1948 that she wrote again in the form. For both of them, then, the event that intervenes between their first and second free verse poem is the public reaction to the initial experiment.[30]

Because in Sayyāb's case we also have the good fortune to have specific dates for all the poems of this period, it is possible to look at his work chronologically. From such an examination certain interesting patterns begin to emerge. First, we find a group of three quite conventional love poems in traditional meters from early 1948—dated in early January, late February, and early March. Their paucity and irregularity of appearance would seem consistent with Sayyāb being deeply involved in the political activities of the Wathba. All these poems are addressed to a woman with blue eyes—behind whose opaque reflective surface the speaker thinks it at first possible to read some coherent identity. But each time he is frustrated in his various strategies designed to frame and contain the subjectivity of his female other.

Then on the 24th of March, we come to a free verse poem, entitled "Asāṭīr" (Myths). The basic argument of the poem does not differ from its immediate predecessors: an inability of the speaking voice to build a coherent dialectic of self and (female) other. But a new element is added to frame the representation of this failure to bridge the ontological gap. This is the intrusion into the interpersonal drama of hegemonic social discourses—the myths of the title:

1) Myths from the death-rattle of time
2) The weavings of a decrepit hand,
3) Narrated by a darkness from the abyss,
4) And sung by two of the dead.
5) Myths like waterless deserts where the mirage
6) Shimmers, and the remnants of comets split [the sky],
7) And I saw there the lightning flash of new-minted gold
8) Caught in the woven shadows [left by stacked loaves] of bread.
9) And I saw myself; while the thick curtain
10) Hid you from me; then hope was lost
11) A destiny miscarried; and two lovers were at an end.

***

12) Myths, like cruel knives
13) Colored by the blood of the wretched,
14) How often they have glittered in tyrants' eyes.[31]

Although the myths clearly interfere in the lover's personal lives, they are also projected as zones of repression in a larger social field. They give off flashes of lightning that become the bright gold coins required for buying the loaves of bread the street sellers peddle. Key to widening the implications of the repressive power inherent in the myths is the assertion here that access to these means of exchange are denied to both the speaker and "the wretched," who are caught in the bright, knifelike controlling gaze of the "tyrants." In the following lines these at-first unaccented and decentered instantiations of the social dominant are figured more specifically as emanating from the religious, or to be more precise a perversion of religious discourse twisted to serve the interests of the "tyrants":

> 15) Because of the dust of years they bore,
> 16) It would be said: "A revelation from the heavens!"
> 17) But if the prophets were to hear,
> 18) The darkness of the abyss would not cackle
> 19) A decrepit myth
> 20) Dragging the centuries
> 21) In a chariot of flame, in madness,
> 22) Flame like madness!

The myths are proclaimed by the "tyrants" to possess the authority of religious revelation by virtue of their age, figured metonymically as dust covering their surface. But the speaker points to the elisions present in this characterization by asserting that, if the prophets—a group as strongly valorized in Islamic consciousness for their role as social reformers as they are as spiritual mediators—were to hear these claims they would put a stop to the use of such specious maneuvers designed to mystify the presence of personal agendas and venality, and they would expose the myths as "decrepit" and invalid rather than venerable and authoritative.

Many have seen this religious framing of the "myths" as a reference to the circumstances of Sayyāb's affair with Lamī'a 'Abbās, since it was supposedly the difference in their religions that prevented them from marrying.[32] But this is to ignore the implications of the highly thematized pull toward a more generalized condemnation of social norms that would open this poem up to a more political reading. We should not forget what Sayyāb says in the introduction to the collection where this poem appears:

> I am one who believes that the artist has an obligation to the unfortunate of the society in which he lives, which he must discharge. Yet I am not willing to make the artist—and especially the poet—a slave to this theory. The poet, if he is sincere in [his desire] to express life in all its aspects, must give expression to the pains and hopes of society, without anyone compelling him to do this. On the other hand, he will also give expression to his own pain and personal feelings, which are in their uttermost depths the feelings of the majority of the individuals in his society.[33]

Clearly, he is giving heuristic instructions to the reader here, to all intents and purposes compelling her or him to read the relation between individuals chronicled in the poems as in some sense metaphoric of the relation of the autonomous self to the rest of society.[34] In other words, we are being advised by Sayyāb to interpret the individual and the collective in his writings as being isomorphic or homologous. In this, we can see Sayyāb still, at least at this point in his career, accepting the general validity of the Arab romantic paradigm of self as microcosm for the social whole.

So, when in the second half of the poem, the speaker turns to address his beloved directly, inviting her to escape with him from the power of myths to an idyllic world with very Keatsian overtones, we should not automatically exclude this section as having a resonance within the speaker's more inclusive cognitive field, as being overdetermined by both social/political and personal valences:

43) Come! the color of the clouds is still
44) Sad—reminding me of a journey:
45) A journey?
46) Come! Come! We will melt time
47) And its hours, in a long embrace,
48) And we will dye with amaranth
49) A sail beyond the horizon.
50) And we will forget tomorrow
51) On your warm, fragrant breast
52) Like the sleepy dreams of a poet.
53) Come! Then the empty sky fills
54) With an echo whispering of a meeting,
55) A susurrus unending.

***

56) On your eyes, a distant hope
57) And something which wants:
58) Shadows,
59) A question muttered along their sides,
60) And a sad yearning
61) Wanting to squeeze the mirage dry,
62) And to tear the myth of the ancients into little pieces.
63) O what torment!
64) Two wings behind the veil.
65) A sail.
66) And the mutterings of farewell.

The speaker seems about to convince the woman to join him in his idyll of sensual, timeless pleasure. But then he looks into her eyes and sees there—

or so he believes—that she is expecting and hoping for someone or something to appear off in the distance. This realization (that she is not looking at him at all) causes the frail structure of words he has built to collapse, quite literally, in the last lines into "a heap of broken images" that his subjectivity can no longer bring into congruence and unify. What threatening thing it was that he saw in the woman's eyes is not entirely clear: it could be simply another lover reflected there, but the phrase "wanting . . . to tear the myth of the ancients into little pieces," suggests—given the social authority ascribed to the mythic discourse in the first part of the poem—that it may equally well be a desire for social or political action that would require individual fulfillment to be put aside in favor of realizing the societal ideal.

Read in chronological context, sandwiched between the other poems Sayyāb wrote during these months, "Myths" registers a particularly intense sense of strangeness, an uncanniness that cannot be accounted for solely by its desire to structure itself as a counter-discourse to hegemonic paradigms *within* Arabic culture that have been perceived as inadequate. For one thing, the epigraph to the poem explicitly labels it "a love story of pagan Greece," and this is not at all consistent with the repertoire of imagery Sayyāb was using in the poems immediately before this, which was modern and spatially unmarked. And the figuring of hegemonic discourses as "myths" appears "out of the blue," so to speak, and vanishes just as quickly, never reappearing in any of Sayyāb's poems again, suggesting some kind of intertextual citation at work here. There is also the formal difference between this poem and its predecessors to be accounted for. Not only is it in the free verse form, but each line comprises short, almost terse, discrete units of speech with few adjectives. This contrasts most strongly with the preceding (and succeeding) poems where long, loose periods, a wealth of adjectives and complex metaphors are the rule. As I have argued elsewhere,[35] there are good grounds for seeing this poem as constructing itself as a counter-discourse to Western modernist literature in general, and to an Imagist poem by the English poet Richard Aldington, called "Choricos," in particular.

The selection of Aldington's poem as an important precursor text for Sayyāb's "Myths" is not so arbitrary as it might at first seem. "Choricos" was included in what was, during the first half of the twentieth century at least, the single most important anthology for shaping the canon of Anglo-American modernism: Harriet Monroe's *The New Poetry*.[36] We know that earlier Sayyāb had freely and not infrequently utilized a similarly authoritative anthology, *Palgrave's Golden Treasury*,[37] as a kind of inspirational archive of source codes to appropriate for citation, translation, and contrafaction in his own poetry. It would not be unusual, then, for an English major in his final years of study at university to have happened upon or been guided to an equally authoritative collection of modernist English poetry. This presupposition is further underwritten by the fact that there are certain intertextual citations in some of Sayyāb's poems from this year that would seem to evoke poems easily available only in this anthology.[38]

The explanatory power of such a presupposition can best be grasped by juxtaposing some verses from Aldington's poem with Sayyāb's:

> The ancient songs
> Pass deathward mournfully.
>
> Cold lips that sing no more, and withered wreaths,
> Regretful eyes and drooping breasts and wings—
> Symbols of ancient songs
> Mournfully passing
> Down to the great white surges,
> Watched of none
> Save the frail sea-birds
> And the lithe pale girls,
> Daughters of Okeanos.
>
> And the songs pass
> From the green land
> Which lies upon the waves as a leaf
> On the flowers of hyacinth;
> And they pass from the waters,
> The manifold winds and the dim moon,
> And they come,
> Silently winging through soft Kimmerian dusk,
> To the quiet level lands
> That she keeps for us all,
> That she wrought for us all for sleep
> In the silver days of earth's dawning—
> Proserpine, daughter of Zeus.[39]

The imagery here is of myths (synecdochically rendered as "ancient songs")[40] personified as the walking dead, passing in a procession toward the ocean where they will depart for the shores of "the land of Proserpine," to join with the other dead of the pagan underworld in a meaningless nonexistence. The speaker clearly identifies with his subject as being what is for him an authoritative sign of a golden age when nature and the human were more closely integrated. The tone, then, is both strongly nostalgic for the past and (implicitly) condemnatory of the present, where there is room no more in his culture for such figures of integration.

What we may have here, in Imagist poetry in general, is a plausible, unproblematized *formal* precursor for Sayyāb's experiment in *al-shi'r al-ḥurr*,[41] but clearly, thematically, what we have is not a straightforward imitation, but a use of the precursor text as grounds for developing a counter-discourse based on inversion, something familiar to Arab readers as one of the varieties of engagement with one's predecessors or contemporaries subsumed under the label of *mu'āraḍa*, or "contrafaction." The inversion is most clearly evident if we focus on the lexicalization of "myth" in the two poems.[42] Aldington's speaker exhibits obvious nostalgia for the Greek pagan myths, which are (to him, at least) emblems of a once organic and integrated past. In this, he anticipates T.S. Eliot's famous anxiety about the growth of a "dissociated sensibility" in modern culture. But to Sayyāb—well aware, through the example of Eden, how mythic nostalgia could be deployed in the service of power—these discourses may not have been so denatured and harmless. Myths must always pose a potential danger for those who cannot seize strategic control of their use, and it may have been his urgent awareness of this danger—perhaps heightened by the instability of the political situation in Iraq in this year, characterized as it was by insistent calls for change—and, given the strongly socialized elements found in "Myths," this could have formed as much a motivating occasion for the poem as any private romantic disappointments he may have been suffering in his relationship with Lamī'a 'Abbās. One can easily imagine Sayyāb happening upon Aldington's poem in Harriet Monroe's anthology and finding in the author's desire to retrieve the "myths"—perhaps by retracing their journey back to the land of their origin, to the Mediterranean, and "re"-possessing it—a potential for the same kind of epistemological violence much more overtly expressed in Donald Maxwell's proposal to people the "empty land" of Eden/Iraq with Indian colonists once it had been revived by Western irrigation technology.

Over the next few months Sayyāb would write two more poems,[43] that would strongly invoke Imagist models, both of which could be read as having political as well as personal overtones. But the bulk of his writing would be given over to another kind of poem, one that suggests rather the paradigm of the dramatic monologue, the canonical example of which would be Robert Browning's "My Last Duchess."[44] The poems that Sayyāb wrote at this time which fall into this category all quite closely resemble one another in their structural outlines. They presume an individualized listener, addressed by the speaker as "you," who is strongly differentiated from the "you" reading the poem. The "you" is invariably marked as female in gender. This feminized auditor—the "other"—is then rendered present to the speaker (and thus, in a sense, problematized for him) by being projected into a dramatic situation or occasion involving interaction or some kind of interplay with the speaker, usually tied to the departure of one or the other.

There is an element missing in Sayyāb's poems, however, that one would expect to find in a conventional dramatic monologue. We find, upon reading them, no strong differentiation between the speaker (the "I" voice in the poem) and the poet himself. Such an assertion of identity between the speaking voice and the controlling consciousness posited in the poem can be seen as more motivated and less arbitrary than might otherwise be the case if we remember that the problem that was becoming increasingly urgent in intellectual life in the Arab world at this time was a potential incommensurability between self and other, and that the examinations of this problem grew out of a tradition of Arab romanticism that had focused on the ideological structuring of a cohesive self as its ultimate reference point.

This lack of distancing would seem remarkable, moreover, only if we take the Browning dramatic monologues as the sole examples on which to construct our notion of the generic norm in Western literature and ignored all subsequent developments. As Robert Langbaum has pointed out in his classic study of the dramatic monologue, *The Poetry of Experience*, the form undergoes numerous (re)appropriations and splittings at the hands of modernist writers like Ezra Pound, Yeats, Robert Frost, Amy and Robert Lowell, and a host of others.[45] But the poet who is valorized by Langbaum as the most original and important contributor to these developments is T.S. Eliot, of whom he says: "the dramatic monologue has been the main form in his work until he assumed what appears to be a personal voice in the series of religious meditations beginning with *Ash Wednesday*."[46]

Certainly, this is suggestive of a possible connection between the two poets, given the influence we saw in chapter three that Eliot's work had upon Sayyāb as early as 1946. Recently, a more detailed mapping of the various operations Eliot performed upon the Browningian body of the dramatic monologue has been pursued by John T. Mayer in *T.S. Eliot's Silent Voices*, and it can only reinforce a sense of the potential relevance Eliot's example might have to understanding Sayyāb's poems to find that it is precisely changes in language structure and syntax that Mayer emphasizes as an important element of Eliot's contribution to the dramatic monologue tradition. In order to accommodate "the twentieth century's sense of psychological realism," Mayer notes, "a poet such as Eliot who was committed to 'make it new' shaped his psychic monologues more spontaneously, with the sharp breaks and discontinuities that baffled "Prufrock's" earliest readers, who, as inheritors of the shaping structures of romantic artifice [in presenting speech], were culturally unprepared for the shaping structures of modernist artifice."[47] Perhaps an echo of this same problem can be found in the evasive strategies of containment found among literary critics when they discuss Arabic free verse. Their focus on its ability to mime more effectively the cohesive thought patterning found in Arabic romantic poetry, and their neglect of its pervasive use in "conversation" poems might be an index of a similar lack of preparedness to deal with something that resembled "the shaping structures of modernist artifice."

But even more importantly, it may be the way that the relationships between the speaking voice (the "I" in the poem), the auditor ("you") and the reader become displaced and reworked in Eliot's dramatic monologues that is relevant to our study of Sayyāb. The critics agree that the two most notable and successful variations on the dramatic monologue in Eliot's early work are "The Love Song of J. Alfred Prufrock," and "Portrait of a Lady." Usually the two poems are discussed together, with the focus being on "Prufrock," as the poem more relevant to tracing certain features found in Eliot's later writings. While both poems do share a sense of experimentation with the dramatic monologue form, it may perhaps be useful—especially in considering them in juxtaposition with Sayyāb's work—to emphasize that they inaugurate their engagement with the form from quite different directions. In "Prufrock," the "you" of the traditional dramatic monologue is internalized and becomes part of the interior consciousness of the speaker (who is nonetheless discernibly demarcated from the poet by having been given a name, "J. Alfred Prufrock"). This is signaled in the very first line of the poem, "Let us go then, *you* and I" (emphasis mine), where Prufrock appears to be speaking to someone else. But as the poem progresses we gradually become more and more sharply aware that "Prufrock's auditor is no auditor in the conventional sense but his deepest self."[48] The structuring of "Prufrock," then, would have offered Sayyāb an example of dramatic monologue where the split between the "controlling consciousness" and the "you" was relocated within the self and not exteriorized.[49]

"Portrait of a Lady"[50] takes quite a different tack, positioning itself more precisely within the dramatic monologue tradition, but even so with an important strategic difference, one that has even more relevance to Sayyāb's poetry than the dramatic situation of "Prufrock." The character of the "Lady" of the title is revealed—like Browning's Duke—largely through the auditor's report to us, the readers, of excerpts from her conversation. But the one she addresses is no silent auditor; rather he intrudes much more substantially upon the reader as the real "center of consciousness" in the poem. Thus a much sharper sense of the inadequacies of the "Lady's" world view is foregrounded.

The poem is carefully divided into three sections, each of which revolves around a conversational encounter between a man and an (as we find out midway through the poem) older woman. The first meeting takes place in December (probably) following a concert the two have attended. Here the Lady speaks of the importance of finding friends who understand her and implies that the young man will be such a friend for her ("To find a friend who has these qualities, / Who has, and gives / Those qualities upon which friendship lives. / How much it means that I say this to you—"). The young man's reaction to these artfully artless conversational gambits is to report the onset of a headache ("Inside my brain a dull tom-tom begins / Absurdly hammering a prelude of its own, / Capricious monotone / That is at least one definite 'false note.'"), indicating his sense of alienation from the social conventions that have authorized the Lady's words.

In the second section the alienation, the sense of discontinuity between surface and depth, is intensified. It is spring, we are told, and the Lady is occupied with rearranging a lush bouquet of lilac flowers as she speaks to her visitor; the subject of her conversation, however, is not life—which would be congruent with the season—but death:

"I am always sure that you understand
My feelings, always sure that you feel,
Sure that across the gulf you reach your hand.

You are invulnerable, you have no Achilles' heel
You will go on, and when you have prevailed
You can say: at this point many a one has failed.
But what have I, what have I, my friend,
To give you, what can you receive from me?
Only the friendship and the sympathy
Of one about to reach her journey's end.[51]

Apart from the ominous portentousness of the reference to the "gulf" between them—whose existence is thus asserted even at the moment it is denied—what the Lady says here reveals the existence of a gap between her and the young man in age, one that would preclude the establishment of any real romantic relationship between them. Yet it is also precisely the distance between their ages that she appears to appeal to, in order to bind the auditor to her by guilt, since he will "go on" after she has "reach[ed] her journey's end."

The ominous portent of separation prefigured in the second section is realized in the third and final section. It is now October, and the auditor has come to tell the Lady he is going away:

> I mount the stairs and turn the handle of the door
> And feel as if I had mounted on my hands and knees.
> 'And so you are going abroad; and when do you return?
> But that's a useless question.
> You hardly know when you are coming back,
> You will find so much to learn.'
> My smile falls heavily among the bric-a-brac.
>
> 'Perhaps you can write to me.'
> My self-possession flares up for a second;
> *This* is as I had reckoned.
> 'I have been wondering frequently of late
> (But our beginnings never know our ends!)
> Why we have not developed into friends.'
> I feel like one who smiles, and turning shall remark
> Suddenly, his expression in a glass.
> My self-possession gutters; we are really in the dark.[52]

Here the poem that began with a seeming identity being asserted between the woman and the young man, or at least a spoken assumption of communicative adequacy, has quickly disintegrated into misunderstanding, missed connections, speech that fails to communicate anything but its own self-reflexiveness, caught up within a network of discourse conventions that circumscribe very narrowly the range of what it is possible to say. The conflicts thus represented—between youth and age, male and female, self and other, and especially language that divides and language that unites—can all be found to play their part in Sayyāb's life during 1948.

If we wish to sketch out the parameters of possible points of engagement between Sayyāb's texts and "Portrait of a Lady," there can perhaps be no more convenient place to begin than the two free verse poems that form the terminal points of this episode: "Sawfa Amḍī" (I Will Go), probably from late March 1948,[53] and "Fī al-Sūq al-Qadīm" (In the Ancient Market), dated

November 3 of that same year. The efficacy of such an approach is underscored by the fact that these two poems appear to be closely related, with the second being a reworking and expansion of the first, an expansion that carries it in directions that are consistent with the general trend of development in Sayyāb's writing as spring gave way to summer and then to fall.

"I Will Go" consists of three stanzas. In each one, a male speaker (who may or may not be identified with the poet) addresses a woman, telling her that he plans to leave her to search for another woman, who "is waiting for" him. Although the voice of the woman being addressed is not recorded in the poem, it is apparent that she says something to him in the blank space between the first and second stanzas, since the male speaker's words in the second stanza, when he asserts that the raging river and the ghosts rising from their graves will not cause him to abandon his quest, would appear adequately motivated only as a response to categories already articulated from another source, most likely the woman's unrecorded speech. The space between the second and third stanzas is even more clearly inscribed as containing/concealing an interaction with his interlocutor, since he quite clearly is responding to her physical gestures of "staring" at him and then attempting to "embrace" him:

1) I will go. I hear the wind calling me from afar
2) In the darkness of the tangled forest—and the long road
3) Stretches out fretfully, and the wolf howls; daybreak
4) Steals the stars just as your eyes steal my soul,
5) Leave me to traverse the night alone.
6) I will go, for she is still there
7) Waiting for me.

***

8) I will go. Neither the raging of the torrent, crashing, terrible,
9) Flooding the valley, nor the ghosts cast by the graves
10) In my path, asking the night where I am going—
11) All of this will not divert me, so go back and leave me,
12) And let me traverse the night as a stranger.
13) Indeed she is staring at the unhappy horizon,
14) Waiting for me.

***

15) I will go. Turn your eyes away, don't stare at me!
16) Indeed, there is a magic in them which forbids my legs to move,

17) Indeed, there is a secret in them which seeks to hold back a broken heart ,
18) And take your arms off of me—what use are embraces
19) If they arouse no yearnings in me?
20) Leave me. Dawn has come, and my comrades are
21) Waiting for me.[54]

Although this poem entirely lacks the overt ironies of "Portrait," the division into three parts, each recording an episode or encounter, the theme of parting as the mainspring of the action, and the ambivalence of the speaker's attitude toward the woman he addresses all suggest a possible positioning of Sayyāb's poem within a frame provided—however indirectly—by Eliot's model.

What we also see here is the same suggestion of a homology between private and public, personal and political, that we found in "Asāṭīr." One minor sign of this is the shift in the characterization of who is "waiting for" the speaker at the end of the poem. In the first two stanzas the "waiting figure" is an otherwise unidentified female. But in the final stanza it has suddenly become the speaker's "comrades (*rifāq*)." This is the word that is usually used as an equivalent for the politically valenced term "comrade" in Communist tracts written in Arabic, and its use in this sense is widely recognized. So when it is substituted here for the much less specifically marked "she," it calls attention to itself as a signifier authorizing a much more sociopolitical reading of the poem than might otherwise be the case. But an even more insistent call for such a reading comes from the presence throughout the poem of two female figures who have claims upon the speaker. This is a pervasive feature of all Sayyāb's poems of this type throughout 1948. There is in each poem a female figure who is present to the speaker and who is represented as being a sensual figure who attracts him physically. He constantly seems to struggle against this woman's claims, however, by invoking the image of another female who is not present—who is waiting for him somewhere else—and who offers him an ideal love not based on sensuality. Usually, Sayyāb's biographers have related these poems to the actual circumstances of his love affair with Lamī'a 'Abbās. While there is probably some truth to this attribution, it cannot explain completely either the splitting of the beloved into a sensual/ideal opposition or the stability of this portrayal over a period when Sayyāb's actual relationship with Lamī'a 'Abbās went through several periods of falling and rising expectations. A more consistent explanation can be obtained, however, by interpreting the competing claims upon the speaker as coming from a conflict in his mind between a real beloved and service to the collective body of society—figured as a second beloved whose attractions are purely spiritual and intellectual, not physical. Such an explanation, at least, would relate to the consistent dilemma Sayyāb must have found himself in throughout 1948: the competing claims of his private feelings for Lamīʻa, and the public claims of what he conceived as his social duty to Iraqi and Arab society, neither of which were easily reconcilable in the volatile atmosphere surrounding the Wathba.

Although "Portrait of a Lady" does not figure a distinct split between a public and private voice, nor does the political have a resonance within its boundaries, it does record the developing conflict of two worldviews—the young man's and the Lady's—whose opposition is ultimately as impossible to reconcile as that between the two characters in Sayyāb's "I Will Go." Thus, one could say that this poem's status as a possible contrafaction of a Western modernist precursor is just as suggestive, intriguing, and ultimately unresolvable in a positivistic sense as is the case with "Myths" and Richard Aldington's "Choricos." However, if "I Will Go" is a contrafaction of "Portrait of a Lady," the strategy used for engagement differs quite markedly from the earlier poem. Here, we are not presented with a straightforward case of inversion and direct contestation, but Sayyāb's other favorite method: supplementation/supplantation, which will be so characteristic of the way he deals with Eliot's example in his poems of the 1950s. This strategy does not suggest, as does inversion, that the precursor is consciously complicit with the hegemonic goals of colonialism, but rather implies that the precursor's work, while still admirable, has somehow forgotten to include an element that the ephebe will now show is essential to an adequate understanding of the situation. This would explain Sayyāb's expressed admiration for Eliot's work, while allowing us to see his activation of that work in his own poetry as something more than simple homage or unproblematic imitation.

Whether or not Eliot was the source, what grew to dominate Sayyāb's poetry more and more as 1948 wore on was a series of meditations on the questions of competing voices. Although this vocal medley continues to be overtly expressed through the narrative of a love triangle, there continue to be allusions and the use of key terms that push us to see these as metaphors for the increasingly vocal ideological tensions Sayyāb would have been exposed to in the society around him at this time. The first Arab–Israeli war, which broke out in the summer of this year, would only have increased this sense of an intensifyingly noisy set of incommensurate discourses, by internationalizing the conflicts already present in Iraqi society, especially as the founding of the state of Israel was widely perceived in the Arab world as being congruent with the desires and interests of the European colonial powers and an extension of their ambitions to control the resources of the Middle East.

Thus it is not surprising to find Sayyāb, at the end of 1948, returning quite overtly to an almost exact repetition of the initial situation he had described in "I Will Go" and this time "letting the scenario play itself out" once again, perhaps in order to see if there would be any change in its dynamics. In this new poem, "Fī al-Sūq al-Qadīm" (In the Ancient Market), Sayyāb chose to use a bipartite structure to organize his meditation upon the problem of voice. To an expanded and much altered version of the psychic monologue from "I Will Go," (strophes 8–11), he added seven introductory strophes that describe the speaker's nighttime perambulations in a deserted village marketplace:

—1—

1) Night, and the ancient market
2) Where the voices have died away: all but the murmurs of the passers-by
3) And the footsteps of the stranger and sad songs scattered by the wind
4) In that inky night.
5) Night, the ancient market, the murmurs of the passers-by,
6) And the light wrung out palely from sad lamps
7) —like the fog on the road—
8) From every wine shop of ancient date,
9) Among the pale faces, like music dissolving
10) In that ancient market.

—2—

11) How often he who is a stranger floated before me
12) In that melancholy market.
13) He saw [something], he shut his eyes, and he disappeared into the inky night.
14) And a shape from a lighted window wavered in rings of smoke,
15) While the wind played with the smoke,
16) The wind played, without interest, melancholy, with the smoke,
17) And a song echoed
18) Distantly, bringing back memories of moonlit nights and palm trees;
19) And I am the stranger—I stay, listening to it [the song] and dreaming of the parting,
20) In that ancient market.

—3—

21) The frail light lies scattered over the merchandise like dust,
22) Casting shadow upon shadow, like a monotonous melody,
23) And the cold colors of the sunset flow liquid over the wall
24) Among the rickety shelves, which resemble the clouds in the sunset.
25) The cup dreams of a drink, of lips,
26) Of a hand colored by the light of the noonday sun, of a lamp or stars.
27) Perhaps they went cold upon it, and life breathed out its last there,
28) On a darkened night: the winds, the stars cold
29) In a chamber where the lamp kept vigil through the night, and morning
snuffed it out.

—4—

30) And I saw, through the smoke, scenes from tomorrow like shadows:
31) Those handkerchiefs moving erratically, as they wave farewell,
32) Or drink down heavy tears; rising to the surface and falling to the
depths
33) Unceasingly in my imagination—a lingering perfume drowses
34) Within them, and they are dyed with freshly flowing blood.
35) The color of the starless night, the burning glow of fire
36) Reveals the bench, then shivering shadows hide it;
37) A face whose pallor is lit by flame
38) Fades, then flickers bright, then disappears from sight.
39) And [somewhere] blood murmurs, as it drips, drips: "he is dead, dead."

—5—

40) Night, the ancient market, the murmuring of the passers-by,
41) And the stranger's footsteps.
42)   And you, O candles, will burn
43) In the unknown chamber, in the night which you will never know,
44) You will cast your light in slow motion, like the autumn evenings—
45) A field where the ripe grain shimmers in waves beneath the light of
sunset,
46) Where the crows gather—
47) You will cast your light in slow motion, like the autumn leaves
48) On moonlit nights drunk with music, in the south:
49) The pounding of the drums, far away,
50) The heavy palm fronds whisper to one another, and fall silent again.

—6—

51) My heart was once like yours [the candles']; it used to dream of flame,
52) Until time gave it a hand and a face in the darkness:

53) The fire of desire and the hand of the beloved (m.).
54) It burned on for life, year after year
55) Passed, and face after face; just as sail after sail
56) Disappears, and still it dreamed silently, silently:
57) Of a breast, of a mouth, of eyes,
58) Of a love shaded by eternity—no meeting, no farewell.
59) But it was [only] a lengthy dream
60) Between stretching out, and yawning [upon awakening], beneath the shadows of the palm trees.

—7—

61) Yesterday, it lasted for a time, then it faded; despair and boredom caused it to be
62) Forgotten; so that how could one dream of brightness: no yearning
63) Affects its starless night, no melancholy, no tears, and no moans.
64) Summer embraced winter, and the two of them left; yet [my heart] remained,
65) Like an abandoned house along whose sides the wind wails,
66) Like a broken staircase that no foot climbs
67) In the melancholy night, and no foot will descend when morning glitters,
68) My heart remained in the twilight : no westering sun, no evening,
69) Until she and the brightness came![55]

First, one should note how Sayyāb foregrounds the question of voice (and foreshadows the second half of the poem) in the very first lines. He establishes the time (the favorite romantic temporality of night, with its potential to manipulate darkness and light in important symbolic ways) and the place (the market, which is old: in other words, it has a history, a temporal dimension as well as a spatial one), which are in themselves unremarkable conventional strategies for opening poems and mainly signal here that the idiolect of Arab romanticism will dominate. Then he adds a detail that at this point seems minor but is proleptically important: "Where the voices have died away: all but the murmurs of passers-by / And the footsteps of the stranger and sad songs scattered by the wind." Thus the market is immediately defined in two ways: it is old and it is a place where (other) *voices* are *not*—or if they *are*, they are immediately naturalized into something else, less threatening to the poet's voice. The voices of the passersby become "murmurs (*ghamghamāt*)," an onomatopoetic word that makes its signified into something natural (the origin of language used to be explained as the onomatopoetic imitation of "nature's" sound) not the result of the operations of a conscious mind. The other sound allowed to enter the poet's market is the songs, which are linked to the "natural" phenomenon of the wind, and in themselves are conventionally seen, because they are incorporated into music, as approaching the pure emotion, the pure "presence" of music in aesthetic theory.

To understand why the market is predicated as being old, we should consider one of the more provocative questions that Iḥsān 'Abbās raises in his critique of this poem: "Why did the poet choose the market as the bearer of his memories, when there is nothing distinctive about the market which sets it off from other places that can arouse memories?"[56] His answer, that "the market is unique in a distinction which is not fully found elsewhere: the scene is at night, the light is squeezed out palely by the sad lamps, the market is old and melancholy, it stretches out before the eyes, it is its nature to arouse melancholy in a soul that is lonely, far from home," actually presupposes the deeper reason for the choice. The market possesses a set of features that allows it to interact meaningfully with the literary tradition's convention locus of memory and loss: the *aṭlāl*. Like the *aṭlāl*, the market is a repository of objects that at first seem meaningless, divorced from their contexts, but then are given significance through the poet's imaginative act, which associates them with a past elegiac vision of unified lovers. Like tent trenches and blackened fire pits, the cups and candles are made *by the poet* into meaningful symbols, not arbitrary signs.

On the other hand, the market is not, as the *aṭlāl* once was, a place of intimacy, of human *(in)dwelling*. It is a place of commodities, where objects are temporarily stored, in order to be bought and sold. This difference is significant because it, again proleptically, connects the first and second half of the poem, where the beloved will say: "I, O one so near, so far, / Am yours alone, but I won't *belong* to you . . . / I *belong* to someone else" [emphasis mine]. This comparison of herself to a commodity becomes a major threat to both her own vision and the poet's vision of her as the ideal beloved, by uniting with whom he can achieve his ideal. Thus, the place and the commercial transactions that take place within it are incompatible with the poet's gesture of making it the setting where he will create his vision. His choice has ominous connotations, though he does not realize it yet.

In the third stanza, the poet begins in earnest to apply the power of his transforming imagination to the objects around him: to cups, handkerchiefs, and candles (as 'Abbās notes, these objects can all be conventionally linked together as being associated with wedding celebrations in the Arab world). Yet, each time he tries to apply that transforming power in any sustained way to these objects, to endow them with meaning, then his meditation is pulled to images of meaninglessness and death, culminating in the internalization of the *aṭlāl* convention (in slightly modernized form) within the poet's own body, as he compares his heart to an abandoned house "along whose sides the wind wails."

In retrospect, compared with what will come, even this negative vision is in some sense a victory for the poet's voice. In the first half of the poem *he* controls the presentation of the material. The poem is constituted as his vision and no one else's. Ultimately, in line 69 he is even able to make the "she," the visionary object, appear. But this powerful imaginative effort is also fatal. The beloved he invokes, the "she" who is to bring reintegration, actually takes over the language of the poem, producing a counter-vision that excludes the poet as subject, and reduces him to an object, like an inanimate thing, incapable of movement:

—8—

70) All that I had from her was that we met a year ago
71) In the evening, and we embraced beneath the street lights.
72) Then her hands fell from me as she whispered, as the darkness
73) Crept forward, extinguishing the sad lamps and the street:
74) "Are you going alone into the darkness?
75) Are you going, though ghosts bar the way, without a comrade?"
76) And I answered her, as the wolf howled far away, far away,
77) "I will go, searching for her; I will meet her there,
78) At the mirage; I will build two abodes there for us."
79) Then she said, as the echo repeated (the secret) she was revealing: "I
am the one you want!"

—9—

80) "I am the one you (m.s.) want; so where are you going?
Why do you travel the empty lands
81) Like a vagabond? I am the beloved (f.); I have been waiting for you.
82) I am the one you want . . ." She kissed me, then she said, with tears
83) In her eyes: "Yet you will never see the dream of youth:
84) The house on a distant hill almost hidden in fog
85) If not for the songs, as they rise half-asleep, and the candles
86) Shed light, in slow, slow motion, from the windows!
87) I am the one you want, and you will stay [here], neither settling down
nor leaving:
88) [This is] a love that, if it gives much, it is miserly with small [things],
89) It contains neither despair nor hope.

—10—

90) I, O one (m.s.) so near, so far,
91) Am yours alone, but I won't be
92) Yours—I hear her; and I hear them behind me, cursing
93) This love affair. I almost hear, O beloved dream,
94) My mother's curses as she weeps. O strange man
95) I belong to someone else—yet you will remain, you will not go!
96) Your feet have been nailed down; they cannot move. And your eyes
97) Can only see my road, O imprisoned slave![''].

***

98) "I will go, so leave me! I will meet her there
99) At the mirage."
100) Then she embraced me, as she whispered: "You will not go."

—11—

101) "I am the one you want; so where are going, beneath the gaze of wolves,
102) Searching for the path far away?"
103) Then I cried out: ["]I will go, as long as [this] longing for the mirage
104) Is in my thirsty heart! Leave me to travel the path far away
105) Until I see her waiting for me. The gaze of wolves will not be
106) More cruel to me than the candles
107) On the wedding night you are waiting for; nor will the darkness
108) And the wind and the ghosts, be more cruel to me than you or mankind!
109) I will go!["] Then her hands fell from me, and darkness
110) Overflowed.
111) But I stood still, my eyes filled with tears![57]

The situation, of course, very much recalls "I Will Go," with one significant difference: here the poet is the silent one, not the woman. Until the last strophe, he is reduced to a single programmatic line: "I will go, so leave me! I will meet her there / at the mirage." Even when he recovers his powers of speech, and reduces her to silence and then abandonment of her claims on him (represented by the dropping of her arms in line 109) it is too late. The darkness of chaos overwhelms the poet's vision, and like Eliot's young man in "Portrait of a Lady," he is left standing still, unable to begin the quest again.

In retrospect, "In the Ancient Market," with its focus on the individual consciousness can be seen as the culmination of the trends found in Arab romanticism, which was still the overwhelmingly popular mode of poetic discourse in Iraq when Sayyāb published it in 1948. The fact that this romanticism was married to the new poetic form, realized in a much longer and more complex poem than either Nāzik al-Malā'ika or Sayyāb had attempted before, can go far to explain the poem's popularity.

As the poem gained in fame, it inspired, as several critics have pointed out, what they call simply "imitations." Although the word *mu'āraḍa* is never used, it becomes clear from statements like 'Abd al-Jabbār Da'ūd al-Baṣrī's that it is this discourse strategy we are dealing with:

> It is worth noting that the first lines [of "In the Ancient Market"] had a tremendous influence on [other] poets, who imitated them, or *sought to outstrip them and entered into an artistic competition with them.* The most notable of these was 'Abd al-Wahhāb al-Bayyātī, especially in his collection *Abāriq Muhashshama* (Broken Pitchers).[58]

The intent to contrafact becomes even more clear when we look at the poems themselves. Shmuel Moreh has very conveniently listed specific poems from the early dīwāns of Sayyāb's contemporary colleagues at the Teachers College, Kāẓim Jawād and 'Abd al-Wahhāb al-Bayyātī, which reproduce the opening tripartite line structure of "In the Ancient Market," and are also in *kāmil* meter (the advent of variable rhyme schemes, such as Sayyāb uses in his poem, made the imitation of a poem's rhyme less readable as a signal of *mu'āraḍa*).[59] There are also several poems in Buland al-Ḥaydarī's early collections that meet this criteria.[60]

On the surface, at least, the *mu'āraḍa* in Jawād's and Ḥaydarī's poems seem to be limited to contrafaction of the more formal features of "In the Ancient Market." This is not the case, however, with Bayyātī's poems, several of which engage directly the themes and worldview that Sayyāb presented in his poem.[61] Of these, the one that was probably most successful (both as *mu'āraḍa* and as an independent poem) in the estimation of the critics was "Sūq al-Qarya" (The Village Market), written sometime before November 1952.[62]

The title itself, incorporating as it does the word "market," already suggests that there may be something going on between these two poems. Bayyātī, by including the word in the title, is telling us that this particular place will be important in the poem, just as Sayyāb had done earlier with his own composition. But even though the place is the same, Bayyātī's title has shorn it of any privileged associations. Sayyāb's market was already in the title more than a simple commercial center because it was "ancient." This potential for valorization was then taken up and expanded upon in the first lines of "In the Ancient Market." Bayyātī's market, in contrast, is characterized solely by being in a village. While this does not automatically preclude its having a history, nor does it directly declare that it is impossible for it to be idealized, it does not proleptically suggest that this will happen, either. Especially for someone aware of the precedent of Sayyāb's poem, the title of Bayyātī's work would create suspense: is this poem linked to Sayyāb's, and, if so, how will this setting be tied to that in the precursor poem?

The suspense, on both counts, is quickly resolved by the structure and imagery used in the very first lines of "The Village Market":

> The sun, and the emaciated donkeys, and the flies
> And a soldier's ancient boots
> Passing from hand to hand . . .

Notably, the first word is a temporal reference, just like Sayyāb's "Night, and the ancient market . . ." Here, the word "sun," as Iḥsān 'Abbās has noted in his reading of this poem,[63] does more than just fix a neutral time. It plays a symbolic role as well: "The scene, therefore, is in the daylight, not at night, which weakens its romantic suggestiveness, because it is only weakly connected with dreams."[64] It is as though Bayyātī has chosen the time of day and symbolized it in an object, the sun, which provides the greatest possible contrast to the world of romanticism in general, and Sayyāb's poem in particular.

The next image, the emaciated donkeys, can be seen as further rejecting, by antithesis, the vision Sayyāb had tried to build at the beginning of his poem. In "In the Ancient Market," the speaker at first perceives a *general* picture: the market as a whole. Then, later, as he moves more deeply into that setting, details began to emerge: the cups, the handkerchiefs, and the candles, each described in sensuous detail. Bayyātī, on the other hand, once the time frame has been established, concentrates on the detail rather than the general totalizing picture. Thus the transforming power of imaginative vision, of the human mind sorting out and magisterially categorizing existence, is refused. In addition, donkeys (particularly emaciated ones) and flies cannot be poeticized. They function as markers of the collocational set whose marker is the characteristic <*—not ideal>, first and foremost. This is also true of the "soldier's ancient boots," an object that points even more openly to Sayyāb's poem by its use of the same adjective, "ancient, old (*qadīm*) that in the previous poem had such a powerful aesthetic freighting.

Returning to the flies, for a moment, we can also see them as being similarly overdetermined in their linkage to Sayyāb's poem. Syntactically, they occupy the same place (third in the series) as the "muttering of the passers-by" in the other poem. Flies, of course, make a sound, droning, not dissimilar to human "mutterings" and is often rendered onomatopoetically in Arabic (though *dandan* is more commonly used for this sound, rather than *ghamgham*). Yet, unlike the human "mutterings," the flies' droning has no meaning, no message. On the other hand, it is far more insistent (its presence is reinforced by the fact that presence of the flies is mentioned several times in the course of the poem) and may even interfere with (and possibly undercut the significance of) the human speech that coincides with it.

There is human speech aplenty in this market as well, again in contrast to Sayyāb's. Bayyātī begins with the words of the peasant who has been looking at the soldier's boots: "At the beginning of new year, / My hands will surely be full of coins, / And I will buy these boots." Here, the contrast may indeed be a simple one. In Sayyāb's poem we have visionary, poetic language; in Bayyātī's poem, quotidian everyday statement. But Bayyātī does not maintain so simple a relationship of antithesis or inversion as the poem progresses. Various types of more formal language also intrude. We have, for example, the "little saint," who speaks in proverbs: "None scratches your skin like your own nail," and "the road to Hell is closer than the path of Paradise." The special nature of proverbial language as both "poetic" and "cliché"—stereotyped meaning—is framed, in this case by animal sounds: it is preceded by "the cry of a cock escaped from its cage," and is followed by the ubiquitous "flies." Thus the problem of voice is doubly enhanced: what status do we grant to these snatches of noise/speech/cacophony/wisdom? The speaker reports them but he gives the reader no easy signposts for ranking them. We must grapple with the question of how we ourselves would classify them and also what the implications are of this reporting for our conception of the speaker. He may seem to be uninvolved (in the best modernist tradition) but he is, as 'Abbās notes, "at the same time selective." Even though the principle of selection may not be obvious, in the end the speaker cannot resist the lure of significance, of introducing "meaning" back into the observations. The last words he records are those of the village women, picking up their baskets of fruit as they leave the market:

> And the women selling grapes gather up their baskets:
> "The eyes of my beloved are twin stars
> And his breast is like springtime roses."

Like the words of the "little saint," these are undoubtedly a cliché—part of a popular poem or song. But they are idealizing, and in placing them as the last reported words in the poem, the speaker in a subtle sense acknowledges the nostalgic pull of that transcendent vision. Thus he is revealed as just as concerned with the uncertainties of the lyric voice as the speaker in Sayyāb's poem. The difference between them appears to be only one of degree, not of kind. The way in which the two speakers are interlinked is reinforced by the very last line of Bayyātī's poem, "And the yawning of the huts in the palm-grove." Iḥsān 'Abbās highlights this connection as part of his analysis : "And if the Stranger in Sayyāb's market spent a long stretch of his life "between stretching and yawning beneath the dappled shadows of the palm trees," to someone standing in Bayyātī's market the whole village appears to be "the yawning of huts in the palm-grove." For Bayyātī to conclude his poem on a line that so closely models a key line in Sayyāb's poem about the loss of the vision, even in an idealized countryside, would seem purposeless unless the two poems were meant to be engaging in some form of *mu'āraḍa*.

It is not difficult to imagine what Sayyāb's reaction must have been to reading Bayyātī's poem. It signaled, in one sense, that he had "arrived," that what he had written was important enough to attract contrafaction. But on the other hand, with his (relatively) detailed knowledge of Anglo-American modernism, Sayyāb would also have been sensitive to the same observation made by Iḥsān 'Abbās several decades later, after he had detailed the resemblances between Bayyātī's techniques and the modernists':

> Whatever the case may be, we see that Bayyātī—a few short years after Sayyāb and Nāzik had set out from the starting point—has commandeered the new poetic form for the benefit of different, outside influences, which go beyond creating a free space for romantic personal emotions, and he has given this new movement the ability to abandon the point of change from within the past, and he has given it the ability to embrace a new point of view—or rather, many new points of view. If Nāzik and Sayyāb participated in the exploration of a new form, then Bayyātī was the first of the innovators in changing the content of that form.[65]

Of course one may point out that by the time Bayyātī wrote his *mu'āraḍa*, Sayyāb's work had also changed dramatically in its concerns. Further, the two poems do represent a fundamental kinship in their theme and in the conclusions they reach. But, no matter how similar the underlying concern of the two poems with the problem of lyric presence and the challenge to the poet's voice, the realization that Bayyātī might have "done it better," in terms of adapting the characteristic style and idiolect of the movement (modernism) that had so influenced them both, must have left a taste of dust and ashes in Sayyāb's mouth. It certainly sounded the death knell for the old consensus of Arab romanticism about the innate homology between the voice of the (solipsistic) self and the voice of the other. Now this identification would become increasingly problematized, emerging as a site of contention and struggle that would occupy much of the energy of Arabic poetry in the next decade.

But the wider implications of Bayyātī's work, and its enabling potential, was almost certainly not apparent to Sayyāb in the late 1940s and early 1950s. Thus, it would be unwise to disregard the possibility that it was the personal aspect of this disabling realization that may have had as much to do with the next events that occur in Sayyāb's life as the political upheavals that swept through Iraq in the years 1949–52. As we shall see, in the next chapter, in all of 1949 and most of 1950 Sayyāb wrote nothing at all, and when he did return to poetry, probably in the latter half of 1950, his work radically shifts in its orientation and direction. Yet this shift, despite its difference from Sayyāb's previous project of creating a self capable of coping the stresses of decolonization, will perhaps have even more important resonances in the context of resistance to colonialist discourse. Sayyāb will, in those years, try to domesticate in Arabic poetry a form it had never before contained: the epic.

CHAPTER EIGHT

The Epic Turn

He rode, I keeping pace with him; and now
He, to my fancy, had become the knight
Whose tale Cervantes tells; yet not the knight,
But was an Arab of the desert too;
Of these was neither, and was both at once.
—Wordsworth, *The Prelude*

Sayyāb began his first teaching job in September of 1948 in the provincial town of Ramādī (this was probably where "In the Ancient Market" was composed). By early 1949, however, the government had grown concerned that there would be new demonstrations (and perhaps violent confrontations) with the Communists, so it began systematically to arrest anyone who had ties to the Party. This, of course, included Sayyāb. He was traced to his father's house in Jaykūr in January of 1949 (where he was spending his end of term vacation) and taken to a concentration camp near Baghdad, where he remained confined until April, when he was released with a large number of other prisoners.

His troubles, however, were far from over once he had been released. He returned to Jaykūr to find his uncle 'Abd al-Majīd sentenced to five years in prison for his activities as commissar *(mas'ūl)* of the Abū al-Khaṣīb chapter of the Party. Then, not long after his return, he was summoned back to Baghdad where he was sentenced by the martial law tribunal to post a bond of 5,000 dinars, with his father as guarantor.[1] Thus, Sayyāb was put on notice that he would continue to be under suspicion by the authorities and that any misstep could end up with his family suffering an enormous financial hardship, or perhaps worse. Nor could he easily find a job, since he could not any longer obtain the requisite certificate of good conduct needed for regular employment, especially in government jobs. This must have strained what were already not very close relations between father and son and could not have made life for Sayyāb in Jaykūr very pleasant.

During the summer months, Sayyāb occasionally found temporary work sampling and inspecting dates in the processing factories in and near Basra. He also seems to have tempted fate by agreeing to become acting commissar for the Party in Abū al-Khaṣīb. The responsibility for keeping the Party organization together immediately after ʻAbd al-Majīd al-Sayyāb's arrest fell on Badr's younger brother Muṣṭafā. But Muṣṭafā was still attending high school in Basra, so he asked his brother to watch over things during the week, while he was away.[2] In a series of newspaper articles written many years later, after he had renounced Communism, Sayyāb recounted how, during this summer, he kept the peasants from deserting the Party by drawing maps showing exactly how the palm groves in the area would be redistributed to them. He also helped at least one member of the Party's Central Committee to try to escape. But the man was caught, confessed, and implicated—not Badr—but Muṣṭafā Sayyāb, who was promptly arrested. After this, the Party's choice for commissar fell on a certain ʻAbd al-Laṭīf Nāṣir, who was on bad terms with the Sayyāb family, thus leaving Badr out in the cold.[3]

About this time, however, Badr was finally successful in getting a regular job. He was hired as a clerk in the offices of Basra Oil. Here, he again became involved in Party activities, especially in the support of a workers' strike against the company. He continued to work at Basra Oil, though, through the remainder of 1949 and on into the spring of 1950. Then, for reasons that remain unexplained,[4] he left this position and returned to Baghdad, once again unemployed except for various temporary jobs, this time mostly for newspapers that needed material translated from English into Arabic. Al-Jawāhirī, in particular, appears to have thrown work his way. This was the continuation of an association that had begun during the Wathba, when al-Jawāhirī published a number of Sayyāb's political poems. Al-Jawāhirī himself, however, was frequently in trouble with the authorities (though his fame and ability to mobilize the masses with his poetry seems to have given him some immunity from personal persecution) and his newspapers were frequently shut down and his license to publish suspended. Finally, through the help of old school friends, Sayyāb was able to obtain a clerk's job in the government's Import Finance Department, which gave him a regular, though minuscule, salary. He continued, however, to work for newspapers.[5]

Sayyāb did not abandon his political involvements when he moved to Baghdad. If anything, his Party activities intensified. Many friends who shared his literary interests were also tied to the Communist Party, especially the members of a group of fellow Basrans, the "Friends of Contemporary Art" (*Usrat al-Fann al-Mu'āṣir*), whose meetings Sayyāb attended regularly. It was from the activities of this group, for example, that Sayyāb became interested in "Les Yeux d'Elsa" (The Eyes of Elsa), a poem by the French author Louis Aragon, which he translated into Arabic from an English translation.[6] Sayyāb also became involved, sometime during 1950–51, with a Communist-linked organization called the Peace Partisans (*Anṣār al-Salām*) . This was one of the major political focal groups around which antigovernment forces began to regroup in the months following the crackdowns of 1949.[7] It was part of the "Ban the Bomb" movement that the Soviet government had begun to promote worldwide in March 1950. Its ostensible *raison d'être* was the furtherance of peace and especially the support of efforts to control nuclear proliferation. Sayyāb's interest in this issue was genuine; he continued to thematize the issue in his poetry and other writings long after he broke his ties to Communism. Many of his poems of the 1950s would portray the horrors of atomic warfare, particularly the "Fukai" poems of 1955, and his interest in the English poet Edith Sitwell may have been initially stimulated by her *Three Poems of the Atomic Age*, which he eventually translated into Arabic and published in 1960.[8] But in 1950–51 his interest in the subject and his allegiance to the Communists coincided in his involvement with the Peace Partisans. It was for them that he wrote, or at least consented to publish,[9] his first serious work since the poems of *Asāṭīr* (Myths).[10] This was the poem that eventually was published under the title "Fajr al-Salām" (Dawn of Peace), a lengthy work that opens by depicting the evils of arms merchants who cause wars in search of profits.[11] This evil is (temporarily) counteracted by the "people" who, through a powerful counter-vision of timeless harmony and peace, are able to will the world of war into nonexistence:

33) There peace gently falls downward, covers all, like a sleeping child's eyelashes
34) Its laughter will fill the fields, and its songs of love,
35) It will throb [like a heartbeat] where the factories wound the heart of darkness,
36) And in the sunstruck cities, it will steal [its way], amidst the crowds,

37) And where the eyes of humankind, staring, meet in harmony and concord,
38) In spite of blazing fire and iron, a flower of peace will have grown![12]

The bulk of the poem deals with the speaker's attempts to communicate this vision of peace to the others around him. In the end he is able to achieve a provisional direct involvement of the audience in his/their vision, which then makes it possible for him to present the final destruction of the tyrants and their henchmen, the arms merchants, at the poem's conclusion.

Among Sayyāb's biographers, there has been a tendency to place special emphasis on this poem, coming as it does after over a year of silence. Iḥsān 'Abbās in particular has stressed the importance of "The Dawn of Peace" as a new departure, the unprecedented appearance of a more politically "committed" kind of poetry in Sayyāb's work. He emphasizes its innovation in content, not form, and contrasts this with the poems published in the collection *Asāṭīr* (Myths), which he says represent just the opposite.[13] This would be a viable assessment, if all we had from Sayyāb's earlier work was *Asāṭīr* and the love poetry from *Azhār Dhābila* (Withered Flowers).[14]

But since his earliest years, Sayyāb had actually been writing, alongside his love poetry, more socially oriented poetry in the neoclassic style known as "poetry of occasion" (works whose composition was tied to specific events, or "occasions"). We have one such poem from as early as 1941, as well as his statement that among the first things he composed in primary school was a political poem. He does not seem to have been as interested in this political poetry as he was in his love poetry during the years 1941–48. He bothered to preserve and publish in his collections only a small smattering of what he must have composed in this vein during the 1940s. It was only by accident, and as a result of specific requests from a friend of his in Basra, that we have a fairly large sampling of the political poetry he wrote in the years 1946–48, which gives us a better idea of just what a significant proportion of his total work this poetry constituted.[15] Even more importantly, a careful perusal of the poetry of occasion from that period suggests that there was not a decisive break in content between it and "The Dawn of Peace."

What differentiates the period 1950–51 from earlier years is that now Sayyāb seems to have entirely stopped writing poetry using the thematics of love to model a pattern for the dynamic interaction of self and other. Overtly political poetry—which he had seen as a lesser poetry, not really worth preserving—now becomes his major focus of interest. While this could probably be seen as simply the most important effect his increasing involvement in Communist political action has on his literary life, the real trajectory of events seems to have been considerably more complex. He indicates himself that he became interested in finding new ways of expressing the relationship between political life and literature as early as 1945, when he says that he read a book in English called *Marxism and Art* (*Al-Mārksiyya wa-al-Fann*),[16] but clearly he did not see ideas like commitment, socialist realism, and proletariat art, which stressed the abandonment of "bourgeoisie" subject matter (like love poetry), as relevant to possible contradictions in his own work or that of his romantic predecessors. He continues, alongside poetry that is overtly political, to write works influenced by "bourgeois" ideals taken from English romanticism and, even worse from a Party perspective, "reactionary" modernist poets like T.S. Eliot.[17] It is only in 1951 that Sayyāb suddenly changes his practice of "separate but equal," and denounces what he calls "subjective (*dhātī*) poetry" to his friend Maḥmūd al-'Abṭa:

> The greatest danger we must fight against are those who broadcast degenerate ideas and try to dupe the masses into believing that there is no use in opposing them, because life is a trifling thing which does not deserve all this concern and that misery is the fate of mankind. . . . [If we] look at the matter carefully, we will find that those who say: 'When will we free ourselves from the colonial powers?' are parallel in their artistry to those who say: 'When will I see my beloved?' In addition, the former are more noble in their feelings and have a wider perspective.[18]

Here, we see an implicit condemnation of his former work that would have been inconceivable as late as the end of 1948.

Nevertheless, Sayyāb in 1950 does not seem to have found continuation of the patterns set in his earlier political poetry—which is what we find in "Fajr al-Salām" (Dawn of Peace)—satisfactory either. His next poetic project would be the unfinished Miltonic poem now called "Al-La'anāt" (Curses),[19] which embarks on a more ambitious undertaking—the domestication of epic into his repertoire of poetic forms.

In one sense, it is not surprising to find Sayyāb developing an interest in the topic of epic poetry during a time when his interest in developing strategies for resistance to colonialism and class exploitation (phenomena that were clearly linked in his mind) were growing. A number of recent studies have shown that European epic poems, especially in the nineteenth century, became primary tools both in the nationalist project of constructing "identities" for the various "peoples" of Europe and in the institutionalization of interpretative patterns for the Renaissance voyages of discovery as the heroically authorizing precursors of mercantile colonialism.[20] To this end, numerous postclassical epics in the vernacular languages of Europe were "discovered"—and where they could not be discovered were "reconstructed," with various amounts of added conjecture and even wholesale imaginative invention (as was the case with the "scandal" of James Macpherson's forgery of the Ossian poems—purported to be a "Celtic" national epic whose discovery placed the Scots and the Irish on an equal footing, culturally, with the ancient Greeks—in the late 1700s).[21]

Sayyāb, as a student in what was at least partially a colonially constructed educational system, would read or at least be made aware of many of these epic poems, and no doubt found himself being subtly indoctrinated with the ideological messages they bore. The European poets he had read in school—as 'Abbās notes[22]—were mostly poets, then, who had produced works that had come into being in a literary world that valorized epic conventions above all others. But many of them were, as well—especially at the Teachers College—poets who were influenced, to a greater or lesser degree, by the idea that epic was a problematic form for post-Enlightenment writers. Goethe, as can be seen in his *Faust*, was probably the last European poet for whom the notion of an epic in the traditional sense was still possible. The English romantic poets were very much concerned with "intensity" as a criterion for art and believed that no epic poem (by virtue of the attenuations introduced by its length if nothing else) could sustain the intensity needed for great art. Nevertheless, they all did attempt works that paid homage to the epic tradition, but these attempts—as numerous critical works have pointed out[23]—remained, either deliberately or not, incomplete. Wordsworth's *Prelude*, for instance, is a poem whose length and allusional structure invoke the epic tradition, particularly Milton's *Paradise Lost*,[24] though its very title signals its wish to refuse—or at least demonstrates its ambivalence about—the label "epic." It announces its aspiration to be the prologmena to an epic but not to be an epic itself. Shelley's *Triumph of Life*, cut short by the author's premature death by drowning, appropriately ends with a question mark, thus neatly, if perhaps inadvertently, foregrounding the problem of epic claims to omniscience and objectivity as generic requirements. Keats begins his epic poem *Hyperion* late in his short life in conscious imitation of Milton's *Paradise Lost*—considered by his generation the last successful epic poem in English[25]—but soon finds himself hopelessly blocked. Writing to a friend, he says: "I have given up on *Hyperion*—there were too many Miltonic inversions in it—Miltonic verse cannot be written but in an artful or rather artist's humor. I wish to give myself up to other sensations."[26] His reference to the "artfulness" of Miltonic verse is not so much an admission of his inability to reach the standard set by Milton as it is a frustration with the sense of *artificiality* the writing of such verse evokes for the romantic poet. Even though Keats later returned to the poem, framing his earlier fragment within a dream-vision modeled this time on Dante, he was equally unsuccessful in completing it. Less than two years later, he died. We have already seen how important all these poets were for Sayyāb in his own affiliative genealogy.

In the Western tradition it was left to Edgar Allan Poe, the American romantic poet and author, to turn this inability to sustain the epic mode into a positive celebration of the lyric as form:

> I need scarcely observe that a poem deserves its title only inasmuch as it excites, by elevating the soul. The value of the poem is in the ratio of this elevating excitement. But all excitements are, through psychal necessity, transient. That degree of excitement which would entitle a poem to be so called, at all, cannot be sustained throughout a composition of any great length.
>
> There are, no doubt, many who have found difficulty in reconciling the critical dictum that the "Paradise Lost" is to be devoutly admired throughout, with the absolute impossibility of maintaining for it, during perusal, the amount of enthusiasm which that critical dictum would demand. This great work, in fact is to be regarded as poetical, only when, losing sight of that vital requisite in all works of Art, Unity, we view it merely as a series of minor poems. . . .
>
> In regard to the Iliad, we have, if not positive proof, at least very good reason, for believing it was intended as a series of lyrics; but, granting the epic intention, I can say only that the work is based in an imperfect sense of art. The modern epic is, of the suppositious ancient model, but an inconsiderate and blindfold imitation. But the day of these artistic anomalies is over. If, at any time, any very long poem *were* popular in reality, which I doubt, it is at least clear that no very long poem will ever be popular again.[27]

Interestingly, a less extreme form of Poe's statement, asserting that European epic can be profitably viewed as incorporating a series of "moments" comprising a variety of genres, can be found in one of the earliest Arabic literary critical statements on the subject, the introduction to Sulaymān Bustānī's 1904 translation of *The Iliad*.[28]

Poe, it will be noted, extends his condemnation from epic as such to any long poem. Not just one genre of lengthy (and usually narrative) poetry is condemned, but all "long" poems are tarred with the same brush. Poe's statement is particularly significant because in this regard, as in many others, he had a profound effect on the critical theories of Baudelaire and the French Symbolists,[29] who then passed their distrust of epic on to their spiritual heirs, the Anglo-American modernists, who found themselves caught up in much the same dialectic as their romantic predecessors, rejecting and emulating epic paradigms at the same time. *The Waste Land* itself is perhaps the foremost example of this. Their struggles in this regard have in recent years been more clearly recognized by literary critics and thus a new generic category has been called into being: the "long poem," taken to include such landmarks as Ezra Pound's *Cantos*, William Carlos Williams's *Paterson*, and Hart Crane's *The Bridge*, alongside the ubiquitous *Waste Land*.[30] The "long poem," then, was a form Sayyāb could have had some acquaintance with from his reading in Eliot, even if he was not familiar with the critical discourse about the epic that had constituted it in the first place.

If all these post-Enlightenment figures in the West share in a broad sense the anxiety of belatedness, of never being able to measure up to the models that came before, this concern was redoubled for a modern Arab poet like Sayyāb. Not only would he have been familiar with the anxieties of English romantics and modernists, through reading their works, but he also had to contend with the particular sets of even more disabling uncertainties involving literature as a tool of identity formation that powerfully afflicted modern Arab poets with regard to epic models.

First, he would have been aware of a need to confront indictments made by Western Orientalists who, more or less subtly, had used the observation that classical Arabic poetry never developed an epic form in the sense codified in a variety of Western literatures (drawing upon the classical paradigms of *The Iliad, The Odyssey* and *The Aeneid*) as a device to downgrade the achievements of Arabic and even call its status as a major world literature into question.[31] What made the strategy of direct disavowals of such charges difficult was the fact that, even though examples of narrative episodes can be found throughout Arabic poetry,[32] narrative does not seem to have been a form particularly valued in the classical canon.[33] Indeed, the *refusal* to narrate (in the sense of recounting an incident from an externally focalized point of view) often appears to have been a deliberately chosen strategy of composition in fictional, as opposed to "truthful" (historical and biographical writings, for example) works written in Arabic during the time of its classical florescence. Perhaps the most illuminating example of this occurs in the Dārat Juljul episode in the *mu'allaqa* of the pre-Islamic poet Imru' al-Qays:

10) Truly there many days for you among them, right good and especially a day at Dārat Juljul,
11) And a day when I slaughtered my riding camel for the virgins
O the wonder of its riding saddle divided into several loads!
12) And the virgins kept on throwing its meat about, and its fat, like fringes of twisted silk.
13) And a day when I entered the camel litter, the camel litter of 'Unayza, and she said: "Woe to you, that you will make me go on foot!"
15) She said, as the camel saddle tilted to the side with both of us together: "You have wounded[34] my camel, Imru' al-Qais; now get down!"
16) I said to her: "Keep going, loosen his reins, and do not keep me far from your twice-tasted fruit.[35]

This passage contains three separate episodes, the last two of which are recognizable narrative segments. First the poet recalls an idyllic past, which he links especially with a place—the pool known as Dārat Juljul. Then he recalls an incident when he slaughtered his riding camel to provide food for some young women, who, when they were preparing the meat for cooking, tossed the bits of the camel's flesh to one another. The poet then compares the bits of fat on the meat to twisted fringes of silk, a comparison that creates an unstable bridge between "natural" and "cultural" objects, an opposition very characteristic of pre-Islamic poetry. Subsequently, in the third segment, he describes a conversation between him and someone named 'Unayza, in a howda. She tries to get him to leave, and he makes sexual advances toward her. The connection between the first line, the identification of a specific place, Dārat Juljul, and the two narratives is made only by the paratactic phrase, "and a day when . . ." Thus, the linkage between all three segments is left ambiguous. They could be connected, but they could equally well have nothing to do with one another.

It is only when we read the commentary that we are told the details that would allow us to reconstruct these lines as a connected narrative sequence:

> Imru' al-Qays was in love with a paternal cousin of his who was called 'Unayza, but he was thwarted in his attempts to obtain a moment alone with her, away from her family's watchful eyes. Until the Day of the Pool, the day of Dārat Juljul, arrived. The tribe packed up their belongings and set out, with the men in front and the women following after, together with the luggage and the slaves. When Imru' al-Qays saw this, he set out after his people, a bow's length behind them. Then he hid himself in a low-lying place until the women went by. And among the young girls was 'Unayza. These turned aside,

> heading to the pool. They dismounted from their camels, dismissed the slaves and entered the pool. Then Imru' al-Qays came up without arousing their suspicions and took their clothes, making a pile of them, upon which he sat down. Then he said: "By God, I will not give one of you girls her clothes, even though she remains in the pool until nighttime, unless she comes out as she is, naked, and takes the clothes for herself." For a long time they refused, but were at last compelled to do so, the last to leave the water being 'Unayza. The women then reproached him for his behaviour, and complained of hunger on account of their long fast. He, therefore, killed his riding camel, which they cooked and ate. Having, therefore, no mount of his own to ride on his way back to the encampment of the tribe, the saddle and other equipment of his camel were divided by the women among themselves for carrying in parts on their camels, he himself falling to the lot of 'Unayza, with whom he insisted on riding on her camel.[36]

Once we are given a narrative to place behind the episodes actually present in the text, then it is a fairly easy job to read these lines as being connected. But these connections are extra-poetic. They are not part of the poem itself. Although the commentary is medieval, it is not coterminous with the poem itself, it is something that was brought to poem from outside.[37] That Imru al-Qays's *mu'allaqa* is conventionally considered to be the oldest Arabic poem to be preserved from the pre-Islamic period lends special force to it as a paradigmatic model of the refusal to narrate.

Examples of commentary being used to "create" narrative is frequent following the pre-Islamic period as well: another good instance is the story of Layla and Majnūn as told in the anthology known as *Kitāb al-Aghānī* (Book of Songs), where the poems are embedded in a (prose) narrative intended to tie them together chronologically. An even more telling signal of a basic reluctance to narrate can be found in the Koran. There are several instances where the Koran seems almost to apologize for introducing a narrative, as in 2:26: "God is not loath to advance the similitude of a gnat or a something above that; as for those who believe, they will know that it is the truth." This verse introduces a distinction between true stories (the kind told by the Koran) and fiction, which becomes culturally relevant. What justifies the act of narration, above all, is for the material thus presented to be *true*. Thus, at the end of the most "narrative" sūra, the story of Joseph, we find: "this is not a fictitious tale, but a verification (*taṣdīq*)[38] of that which is before him, and a detailed exposition of everything, and a guidance and mercy to a people who believe" (12:111). The Koranic discourse about stories thus appears reactive, geared to defending Muḥammad from an accusation of "making up" stories: the act of storytelling must be justified by some overriding imperative and the justification for telling stories is based primarily on their truth content. Thus, fictional narrative is seen to occupy a very lowly generic space indeed (though it should be noted that this is something that appears to exist before the Koranic event, rather than occurring as a consequence of it; in fact the Koran could be seen as giving a limited valorization to narrative—provided it was truthful—that it may not have possessed prior to this).

As I briefly mentioned earlier, when Orientalists began to study medieval Arabic writings in the nineteenth century, this seeming lack of narrative, and more particularly narrative as manifested in epic, was seized upon as evidence of an inferiority in Arabic literature. None was worse in this respect than Ernest Renan, whose frequent pronouncements on this lack were always generalized into a judgment of absolute inferiority for the "Semites" (comprising both Arabs and Jews) vis-à-vis the more creative "Indo-Europeans":

> Ainsi la race sémitique se reconnaît presque uniquement à des caractères négatifs: elle n'a ni mythologie, ni *épopée*, ni science, ni philosophie, ni *fiction*, ni arts plastiques, ni vie civile; en tout absence de complexité, de nuances, sentiment exclusif de l'unité. Il n'y pas de variété dans le monothéisme.[39]

One can see here quite clearly the Orientalist propensity, as described by Edward Said, to generalize from a specific *nonoccurrence* (lack of narrative and epic, listed among other qualities) to a global *deficiency* ("an absence of complexity and nuance") in the culture under examination. Since Renan had a prestigious academic position in the West (already the site of tremendous authority because of its technological dominance), his statements could not be dismissed out of hand as those of a marginalized figure. Instead, numerous efforts were mounted by Arab intellectuals in the late nineteenth and early twentieth centuries to (1) naturalize the epic genre (or at least narrative) within Arabic poetry and (2) to explain why it had not appeared previously[40]—and this would form the intellectual backdrop against which Sayyāb's generation would find themselves enacting their own responses to this "problem" of the presence/absence of epic as index of (national) identity.

The first conscious attempts to "make epic possible" in Arabic poetry can be traced back at least to the last decades of the nineteenth century. In 1894, the neoclassic poet Aḥmad Shawqī was sent by the Khedive 'Abbās to represent Egypt at the International Congress of Orientalists in Geneva. At this congress, he publicly recited a poem, "Great Historical Events of the Nile Valley," which, among other things, was apparently intended to show to an audience of skeptics that narrative—if not epic—poetry was assimilable into Arabic verse. The Orientalists, however, appear to have been unimpressed, and Shawqī's attempt was regarded as a failure.[41] At virtually the same time, Sulaymān al-Bustānī, of the famous Lebanese literary family, was translating *The Iliad* into Arabic verse. This translation, published in Cairo in 1904, contained an important introduction that attempted a critical assessment of Arabic poetry as well as an overview of the nature of epic verse. It had an important impact on subsequent attempts to naturalize the epic, particularly in the case of Bustānī's fellow-countryman, Khalīl Muṭrān, who became known as the father of narrative poetry in Arabic. Muṭrān followed Bustānī's lead in asserting that the only thing that had prevented the emergence of epic in Arabic were the restrictions placed on the poem's rhythmic form, in particular the requirement of monorhyme.[42] About a decade after the publication of Bustānī's translation of *The Iliad*, Muṭrān recited before an audience of intellectuals at the American University in Beirut his most famous poem, *Nayrūn* (*Nero*) in which he tried to show the poverty of the classical monorhyme as a mold for epic style in practice, through the composition of a 327-line *qaṣīda* rhyming in the letter *rā'* about the tyrannical Roman emperor, by the end of which the rhyme words became more and more incomprehensible or outlandish, provoking his audience to gales of laughter. After Muṭrān's *tour-de-force*, it was clear that the traditional *qaṣīda* form would never be acceptable for the composition of either narrative or epic poetry of any length.[43]

Experimentation in writing various kinds of narrative poetry continued during the interwar years. The Apollo group was particularly prolific in this regard. Aḥmad Zākī Abū Shādī, the leader of the group, saw himself as a disciple of Muṭrān, and consciously set out to heed his call for a change in the structure of the *qaṣīda*, to make it capable of absorbing lengthy compositions.[44] He varied the rhyme schemes, and in some of his later poems experimented with combining different kinds of meters in one composition. However, the reaction of critics and audiences to these initiatives was lukewarm.[45] Nor did the narrative or dramatic poems by any other members of the Apollo group, including those of Ibrāhīm Nājī and 'Alī Maḥmūd Ṭaha—poets who were so influential on Sayyāb in his early years—have significantly more success. Yet it is important to note that

Ṭaha's closet drama, *Arwāḥ wa-Ashbāḥ* (Spirits and Ghosts), would inspire Sayyāb to imitate it quite closely in 1944–45, with his poem *Bayna al-Rūḥ wa-al-Jasad* (Between Soul and Body).[46] But Sayyāb seems to have been one of the few who found this poem by Ṭaha impressive.[47] It, like many other attempts at writing narrative verse in the 1930s and 1940s (too numerous to detail here), seems to have surfaced briefly and all too quickly sunk without a trace. By 1950 it must have begun to appear, to the younger generation of poets especially, that narrative poetry—much less epic—would never become a viable part of Arabic literature.

In this context, it would seem logical that Sayyāb's discovery of a new kind of metrical pattern, one that was far more elastic than previous models, would have immediately inspired him to see whether or not it could be adapted to lengthy, narrative poems—and perhaps even to epic. In fact, we do see in his 1948 poems a few tentative steps in this direction. It is surprising, then, to find him writing both "Fajr al-Salām" and its even more epiclike companion "Al-La'anāt" in traditional meters. It would only be with "Ḥuffār al-Qubūr" (The Gravedigger—1951) that he finally married free verse with narrative and produced a truly innovative work in the epic/narrative vein.[48] It was almost as though he had to put himself once more through a period of apprenticeship, working on the techniques of writing long poems before he could commit himself to taking the final step. We know that at this time he confided to at least one of his friends an interest in "long poems"; that this interest had been kindled by his reading in Western poetry, and that he felt that "the long poem was the most appropriate form to express the complex nature of contemporary life, full of struggle."[49] "Al-La'anāt" shows that his enthusiasm, at least for a brief period, focused specifically on the epic form based on traditional European conventions, as opposed to any other kind of "long poem."

Perhaps of even more interest, given the colonial/national valencing of the epic paradigm, is the fact that both "Al-La'anāt" and the later "Ḥuffār al-Qubūr"—with such different bases of formal patterning—only deal indirectly and symbolically with the discursive violence implicit in the imposition and maintenance of colonial rule. The same stricture would not apply to his next experiment in this style, the nearly 500-line poem eventually entitled "Al-Mūmis al-'Amyā'" (The Blind Whore).

This poem tells the story of Salīma, a woman who works as a prostitute in the enclosed and restricted red-light district of postwar Baghdad.[50] The introductory lines of the poem, particularly by their persistent recourse to allusions from Greek mythology, signal a desire to evoke epic associations in their setting of the scene:

1) Night closes in once more, then the city and the passers-by
2) Drink it down to the dregs, like a sad song.
3) The street lamps, like oleanders, have blossomed,
4) Like the eyes of Medusa[51] malevolently turning every heart to stone,
5) Like the omens that foretold fire to the inhabitants of Babylon.
6) From what forests did this night come? From what caves?
7) From what wolf's den?
8) From what nest among the graves did it rise, flapping its wings, dark brown like a crow?
9) Cain![52] Hide the telltale blood with flowers and transparent fabrics,
10) With perfume if you like, or women's smiles.
11) From the shops and the cafés, pulsing with light,
12) [Comes] a blind woman, like a bat at the height of day: this is the city,
13) And night has made her more blind.
14) And the passers-by:
15) Ribs curving around fears and doubts,
16) Tired eyes searching for a dream in other eyes,
17) Counting bottles glittering in the taverns,
18) Dead men, afraid of the resurrection.
19) They say: "We will run away," but they take refuge in graves from the graves.
20) Who are these passers-by?
21) The grandsons of Oedipus[53] the Blind and his sighted heirs.
22) Jocaste is a widow as before, and on the gate of Thebes
23) Still the terrible Sphinx casts shadows of fear.
24) And death pants in an eternal
25) Question, the same as before, but its ancient meaning has died—
26) Because the answer rotted too long on those lips. And what is the answer?
27) "I" said some of the passers-by.[54]

Although the wraith-haunted atmospherics of the initial description would seem to owe a great deal to the example of Goethe's *Faust*,[55] they also strategically deploy two important sets of allusions to the world of Greek myth: to the legend of Medusa, whose gaze turned men to stone, and to the story of Oedipus, the Theban king who killed his father and married his mother. Certainly, one could see these two story-sets gaining as much evocative power from the fact that they are not linked to the major topoi found in the classical epics as for any positive discursive patterning they might possess. They represent instead the "other" genres of classical literature: in the case of "Oedipus," the drama, and in the case of Medusa, myth itself. One might see them, then, as possessing the potential for a kind of oppositional counter-discourse to the ratification of epic values. What the two stories would seem to most economically project as they occur here is a kind of critique of epic temporality. If, as David Quint argues, *The Iliad*, *The Aeneid* and their Renaissance progeny like Tasso's *Gerusalemme liberata* and Camões *Lusíades* perpetuate a teleological temporal vision of imperial destiny fulfilled, one that gains part of its power through repetition in epic after epic,[56] what the speaker seems to be doing in Sayyāb's poem is to argue quite the opposite: that to impose the Greco-Latin paradigms of experience on the modern world is to condemn it sterile reenactments of ancient crimes.

Nor do the biblical myths fare any better in the poem as experiential models. Parallel to the classical framing, we are confronted with two major referential frames employing biblical allusion in this section: one to Babylon and its prophesied destruction in the Book of Revelation, and the other to the story of Cain, who kills his brother Abel in a fit of anger after God refuses his sacrifice, preferring instead his brother's offering. In both cases, the same cyclical temporality of repeated sins as was posited with the Medusa and Oedipus allusions is emphasized. Furthermore, to this temporal grounding is added the observation that the men in the city streets are "Dead men, / Afraid of the resurrection." Clearly, these are not individuals who would welcome a visitation of the purifying fires of apocalypse. And, like Oedipus, Cain emphasizes an unnatural family relationship—clearly pointing in a colonial context to the "unnatural" hatred of the Western colonizer for his fathers/brethren among the Arabs (as well as, of course, other colonized groups), whose genealogical filiations with his own culture he would often violently deny, as we saw in the case of Renan.

As if to ratify this connection of his own narrative to the critique of the entire gamut of Western epic values, Sayyāb will end the next section of "The Blind Whore" with an extended set of allusions to a work that defines in a certain sense the terminus (as Homer and the Greeks define the origin) of the history of unproblematized valorization of epic paradigms in the European tradition: Goethe's *Faust*. Before this, though, Sayyāb describes more specifically the prostitutes who inhabit the grim landscape of his Baghdad/Babylon. He emphasizes, through a series of binary oppositions, which compare them to inhabitants of the "natural" world (butterflies, birds, flowers), the contrast between their innocent past and their degraded present. This culminates in a vision of Eden as the time/place where the exploitation of women in the service of male desire is authorized, through a seemingly incontrovertible mythic/historic precedent, so that each of these females is figured as:

61) . . . a virgin apple, [who] would with the years entwine
62) Like twin snakes the loins of a thousand weary men
63) Who have left, as Adam did, a bliss in the fields.[57]

This use of Eden as the means to identify male desire with the agent of female destruction, evokes as well the conventional association between women and land in Arabic literature. The connection will be made explicit in lines 158-169 of the poem, where Salīma reminisces about how she and her next-door neighbor, Yasmīn, became prostitutes:

158) It was decreed that she should live by means of her honor (*'irḍ*), like
159) So many others of these unfortunates. And the Lord of the two worlds desired
160) That no one else—among thousands of others—should be her father,
161) And He fated him to be hungry
162) While the grain was ripening in the fields, from morning to night,
163) And that he should steal, then that they should kill him (and she raises her face to the heavens,
164) Like a petitioner, as she weeps in the darkness without tears).
165) And God, the Almighty, desired
166) That distant cities and seas hurl into Iraq
167) Thousands upon thousands of soldiers, so that they could violate, in an alley, out of all other alleys,
168) And out of all other maidens, the bread vendor's daughter,
169) This wretched girl, Yasmīn.[58]

Here we find an implicit reference to the traditional linkage between the word *'irḍ*, standing for a woman's sexual honor, and its near-homonym, *arḍ*, meaning "land." The two are mediated here by the military power of colonialism. Salīma depicts herself as relying on the exchange value of her body, her *'irḍ*, for food in the opening lines of this passage. This then leads her to equate her fate with that of her neighbor, Yasmīn, who lost her *'irḍ* when the occupying (British) soldiers dispossessed her and her people of their *arḍ*, the land of Iraq.

This development, however, is anticipated by the "Faust section" at the opening of the poem, which also continues the theme of a more generalized male exploitation of the female:

76) The Faust[59] within their (fem.) depths brings back a sad song.
77) Money, the devil of the city, is Faust's new lord:
78) He has so many servants that the cost has come down—
79) Bread and rags are the portion meted out
80) For his cringing servants, not pearls and youth,
81) And the crooked whore, not Helen,[60] and cursed thirst,
82) Not the knowledge of winged joy, of sin, of punishment—
83) The horses neigh restively, beating the paving stones
84) With their hooves.[61] Come here! the cabman is looking for a fare,
85) And the wind is a screech, and the whore has been without a customer a long time since.
86) If you won't take her to bed—everyone else has turned away from her—
87) How will she live? Like you, she cannot survive without food
88) Do not worry that she might be frightened by the leprosy
89) Eating up your broad, rotten chest. And you, her brother,
90) What do you want? What are you searching for, among the faces? And you, her father,
91) Stab the air with your dagger—the two of you will never kill her.
92) She will never die:
93) Her abductor will keep on chasing her, and the houses will cast her forth.
94) She will keep on—as long as the arrows of gold whistle through the air—
95) Running, with Apollo[62] following her again, like fate,
96) And she will keep on whispering as his hands are about to seize her:
97) "Father . . . help me!" But you will not listen to her cries.
98) If you were [just] the blood and sweat to spray upon her forehead
99) And change her into a real woman, not a commodity for sale,
100) [Then] you would have crowned her brow with glory and heroic deeds.[63]

Here, at the beginning of the poem, both the narrator's normative voice and Salīma's seem to speak as one, concurring that she is the martyred victim of male lust, passively enmeshed in a situation not of her own making. But the allusion to *Faust*, and in particular its episode of Margarete, who is seduced and abandoned by Faust at the behest of Mephistopheles, has a greater proleptic significance for the course of "Al-Mūmis al-'Amyā'" than might at first be apparent. In modern Arabic poetry of the 1950s, Faust seems to have assumed the status of a figure emblematic of the restless, questing spirit of the West, spellbound by its own technological achievements, seeking its own epistemological empowerment with little thought for those who might have to be sacrificed along the way.[64] In Goethe's play, Faust discovers through a vision that Margarete, his seduced and abandoned lover, is in prison, condemned to die, and he resolves to rescue her. He forces the reluctant Mephistopheles to transport him to her cell. But when he enters, he finds his former love has gone mad and he cannot convince her to leave with him. In a confused, barely coherent monologue, Margarete inadvertently betrays the cause of her imprisonment—and perhaps her madness as well. She has drowned the illegitimate child that resulted from their lovemaking. The fact that she has revealed herself as an unnatural mother and a murderer must to a certain extent undermine her claim to be an innocent victim, lacking in responsibility for her plight.

This is the crucial plot element that Sayyāb will reenact at the end of "The Blind Whore," when Salīma is shown to have allowed her daughter—ironically named "Amal" (Hope)—to die through neglect. Thus, by strategically using a plot motif from Goethe's masterwork, a work that, even though it is officially a drama, is saturated with potent echoes of epic conventions, Sayyāb widens his scope to narrate a condemnation of not only early examples of Western epic, but the entire spectrum of that tradition. Yet this revelation about Salīma, however much it may advertise the fissures in epic claims to provide providentially valuable patterns to its practitioners through its tradition of thematic repetition, also makes the reader question the adequacy of Salīma's interpretation of the world she lives in, with its simple binary oppositions of good and evil. In this, Sayyāb would seem also to be questioning the validity of earlier narrative poems constructed by Arab poets of the neoclassical period, at a time when the overriding goal was to create a consensually acceptable portrait of an unproblematically unified Arab self that could withstand the assaults, both overt and covert, of colonial discourse. Many of the best known of these poems, like Khalīl Muṭrān's "Fatāt al-Jabal al-Aswad" (The Maid of Montenegro) or Ma'rūf al-Ruṣāfī's "Umm al-Yatīm" (The Orphan's Mother), had given voice to this image of a cohesive self through the discourse of a woman depicted as having heroic stature. So, for Sayyāb to present his readers with a decidedly unheroic, inconstant Salīma was to challenge not only the power of the colonizer's epic paradigms, but in another way to challenge earlier versions of "the nation" within his own literary tradition.

To effect his challenge to past versions of reality Sayyāb deployed an array of new and experimental techniques unprecedented in the history of Arabic narrative poetry, which had tended to rely on straightforward retailing in the third person of the events that were the subject of the poem as they had happened, coupled with direct verbalized speeches by the characters, to construct its narrative trajectories. In contrast to these earlier conventions, Sayyāb would use in "The Blind Whore" two radically different techniques: the reordering of the story line, or fable (resulting in a heightened degree of focalization and an intensification of the suspense), through devices such as flashback and proleptic anticipation, and a resort to the narrative representation of consciousness through the technique known "free indirect discourse."

Free indirect discourse is a very sophisticated narrative technique, often linked to the development of the modern novel. It has the advantage of being able to render "the inner life of a fictional figure" directly, without relinquishing narratorial control of the shape of the discourse. This is accomplished most often by combining third person pronouns and present tense verbs with rhetorical structures that suggest direct representation of the character's thoughts. Using free indirect discourse, one can accomplish very quick and subtle shifts from the character's to the narrator's point of view without unnecessarily jarring the reader's sensibilities. This is a far cry from the abrupt movements between the narrated sections of earlier "story" poems in Arabic and the sections of those poems where the characters spoke, as well as Sayyāb's own previous experiments in this area, like "The Gravedigger" (1952), where there was no attempt to represent the gravedigger's inner thoughts—they were always verbalized, which led fairly often to situations that violated the verisimilitude of speech.

The first sustained use of free indirect discourse in "The Blind Whore" occurs in the section beginning with line 110, where Sayyāb, having described the whores and their innocent childhoods, returns to the present and the city street. He shifts his attention temporarily to another habitué of the street, the bird-seller: a man hawking wild birds shot by hunters in the southern marshes of Iraq, where huge flocks congregate during the seasons of migration. As this bird-seller tries to entice Salīma to buy, she asks him to come close to her so that she can touch the birds she cannot see. When she strokes her hands along their feathered wings, it suddenly invokes a memory, rendered vividly in the present tense, of her father's death:

126) And she touched speckled wings, then spread them wide with her
hands,
127) Remembering—as she smoothed them—other wings

128) She used to see, beating strongly. She used to see them fully with her eyes,
129) A flock of migrating ducks, thrusting southward
130) Their joyous necks, their intermittent cries
131) Almost making the silence of the sunset deeper, fading away across the flat ground
132) Among the mist, as the rushes whisper a mournful echo.
133) A shot rocks
134) The whispered silence; then everything grows still; then it riots insanely:
135) It is [only] a duck, why did you start? What else could it have been?
136) Perhaps your father shot it; if so, then you will eat your fill,
137) And she runs lightly along the river to meet her father:
138) He is reaping behind that hill. He will be angry if he sees her.
139) The day has passed and she did not help him, and there is no one but her to help him,
140) She climbs the hill; she almost blasphemes because of her grief.

***

141) O memories—why do you visit those who are blind, those unable to sleep?
142) Do not tarry: the torture is that you pass so slowly.
143) Tell her how he died; how he became smeared with blood—he, the ripe grain and the evening—
144) As the peasants' eyes twitch humiliated in their sockets,
145) And the mumbles: "He caught him stealing," and the lips jerk,
146) Dishonoring her dead. Then she cries out: "O God, O God,
147) If it had been anyone but the Shaykh!" And she fell down, fastening two lips
148) Upon the dead man, swearing vengeance for him in pain, sorrow and hurt.
149) The whispers of the ripe wheat, the brooks and the palm trees seemed like
150) The echoes of the dead, murmuring: "He caught him stealing" through the fields,
151) Where the threshing floors open the veins of the dead, ever widening.[65]

This section of the poem begins conventionally enough with externally rendered third-person description of how Salīma reaches out to touch the dead bird's wings. This is where the narrative begins its move into the recollective phase, which gives us the first indication in the plot—halfway through the poem—of the initial situation that stands at the beginning of the fable.

The description of the flying birds in the following lines then becomes an opportunity to shift gradually into the direct representation of consciousness, where the descriptive adjectives "*joyous* necks," "*mournful* echo," are but the most obvious markers that the perceptions being given to the reader are being filtered through a particular point of view, one that has had a greater involvement in the events being recounted than the impersonal voice of the poet/narrator. At this point, however, we are as yet unsure whether we are still in the mind of the narrator, or have shifted to Salīma's perspective. But by the time she hears the shot and runs toward where her father is working, we have moved steadily toward a perspective that comes closer and closer to free indirect discourse, or narrated monologue, until in line 138 "He is reaping behind that hill. He will be angry if he sees her" there is no doubt that we are seeing the world through Salīma's eyes and listening to words meant to represent her unmediated thoughts. The only change necessary to make these words first-person speech spoken by Salīma herself would be to change the pronoun "her" to "me."

We find similarly sophisticated manipulations of both temporality and narrative point of view throughout the rest of "The Blind Whore" as well. Once her father is dead, there is no one to protect Salīma, and she is raped by foreign soldiers. Dishonored, she begins to work as a prostitute, where we are told that she is constantly made to feel the lowliness of her position. As she thinks about her state, she longs for a "respectable" life as someone's wife, but then the narrative is deflected once again into her recollection about what a policeman's wife has told her about that "respectable" life:

182) If only there were some porter who would marry her, returning in the evening
183) With bread in his left hand and love in his right.
184) But another unhappy woman once told her
185) About her house and her two daughters, as she sobbed,
186) About her husband the policeman whom sunset carried to the whores,

....

195) As she continues to wait for morning and his two arms with the morning
196) She listens—hugging her two daughters in the darkness—to the wolves howling

197) And the winds moaning like the dead and wailing like women captives,
198) And they [the winds] gather the ghosts from the pits on the heath and the caves
199) And from the graveyards and the deserts in their hundreds and thousands.
200) Then her hair stands on end in terror, and she hides her eyes with the covers,
201) And he returns, as the sad false dawn spatters with lighted dew
202) The palm fronds—he returns, groaning from having to stay awake all night and from fatigue—
203) Like a cloud that has spent its power in the desert while hungry villages
204) Across the hills were looking for it—so that he can sleep till evening.[66]

Here we find an even more complex layering of narrative point of view, where Salīma seems to represent her recollection of the other woman's story in language that renders the woman's unvoiced feelings rather than her explicit statements. By line 197, "and the winds moaning like the dead . . ." we are no longer listening to a narrative of a narrative, but are—in the present tense—directly situated inside the woman's consciousness.

There is also one notable instance in the poem where the deviation from normal temporal progression is not a flashback, but a prolepsis: a movement into the discourse of prophecy. This is where Salīma contemplates suicide as a release from her misery, and she imagines a reunion beyond the grave with her father:

210) O if only her life would come to an end and her sorrows be folded up,
211) "If I could, I would kill myself," a whisper with strangled echo.
212) Another whispers: "And Hell? Could you endure its flames?
213) And when your grave is darkened and grows narrower and narrower, to the depths
214) Until lifeblood explodes from your fingers in gouts of fire,
215) And the two angels ask: "Why did you kill yourself, you sinner?"
216) And they will cast you into the inferno, to atone for your crime.
217) Then will you cry out: "Father!" and he will shake the dust from his hands
218) And hasten to you, shouting: "I have come to you, Salīma!"
219) She has lost even her name, concealed by another, borrowed one,
220) Ever since she became blind, she has been Ṣabāḥ.[67]
What a bitter irony![68]

The potential for irony and the rendering of multiple levels of awareness inherent in the use of free indirect discourse is graphically portrayed in this passage. Most of it is free indirect discourse: third-person pronouns, but Salīma's—not the narrator's—consciousness. The last two lines, however, are difficult to naturalize as part of Salīma's mind. They are, in fact, a shift back into the narrator's consciousness, and the shift in perspective is used to make a comment about an irony concerning her new name. She has been given the name "Ṣabāḥ," which means "morning," the coming of light, but this christening has coincided with her becoming blind, unable to see. Given that an equation between light and good (coupled with an equation between dark and evil) already established earlier in the poem, the ambivalence this naming lends to the truth-value of Salīma's subsequent statements should be clear. She is light/morning at the same time she is blindness/darkness.

This passage can be interpreted as crucial to the poem in the sense of being a turning point in the narrative, but it also has importance as an object of study for understanding how Sayyāb's manipulation of narrative *technique* was developing at this stage of his career, for it shows both his strengths and weaknesses at work. On the one hand, he has become much more adept at representing the process of consciousness at work in another mind. Salīma's internal debate over the question of suicide is dynamically rendered as a process, in language that is rhetorically well shaped to convey its purpose. The first inner voice (the one advocating suicide) is convincingly understated, neutrally giving expression to a culturally unacceptable thought. This contrasts dramatically with the hyperbolic, highly figurative language of the voice that reminds her that she will be punished with eternal damnation if she dares to commit such a sin. The second voice speaks with the well-honed, vivid language of an authoritative tradition that has had centuries to craft its rhetoric for maximum effect.

It is worth noting, however, that the authoritative tradition of heavenly judgment of individuals (which can take place at any time) is deflected in lines 217–18, and it is deflected by the introduction of a quasi-apocalyptic motif (a rhetorical tradition consisting of even more dramatically figurative language). When Salīma is about to be cast into hell, one of the voices (and we are not told which one), asks her whether, when she cries out for help, her father will come to save her. This suggests, then, not the moment of individual judgment, when the sinner stands alone before the two interrogating angels in Islamic tradition, Munkar and Nakīr, but the collective resurrection on the day of the Last Judgment, when intercession on behalf of others becomes possible. Salīma's father, then, at the moment of apocalyptic rebirth can intervene on her behalf—perhaps successfully because he himself was murdered, and therefore a victim of a kind of injustice that will cancel out the sin of Salīma's self-murder. But, ironically, this rescue fails because he does not recognize her in her new identity as "Morning"—he is as blinded by the light in front of him as his daughter now is in her darkness. Interestingly, this recalls the opening image of the poem, where the street lamps, as they switch on, are compared to Medusa's eyes: instruments that freeze, and therefore negate, the dynamic movement necessary to life. Thus unlike many of Sayyāb's other poems, especially his earlier ones, in "The Blind Whore" light can be as dangerous, as symptomatic of evil and death, as darkness.

The collapse of Salīma's vision of rescue silences both her inner voices at this point, and the narrator's voice, as we have already seen, must take over the narrative duties, in order to keep the story moving. His authoritative voice pronounces the end of the apocalyptic episode:

221) [Distant] is the morning in that darkness without day where she lives
222) Without stars or candles or windows, without fire.
223) Why, after that, should you fear, girl, to meet your Lord or his inferno?
224) The grave would be a darkness gentler and easier to bear than yours, blind woman,
225) O common property, like quarry caught out in the open, O captive,
226) You look every way, but there is no escape.[69]

Aside from its thematic importance, in establishing that death would be preferable to life for Salīma, the most interesting aspect of this passage is the shift in pronouns from the third person to the second person in line 223.

Already, in lines 212–20, we were given one extended section where second-person pronouns were used, by the second of Salīma's inner voices. There, because second-person address is often used in inner monologue to express self-contempt ("He said to himself: "You fool!""), the rhetorical strategy worked well to reinforce the theme of the passage: Salīma's self-condemnation for contemplating the sin of suicide was externalized and she addressed herself as "you," because all of her arguments were externally generated, coming from the religious tradition.[70]

Here, though, the speaking situation is quite different. It is now the narrator who addresses Salīma as "you." Nor is this all. He also employs the rhetorical device of apostrophe—"O blind woman," "O prisoner"—in foregrounded positions at the end of successive lines. Here, the apostrophe can be seen as a sort of hyperbolic assertion of "you-ness," a way of confronting the reader inescapably with the fact that he or she is no longer being addressed—the narrator has figuratively turned his back and is speaking to another audience. The shift into second person also has another effect in this passage: it transforms Salīma from a subject—a mind thinking thoughts that the fiction of free indirect narration had given us access to—into an object, an "other" that can be spoken to, exhorted, reproached, but whose mind remains a mystery to the speaker.

The shift into "you" here directly violates the conventions of narrative verisimilitude, in Arabic as well as European literature, conventions that Sayyāb has followed with relative faithfulness up to this point in the poem. A narrative may be related in the third person or the first person, it may even incorporate a "you" that stands in for "the gentle reader," but the characters in the narrative virtually never have their story told to them in the second person by the narrator. This sort of speech convention (extended use of "you") is much more closely tied to the lyric genre than any narrative kind. As a matter of fact, a very persuasive case has recently been made by Jonathan Culler that apostrophe—the kind of hyperbolic second-person address briefly discussed above—is the ground trope of lyric:

> . . . one [may] distinguish two forces in poetry, the narrative and the apostrophic, and that the lyric is characteristically the triumph of the apostrophic. A poem can recount a sequence of events, which acquires the significance lyric requires when read synecdochically or allegorically. Avoiding apostrophe, Wordsworth wrote lyrical ballads: anecdotes which signify. Alternatively, a poem may invoke objects, people, a detemporalized space with forms and forces which have pasts and futures but which are addressed as potential presences. Nothing need happen in an apostrophic poem, as the great Romantic odes amply demonstrate. Nothing need happen because the poem itself is to be the happening.[71]

As Culler makes clear earlier in his discussion, "the poem itself is . . . the happening" because it transforms the addressed object from something absent to the poet, either temporally or spatially, into a "presence," something that is there before him, something that can be addressed. This negates the temporality of past-present-future, on which narrative depends. All is transformed in the apostrophic lyric into an eternal "now." Such an operation, of total focus on the making of the absent present through language, is very similar to that performed by a prophet, whose vision of a more glorious, godly future is communicated to his audience as a potential present, a reality. As Culler himself emphasizes, however, the function of apostrophe in poetry is often not so much to assert that the poet's vision is real, as it is "to dramatize [his] calling, to summon images of [his] power so as to establish [his] identity as poetical and prophetic voice."[72] In fact, Culler argues, much of the dramatic tension and interest in this kind of poem is generated by the inability of the poet to actually instantiate and sustain an enduring prophetic vision, once he has established his credentials as that kind of speaker.

Sayyāb's move here, then, at this point in "The Blind Whore," to create a narrator whose authority approaches that of a prophet, is very daring. He clearly seeks to push beyond the ordinary boundaries of narrative, to experiment with making it do things it has rarely been called upon to do before. But he pays a price for this experimental spirit. By increasing the power and authority of his narrator's voice, he decreases the power of Salīma's. We see her now as an object, hierarchically inferior to the implicit "I" of the narrator, and when she speaks, whatever she says we must question. As Sayyāb says, she is trapped, "with no escape" (line 226), but the bars that hold her are generated by the move from a dynamic narrative, where change and development of her character were possible, to the static world of propositional, generalized statement, in its own way a "master narrative" of what the lyric as genre seeks.

It is ironic, perhaps, that in "The Gravedigger" Sayyāb's unwillingness to experiment ended up fatally limiting the ability of the poem to engage dynamically with the problems it raised about change (as opposed to cyclical experience) and its importance to human life. In "The Blind Whore," the opposite problem—too radical an experimentation with narrative conventions—leads to much the same result. After the apocalyptic vision is short-circuited (in part by the change in the narrator's stance at this crucial juncture), when Salīma's story resumes we find many of the possibilities for escape from the sterile patterns of cyclical repetition, or from linear time teleologically driving toward death, incapable of being actualized. Thus Sayyāb's willingness to experiment in this poem, which worked so well in the areas of meter and of the deployment of figurative language, also becomes in this case the poem's greatest weakness.

The poem itself dramatizes this weakness in a story the narrator tells toward the end of the poem (lines 280–302). In the interval, Salīma has decided not to kill herself so that she can take revenge upon men for making her what she is, by infecting them with the sexual diseases that her body now carries. Then she regrets her resolve, deciding that most of her customers are poor villagers just like herself. Her revenge should be reserved for foreigners, men like those who raped her, and the rich inside her own country who exploit both the whores and their customers. These "tyrants" create the oppressive systems of control (metonymized as "walls"), which imprison the people:

280) And she feels in her blood the melancholy of all those rainy winters,
281) Of the tread of drunken feet; like a prisoner behind a wall
282) Who listens to the drumbeats dying in the glowing dusk.
283) She and the whores are on one side of the wall, the drunkards are on the other,
284) One looking for men, the other for women,
285) Their (f.) fingers are bloody: they dig but the stones do not yield.
286) And the wall chews them (f.) up, then spits them out as mounds of mud—
287) A monument to Adam's shame and the expulsion of the prophets,
288) And a broken marker for the grave containing the remains of Abel as embryo.
289) They used to tell her of a wall like this in childhood stories:
290) Yagog[73] used to sink his long fingernails into it, in rage,
291) And bite its silent stones; and Magog's heavy hand
292) Used to fall, as fiercely as could be, on its massive blocks,
293) And the wall would remain, it could not be thrown down for a thousand years,
294) But "God Willing"
295) —a child so named—
296) Would arise one morning and tear out this great wall by the roots.
297) The child's hair has grown white; yet her wall is still as God's creatures [first] saw it
298) Before Yagog. It is a twin to Hell.
299) It stole the stones from houses in the plains and in the mountains
300) In whose rooms children used to leap and prattle,
301) And mothers gave birth, and fathers smiled at the future,
302) Not a stone of them is left; they are wind and ghosts.[74]

The story of Gog and Magog, which makes up the grounding for a large part of this passage, is connected with the eschatological events of the Last Judgment in the Koran. In sura 18:93–101, we are told that Dhū al-Qarnayn,[75] on his journey to the ends of the earth, came across a people who were being menaced by two tribes of horrible creatures, called Yājūj and Mājūj. Dhū al-Qarnayn agreed to build a wall for these people, made of brass and iron, that will keep Yājūj and Mājūj away from them. But he warned them that the wall will fall on the Last Day, and Yājūj and Mājūj will be free to overrun the land. In the original story, then, the wall is something that protects; its destruction will herald the dangers attendant upon the end of life as we know it.

Yet, in Salīma's retelling of the story, the destruction of the wall is pictured as desirable and the construction of the wall does not prevent destruction, it causes it. Nevertheless, despite Salīma's clear desire for an apocalyptic dénouement, the opportunity for change is again frustrated. Although the child named "God Willing," whose destiny it is to destroy the wall,[76] has been born, he has grown old while the wall still stands. Salīma's imaginative powers are here much reduced even from what they had been when she imagined her father coming to her rescue. She has become a flawed narrator, in the sense that she cannot transcend the words and the narratives that reinforce the power of what she has vowed to revenge herself against. She can only tinker with their stories, not create new narratives of her own. Thus she inverts the traditional significations of the story: the wall originally said to have been built to protect the people, now turns out to have been built from stones taken from the ruined houses of once-happy families, whose lives were destroyed by the destruction of their homes. What she cannot do, however, is invent a new story of her own.

It is as though, by tacitly admitting the authority of this Koranic narrative of control—and even enhancing it—Salīma surrenders her desire to take revenge or destroy those who have oppressed her. She retreats into narcissistic fantasies, ending in a declaration that money rules all:

399) O, if only the dead had eyes, [made] from the dust motes of the abyss,
400) They would see my misery.
401) Then my father would see his pure blood swallowing up oozing drops of other blood,
402) Like mud in a swamp. No other father would drive away the suitors
403) Because this one's mother's grandmother was a slave,
404) Or because the wife of that one's maternal uncle was the daughter of the maternal aunt of these!
405) You drunkards, I won't refuse any customers at all
406) Except guests without money.
407) I am a flower of the swamps, I gulp mud and clay
408) And shine with the light of morning.". . .[77]

Here, a darker side of the previously idolized father-daughter relationship is hinted at. Salīma implies that her father's concern for the family honor kept her from contracting a decent marriage, one that might have prevented her far-worse degradation into prostitution. His concern with one system of social control, the prohibition against marrying "out of one's class," is then juxtaposed with Salīma's obsession with an even more pervasive means of social control: desire for money. Here, too, Salīma is revealed to be morally as well as physically blind. She does not realize, as she condemns her father's wrong-headed obsession, that she herself is equally prey to an even more destructive obsession.

In case this defect in Salīma's perception of her world has escaped the reader, the narrator now reveals one last important bit of the narrative of her life—which actually occurred long before—in order to drive the point home. Salīma has had a child, a daughter who died as a baby. The narrator, stepping back into the second-person feminine singular form of address, holds the unhappy fate of this child up as a direct reproach to Salīma:

427) Twenty years have passed, and you are starving, you will eat
428) Your own children from hunger, and [you are so] thirsty that you will drink
429) The milk of your own breasts, as it bleeds from the noses of the unborn children.
430) Like a farmer who has devoured his seed
431) And has gone on to pull out the [plants by their] roots
432) In his hunger, then spring came but the flowers did not blossom,
433) Nor did the ripe wheat breath deep—there was nothing but stones,
434) But sand, but desert.
435) You have betrayed life, unknowingly, in your struggle to live.
436) How often your children's death has turned your own away from you. You cut
437) The cord of life, to destroy it and weave another,
438) A cord through which you will connect yourself to life. You sleep with a man
439) But there is no fruit but tears, and you eat
440) And your eyes are open all night, but you cannot see, and you cry out but you have no lips,
441) And tomorrow you will be hung with your own cord.
442) And tomorrow, and yesterday, and for a thousand yesterdays as though time had erased
443) The boundaries of the yesterdays and tomorrows that were yours, then it turned around in its circle, and there were no more boundaries
444) Between your night and day: there was nothing, then, but existence.

445) But darkness and the footsteps of your customers' bodies, and the money,
446) And no time but the bench and the bed, and no place.
447) Why do you count the sleepless, monotonous nights?
448) What is a lifetime, what are the days, to you? What are the months, the years?
449) "Hope" died, so there is no hope. You have lost your beloved flower.
450) When you used to count, yesterday, it was her lifetime you counted.
451) There is still a freshness in your nipple
452) From her tiny mouth, and laughter in the bed.
453) She was your comfort in misfortune,
454) And the spring of your blasted waste land.
455) She was the one pure thing in your profligacy, a breeze in the noon-time heat,
456) Your promised salvation, and the great divine twilight before the dawn.
457) What wisdom was there in her coming into existence and then dying?
458) Was it that she drank milk muddied by sin and spit?
459) Or the saliva that the jaws of wolves left in your breasts?
460) The adulterers used to lie with you as she cried without food,
461) So that it was as though, although she was innocent,
462) She shared with you in your punishment, so that she should expiate the sin.
463) Are you happy that she shares your fate? Leave her in the earth,
464) In the darkness of the tiny tomb, sleeping there without any return.
465) Light and little children and smiles belong to the rich [only],
466) Hunger, disease, homelessness are the lot of the workers.
467) And you are the daughter of workers.[78]

Here, at last, the reason for Salīma's—and the narrator's—constant recurrence to images of childhood is revealed. Salīma's own childhood, truncated though it may have been, was full and happy beside the even more miserable, more abruptly terminated, childhood of her daughter, ironically named "Hope." Salīma's obsession with her own childhood masks a more troubling refusal to think about her daughter's.

Reading this poem in the context of the failure of the 1952 Intifāḍa, one could easily construct an allegorical reading for this passage. Salīma is the people of Iraq, her child the Intifāḍa itself—the rebellion that died for lack of nourishment/support from those who brought it into being. But one does not really need to read this passage allegorically. The rhetoric of time used here insistently conveys the same message in a way less bound to particular circumstances. The same Salīma who dreams so wistfully of an idyllic past, of a strong parent-child relationship, who even at one point projects that relationship beyond the grave, into her vision of rescue by her father, refuses to extend that same protectiveness to the next generation, to become a mother to her own child. In doing so, she forces time into an eternal cyclical movement that "erases the boundaries of the yesterdays and tomorrows"—a line that recalls Sayyāb's concern with the problematic nature of boundaries in some of his earliest writing. Without the individual's willingness to change the mental categories with which she defines her identity—put in simpler terms, without a willingness to "grow up"—nothing will change. But, apparently, *telling* Salīma this, speaking to her as a "you," does not lead to change. The poem ends:

468) The clamor has died. And you are yet waiting for the adulterers,
469) You listen carefully, then you hear
470) The resonant echo of the iron locks dying, wearily, away:
471) The door has been shut.
472) Night has passed: so you must wait for another.[79]

So the authoritative prophetic voice, the one that claims the right to use "you" as a form of address, that is closely identified, therefore, with the unmediated voice of the poet himself, can offer no better vision than the flawed one of Salīma. His narrative of her life holds out no more hope than her story of Yājūj and Mājūj: both end in silence. Thus, both poet/prophet and the "daughter of the workers," representative of the only "innocent" class in the schematic of the Communist ideology with which Sayyāb was most familiar, are denied the right to be unproblematic saviors. In essence, then, "Al-Mūmis al-'Amyā'" is a narrative poem that uses epic allusion to critique the false teleology of narrative assumptions about linear progression and change. Temporality here cannot be redeemed by apocalypse; it is trapped in a barren cycle endlessly repeating patterns drawn from a bankrupt past. Moreover, the shifting back and forth between third-person narration and second-person address would seem to indicate a fundamental uneasiness on Sayyāb's part with the narrative poem as a vehicle for representing what he wanted to represent. All this is highly congruent with the frustrations of Iraqi revolutionaries of the early 1950s—who saw no escape from the hegemony of colonial rule by the British, who had responded to earlier pressure by moving from the foreground to the background of the Iraqi political map, but had continued from that less visible position to exercise as much dominance over Iraqi reality as before. And these reasons may be as good as any for Sayyāb's disenchantment with narrative, which sets in quickly after the completion of "The Blind Whore." Another, more positive, reason for this shift to lyric and (for the most part) short poems, many have been that shorter poems—as the Anglo-American modernists had earlier discovered—provided a much greater potential for controlled experimentation with the manipulation of poetic voice and the concentration of imagery.[80]

Whatever Sayyāb's motives may have been in this case, the fact remains that the rest of the poems from the period during and immediately following his Kuwaiti exile eschew the narrative paradigm entirely and, with the partial exception of "Hymn of the Rain," reach back for their models into earlier periods of his own work. When he returns, in 1955, to writing another "long poem," it will be much more consciously modeled on the Anglo-American modernist "long poem," which has as its goal the emulation of the social significance of epic, of writing a significant "public" poem without using overt narration. The "long poem" would offer to Sayyāb new and more expressive modes for rendering the newly problematized voices of postwar Iraqi society, which emerged as decolonization took hold.

The reason that Sayyāb himself suggested, however, for his abandonment of the long form, was much more prosaic and commercial in origin. He seems to have been afraid that he would lessen the chances that his work will be published if he continues to write poems too long to be published in one issue of a literary magazine. This certainly seems to have been behind the somewhat awkward phrasing he used in a letter to the editor of *Al-Ādāb* magazine, Suhayl Idrīs, where he tells Idrīs about "Hymn of the Rain," a new poem he would like to get published:

> Accompanying this letter I am sending you a poem called "Hymn of the Rain." I hope that it will meet with your approval and that it will be appropriate for publication in *Al-Ādāb*. I am very embarrassed at the idea that this poem of mine might take up a space in *Al-Ādāb* that could be filled by something better and more deserving than my poem, but what can be done, when the dominant characteristic of my poems are their length? Perhaps this is one of the reasons that made me hesitate to send it to you after my return from Kuwait a few months ago.[81]

Although "Hymn of the Rain" is far shorter than "The Blind Whore" (120 lines vs. 472 lines), Sayyāb by this time (March 1954) actually presents the poem's length as a potential drawback, rather than evidence of its significance as a serious work.[82] Interestingly, in view of his later experiments with poems that more clearly owe their allegiance to the modernist long poem, he asserted shortly before he died that "Hymn of the Rain" was originally a much longer poem, "characterized by a tone of [political] commitment (*iltizām*)," from which he "omitted a number of sections (*maqāṭiʻ*)."[83] The resemblance between this description and the story of how Ezra Pound drastically pruned T.S. Eliot's original version of *The Waste Land* is striking. Whether or not Sayyāb's framing of his story about "Hymn of the Rain" was consciously influenced by Eliot's example is not the important question here; what is important is that both poets chose to disassociate themselves from the tradition of chronologically organized narrative poetry and to valorize instead other methods of shaping their poems.

In the end, the "long poem" seemed to have been insufficient as a generic model, and Sayyāb found his greatest success in the series of poems from the late 1950s, which married the multiple voicing characteristic of "long poems" with some of the generic conventions of the "greater romantic nature lyric" (including its shorter length). Like Wordsworth's "Arab" in the "Arab Dream" episode from Book 5 of *The Prelude* (see epigraph), Badr's relationship to both the narrative and epic traditions was shot through with ambivalence and inconstancy.

But even if one considers Sayyāb's "epic period" to have been one of ultimate failure, it nevertheless (like the more successful period of free verse) was decisively conditioned by its need to respond to the discursive structuring of Western colonial practices in Iraq and the Arab world more generally. And perhaps it would not be wrong to see this need enhanced, rather than reduced, by the tensions that appeared during the transition to a truly postcolonial period, which brought new questions with necessarily laying earlier ones to rest. Much can be gained here, as we have seen in earlier chapters as well as this one, by acknowledging the importance of this element in Sayyāb's work, and the only thing we would stand to lose are those blinders that keep us from seeing his poetry whole, rather than distorted or truncated by our own refusal to accept it on its own terms.

CHAPTER NINE

Conclusion

Mon enfant, ma soeur,
Songe à la douceur
D'aller là-bas vivre ensemble!
Aimer à loisir
Aimer et mourir
Au pays qui te ressemble!
Les soileils mouillés
De ces ciels brouillés
Pour mon esprit ont les charmes
Si mystérieux
De tes traîtres yeux,
Brillant à travers leurs larmes.
—Baudelaire, "Invitation au Voyage"

The years following the publication of "Unshūdat al-Maṭar" (Hymn of the Rain) in 1954[1] were ones in which Sayyāb received increasing recognition throughout the Arab world for his work. His poems were now being regularly published in the leading literary journals of the day, especially in *Al-Ādāb* and *Majallat Shi'r*, an avant-garde magazine started by the Lebanese poets Adūnīs ('Alī Aḥmad Sa'īd) and Yūsuf al-Khāl in 1957. Both Adūnīs and al-Khāl befriended Sayyāb (as Suhayl Idrīs had done before them), regularly corresponding with him, helping to publish his poetry in book form, and making the arrangements when he came to Beirut for medical treatment once the symptoms of his illness became too obvious to ignore any longer.

In 1958 his reputation was enhanced even further when his poem "Madīna Bilā Maṭar" (City Without Rain)[2]—which incorporates apocalyptic imagery into a vision recounting the punishment and attempted destruction of the inhabitants of ancient Babylon by their vengeful gods, only to have the doom averted at the last moment by the recuperative gesture of an innocent young girl—was published in *Al-Ādāb* on the eve of the July 1958 Iraqi revolution. This uprising finally toppled the hated Nūrī al-Sa'īd regime that Sayyāb had fought against for so long, and the new regime of 'Abd al-Karīm Qāsim briefly held out hope for a truly independent and autonomous Iraqi state, where the resources of the country would be used for the benefit of all its citizens. For many, "City Without Rain" seemed like a prophecy of what might be possible in the new Iraq, and Sayyāb was the prophet who had seen its approach before anyone else.

Despite his growing reputation in those years, Sayyāb found his life on the material level a continual struggle to make ends meet. In mid-1955 he married, a relative by marriage (her sister was married to his uncle) named Iqbāl who was a primary-school teacher in Sayyāb's grandfather's home village of Abū al-Khaṣīb. At the end of 1956, the couple had a daughter, Ghaydā'. A son, Ghaylān, followed in November of 1957 and a final child, another daughter, 'Ālā', was born in July 1961.

Although his growing family may have made Sayyāb's financial situation even more precarious than it had been, it also intensified his interest in the theme of children and childhood in his poetry. The literary image of the child had already emerged even in Sayyāb's earliest poems as a potent figure of energy who could be counterposed to the colonizers' claims to survey their newly acquired domains through the "innocent" eyes of youth (which occurred, for example, so frequently in the children's literature of Empire, with its adventure stories of H. Rider Haggard, or the Tarzan series, or Rudyard Kipling's *Kim*, to name only a few of the most popular where the colonizer *becomes* the child). Now this child (often identified by the name of one of his own children) comes more and more to dominate his work as a symbol of hope for the future when all else fails.

Here, yet again, we can see that by a certain point in Sayyāb's career, the "problems," the "sites and sources of cultural disquiet" engendered by colonialism have so inscribed themselves in the fabric of his world that it often becomes extraordinarily difficult for us to separate the public from the private, the personal from the social voice. As I have endeavored to show in the preceding two sections of this book—first through an examination of how the theme of place evolved and developed in Sayyāb's poetry, and second through an examination of how the processes of influence worked to create new ways of expression and above all a new sense of self in Sayyāb's writing—reactions to the fact of colonial hegemony pervaded Sayyāb's work, even in places and at times where it would be least expected: for example, in his experimentation with meter and the discovery of the principles of *al-shi'r al-ḥurr*.

In the process, I hope it has also become clear that there was a period in Sayyāb's career (during the late 1950s through 1961) when the fight against colonialism was overtly at the thematic center of his poetry and constituted its most highly foregrounded element. The groundwork, however, for this development had been prepared long before in his earlier writings, where colonial preoccupations are figured less directly but are nevertheless omnipresent beneath the surface. The unmistakably anticolonial stance of "Madīnat Sindibād" (City of Sindbad) or "Tammūz Jaykūr" are best understood as a continuity emerging from the matrix of poems like "Fī al-Sūq al-Qadīm" (In the Ancient Market) or even "Aṣīl Shaṭṭ al-'Arab" (Late Afternoon on the Shaṭṭ al-'Arab).

Likewise, when one looks beyond the period of explicit anticolonialism to work from the last phase of Sayyāb's career, its increasingly personal tone should not obscure the fact that it is not so much a "retreat" into the attitudes found in Arab romanticism of the 1930s and 1940s as it is a return to the romantics' concern with the need to develop strong and consistently cohesive subject positions in response to colonial projections of the fragmented, inchoate Arab self. Unlike the romantics, however, for Sayyāb and his generation of poets the solipsistic self, no matter how strong, was inadequate to the new challenges of the postcolonial world, where the fictiveness of the "nation" as untroubled unity had to be acknowledged and new strategies developed to give an opportunity for expression to the many voices making up that nation. Otherwise, their fragile coalition risked disintegration.

On the other hand, in the last part of his life, Sayyāb's attention was increasingly turned inward as thoughts of death—the experience that all must face at least partially alone—became the constant company of his daily life. Although "others," of course, had experienced death, their voices could not bridge the gap to speak across that final boundary. Thus, while Sayyāb composed almost constantly during this time, producing some very moving verses that chronicle his struggle with the inexorable ravages of ALS—his alternations between hope and despair, his desperate search for a spiritual presence that might guide him and give him reassurance, his attempts to come to terms with the people from his past and evoke their presence—very few of these poems can be significantly enhanced by attempts at interpreting them through the focalizing lens of the characteristic thematic preoccupations of colonial discourse or an analysis of possible links to the patterns of power and resistance theorized in the writings of postcolonial critics.

There are, however, occasional exceptions to this generalization, even in Sayyāb's final months. One such exception is the title poem of the last collection of his poetry to be published during his lifetime, *Shināshīl Ibnat al-Jalabī* (The Enclosed Balcony of the Nobleman's Daughter).[3] For me, at least, this has always seemed a work of summation (especially as it was chosen as the eponym by Sayyāb for what he knew was his last volume of poetry), an attempt by Sayyāb to put into written form what poetry and writing over the course of over thirty years had meant to him. It seems especially apt to consider it here, in full, because it returns to so many of the themes we have seen as preoccupations of Sayyāb in earlier poems: the images of childhood and youth, of place (thematized in part through the use of language, in that he employs many terms that belong specifically to the local dialect of Basra and its environs), the problems of narrative, of "telling one's story," and especially the relationship of self to other, whether it be the colonial other (in this case, Wordsworth, and especially his "Ode: Intimations of Immortality") or the other of one's group (the character in the poem called "Aḥmad the caretaker"):

1) I remember the village winter, where drops of light came sprinkling
2) Through the narrow rifts in the clouds, like melodies
3) Sliding between the strings of an instrument set atremble by the darkness
4) It had sung before—in the morning . . . why am I being so calculating? . . . as a child I would simply smile
5) At my nights and days, their exultant boughs thickly laden with catkins.
6) And we—as our booming grandfather laughed or sang in the shade of the reed pavilion[4]
7) And his tenants waited for "Your bounteous rain, O Lord," and my brothers in forest haunts
8) Hunted rabbits and butterflies and Aḥmad the caretaker[5]—
9) We would gaze into the reed pavilion's tawny reflection in the river
10) And we would raise our eyes to the clouds: they will send their raindrops streaming forth,
11) The heavens will thunder, the river depths will ring, the palm crowns will stir,
12) Lightning will flare, kindling them blue, then green, then it will disappear.
13) And the heavens will open gate upon gate for its "bounteous rain," from which
14) the river will come back, laughing, filled full,

15) Crowned with bubbles, it will come back green, it will come back brown, choked with melodies and sighs
16) And under the palms where fronds are still dripping, making a second rain,
17) The bubbles dance as they burst—look, they are dates
18) Falling into the Virgin's[6] hand as she eagerly shakes
19) The slender palm trunk (Your child's crown will be light, not gold,
20) His love of others will crucify him, he will heal the blind
21) And he will raise from the depths of the grave a dead man, crushed by the weariness
22) Of a long journey to the darkness of death, he will clothe his bones with flesh
23) And kindle a fire in his icy heart, through his love the other will spring forth!)

***

24) The sky flashed lightning, and there where the river bends
25) The balcony of the nobleman's daughter appeared
26) And floated, circling, suspended in the air without support, kissing the water,
27) Surrounded by blossoming flowers
28) (Dewy necklaces of ivy with glints of white)
29) And the lovely lady's nurse, whose eyes are outlined with excitement and lack of sleep.

***

30) O rain so silken[7]
31) Weep, daughters of the nobleman
32) O rain so white
33) Weep, daughters of the knight
34) O rain of gold.

***

35) The roads have been cut, this "bounteous rain's" scissors have cut and covered them,
36) And the footbridges cling to the palm trunks in the rain
37) Like drowning men from Sindbad's ship, like a green story Aḥmad the caretaker
38) Puts off and abandons till tomorrow, as he hands cups of tea
39) Around the room, fingers his rifle, coughs, then his eyes cross to the balcony

40) And pierce the darkness.
41) He cries out: "Grandfather"—(my brother in gossip):
42) "Shall we sit here long, waiting in the wet darkness of the pavilion?
43) When will the rain stop?"

***

44) The sky thundered, and the balcony of the nobleman's daughter
45) Circled and burst apart.
46) Then on the horizon the clouds' rainbow peak
47) Appeared. There, where the beautiful lady's balcony used to catch and hold the eye,
48) There was nothing to see but the twilight's rosy glow.

***

49) Thirty years gone, and I have grown old: how much love, how much passion
50) Has flamed in my heart!
51) Yet, whenever the thunder claps its hands
52) I strain my eyes, watching: perhaps the balcony will glitter
53) And I will see the nobleman's daughter, coming to our rendezvous!
54) But I have not seen her. My desires are mere air, vanities,
55) A plant without fruit or flowers.[8]

Although this poem can certainly stand on its own as a lament for an idyllic past that is only recognized once it is lost, it gains much greater evocative power if it is considered in conjunction with one of William Wordsworth's most famous poems: "Ode: Intimations of Immortality" (which Sayyāb, as an English major, would almost certainly have been required to read in college if not high school). The beginnings of the two poems are remarkably similar, each using a meditation upon an image of a natural scene remembered from childhood as a scaffolding upon which to erect an otherworldly vision. Sayyāb's clouds, through which his musical light pours in a symphony of metaphoric harmony, are perhaps slightly more concrete and specific than Wordsworth's landscape, but the impression left behind by both are comparable, as the opening stanza of the *Ode* shows:

There was a time when meadow, grove and stream,
The earth, and every common sight,
        To me did seem
    Appareled in celestial light,
The glory and freshness of a dream.

It is not now as it hath been of yore—
    Turn whereso'er I may
        By night or day,
The things which I have seen I now can see no more.[9]

As in both poems the original vision is remarkably similar, so too do they share an abrupt termination of the potential of that vision. But in each case the reason for that short-circuiting is different. Wordsworth's problem is conventionally seen, by himself and others, as the inability of the adult, caught up in the minutiae of worldly life, to sustain his connection with the preternatural awareness of the child who still recollects something of his existence as an immortal soul prior to birth. For Wordsworth, the fullest form of the vision belongs to the child, and his adult self can only dimly suggest, with words that notably lack any precise concreteness, what the experience must have been like.

The case is quite different for Sayyāb. For him, it is the adult self who creates—or rather manipulates—the vision of universal harmony and oneness, although this very access to visionary language, from his point of view, seems to interfere with the experience of convergence. So he chastises himself for being "calculating" and depicts his child-self instead in lines 4 and 5 as "simply smil[ing] / At my nights and days," that is, reacting to them as one might to another human being with whom communication is possible. And they, in response perhaps, take on the attributes of living trees with their branches in bud, in a veritable revel of metaphoric transference.

The only hint of some potential flaw in this idyll comes in line 8, where the speaker talks of how his brothers "hunt" rabbits and butterflies. That there is violence implicit in the verb *ṣāda* (hunt) is not necessarily to be taken very seriously, for *ṣāda* is as likely to imply the chase of the quarry as its capture. To have his brothers, however, hunting Aḥmad, a person, is more troubling because it suggests that they see him as truly an "other," not one of themselves and perhaps not fully human. This suggestion of some incommensurability between the speaker's point of view and Aḥmad's will, moreover, not be left to lie latent in the poem but will be taken up and thematized in lines 35–43, in what is probably the most crucial section of the poem and the one that is most directly aimed at deconstructing the Wordsworthian fiction of the child's untroubled access to the unfallen world of unity.

Before the speaker reaches that point in the poem, though, he rather unexpectedly takes one more detour into the language of prophetic vision that he had already dismissed in the opening lines as "calculating." This time, however, he relies on, not the descriptive mode of his prologue, but the even more totalizing mode of narrative. Although he does not recount the whole incident for the audience, he uses allusion (and even underscores the allusion with a footnote) to activate the redemptive narrative of how the Virgin Mary is safely delivered of her child in the Koran. The power of this allusion then allows him, by very adroit manipulation of metonymic slippage, to shift into the narrative of Jesus' resurrection of Lazarus (one might note here how the speaker's use of "you" to address Mary recalls the troubling narrative totalization created by an identical mode of address to Salīma in "Al-Mūmis al-'Amyā'"). The strategic deflection, in its turn, permits the speaker to arrive at the point of rebirth and redemption (whether for himself or others is not clear) in a dizzyingly short space, without having to examine the parameters of his own subject position or to encounter any doubts or setbacks along the way. And thus he is able, through the power of a narrative teleology, which asserts that everything will happen "just so," to experience—albeit briefly— his personal redemptive vision of the balcony of the nobleman's daughter as it floats, "circling, suspended in the air without support, kissing the water" (line 26).

Wordsworth's poem maps out a strategy of appropriation of the dominant subject position in order to reclaim the redemptive vision that is remarkably similar to Sayyāb's speaker. Once Wordsworth has sketched out the lineaments of the child's visionary ability and laments how the process of growing up robs the individual of his power to recapture the intimations of that past glory, which "fade into the light of common day," he deflects the description into a lengthy portrayal of the apprentice poet, whom one can find, even as a child of six, busy with

Some fragment from his dream of human life,
Shaped by himself with newly-learned art;
  A wedding or a festival,
  A mourning or a funeral;
    And this hath now his heart,
  And unto this he frames his song:
    Then will he fit his tongue
To dialogues of business, love, or strife;
  But it will not be long
  Ere this be thrown aside,
  And with new joy and pride
The little Actor cons another part
Filling from time to time his 'humorous stage'

> With all the Persons, down to palsied Age,
> That Life brings with her in her equipage;
> As if his whole vocation
> Were endless imitation.

There is no mistaking this speaker's view of poetry that would seek to imagine even the possibility of other voices besides that of the lyric "I" appearing in a given poem. Such "dialogues" lead only to "strife," and a life wasted in a sterile round of "endless imitation." It is only by recalling the image of the child to the poem through apostrophic address (where the child is rather chillingly invoked in retrospect as "Thou, over whom thy Immortality / Broods like the Day, a Master o'er a Slave, / A Presence which is not to be put by") that the speaker is able to repossess his original vision, this time from the less ecstatic but more balanced viewpoint of the mature "philosophic mind," which then allows him to conclude the poem with a renewed confidence in the power of the self to encompass the other:

> Thanks to the human heart by which we live,
> Thanks to its tenderness, its joys, and fears,
> To me the meanest flower that blows can give
> Thoughts that do often lie too deep for tears.

It is vital to note that in this concluding passage, despite its optimistic tone, this version of the speaker's self can still only approach the other—in this case, the flower—as instrumentality, as an object presence whose value lies solely in its ability to serve as a scaffolding for giving focus to the speaker's noble sentiments.

It is precisely this solipsistic trap that Sayyāb's speaker strives to avoid by allowing the voice of Aḥmad the caretaker authorization to speak directly in the text of the poem itself. Or, to put it another way, Sayyāb would have us realize the fictiveness of that sovereign subject, which the romantic mind of those like Wordsworth had so eagerly sought, and shows us its limitations by allowing another voice to interrupt his primary speaker. But for this he also pays a price, in the sense that this opening up to the "other" voice also destroys the illusion of congruence between the subjects on which the power of his speaker's vision was predicated. For Aḥmad most emphatically does not share the speaker's point of view. He is not interested in the binding effects of shared narratives—he puts off the "green story" he was in the midst of telling "until tomorrow" once the rain begins to fall. Even more pointedly, he can hardly wait for the rain (which to the speaker prefigured the renewal of fertility in the land and the promise of a new life) to stop, and his outburst to the speaker's grandfather, beginning in line 42—"Shall we sit here long, waiting in the wet darkness of the pavilion? / When will the rain stop?"—leads directly to the disappearance of the balcony in lines 44 and 45.

The speaker is thus led to conclude the poem by expressing the sentiment that *his* quest, unlike Wordsworth's, has ended in failure. And if we limit ourselves to his point of view alone, we must agree. The balcony cannot be made to appear by the power of one mind alone. But Sayyāb, the presence behind the speaker, has opened up to our view what was in his time—and may still be—a more relevant and more perplexing question: what is the value of the single vision, if others cannot find the point of purchase that would allow them to share it? And even more urgent: is there a way for those who would seek to influence their culture through written works (whether or not limited to Arabic) to open new avenues that would allow other voices to speak and thus avoid a hegemonic monopolization of the discourse?

Such questions, I believe, have yet to be answered by any literature or literary figure in the world today. But this was, in a very real sense, Sayyāb's last legacy to Arabic poetry: a challenge to find some way to open the field of literary discourse to a multiplicity of voices, even if they do not and cannot agree. Otherwise, he seems to say here, the hegemonic oppression that was colonialism (which certainly counted as one—but only one—of the oppressions experienced by Aḥmad the caretaker in the course of his life) will simply re-emerge in other, but just as pernicious, forms. Sadly, the continued interest in his poetry and the relevance so many people seem to feel it has to their lives even today would seem to indicate that his plea is still just as far from being answered as it was on the bleak December day when Sayyāb died in 1964.

Notes

PREFACE

1. "Tajribatī fī Sujūn al-'Irāq," ed Nijm 'Abd al-Karīm, *Al-Majalla* 556 (Oct. 9, 1990):18–22.

2. These two verses echo a famous line by a well-known classical Arab poet, 'Alī ibn al-Jahm: 'Uyūn al-mahā bayna l-Ruṣāfati wa-l-jisr // jalabna l-hawā min ḥaythu adrī wa-lā adrī (The wild cow's eyes . . . // bring passion from whence I know and know not)."

1. EMPTY SPACES AND UNVEILED PLACEHOLDERS

1. See, for example, Michel Foucault, *Power/Knowledge: Selected Interviews and Other Writings 1972–1977*, ed. Colin Gordon (New York: Pantheon Books, 1980) especially the interview with the editors of the journal *Hérodote*, "Questions on Geography" (63–77), where he is led to analyze his own poststructuralist strategies of interpretation in terms of their dependence on tropes of spatialization, concluding that "[g]eography acted as the support, the condition of possibility for the passage between a series of factors I tried to relate" (77). More often, such metaphors of place are incorporated into descriptions and analyses without their conditioning presence being made explicit. See, for example, Giles Deleuze's description of symbiotic relations in terms of "deterritorialization" and "reterritorialization" in *A Deleuze Reader*, ed. Constantin V. Boundas (New York: Columbia University Press, 1993), 32.

2. Fredric Jameson, *Postmodernism Or, the Cultural Logic of Late Capitalism* (Durham: Duke University Press, 1991), 154. Jameson is quite right to stress later in the same passage that what is at stake in postmodernism is not

just a simple either/or dichotomy of temporality vs. spatiality, but that "the distinction is between two forms of *interrelationship between time and space* rather than between these two [as] inseparable categories themselves. . . . What one means by evoking [postmodernism's] spatialization is rather the will to use and to subject time to the service of space, if that is the right word for it." (emphasis mine).

For an insight into the development of the notion of temporality as "a dominant" of modernism, see Harry Levin's seminal essay, "What Was Modernism?" (*Refractions: Essays in Comparative Literature* [London: Oxford University Press, 1966])—one of the earliest attempts to see beyond modernism to what would replace it. In this essay, Levin emphasizes the importance of temporality in the modernist movement, at one point remarking: "Time was of the essence, not only for the metaphysician Bergson, but for the innumerable poets, novelists, painters, and scientists who worked in the dimension he formulated. Vainly did Wyndham Lewis assail the time-consciousness of his contemporaries" (286).

3. Edward Said, "Yeats and Decolonization," in *Nationalism, Colonialism and Literature* (Minneapolis: University of Minnesota Press, 1990), 76.

4. Studies of these ambivalences on the part of the colonizer form probably the most thoroughly documented aspect of Western postcolonial theory, which may say something important about its own hegemonic tendencies. For the most extensive theoretical treatment of the question, see Homi Bhabha's *The Location of Culture* (London: Routledge, 1994), a recently published collection of the essays he has written on the subject over the last decade.

5. In the case of Iraq under British control, the most extensive primary source for the nascent development of the colonial educational system can be found in Abū Khaldūn Sāṭi' al-Ḥuṣrī, *Mudhakkirātī fī al-'Irāq*, 2 vols. (Beirut: Dār al-Ṭalī'a, 1968). For some illuminating observations about the struggle over language of instruction in the Egyptian schools under British occupation, see Imīl Badī' Ya'qūb, *Jubrān wa-al-Lugha al-'Arabiyya* (Tripoli, Lebanon: Jarrūs, 1985), 29–34.

6. Foucault, "Questions on Geography," *Power/Knowledge*, 73.

7. Richard Terdiman, *Present Past: Modernity and the Memory Crisis* (Ithaca: Cornell University Press, 1993), vii.

8. This, of course, is how they are portrayed by M.H. Abrams in the classic study *The Mirror and the Lamp: Romantic Theory and the Critical Tradition* (Oxford: Oxford University Press, 1953). See especially 159–77.

9. Bill Ashcroft, Gareth Griffiths, and Helen Tiffin in *The Empire Writes Back: Theory and Practice in Post-Colonial Literatures* (London: Routledge, 1989) have highlighted this point as the central element of their early and influential analysis of the postcolonial phenomenon when they say "A major feature of post-colonial literatures is the concern with place and displacement. . . . The most widely shared discursive practice within which this alienation can be

identified is the construction of "place." The gap which opens between the experience of place and the language available to describe it forms a classic and all-pervasive feature of post-colonial texts" (9).

10. Ibrāhīm al-Sāmarrā'ī, *Lughat al-Shi'r Bayna Jīlayn* (Beirut: Al-Mu'assasa al-'Arabiyya li-al-Dirāsāt wa-al-Nashr, 1980), 212. This is a reprint of the first edition, originally published without a date. Internal evidence, however, would indicate that the section on Sayyāb was written sometime between 1948 and 1950, because it mentions Sayyāb's first collection, *Azhār Dhābila* (1948) but not his second, *Asāṭīr* (1950). In his *A Critical Introduction to Modern Arabic Poetry* (Cambridge: Cambridge University Press, 1975), 283 n. 81. M.M. Badawi opines that al-Sāmarrā'ī's work was published before 'Abd al-Wahhāb al-Bayyātī's poetry became well-known—that is, the early 1950s. For another early discussion linking Sayyāb's poetry to concerns of place, see Muḥyī al-Dīn Ismā'īl, "Al-Shi'r al-'Irāqī al-Ḥadīth," *Al-Ādāb* 3, no. 1 (January 1955): 49–57, where he characterizes Sayyāb's poetry as being "iqlīmī," or regionalist, and says that this "regionalism" is a direct response to the environment in which Sayyāb grew up (55).

11. Rafā'īl Buṭṭī, "Introduction," in Badr Shākir al-Sayyāb, *Azhār Dhābila wa-Qaṣā'id Majhūla*, ed. Ḥasan Tawfīq (Beirut: Al-Mu'assasa al-'Arabiyya li-al-Dirāsāt wa-al-Nashr, 1981), 22.

12. Sāmarrā'ī, 212.

13. Lūwīs 'Awaḍ, *Al-Thawra wa-al-Adab* (Cairo: Dār al-Kitāb al-'Arabī, 1967), 74.

14. See, for example, Ḥasan Tawfīq, *Shi'r Badr Shākir al-Sayyāb: Dirāsa Fanniyya wa-Fikriyya* (Beirut: Al-Mu'assasa al-'Arabiyya li-al-Dirāsāt wa-al-Nashr, 1979),125; 'Abd al-Jabbār Dāwūd al-Baṣrī, *Badr Shākir al-Sayyāb: Rā'id al-Shi'r al-Ḥurr* (Baghdad: Dār al-Jumhūriyya, 1966), 7–8 and 16–17; and Sīmūn Jārjī, *Badr Shākir al-Sayyāb fī Ḥayātihi wa-Shi'rih* (n.p.: Manshūrāt Aḍwā', 1966) 24, among others. Significantly, in light of what we will find in the second chapter of this study, Jārjī speaks of Jaykūr as Sayyāb's "paradise lost (*firdawsuhu al-ḍā'i'*)."

15. 'Īsā Bullāṭa, *Badr Shākir al-Sayyāb: Ḥayātuhu wa-Shi'ruh* (Beirut: Dār al-Nahār, 1971; rpt., Baghdad: Dār al-Shu'ūn al-Thaqāfiyya al-'Āmma, 1987) and Iḥsān 'Abbās, *Badr Shākir al-Sayyāb: Dirāsatun fī Ḥayātihi wa-Shi'rih* (Beirut: Dār al-Thaqāfa, 1969). Much of the information found in these two books has now been made available in German in a recently published study by Leslie Tramontini, *Badr Šākir as-Sayyāb: Untersuchungen zum poetischen Konzept in den Diwanen azhār wa-asāṭīr und unšūdat al-maṭar* (Wiesbaden: Otto Harrassowitz, 1991). I obtained a copy of the monograph too late, however, to fully integrate its insights into the present work.

16. See Bullāṭa, 17f and 'Abbās, 17. 'Abbas can even be seen as trying a rhetorical strategy to counter other critics' acceptance of Sayyāb's idealization of his natal village in his poetry by repeatedly emphasizing the unattractiveness of

the village and its surroundings, pointing out that it is just a collection of houses made of mud and brick, surrounded by palm trees, which "has nothing to catch the eye, nothing to distinguish it from any other village in southern Iraq."

17. See, for example, Foucault, "Two Lectures," *Power/Knowledge*, 90.

18. Foucault, "Prison Talk," *Power/Knowledge*:, 52.

19. For an early and highly influential example of such analysis of the "textuality" of empire, see Gayatri Chakravorty Spivak, "The Rani of Sirmur," in *Europe and Its Others*, vol. 1, ed. Francis Barker et al., (Essex: University of Essex, 1985), 128–51.

20. See "Joseph Conrad: Introduction," in *The Shaping of Fiction*, ed. Robert M. Bender (New York: Washington Square Press, 1970), 91.

21. Interestingly, the Orientalist Gertrude Bell (who had a large role in the creation of Iraq under British mandate) recounts a very similar occasion of "mapping" in a letter to a colleague (Sir Reginald Hall, who eventually became a Vice Admiral in the British navy): "Dear Captain Hall: . . . Before I went to Basrah I remember your putting your finger on the Baghdad corner of the map and saying that the ultimate success of the war depended on what we did there. You are one of the people who realised how serious are the questions we have to face. . . ." (Gertrude Bell, *Letters*, ed. Lady Bell [New York: Boni and Liverwright, n.d.], 1:368). What she would seem to be referring to here (though it is never made explicit) is the fears of the British Navy during and after World War I that their major supplier of oil, Iran, might fall under hostile control (first Turkish/German, then Bolshevik) and their consequent desire to gain control over potential alternative supplies in Iraq, especially in the north around the Mosul, which they took at great cost after the armistice had actually been declared. That the British suspected the presence of oil in Iraq well before such fields were proved can be seen from references made in Donald Maxwell's book about his trip to Iraq at the end of the war, *A Dweller in Mesopotamia* (London: John Lane, 1921), 122, and also—in a more "official" sense—from a British Cabinet Memorandum of June 1921, which mentions that the Germans were working wells in Iraq that were yielding as much as 10,000 gallons a day during the war (quoted in Peter Sluglett, *Britain in Iraq: 1914–1932* [London: Ithaca Press, 1976], 106). There were also somewhat more vaguely inspired fears early in the war that the Germans (as allies of the Turks) might work to complete the "Berlin-to-Baghdad" rail line and extend it south to Basra, with the goal of controlling the Persian Gulf waters and interfering with British lines of communication with India. For an early of articulation of this apprehension, see "The Baghdad Railway," in *The Edinburgh Review* 422 (October 1907): 371–98, especially page 395.

22. Bhabha, 212.

23. See, for example, Milton Viorst's article in *The New Yorker* (October 12, 1987), 94. (It is true that Viorst here is citing the words of an Iraqi military commander, but he passes them on without comment or question.)

24. See Anthony Cordesman's *The Iran–Iraq War and Western Security 1984–87: Strategic Implications and Policy Options* (London: Jane's Publishing Co., 1987).especially 3–4, 64, 123, and 148–49.

25. Cordesman, 10.

26. Samir al-Khalil, *Republic of Fear* (Berkeley: University of California Press, 1989), 290.

27. It is worth noting that this term—"droves"—in its original collocation is used to describe animals.

28. Penny Kemp, "For Generations to Come: The Environmental Catastrophe," *Beyond the Storm: A Gulf Crisis Reader* (New York: Olive Branch Press, 1991), 325.

29. Edward Said, "Foreword," *Beyond the Storm: A Gulf Crisis Reader* (New York: Olive Branch Press, 1991), 3.

30. Al-Qur'ān, Sūrat al-Takwīr (The Bundling). The translation is mine.

31. Earlier texts, such as those found in 'Abbās al-'Azzāwī's compilation of contemporary nineteenth-century sources in *Tārīkh al-'Irāq Bayna al-Iḥtilālayn*, vol. 6 (Baghdad: Sharikat al-Tijāra wa-l-Ṭibā'a, 1954) tend to see the events of this year as no worse than those of other periods, like the famine of 1200 A.H.

32. "Akhbār wa-Qadāyā," *Majallat Shi'r* 1, no. 2 (summer 1957): 111.

33. Badr Shākir al-Sayyāb, *Dīwān* (Beirut: Dār al-'Awda, 1971) 1:477. All translations from Sayyāb's poetry are mine unless otherwise noted.

34. Shortly before his death Sayyāb gave an account of the poem's composition to his friend Mu'ayyid al-'Abd al-Wāḥid. See Jārjī, 54.

35. "Speaker" and "persona" are technical terms—once controversial, now widely accepted—used to identify the speaking voice in a lyric poem when it is important to differentiate between this voice and that of the real author. This is important because too close an identification between the author and his writing can sometimes lead to mistaken assumptions. The speaking voice is almost always, even in poems where there is encouragement to identify the speaker with the author, in some sense a construct or fiction, since the speaker must of necessity be, temporally at least, more limited in his personality and experiences than the actual author, who goes on existing—and adding to his experience—after the poem's composition and the closure of the speaker's formation as a character. In addition, the speaker's thought processes—as mimed in the poem—will not coincide with the actual author's because they will be simpler, if for no other reason. Anything not relevant to the poem's trajectory will be excised. As Mikhail Bakhtin said: "We must never forget this, must never confuse—as has been done up to now and as is still often done—the *represented* world with the world outside the text (naive realism); nor must we confuse the author-creator of the work with the author as a human being (naive biographism); nor confuse the listener or reader of multiple and varied periods. . . ." (*Dialogic Imagination*, ed. and trans. Michael Holquist and Caryl Emerson (Austin: University of Texas Press, 1981), 253).

36. Sayyāb, *Dīwān* 1:491.

37. The use of this word here attains its special resonance from the fact that the literal meaning of the word apocalypse is "unveiling." Thus, the more traditional "millennial" form of apocalyptic "unveils" the paradisiacal vision of a world transformed, a new heaven where those who have been saved may live free of the toils of time, death, conflict, and violence.

38. Christopher Sharett, "Introduction: Crisis Cinema," *Crisis Cinema: The Apocalyptic Idea in Postmodern Narrative Film*, ed. Christopher Sharett (Washington, D.C.: Maisonneuve Press, 1993), 4.

39. Barry Brummett has an interesting discussion of this point in *Contemporary Apocalyptic Rhetoric* (New York: Praeger, 1991), 92–93.

40. This term seems to have originated with Richard Terdiman's book *Discourse Counter-Discourse: The Theory and Practice of Symbolic Resistance in Nineteenth-Century France* (Ithaca: Cornell University Press, 1985). See, for example, Linda Hutcheon in her article "Circling the Downspout of Empire: Post-Colonialism and Postmodernism" *Ariel* 20, no. 4 (October 1989): 156 (where she cites Terdiman as the source for her use of the word), but it is implicit in much of Foucault's later writing, especially in those places where he speaks of "subjugated knowledges." See, for example, "Two Lectures" in *Power/ Knowledge*, 82–83.

41. Foucault, "Two Lectures," *Power/Knowledge*, 92.

42. Foucault, "Power and Strategies," *Power/Knowledge*, 142.

43. Probably the earliest full treatment of postcolonialism using Foucault's concept of resistance to deal with any aspect of Arabic literature is Barbara Harlow's *Resistance Literature* (New York: Methuen, 1987), an extremely insightful book whose major drawback for this study is that it deals mainly with contemporary Arabic literature since the 1960s and makes little attempt to include a historical perspective in its theorizing. Edward Said, drawing on Harlow, incorporates considerable discussion of the phenomenon of resistance, with some reference to Arabic literature, in his recent *Culture and Imperialism* (New York: Vintage Books, 1994) (see especially the third chapter, "Resistance and Opposition"), but his emphasis is on the literature of the colonizer and he does not present systematic treatments of the other side.

2. THIS OTHER EDEN

1. See Gen 2:13–14; also, uses of the word "*furāt*" (the Arabic name for the Euphrates) to mean "sweet water," and associated with tableaus representing God in his role as creator, can be found in the Koran 25:53, 35:12, and 77:27. One of the earliest treatises using biblical authority to place the former location of Eden specifically in Mesopotamia was by a teacher of Oriental languages in England,

John Hopkinson, who wrote a book entitled *Synopsis Paradisi* in 1593 (for more information see Joseph Duncan, *Milton's Earthly Paradise: A Historical Study of Eden* [Minneapolis: University of Minnesota Press, 1972], 96f).

2. Maxwell, 101–2.

3. The following extract from "The Baghdad Railway" will give an idea of the disjunctive maneuvers involved in such a procedure: "Among the many lands which their fiery courage gave them the pick of, it is natural that the desert tribesmen should fix their affections with a particular fervour on ancient Babylonia. Fabled to be the Garden of Eden, the Bedouins might see in these groves and gardens and murmuring waters all the features with which their imagination had invested the idea of Paradise. . . . All [their cities and towns] have declined and fallen away, or utterly perished. The sites of some are still marked by straggling villages or by the reed-woven huts of sedentary Arab tribes; but of many every vestige has disappeared, and their very positions are matter of conjecture. Already they have followed into oblivion the mightier cities of ancient Babylonia. It would be difficult indeed to find pages more melancholy than those in which travellers have recorded their impressions of the now universal desolation" (382–83).

4. Sayyāb, *Dīwān*, 2:400–403.

5. Bhabha, 86 [emphasis added].

6. Sayyāb, *Dīwān*, 1:479–81.

7. David Malouf (an Australian author of Lebanese heritage), for example, retells *The Tempest* in his play *Blood Relations*. For more examples of this revisionist rewriting of Shakespeare, see Ashcroft, et al., *Empire*, 189–91. Sayyāb himself is not uninterested in this discursive practice, see the analysis of "Min Ru'yā Fūkāy" (From the Vision of Fukai) in Terri DeYoung, "And Thereby Hangs a Tale: A Study of Myth in Modern Arabic Poetry," Ph.D. diss., University of California, Berkeley, 1988, 123–28.

8. Derrida calls this term "dangerous" because "supplementation" can all too easily (and, according to Derrida, must) permute into "supplantation." As he says ". . . the concept of the supplement . . . harbors within itself two significations whose cohabitation is as strange as it is necessary. The supplement adds itself, it is a surplus, a plenitude enriching another plenitude, *the fullest measure of presence*. It cumulates and accumulates presence. . . . But the supplement supplements. It adds only to replace. It intervenes or insinuates itself *in-the-place-of*; if it fills, it is as if one fills a void" (Jacques Derrida, *Of Grammatology*, trans. Gayatri Chakravorty Spivak [Baltimore: Johns Hopkins University Press, 1976], 144–45).

9. See Terri DeYoung, "A New Reading of Badr Shākir al-Sayyāb's 'Hymn of the Rain,'" *Journal of Arabic Literature* 24, no. 1 (March 1993): 39–61, for a more thorough and complete reading of the text as an independent work.

10. Sayyāb, *Dīwān*, 1: 458.

11. Sayyāb, *Dīwān*, 1: 418.

12. A detailed discussion of the topography and statistics on agriculture in Basra province may be found in Ḥāmid al-Bāzī, *Al-Baṣra fī al-Fatra al-Muẓlima* (Baghdād: Dār Manshūrāt al-Baṣrī, 1969), 34–36.

13. Cecil Byford, *The Port of Basrah* (London: Waterlow and Sons, 1935), 79–80.

14. The versions of the Eden story that appear in most commentaries on the Koran very strongly underwrite the association of Eden with boundaries. After the Fall, Eden is walled in; a boundary is thus erected between it and mankind, which can only be crossed following the Day of Judgment, when the Prophet Muḥammad will lead the righteous to one of the gates in this wall and will break it down.

15. For an insightful picture of Baghdad and the Abbasids in the days of their glory, see Marshall Hodgson, *The Venture of Islam* (Chicago: University of Chicago Press, 1974), 1:280–98.

16. See Yūsuf 'Izz al-Dīn, *Al-Shi'r al-'Irāqī Ahdāfuhu wa-Khaṣā'iṣuhu fī al-Qarn al-Tāsi' 'Ashar* (Cairo: al-Dār al-Qawmiyya li-al-Ṭibā'a wa-al-Nashr, 1965) 12, 134–35; and Ibrāhīm al-Wā'ilī, *Al-Shi'r al-Siyāsī al-'Irāqī fī al-Qarn al-Tāsi' 'Ashar* (Baghdad: Maṭba'at al-'Ānī, 1961) 14, 42–43 and 53–54 for assessments of the general effect Iraq's new status as a borderland had on its cultural and political positioning vis-à-vis the metropole.

17. Freya Stark, *East is West* (London: John Murray, 1945), 198–99.

18. For the story of Sayyāb's sojourn in Iran, see Bullāṭa, 66–67; and 'Abbās, 173 and 177.

19. As he had likewise done for Ottomans, editing *their* official newspaper, *Al-Zawrā'*, in the late 1880s and early 1890s. Relations between him and the British eventually became extremely warm and cordial. Gertrude Bell, for instance, refers to him on more than one occasion as "our" poet. For a sampling of her descriptions of Zahāwī's public recitations, see Gertrude Bell, *Letters*, 2:561–62, 593–94, and 606–7.

20. See 'Abbās al-'Azzāwī, *Tārīkh al-'Irāq Bayna al-Iḥtilālayn*, vol. 8 (Baghdad: Sharikat al-Tijāra wa-al-Ṭibā'a, 1956), 223.

21. The assessment by Sayyāb's friend and classmate at the Teachers' College, Muḥyī al-Dīn Ismā'īl, in his article entitled "Malāmiḥ min al-Shi'r al-'Irāqī al-Ḥadīth," is typical of the low esteem in which Zahāwī was held. See especially page 50.

22. See 'Azzāwī, 8:106 (his father's obituary notice).

23. 'Azzāwī, 8:96

24. 'Azzāwī, 8:117.

25. See Qāsim al-Khaṭṭāṭ, Muṣṭafā 'Abd al-Laṭīf al-Saḥaratī, and Muḥammad 'Abd al-Mun'im al-Khafājī, *Ma'rūf al-Ruṣāfī: Shā'ir al-'Arab al-Kabīr* (Cairo: Al-Hay'a al-Miṣriyya al-'Āmma li-al-Ta'līf wa-al-Nashr, 1971), 41.

26. Al-Khaṭṭāṭ et al., 44.

27. Al-Khaṭṭāṭ et al., 47. This is probably the text found in *Dīwān al-Ruṣāfī* (Cairo: Al-Maktaba al-Tijāriyya al-Kubrā, 1963), 504, described as a "translation of a Turkish poem by Tawfīq Fikrat."

28. Prior to the restoration of the constitution, it had been almost impossible for private citizens to import printing presses into the Ottoman dominions, so the history of Iraqi newspapers really only begins in 1908.

29. Al-Khaṭṭāṭ et al., 56.

30. We find it mentioned, for instance, that he translated a "novel (*riwāya*)" by the Turkish author Nāmik Kamāl. He also became embroiled in several literary controversies, as when, for example, during World War I the Turkish poet Sulaymān Naẓīf composed a poem upon the surrender of Baghdad castigating the Iraqis for their cowardice, and Ruṣāfī composed a famous ode, "Niwāḥ Dajla" (The Lamentations of the Tigris), defending his fellow countrymen. See Ruṣāfī *Dīwān*, 418–19.

31. Al-Khaṭṭāṭ et al., 99.

32. Fayṣal, along with his father Ḥusayn, Sharīf of Mecca, and his younger brother 'Abdallah (who eventually became king of Jordan) had led the Arab revolt against the Ottomans during World War I, with the help of T.E. Lawrence (Lawrence of Arabia). Fayṣal set up his capital in Damascus, which was (he thought) to become the nucleus of a new, independent Arab state, but he was ousted from there in 1920 by the French, who were claiming all of Syria as their "mandate" under the Sykes-Picot Agreement.

33. Al-Khaṭṭāṭ et al., 11.

34. He has apparently given a variety of birth dates, from 1900 to 1906. For complete particulars of his background and youth, see Hādī al-'Alawī, "Min Riḥlat al-Fikr wa-al-Taḥawwul," in *Muḥammad Mahdī al-Jawāhirī: Dirāsāt Naqdiyya*, ed. Hādī al-'Alawī (Baghdad/Najaf: Maṭba'at al-Nu'mān, 1969), 21–22.

35. See Bullāṭa, 63; and Tawfīq, 85.

36. See Jabrā Ibrāhīm Jabrā's complex and nuanced evaluation of al-Jawāhirī's relationship to both the neoclassical school and the modernists, including Sayyāb, in his article "Al-Shā'ir, wa-al-Ḥākim wa-al-Madīna" published in the collection *Muḥammad Mahdī al-Jawāhirī: Dirāsāt Naqdiyya*, 43–80, and also an article ascribed to Sayyāb about modern Iraqi poetry, in Jārjī, 102.

37. Jabrā, 65.

38. "Anā l-'Irāq, lisānī qalbuhu, wa-damī furātuhu . . ." quoted in Jabrā, 48.

39. By tacit agreement, the office of Minister of Education during the Mandate period, and in subsequent decades, was held generally by a Shi'ī, as if to forestall any demands on their part, as the majority of the population in Iraq (not just the south) for a greater share in the government, which was dominated by Sunnīs.

40. This word, although widely used in Iraqi colloquial Arabic, is Persian in origin and Ḥuṣrī deploys it very effectively here to underscore Jawāhirī's essential "Persianness," even at the moment when he is on the verge of giving up his Iranian citizenship.

41. Ḥuṣrī, 1:589.

42. For a description of Ḥuṣrī's Turkish education, and he and his family's preference for Turkish as a language of communication (at least prior to 1919), see William L. Cleveland, *The Making of an Arab Nationalist: Ottomanism and Arabism in the Life and Thought of Sati' al-Husri* (Princeton: Princeton University Press, 1971), 14–16 and 39–40.

43. This essay has recently attracted much attention among those interested in nationalism and its relationship to modern literature and culture. It has been translated into English and republished in *Nation and Narration*, ed. Homi K. Bhabha (London: Routledge, 1990), 8–22. The passage quoted above is found on page 11 of *Nation and Narration*.

44. From "Neocolonialism and the Secret Agent of Knowledge: An Interview with Gayatri Spivak," *Oxford Literary Review* 13 (1991): 222.

45. This is one of those instances of elision that I spoke of above. In purely statistical terms, this statement could be considered correct. But it would not apply to, for example, Kurdish children whose home language was very close to Persian and quite far from Arabic (which belongs to an entirely different language family). The use of Arabic in state schools has always been a point of conflict between Iraqi Kurds and the central government. Likewise, many of the families in the Shī'ī religious and educational centers of Najaf and Karbalā' have always spoken Persian rather than Arabic. Then there is the question of Christian minorities and their use of older Semitic languages like Syriac. The linguistic mix in Iraq is a very complex one, as is the case with many "border" lands, nor does it respect neat geographical boundaries. So what may have been a liberationist move for one linguistic group was almost bound to be potentially recuperable as an oppressive move for another.

46. This was at the beginning of the British occupation in 1919. English instruction at that time began with eight hours a week in the Iraqi equivalent of the third grade, increased to nine hours in the fourth grade and ten hours in the sixth grade (see Ḥuṣrī,1:107). By 1922–23, the hours remained the same (in the sixth grade, three more hours were spent per week on English instruction (9) than on Arabic (6), but English instruction did not begin until the fifth grade (Ḥuṣrī, 1:212). In 1936, the number of hours spent on English at the primary level was reduced to six, making it equal to Arabic. It continued at the same level until the last two years of high school, when it was increased to seven (Roderic D. Matthews and Matta Akrawi, *Education in Arab Countries of the Near East* [Washington D.C.: American Council on Education, 1949]), 149 and 167. Thus a student like Sayyāb, who began school in 1932, would have spent, every year

after the fifth grade, as much time studying English in school as he would have on Arabic.

47. The difference between generations is underscored by the fact that al-Jawāhirī knew the Persian of Khayyām well and even translated part of the *Rubā'iyyāt* into Arabic. See Muḥyī al-Dīn Ismā'īl, 53.

48. For example, in one book that was in use in the Mandate Period, there is considerable material devoted to the period when Crusaders from Europe invaded the Levant (an event that barely touched the contemporary Iraqi society), but practically nothing is said about the later 'Abbasid caliphate or the struggle between the Ottomans and the Safavis. Equally, this same book devotes several chapters to the reforming Egyptian governor Muḥammad 'Ali (whose son occupied Syria with his father's army for nearly a decade) but does not even mention the Iraqi Mameluk governor Dawūd Pasha, who also sought to break away from Ottoman suzerainty but was defeated in 1831. See Muḥammad 'Izza Darwaza, *Durūs al-Tārīkh al-'Arabī min Aqdam al-Azmina Ḥattā al-Ān* in *Mukhtārāt Qawmiyya li-Muḥammad 'Izza Darwaza*, ed. Nājī 'Alūsh (Beirut: Markaz Dirāsāt al-Waḥda al-'Arabiyya, 1988), 55–217.

49. Yūsuf 'Izz al-Dīn, *Al-Shi'r al-'Irāqī al-Ḥadīth* (Cairo: Dār al-Ma'ārif, 1960), 212.

50. Sidonie Smith and Julia Watson, "Introduction: De/Colonization and the Politics of Discourse in Women's Autobiographical Practices," *De/Colonizing the Subject: The Politics of Gender in Women's Autobiography*, ed. Sidonie Smith and Julia Watson (Minneapolis: University of Minnesota Press, 1992), xvi.

51. At least he complains of precisely those problems (slowness and poor quality of reproduction) when, for the publication of his second collection of poems, he used an Iraqi printer. See Badr Shākir al-Sayyāb, letter to Ṣāliḥ Jawād al-Ṭu'ma, dated May 7, 1947, *Rasā'il al-Sayyāb* (Beirut: Dār al-Ṭāli'a, 1975), 53–54.

52. For a full account of the particulars of the coup, its causes and its aftermath, see Hanna Batatu, *The Old Social Classes and the Revolutionary Movements of Iraq* (Princeton: Princeton University Press, 1978), 30 and 345; and Reeva Simon, *Iraq Between the Two World Wars: The Creation and Implementation of a Nationalist Ideology* (New York: Columbia University Press, 1986), 146–47. It is worth noting that one of the results of this coup was that the British reoccupied Basra, and it is likely that Sayyāb, who was living there at the time as a high school student, witnessed their reentry in force into the city.

53. The text of the poem may be found in Sayyāb, *Dīwān*, 2:108–11.

54. 'Aqqād was from an early period active in the Wafd Party, which played a leading role in opposing British rule in Egypt following World War I. He wrote for its newspapers, composed a biography of Sa'd Zaghlūl, the Wafd leader, and was even a member of Parliament and leading speechmaker for the Wafd in the

late 1920s and 1930s. See Afaf Lutfi al-Sayyid-Marsot, *Egypt's Liberal Experiment: 1922–1936* (Berkeley: University of California Press, 1977), 134.

55. See, for example, 'Abbās Maḥmūd al-'Aqqād's highly influential later assessment of Shawqī and the other late neoclassical poets, *Shu'arā' Miṣr wa-Bī'ātuhum fī al-Jīl al-Māḍī* (Cairo: Maktabat al-Nahḍa, 1937) where he describes these poets as being "superficially Europeanized, but the influence did not penetrate very deeply." He concludes this key passage by saying that "they are among the people who were least able to understand the European mind and the European genius, even though they were in clothes and manners more European than the Europeans" (183–84). 'Aqqād then follows this judgment up by saying that the generation after Shawqī (his own) differs from their predecessors in being a generation that is extremely well-read in European, especially English, literature (192–93). This latter passage has been partially translated in Badawi, 87.

56. The definitive work on the Iraqi Communist Party is Hanna Batatu's *The Old Social Classes and the Revolutionary Movements of Iraq*. For relations between the Communists and the Nūrī al-Sa'īd group during World War II, see especially 485–92 and 523–31 of this book.

57. Quoted in Batatu, 370, from the Proceedings of the Iraqi House of Deputies, session of 7 June 1937, as reported by *Al-Ahālī*, Year 6, No. 606 of 8 June 1937.

58. Sayyāb, *Rasā'il* (Letter to Suhayl Idrīs, 19 June 1954), 62.

59. Badr Shākir al-Sayyāb, "Wasā'il Ta'rīf al-'Arab bi-Nitājihim al-Adabī al-Ḥadīth," *Al-Ādāb* 4, no. 10 (October 1956): 22.

60. See Sayyāb's short autobiographical sketch included in Jārjī, 17–20, especially page 18.

61. For more information on the relationship between Sayyāb and 'Alī Maḥmūd Ṭaha, see chapter 5 of this study, and Terri DeYoung, "Mu'āraḍa and Modern Arabic Poetry: Some Examples from the work of Badr Shākir al-Sayyāb," *Edebiyat* n.s. 5 (1994): 222–29.

62. Sayyāb was required to study a year of Latin in the Teachers College, and Catallus was probably one of the class texts. See Iḥsān 'Abbās, 54–55.

63. The titles of the poems (along with probable dates of composition) are: "Dhubūl Azāhir al-Diflā" (The Withering of the Oleander Flowers) (June 7, 1944), "Al-'Ushsh al-Majhūr" (The Abandoned Nest) (July 27, 1944), "Jadwāl Jaffa Mā'uh" (A Brook Whose Water Has Dried Up) (August 12, 1944), "Aṣīl Shaṭṭ al-'Arab," (Late Afternoon on the Shatt al-Arab) (August 30, 1944), and "Majrā Naḍīr al-Ḍiffatayn (The Stream with Two Bright Banks) (October 17, 1994). For Bullāṭa's description of the discovery of the poems, see his *Badr Shākir al-Sayyāb*, 38.

64. For the text of the poem see *Dīwān al-Sayyāb*, 2:296–99. The title of the poem is given in the *dīwān* as "Amīr Shaṭṭ al-'Arab," but this is almost certainly a misreading of the manuscript, since the poem never once speaks about a "prince

(*amīr*)," but from the very first line the time of day is established as being in "the late afternoon (*aṣīl*)." It has been so emended by Tawfīq Ḥasan in his edition of *Azhār Dhābila*, 216.

65. Literally, the second hemistich says: ". . . and the departure has begun to urge it forward." The verb "urge" used here is frequently employed in classical poetry specifically for the way a camel driver urges the caravan animals on with a rhythmic chant or a few well-chosen prods with a stick if the animal is laggard.

66. The word literally means "flat surface," but the context suggests garment-like connotations because the river is being "bodified" here.

67. The Arabic has literally "the *ribs* of the waves" here.

68. "Reeds" [poet's note].

69. "The small boat [used on] the Shatt al-Arab. I decided to mention it because the word *zawraq* does not truly convey the image of what I saw. And why shouldn't we mention the *balam*, when the Egyptians have mentioned the Venetian *zawraq*, the "gondola," and the English use the word *balam* in their language?" [poet's note].

70. According to Ḥasan Tawfīq (*Sayyāb*, 337), this line is a mu'āraḍa of a line from the beginning of the pre-Islamic poet 'Antara's *mu'allaqa*, describing his beloved 'Abla's mouth:

> idh tastabīka bi-dhī ghurūbin wāḍiḥi // 'adhbun muqabbaluhu ladhīdhu l-maṭ'ami
>
> (When she captures you with a mouth of lustrous teeth, clear to see, sweet is the place of kissing, delicious to the taste).

This linkage of the river to the human beloved celebrated by a famous poet from the Arabic literary tradition should be seen as highly relevant to the arguments I will be discussing about Sayyāb's use of both personification and the traditions of the past to construct an identity.

71. Sayyāb, *Dīwān* 2:296–99.

72. This is reinforced by the fact that the verb used here, *rāwaḥa*, strongly collocates with human activities, since it is used for the action of shifting from one foot to another and, in military contexts, for marking time in marching in parade formations.

73. William Wordsworth, "Preface to the Second Edition of *Lyrical Ballads* (1800)," *The Poetical Works of William Wordsworth*, ed. William Knight (Edinburgh: William Paterson, 1883), 4:278.

74. For a complete history of this controversy with special attention to Egypt, see Imīl Badī' Ya'qūb, *Jubrān*, 28–36. Vis-à-vis the Iraqi experience, Sāṭī' al-Ḥuṣrī describes several clashes with his British educational "adviser" over what language should be used in the new school system. See *Mudhakkirātī*, 1:67–68 and 212–13.

75. The authors of *The Empire Writes Back* speak of this phenomenon very helpfully when they say: "Within the syncretic reality of a post-colonial society it is impossible to return to an idealized pure pre-colonial cultural condition. . . . The post-colonial text is always a complex and hybridized formation. It is inadequate to read it either as a reconstruction of pure traditional values or as simply foreign and intrusive. The reconstruction of "pure" cultural value is always conducted with a radically altered dynamic of power relations" (Ashcroft et al., 110).

76. Bakhtin, *Dialogic Imagination*, 358.

77. A common periphrasis for Paradise in the Koran is "Gardens of Bliss."

78. This word is taken from Koran 2:35 where God recalls His commandment to Adam and Eve when they entered the Garden: "And We said: Adam, you and your mate live in the garden, and eat whatever is there with full pleasure, just as you wish, but do not come near this tree, lest you two become tyrants."

79. In the *Dīwān* (2:204 and 594) the poem is listed as "Ẓilāl al-Ḥubb (Shadows of Love)," but this is less likely as a title, since *ḍalāl* is used in the text in connection with love (line 4) while *ẓilāl* is not.

80. See, for example, Abū 'Abd Allāh al-Qurṭubī, *Al-Jāmi' li-Aḥkām al-Qur'ān* (Cairo: Dār al-Kātib al-'Arabī, 1967), 1:309, and Abū Ja'far Muḥammad ibn Jarīr al-Ṭabari, *The Commentary on the Qur'ān* trans. J[ohn] Cooper (Oxford: Oxford University Press, 1987), 249.

81. Ṭabarī makes precisely this linkage of "tyrants" and "transgressors" of boundaries or limits in his commentary on the Koran, 249.

82. This is very different from the Koran, of course, where the transgression is against the prohibitions, or limits/boundaries, set by God.

83. Ibn al-Muqaffa', *Al-Adab al-Kabīr* (Beirut: Dār Ṣādir, 1987), 63–64.

84. For a description of this theme, see E[rnst] R[obert] Curtius, *European Literature and the Latin Middle Ages* (Princeton: Princeton University Press, 1953) 83–85; for historical examples of it, see [Cicero], *Ad Herennium*, trans. Harry Caplan. (Cambridge: Harvard University Press Loeb Classical Library, 1954), 229–45.

85. This is Ṭahṭāwī's terminology. He equates "barbarism" with the nomadic lifestyle and "civilization" with city-dwelling, two concepts that become central to Muslim historiography after their use by Ibn Khaldūn. In fact, the whole conceptualization in its details of categorization (though not in its teleological argumentation) is somewhat reminiscent of Ibn Khaldūn, whom he had apparently read. See Rifā'a al-Ṭahṭāwī, *Takhlīṣ al-Ibrīz fī Talkhīṣ Bārīz* in *Uṣūl al-Fikr al-'Arabī al-Ḥadīth 'Ind al-Ṭahṭāwī, Ma' al-Naṣṣ al-Kāmil li-Kitābih: 'Takhlīs al-Ibrīz'*, ed. Maḥmūd Fahmī Ḥijāzī (Cairo: al-Hay'a al-Miṣriyya al-'Āmma li-al-Kitāb, 1974), where Ṭahṭāwī compares Montesquieu to Ibn Khaldūn (334), as well as his later championship of the publication of the *Muqaddima* in Egypt during the 1850s.

86. The Arabic text reads: "Fa-kullumā taqādama al-zamanu fī l-ṣu'ūd, ra'aytu ta'akhkhura l-nās. . . ," Ṭahṭāwī, 146.

87. "Wa-kullumā nazaltu wa-naẓartu ilā l-zaman fī l-hubūṭ. . . ," Ṭahṭāwī, 146.

88. Ṭahṭāwī, 147.

89. Sara Suleri, *The Rhetoric of English India* (Chicago: University of Chicago Press, 1992), 34.

90. Sayyāb, *Rasā'il* (letter to Khālid al-Shawwāf, dated July 26, 1944), 28.

3. JAYKUR STRETCHES OUT TO MEET MARGATE SANDS

1. From Bombay to Sydney to Baghdad and Cairo, no poet of Anglo-American modernism is better known or has been more influential on colonial literatures in ways both great and small than T.S. Eliot. This is despite the ambivalent attitude he often seems to take to the "primitive" and an espousal of the values of elitism that would seem ominous for multicultural dialogue (for an astute analysis of this aspect of Eliot's writings, see Gregory S. Jay, "Post-modernism in *The Waste Land*: Women, Mass Culture, and Others," in *Rereading the New: A Backward Glance at Modernism* ed. Kevin J.H. Dettmar [Ann Arbor: University of Michigan Press, 1992], 221–46). Perhaps part of the explanation for this can be seen in the fact that many of these poets seem to have sought, as did Sayyāb, as much to contest the hegemony of Eliot's vision as to espouse it uncritically. See, for example, the poetry of Nun Mim Rashid in D.J. Matthews, C. Shackle, and Shahrukh Husain, *Urdu Literature* (London: Urdu Markaz, 1985), 129–30; and the poetry of Sudhindranath Datta and Jivanananda Das in *Studies in Modern Bengali Poetry* ed. Nirmal Ghose (Calcutta: Novela, 1968), 21–70.

2. The above represents a combination of the two most explicit statements he made about his conception of *The Waste Land*. In a lecture Sayyāb gave at the Second Arab Writer's Conference (1956) in Damascus, "Wasā'il Ta'rīf al-'Arab bi-Nitājihim al-Adabī al-Ḥadīth," later published in *Al-Ādāb* 4, no. 10 (October 1956): 22–24, 100–101, he says: "So the unique English poet T.S. Eliot analyzed (*ḥallala*) his society—no, the entire society of Europe—deeply and sincerely, incorporating many truths, in his wonderful poem *The Waste Land*, which he wrote in the aftermath of World War I" (23). A similar evaluation of the poem is expressed in a 1962 interview he gave in Beirut, where he said: "T.S. Eliot in his poem 'The Waste Land' satirized (*hajā*) the Western capitalist world far more bitingly than the Communist poets ever did." ("Badr al-Sayyāb wa-al-Shi'r al-Ḥadīth wa-al-Iltizām," quoted in Jārjī, 99).

3. Quoted in F.O. Matthiessen, *The Achievement of T.S. Eliot: An Essay on the Nature of Poetry* (Oxford: Oxford University Press, 1935), 106, and Bernard Bergonzi, *T.S. Eliot* (New York: Collier Books, 1972), 93. See also C. Day Lewis, *A Hope for Poetry* (Oxford: Basil Blackwell, 1934; rpt. 1945) where he says "It is

very much to Eliot's credit as a poet that he detected this death-will in western civilization before it rose to the surface in the disillusionment of the later war years" (18). Stephen Spender, a member of the "'thirties generation" of English poets, writing in an appreciation on the occasion of Eliot's death in 1965, tries to sum up the impression made on his contemporaries when he says: ". . . *The Waste Land* was exciting . . . because it was concerned with the life which we felt to be real. It carried the equipment of the world beyond the screen, a landscape across which armies and refugees moved" ("Remembering Eliot," *Encounter* 24, no. 4 [April 1965]), 5.

4. Stephen Spender recounts an illuminating anecdote about how an undergraduate at a meeting of the Oxford Poetry Club asked Eliot what he meant when he wrote a particularly oblique and seemingly quite allusive line from the poem *Ash Wednesday*: "Lady, three white leopards sat under a juniper tree?" Eliot responded by saying "I mean, 'Lady, three white leopards sat under a juniper tree . . .' (Spender, "Remembering Eliot," 4).

5. Matthiessen, 106; and Bergonzi, 93.

6. John Porter Houston, *French Symbolism and the Modernist Movement* (Baton Rouge: Louisiana State University Press, 1980), 123.

7. Probably the best guide to the more recent responses to *The Waste Land* can be found in Gregory S. Jay's article mentioned at the beginning of this chapter, "Postmodernism in *The Waste Land*: Women, Mass Culture, and Others."

8. This has been the case despite the fact that Eliot made a very telling reference to "land" as a theme in a late lecture, in the context of a discussion of Thomas Hardy's writing: "Landscape is a passive creature which lends itself to an author's mood. Landscape is fitted . . . for the purposes of an author who is interested not at all in men's minds, but only in their emotions; and perhaps only in men as vehicles for emotions" (T.S. Eliot, *After Strange Gods: A Primer of Modern Heresy* [New York: Harcourt, Brace, and Company, 1933], 59). Such observations would be very suggestive for any attempt at understanding Eliot's manipulation of landscape representation in both *The Waste Land* and *The Four Quartets*.

9. His many references to critical works by Stephen Spender, for example, show not only his fondness for that writer's essays but also would suggest a systematic attempt to assimilate his entire *ouevre*. For his reference to reading "Tradition and the Individual Talent," see his discussion of the essay in a letter dated May 4, 1958, to Yūsuf al-Khāl, *Rasā'il al-Sayyāb*, 80.

10. F.R. Leavis, *New Bearings in English Poetry: A Study of the Contemporary Situation* (London: Chatto and Windus, 1942), 103.

11. Matthiessen, 37–38.

12. Hugh Kenner, *The Invisible Poet: T.S. Eliot* (New York: McDowell, Obolensky, 1959), 180–81.

13. For characteristic examples of the ambiguous nature of more recent readings of *The Waste Land*, see Calvin Bedient, *He Do the Police in Different*

Voices: The Waste Land *and Its Protagonist* (Chicago: The University of Chicago Press, 1986), especially page 218; and John T. Mayer, *T.S. Eliot's Silent Voices* (Oxford: Oxford University Press, 1989), especially pages 290–91.

14. For a detailed description of 'Awaḍ's article in the context of other early writings in Arabic about Eliot and a well-nuanced assessment of the role it played in introducing the poet to Arab readers, see Muhammad Abdul-Hai, *Tradition and English and American Influence in Arabic Romantic Poetry* (London: Ithaca Press, 1982), 225–27.

15. See Abdul-Hai, 226.

16. Besides "The Hollow Men," translated lines include long sections from the middle and end of "The Love Song of J. Alfred Prufrock," the first eighteen lines of *The Waste Land*, the first fifteen lines of "Burnt Norton" from *The Four Quartets*, the last nine lines from the second section and the last thirteen lines from the third section of the same poem, and a shorter section from "The Dry Salvages," the lines from the second section beginning "The moments of happiness—not the sense of well-being," and ending with "We can assign to happiness. . ." What unites these quotations in an interesting way is their concern with the temporal and with describing the human experience of time.

17. Evidence would include the fact that the first explicit mention of the term "Waste Land," along with its attribution specifically to T.S. Eliot, can be found in a poem probably composed in 1946, "To the Beauty of the Castle" (see note 20).

18. See Bullāṭa, 44, and Tawfīq, 67–68, for details of this episode.

19. *Rasā'il al-Sayyāb*, 50.

20. The poem's title is "Ilā Ḥasnā' al-Qaṣr" (To the Beauty of the Castle). For complete text of poem and note, see Sayyāb, *Azhār Dhābila wa-Qaṣā'id Majhūla* ed. Ḥasan Tawfīq, 95. For the reference in 'Awaḍ's article, see Lūwīs 'Awaḍ, "T.S. Iliyūt," *Al-Kātib al-Miṣrī* 1, no. 4 (January 1946):568.

21. See, for example, Badawī, 251.

22. *Azhār Dhābila*, ed. Tawfīq, 95.

23. By this time Sayyāb had become a member of the Iraqi Communist Party. See Bullāṭa, 40–41 and 44; 'Abbās 89–90, 128, and 172–80.

24. For analyses of this relationship between Eliot's poetry and the dramatic monologue form, see Robert Langbaum, *The Poetry of Experience: The Dramatic Monologue in Modern Literary Tradition* (New York: W.W. Norton, 1957), 76–77 and 189–92, and Mayer, 8–9 and passim.

25. Tawfīq, *Sayyāb*, 332.

26. He had earlier attended Cambridge University, where he had received a B.A. in 1943 and an M.A. in 1948. For more complete biographical information, see Issa Boullata, "Jabrā Ibrāhīm Jabrā," *Encyclopedia of World Literature in the Twentieth Century* Vol. 5: Supplement and Index (New York: Continuum Publishing Company, 1993), 329–330.

27. Adonis was the Greek name for a mythic figure who was known in earlier Mesopotamian traditions as Tammuz. In the Greek myth Adonis was the beloved of the goddess Venus, but before that (as Tammuz) he had been the consort of the Babylonian/ancient Semitic goddess Ishtar.

28. Jabrā would later publish these sections and the rest of the translation of part 4 (in 1957). See 'Abd al-Riḍā 'Alī, *Al-Usṭūra fī Shi'r al-Sayyāb* (Beirut: Dār al-Rā'id al-'Arabī, 1978), 51 and Salma Khadra Jayyusi, *Trends and Movements in Modern Arabic Poetry* (Leiden: E.J. Brill, 1977), 2:731–33.

29. Jabrā Ibrāhīm Jabrā, *Al-Riḥla al-Thāmina* (Beirut: Al-Maktaba al-'Aṣriyya, 1967), 24.

30. Although F.O. Matthiessen perceptively notes (in a passage about this same scene from "The Fire Sermon") that this process works both ways. Quoting a line taken from a previous work in a new context also forces a rereading of the precursor text and the "idealized . . . begin[s] to be seen with new eyes" (49).

31. Sayyāb mentions this passage specifically in a letter to Suhayl Idrīs four years later. See *Rasā'il Sayyāb*, 83.

32. This is the name still given to the month of July in the traditional calendar used to mark the divisions of the solar year in the Fertile Crescent area (modern-day Lebanon, Syria, Palestine, Jordan, and Iraq).

33. James Frazer, *The Golden Bough Part IV: Adonis, Attis Osiris* (New York: The Macmillan Company, 1935; 3rd ed.), 1:230–31.

34. In passing, it might be noted that colonial enterprises in one form or another had contributed a great deal to this store of information. See Robert Ackerman, "The Cambridge Group: Origins and Composition," in *The Cambridge Ritualists Reconsidered* (Atlanta: Scholars Press, 1991), where he says: ". . . the end-of-the-century scramble for colonies among the imperial powers . . . threw off as a by-product unexampled quantities of ethnographic data about so-called primitive peoples which in turn permitted generalizations of a scope quite unimaginable at any earlier time" (4). Although Sayyāb may or may not have been aware of this aspect of Frazer's work, it illustrates the ways in which modernism (for not only Eliot, but Ezra Pound and many other modernist writers appropriated work from Frazer) could be invisibly complicitous with colonialism: its celebrated disinterestedness and "openness to the other" was conditioned from the start by the colonial discourses of containment and exploitation.

35. John Vickery, *The Literary Impact of* The Golden Bough (Princeton: Princeton University Press, 1973), 26.

36. Fukai was a character that Sayyāb created for these poems, a "writer at the Christian mission in Hiroshima who was driven mad from terror at what he saw following the dropping of the atomic bomb" (poet's note, *Dīwān*, 1:355). His consciousness unites the three poems "Min Ru'yā Fūkāy" (From the Vision of Fukai), "Marthiyat al-Āliha" (Elegy for the Gods), and "Marthiyat Jaykūr" (Elegy for Jaykūr) as their focalizing agent. Although Sayyāb indicated at the

time of their publication in *Al-Ādāb* magazine (January through April 1955) that they were part of a larger long poem he was writing called "The Vision of Fukai," no new installments were written, and when the three poems were first published in book form in Sayyāb's 1960 collection *Unshūdat al-Maṭar*, they were not grouped together, nor was any indication given that they had originally been conceived as a linked series.

37. Sayyāb, *Dīwān* 1:361.

38. T.S. Eliot, *Collected Poems: 1909–1962* (New York: Harcourt Brace and Company, 1963), 54.

39. In Arabic, al-Ma'arrī's line reads "Wa-l-ladhī ḥārati l-bariyyatu fī-hi ḥayawānun mustaḥdathun min jamādi."

40. The line reads in Arabic "Wa-l-ladhī ḥārati l-bariyyatu fī-hi bi-t-ta'āwīli kā'inun dhū nuqūdi."

41. Ra'īf al-Khūrī, "Qara'tu al-'Adad al-Māḍī," *Al-Ādāb* 3, no. 2 (February 1955): 65.

42. 'Abd al-Raḥmān Rabāḥ al-Kayālī, "Hawla Qara'tu al-'Adad al-Māḍī," *Al-Ādāb* 3, no. 6 (June 1955): 68.

43. Maḥmūd Amīn al-'Ālim, "Qara'tu al-'Adad al-Māḍī, " *Al-Ādāb* 3, no. 3 (March 1955): 66.

44. Al-'Ālim, 67.

45. A complete and substantially accurate (with one exception that will be discussed below) translation of the poem can be found in *Modern Arabic Poetry: An Anthology*, ed. Salma Khadra Jayyusi (New York: Columbia University Press, 1987), 437.

46. Here I find myself forced to disagree with Lena Jayyusi and Christopher Middleton's translation. The Arabic in the *dīwān* reads: Fa-kayfa yuḥissu insānun yarā qabrah? / Yarāhu wa-innahu la-yaḥāru fīh: / A ḥayyun huwa am mayyitun? fa-mā yakfīh / An yarā ẓillan la-hu 'alā r-rimāl, / Ka-mi'dhanatin mu'affara. Which they translate as ". . . How / does a person feel when he sees his grave? / He sees it and is perplexed. Is he / alive or dead? For it is not enough / that he should be impressed by what he sees across the sand, / A dusty minaret . . ." This vitiates, however, the precision of Sayyāb's Arabic imagery in the last two lines, which I believe should rather be translated as ". . . For it is not enough / For him to see *he has* a shadow on the sand / *Like* a dusty minaret . . . " [emphasis mine]. In the original Arabic, then, the observer and the minaret are fused into one through the vehicle of the shadow, and this provides the ground for the symbolic significance the minaret takes on in the rest of the poem. The translation, however, maintains a certain distancing between the man and the minaret that makes it more difficult to recognize what Sayyāb is doing here.

I also find myself in partial disagreement with Iḥsān 'Abbās's reading of these lines in his book *Badr Shakir al-Sayyāb* when he says that they "depict a man who is *in reality* dead . . ." [my emphasis] (271–72), because I think that the whole tropological structure of the poem depends on this question being uncertain in the speaker's mind (i.e., not a rhetorical question), at least in the beginning.

47. Sayyāb, *Dīwān*, 1:395.

48. Sayyāb, *Dīwān*, 1:398.

49. This is the Arabic spelling of the name for the Alhambra, the famous palace in Granada belonging to the last Muslim ruler in Europe. It fell to King Ferdinand and Queen Isabella in 1492, the same year as Columbus set sail for the Indies and discovered the New World. It is now preserved as a museum: a fitting symbol of the "dead" past, here transformed by being made relevant to the present.

50. Sayyāb, *Dīwān*, 1:400–402.

51. The classic description of this poetic kind is to be found in M.H. Abrams "Structure and Style in the Greater Romantic Lyric" (included in *Romanticism and Consciousness*, ed. Harold Bloom [New York: W.W. Norton, 1970], 201–29), especially in his characterization of these poems as "present[ing] a determinate speaker in a particularized, and usually a localized outdoor setting, whom we overhear as he carries on, in a fluent vernacular which easily rises to a more formal speech, a sustained colloquy, sometimes with himself or with the outer scene, but more frequently with a silent human auditor, present or absent. The speaker begins with a description of the landscape; an aspect or change of aspect in the landscape evokes a varied but integral process of memory, thought, anticipation, and feeling which remains closely involved with the outer scene. In the course of this meditation the lyric speaker achieves an insight, faces up to a tragic loss, comes to a moral decision, or resolves an emotional problem" (201).

52. That there is a resemblance between Eliot's techniques for representing the "disassociated" modern consciousness and the most common form for the traditional Arabic poem should not be lost on the reader here. Although it is a hypothesis impossible to prove, the idea that the rejection of the "Fukai" poems—Sayyāb's first attempts to use this modernist mode of representing thought—may be due in part at least to the fact that they reminded their readers of the now inadequate models of traditional Arabic poetry is a seductive one. It certainly is suggestive that the reviewers' most-often-voiced objection to the "Fukai" poems is that they are "disorganized" and "unintegrated." Further, the fact that in some parts these poems used traditional meters and the hemistich form is frequently brought to the reader's attention and made the object of negative comments in the critics' discussions of the poems.

53. In this regard, note how Sayyāb uses personification in the last lines of the poem to turn the land into a woman about to give birth.

54. By "Islam" here I mean normative Islam, not folk practices in the Islamic world, to which Frazer frequently refers.

55. The clearest example of the more general signification is found with the Koranic prophet Khiḍr, whose very name comes from the same Arabic root as the word for green. As he is portrayed in the Koran, this prophet is closely associated

with events linked to rebirth or the coming of new life to something dead. See the traditional commentaries on Sura 18 (al-Kahf), verses 60–65, and the *Encyclopedia of Islam*, art. "Khiḍr."

56. Frazer, 5:81.

57. Sayyāb, *Dīwān*, 1:400.

58. See Stephen Greenblatt, *Marvellous Possessions: The Wonder of the New World* (Chicago: University of Chicago Press, 1991), 134.

59. For a complete exploration of the colonial sources of *The Tempest*, see Leslie Fiedler, *The Stranger in Shakespeare* (New York: Stein and Day, 1972), 199–253. An analysis of the connection between the name Caliban and the word cannibal can be found on page 205.

60. Hayden White, *Tropics of Discourse: Essays in Cultural Criticism* (Baltimore: Johns Hopkins University Press, 1978), 188.

61. It should be noted that Sayyāb, too, must have been strongly affected by this passage, since he uses these lines from the Koran as an epigraph to his 1954 poem "Al-Mukhbir" (The Informer).

62. One of the frequent discursive strategies of "high" Orientalism is to describe Islam as being impoverished in terms of symbolism and to compare it unfavorably with the "richness" of Christian symbolism.

63. For a more detailed discussion of this aspect of "Christ After the Crucifixion," see DeYoung, "And Thereby Hangs a Tale," 137–54.

64. See, for example, the discussions of Stephen Slemon, "Magic Realism as Post-Colonial Discourse," *Canadian Literature* 116 (Spring 1988): 14–15; and Suleri, 113.

65. Sayyāb, *Rasā'il* (letter to Suhayl Idrīs dated May 7, 1958), 82–83.

66. See Michel Foucault, *Technologies of the Self: A Seminar with Michel Foucault*, ed. Luther H. Martin, Huck Gutman, and Patrick H. Hutton (Amherst: University of Massachusetts Press, 1988) for an indication of how preoccupied Foucault was with this subject in the period just before his death, and what the terminology meant to him in the context of his research.

4. ODYSSEUS RETURNS AS SINDBAD

1. Quoted in Issa J. Boullata, "The Poetic Technique of Badr Shākir al-Sayyāb (1926-1964)," in *Critical Perspectives on Modern Arabic Literature* ed. Issa J. Boullata (Washington D.C.: Three Continents Press, 1980), 241. It should be noted that the figure of Odysseus had, even by the early 1960s, developed an enormous symbolic significance for modern Arab poets, a significance that has only grown with the passage of time. For a cogent review and analysis of this phenomenon, see the recent paper by As'ad Khairallah, "The Greek Cultural Heritage and the Odyssey of Modern Arab Poets," in *Tradition and Modernity in*

Arabic Literature, ed. Issa Boullata and Terri DeYoung (Fayetteville: University of Arkansas Press, 1997), 43–61.

2. A letter Sayyāb wrote to the author 'Āṣim al-Jindī, dated September 11,1963, gives us more of a sense of the state of mind out of which this declaration arose: "I am not writing, these days, anything except purely personal (*dhātī*) poetry. I am no longer "committed" (*multazim*). What harvest did I reap from commitment? This disease and this poverty? . . . Do not think that I am pessimistic. The opposite is true. But my attitude toward death has changed. I am no longer afraid of it. Let it come when it wants. I feel that I have lived for a very long time: that I accompanied Gilgamesh on his adventures, and befriended Odysseus (*'Ūlīs*) during the time he was lost. And I have lived all of Arab history. Is this not enough?" *Rasā'il al-Sayyāb*, 177. It should also be noted that the above constitutes something of an overstatement. Sayyāb continued to use allusions to a number of different myths and mythical figures besides Sindbad and Odysseus in his later poems (especially if we include in this category biblical/Koranic allusions). Figures that appear in poems written after 1962, when Sayyāb's work began to change as a result of his awareness of his illness, include Cain (*Dīwān*, 1:251), the Magi, the Flood, Noah (1:212–16, and 1:258), Zeus, Proserpine, and Aeneas (1:238–41), not to speak of the magnificent series of ten poems where the speaker is Job (*Dīwān*, 1:248–76), considered by many to be the best of Sayyāb's late work. It would be fair to say that these mythic allusions are, however, notably less frequent than in the immediately preceding period of Sayyāb's career.

3. See 'Abbās, 268; and Bullāṭa, 190.

4. Ḥasan Tawfīq has been a particularly strong advocate of this position. See, for example, pages 168–69 of his book. The connection between "introspection" and romanticism as characteristics of Sayyāb's work can be seen as better motivated if we recall that many of the characteristic patterns of romantic writing involve *internalizations* of literary themes—like the "quest"—that were externalized in earlier eras. For discussions of two instances that have particular relevance to Sayyāb's work, see Harold Bloom, "The Internalization of Quest Romance," in *Romanticism and Consciousness*, ed. Harold Bloom (New York: W.W. Norton, 1970), 3–24; and M.H. Abrams's analysis of the "internalization" of apocalyptic imagery in *Natural Supernaturalism: Tradition and Revolution in Romantic Literature* (New York: W.W. Norton, 1971), 327–72.

5. Sayyāb would die at the early age of 37 in 1964, after a three-year struggle with the degenerative muscular disease amyotrophic lateral sclerosis (ALS)—commonly known as "Lou Gehrig's disease" in the United States.

6. Charles Segal, *Singers, Heroes, and Gods in the* Odyssey (Cornell: Cornell University Press, 1994), 62.

7. See Iḥsān 'Abbās, 68, for a discussion of Sayyāb's use of Palgrave here. The poem was published in Sayyāb's first *dīwān*, *Azhār Dhābila*, and then republished (after extensive revisions) in *Azhār wa-Asāṭīr*.

8. When this poem was re-published in *Azhār wa-Asāṭīr*, Sayyāb revised some of the lines slightly. The differences, while giving interesting evidence of how Sayyāb worked to change his poetry, have little impact on my argument here, and therefore I have not noted them. For those interested in comparing the two versions, see *Azhār Dhābila*, ed. Tawfīq, 136–49.

9. Sayyāb, *Dīwān*, 1:13–14.

10. Sayyāb, *Dīwān*, 2:396.

11. Hārūn al-Rashīd, Abbasid caliph famous for his wealth and patronage of literature.

12. Sayyāb, *Dīwān*, 1:407.

13. Sayyāb, *Dīwān*, 1:408.

14. Sayyāb, *Dīwān*, 1:563–64.

15. Sayyāb, *Dīwān*, 1:147.

16. Sayyāb, *Dīwān*, 1:597–601.

17. Sayyāb, *Dīwān*, 1:602–7.

18. Sayyāb, *Dīwān*, 1:218.

19. For an extended discussion of this dual depiction of Odysseus in classical Greek and Latin literature, see W.B. Stanford, *The Ulysses Theme: A Study in the Adaptability of a Traditional Hero* (Oxford: Basil Blackwell, 1954), especially pages 90–95 and 104–17.

20. Dante, *Inferno* 26:97–99 (. . . vincer poter dentro da me l'ardore / ch'i'ebbi a divenir del mondo esperto, / e de li vizi umani e del valore;); see Dante Alighieri, *Inferno*, trans. with notes by Allan Gilbert (Durham: Duke University Press, 1969), 219 and 221 for English translation. Clearly, Ulysses' desire here is for knowledge, which as we have seen can never be wholly unimplicated in a desire for power.

21. Dino Bigongiari, "Dante's Ulysses and Columbus," edited and introduced by Henry Paolucci in *Columbus, America, and the World*, ed. Anne Paolucci and Henry Paolucci, Review of National Literatures, no. 16 (New York: Griffon House Publications, 1992), 119.

22. He frequently mentions Dante's work as having influenced him and, given his fascination with Milton, which clearly motivated him to read at least part of *Paradise Lost*, it would not be amiss to hypothesize a similar experience with Dante.

23. Sayyāb never mentions having read the Tennyson version of Ulysses. It was, however, used throughout the British Empire as a curriculum text, and it thus would not have been unlikely that an English major at the Baghdad Teachers College would have been required to read it. For an illuminating discussion of the dissemination of "Ulysses" in Britain's colonial empire, see Matthew Rowlinson, "The Ideological Moment of Tennyson's 'Ulysses,'" *Victorian Poetry* 30, nos. 3-4 (Autumn-Winter 1992): 265–267.

24. See, for a convenient summary of all Tennyson's sources for the poem as well as a convincing argument that Dante was the most important of them, Tony

Robbin's article, "Tennyson's 'Ulysses': The Significance of the Homeric and Dantesque Backgrounds," *Victorian Poetry* 11, no. 3 (Autumn 1973): 177–93, and especially 187–90.

25. Two facts make this a more plausible hypothesis than might otherwise be supposed. First, when the *1842 Poems* (which included "Ulysses") was published, one of the most widely disseminated reviews to actually mention the poem by name said; "Yet we know not why, except from schoolboy recollections, a modern English poet should write of Ulysses rather than of the great voyagers of the modern world, Columbus, Gama, or even Drake." Quoted in Alfred, Lord Tennyson, *The Poems of Tennyson in Three Volumes*, ed. Christopher Ricks (London: Longman, 1987), 3:49. Thus, there was a connection established early on in the minds of readers between Tennyson's "Ulysses" and the figure of Columbus. Later, this linkage was reinforced when, in 1880, Tennyson wrote a dramatic monologue entitled "Columbus" in response "to entreaties from certain prominent Americans that he would commemorate the discovery of America in verse" (*Poems* 3:49). This latter poem contains several allusions to the text of "Ulysses." A brief discussion of the relationship between the two poems can be found in Roger B. Wilkenfeld, "'Columbus' and 'Ulysses': Notes on the Development of a Tennysonian Theme, "Victorian *Poetry* 12, no. 2 (Summer 1974): 170–74.

26. This was an interest shared by Sayyāb. See chapter 7 of this study.

27. See Patrick Brantlinger, *Rule of Darkness: British Literature and Imperialism, 1830–1914* (Ithaca: Cornell University Press, 1988), 35–36 and 143.

28. Alfred, Lord Tennyson, *Complete Poems* (New York: R. Worthington, 1885), 61.

29. Rowlinson, 267.

30. For an interesting discussion of this concept—especially as it relates to Sayyāb's depiction of his natal village, Jaykūr—see Tramontini, 93–96. Tramontini rightly points to the interaction of "public" myth and "private" myth as a significant feature in Sayyāb's work.

31. It is worth noting here that women in the Arab/Islamic world have long been associated symbolically with the land, just as in the Western tradition. Although the linkage may be even older than the advent of the Koran, verse 223 in Sūrat al-Baqara underwrites the authority of this trope in Koranic contexts: "Nisā'ukum ḥarthun la-kum" (Your women are a tillage for you). Al-Qurṭubī cites the following verse by the grammarian al-Tha'lab in his explication of this verse:

Innamā l-arḥāmu arḍūna la-nā muḥtarathātu
fa-'alaynā z-zar'u fīhā wa-'alā l-lāhi n-nabātu.

(The wombs are naught but lands for us, places for tilling:
ours is the sowing, God's the growing).

This line makes clearer the metaphoric equivalence between woman and land that was understood as being derived from the Koranic verse (for further discussion, see Qurṭubī, 2:901). For a brief examination of the use of this theme in modern Arabic (and especially Palestinian poetry) see Khalid Sulaiman, *Palestine and Modern Arabic Poetry* (London: Zed Books, 1984), 156-57.

32. The closest literal English equivalent to the Arabic word used here, *nashwān*, would be "intoxicated." It has become a technical term in Sufism, used to describe the rapture (akin to the first flush of physical inebriation from drinking alcohol) felt by the seeker when he or she first begins to the feel oneness with God. In this case I have not translated it as "drunk" or "intoxicated," because Sayyāb also seems to have in mind the visual image of the rising sun's rays being caught and reflected off the panes of glass in the window. Thus, a word like "radiant," which in English collocates both with light reflection and inner, transfigurational emotional states seemed most appropriate.

33. Sayyāb, *Dīwān*, 1:117–18.

34. As a technical term in Islamic theology, this word refers to the journey on which the Prophet Muḥammad was taken one night by God, in which he visited the seven heavens. God transported Muḥammad to Jerusalem on the back of the marvelous steed Burāq, and from there he ascended to heaven.

35. Sayyāb, *Dīwān*, 1:119.

36. "A lake in Malaysia in whose depths the temple sank"—poet's note.

37. Sayyāb, *Dīwān*, 1:179–81.

38. "The river which leads to Lake Chine"—poet's note.

39. Sayyāb, *Dīwān*, 1:183.

40. "The cave where the revelation descended upon Muḥammad"—poet's note.

41. "Ganymede, the Greek youth to whom Zeus (the chief of the gods) sent an eagle in order to kidnap him. He became a cupbearer to the gods"—poet's note.

42. Literally, "reddish wine."

43. Sayyāb, *Dīwān*, 1:184–85.

5. THIS BOY'S LIFE

1. Bāzī, 180–181. Buraq was the name of the steed on which Muḥammad rode during his ascension (*mi'raj*) to the heavens.

2. Amatzia Baram even goes so far as to make the assumption that Sayyāb actually was a Shi'ī in his book *Culture, History and Ideology in the Formation of Ba'thist Iraq, 1968–89* (Oxford: St. Anthony's College in association with Macmillan, 1991), 87, undoubtedly based on his understanding that Sayyāb was from southern Iraq.

3. But he also wrote a series of poems dealing with Kurdish themes when he was working for one of al-Jawāhirī's newspapers.

4. For descriptions of this conference and Sayyāb's role in it, see Bullāṭa, 122–26 and 'Abbās, 342–44.

5. See 'Abbās, 174.

6. For a comprehensive picture of these groups and their relations to each other, see the chapter on "Shaikhs, Aghas and Peasants" in Batatu, 63–152.

7. 'Abbās, 18.

8. Bullāṭa, 18–19.

9. Bullāṭa, 30.

10. See Rajab Barakāt, *Ṣiḥāfat al-Khalīj al-'Arabī* (Baghdad: Maṭba'at al-Irshād, 1977), 140–41.

11. Bullāṭa, 30.

12. Barakāt, 141.

13. Quoted in Jārjī, 38–39.

14. Jārjī, 30.

15. Jārjī, 35–36.

16. Jārjī, 32.

17. Jalīl Kamāl al-Dīn, "Bayna al-Sayyāb wa-Dustīyūsfskī," *Al-Ādāb*, 22, nos. 7–8 (July–August 1975): 39.

18. 'Īsā Bullāṭa wisely chooses to remain on safer ground, choosing to state explicitly from the outset that his only purpose is biographical and not one of literary interpretation. See Bullāṭa, 11.

19. Edward Said, *The World, the Text and the Critic* (Cambridge: Harvard University Press, 1983), 15–20.

20. Bullāṭa, 53. The poem was "Ri'a Tatamazzaq" (A Torn Lung). See Sayyāb *Dīwān*, 1:42.

21. Jārjī, 18.

22. Tawfīq, 332.

23. *Rasā'il Sayyāb*, 24–25 (the letter dated July 11, 1944), and 29 (the letter dated July 26, 1944).

24. Ḥasan Tawfīq gives a complete list of Sayyāb's quotations from al-Ma'arrī, see Tawfīq, 336–37.

25. His earliest citations from classical poets, of 'Antara in "Ḍalāl al-Ḥubb" and Imru' al-Qays in the 1944 poem "Al-Masā' al-Akhīr" (The Last Evening) would appear to be even less oppositional than his later usage of classical poetry, since their presence in the respective poems seems predicated upon a desire simply to call upon the valorized presence of the "canon" as a defense against intrusive threats from without (in the latter poem it is the attack upon the lovers' bliss by the Greek god Cupid).

26. Tawfīq, 327.

27. This is the final installment of the series of Fukai poems. See chapter 3 of this study, 76–79.

28. Said, 16–17.

29. For a discussion of how these two poets are present in Sayyāb's political verse, see Tawfīq, 172–73.

30. Sayyāb, *Dīwān*, 1:418-419.

31. Aḥmad Shawqī, "Nakbat Dimashq" (The Tragedy of Damascus), *Al-Shawqiyyāt* (Cairo: Maṭba'at Al-Istiqāma, 1964), 2:76.

32. See Tawfīq, 337–42.

33. For examples of such definitions, see Aḥmad Shāyib, *Tārīkh al-Naqā'iḍ fī al-Shi'r al-'Arabī* (Cairo: Maktabat al-Nahḍa,1954), 6–8; Ibrāhīm 'Awaḍayn, *Al-Mu'āraḍa fī al-Adab al-'Arabī* (Cairo: Maṭba'at al-Sa'āda, 1981), 8–10; and Muḥammad Maḥmūd Qāsim Nawfal, *Tārīkh al-Mu'āraḍāt fī al-Shi'r al-'Arabī* (Beirut: Dār al-Furqān, 1983), 13. Usually it is implied, or an explicit rider may even be attached to this definition stating that the gap between composition of the original and the *mu'āraḍa* may be virtually nonexistent, and that the two authors may be contemporaries. See Nawfal, 13; Awaḍayn, 9 and 47.

34. Nawfal and Awaḍayn occasionally acknowledge the issue, but consistently minimize the confrontational aspect whenever possible, usually concluding any discussion by stressing the interpretation of *mu'āraḍa* as homage or apprenticeship technique, as when Nawfal adds, after defining *mu'āraḍa* on a strictly formal basis: "This [i.e., *mu'āraḍa*] is only the result of the later poet's *admiration* for that [earlier] poem" [emphasis added] (13). For more examples of the same approach, see Awaḍayn, 35–59.

35. Abū al-Qāsim al-Ḥasan ibn Bishr al- Āmidī, *Al-Muwāzana bayna Abī Tammām wa-al-Buḥturī* (Cairo: Dār al-Ma'ārif, 1972), 6 (emphasis added).

36. One of the most useful treatises in this respect (i.e., of better understanding *mu'āraḍa*) is the one by Abū Sulaymān al-Khaṭṭābī (d. 998 A.D.), "I'jāz al-Qur'ān," which is included in *Thalāth Rasā'il fī I'jāz al-Qur'ān*, ed. Muḥammad Khalaf Allāh and Muḥammad Zaghlūl Sallām (Cairo: Dār al-Ma'ārif, 1968), 21–71, along with two more famous brethren by al-Rummānī ("Al-Nukat fī I'jāz al-Qur'ān," 75–113) and 'Abd al-Qāhir al-Jurjānī ("Al-Risāla al-Shāfiya fī al-I'jāz," 117–58).

37. For versions of the anecdote, see, for example, al-Khaṭṭābī, 58–59, and al-Jurjānī, 129-30. Other sources can be found in Nawfal, 16.

38. Nawfal, 16, quoting from Ibn Qutayba, *Kitāb al-Shi'r wa-al-Shu'arā'* (Leiden: E.J. Brill, 1904), 107.

39. As late as the 1970s, probably the most extensive definition of *mu'āraḍa* was found in the brief comments made by Aḥmad al-Shāyib in his book devoted to the related technique of *munāqaḍa* (flyting) (6–8). The lack of available sources, for example, is reflected in the article on *mu'āraḍa* in the new *Encyclopedia of Islam*. In the early 1980s, however, three books quickly appeared one after the other which dealt exclusively with *mu'āraḍa*: Ibrāhīm 'Awaḍayn's *Al-Mu'āraḍa fī al-Adab al-'Arabī*, and his *Al-Mu'āraḍa fī Shi'r*

Shawqī, along with Muḥammad Maḥmūd Qāsim Nawfal's *Tārīkh al-Mu'āraḍāt fī al-Shi'r al-'Arabī*. Both authors pay a certain degree of attention to *mu'āraḍa* as contrafaction of themes, but 'Awadayn is clearly more comfortable with the traditional formalist definition and less willing to look at *mu'āraḍa* in new ways.

40. This is in direct contrast to the few Western discussions of *mu'āraḍa*, where the assumption is almost automatically made that contrafaction of thematic elements is necessarily part of the global phenomenon of *mu'āraḍa*. See, for example, Margaret Larkin, "Two Examples of *Rithā'*: A Comparison between Aḥmad Shawqī and al-Mutanabbī," *Journal of Arabic Literature*, 16 (1985): 18–39; and Harlow, 24.

41. Probably the closest correspondence to *mu'āraḍa* in Western culture is the medieval (largely musical) practice known as "contrafaction," in which new lyrics were set to older melodies. The analogy between this practice and *mu'āraḍa*, where the formal parameters of the poem—its meter and rhyme—remain the same while the treatment of thematic elements in the poem change, is obvious. Therefore, I propose in the following discussion to use "contrafact" to refer to the act of making a *mu'āraḍa*—rather than attempt an awkward neologism like " *mu'āraḍ*ize." In this I am following a precedent set by many of those who deal with the *muwashshaḥāt* of Hispano-Arabic poetry (a good number of these poems being *mu'āraḍa*s).

42. Adūnīs ('Alī Aḥmad Sa'īd), "Muḥāwala fī Ta'rīf al-Shi'r al-Ḥadīth" (An Attempt to Define Modern Poetry), *Majallat Shi'r* (Beirut) 2, no. 3 (summer 1959): 79.

43. Sasson Somekh, "The Neo-Classical Arab Poets," *Modern Arabic Literature*, ed. M. M. Badawi (Cambridge: Cambridge University Press, 1992), 59.

44. See the first five chapters of 'Abbās Maḥmūd al-'Aqqād and Ibrāhīm 'Abd al-Qādir al-Māzinī, *Al-Dīwān* (Cairo: Dār al-Sha'b, n.d.).

45. The poetics of the Arab romantics and their interest in translation of Western works (rather than *mu'āraḍa*) is well described by Badawi, 115–45. Early poems by Sayyāb that have been described by various authors as *mu'āraḍa*s include: "Al-Kharīf" (Autumn), "Al-Shitā'" (Winter), "Bayna al-Rūḥ wa-al-Jasad" (Between Body and Soul), "Nahr al-'Adhārā" (The River of the Virgins), and "'Āshiq al-Wahm" (In Love with an Illusion). Both Tawfīq, 337–42, and 'Abbās, 87–88, are relevant here.

46. Tawfīq, 337.

47. For an illuminating discussion of how the European literary evocation of ruins changed over time, see Roland Mortier, *La poétique des ruines en France* (Geneva: Droz, 1974), *passim*.

48. 'Alī Maḥmūd Ṭaha, *Dīwān* (Damascus: Al-Mu'assasa al-Thaqāfiyya li-al-Nashr wa-al-Tawzī', 1962), 337.

49. Maḥmūd Sāmī al-Bārūdī, *Dīwān* (Cairo: Dār al-Kutub, 1940), 1:79.

50. Ma'rūf Ruṣāfī, *Dīwān*, 213.

51. Ṭaha conflates here Adam's eating of the fruit from the first Tree, which gave him knowledge of good and evil, with his attempt to eat from the Tree of Eternal Life.

52. The phrase "*da' 'anka*" (Leave off this, stop this), was the most common formula used to signal a transition from the *nasīb* to the other themes treated in the traditional *qaṣīda*.

53. Sayyāb, *Azhār*, ed. Tawfīq, 117.

54. For the waves breaking at the beloved's feet, see Ṭaha, *Dīwān*, 351; for the image of the disappearing land, see 355.

55. One famous instance of this usage is in the title of Ibn al-Jawzī's well-known medieval treatise *Dhamm al-Hawā* (Censure of Illicit Desire).

56. Sura 26 of the Koran (The Poets) declares poets inferior to prophets, so they could hardly hope to compete with God himself. Yet, the Koran (like the Bible) imputes a creative power to words ("If He wants to put something into effect, He only *says* to it 'be!' and it is" (2:117)—emphasis added). This gives words the same sacred quality in Islam that they have in its sister scriptural religions, Judaism and Christianity. The poet (whose tools are words) is thus confronted in all these cultures with a tension between sacred and nonsacred uses of language, which often renders his own use of language problematic.

57. 'Abbās, 3.

58. Bullāṭa, 25.

59. This work is usually referred to as *Palgrave's Golden Treasury*, and was easily available throughout the Arab world, but especially in Egypt and Iraq, where it seems to have been the text that introduced English literature to a number of Arab writers, starting with the Dīwān school. The edition I have used is from 1924—a version that Sayyāb might very plausibly have had access to (Francis T. Palgrave, *The Golden Treasury of Songs and Poems, Selected by Francis T. Palgrave, Revised and Enlarged with Additional Poems* [New York: Thomas W. Crowell Co., 1924]).

60. The song from *The Tempest* sung by Ariel as a lament for Ferdinand's father, "Full fathom five thy father lies . . . ," which Sayyāb quotes at the beginning of "From the Vision of Fukai," is found in Palgrave (40)—though it is possible he took it from *The Waste Land*.

61. Sayyāb probably used "The Passionate Shepherd to His Love" (6–7) as a base for his own poem "Ughniyat al-Rā'ī" (The Shepherd's Song). Both poems are structured as invitations to a woman to go with the poet into the pastoral countryside where they can live as lovers safe from prying eyes. There are several very specific correspondences of imagery. For instance, Sayyāb changes Marlowe's promise to clothe his beloved to a promise to weave her a sail, but

both would make their fabric from "the wool of our flocks," ". . . the finest wool / Which from our pretty lambs we pull." See Sayyāb, *Dīwān*, 2:152.

62. Sayyāb translates his "Cupid and Campaspe" (43) virtually verbatim and includes it as a stanza in his long poem "Ahwā'" (Passions), published first in *Azhār Dhābila* (lines 161–68) and later republished in *Azhār wa-Asāṭīr*. See also *Dīwān* 1:12–20.

63. Jārjī, 19.

64. See Jārjī, 99 and Tawfīq, 332. It should be remembered that at the end of World War II Edith Sitwell's reputation was much higher than it is today. She also recorded many of her poems on LPs, a format that seems to have held much appeal for Sayyāb. For the rise and fall of her poetry in the eyes of critics after the war, see Geoffrey Elborn, *Edith Sitwell: A Biography* (London: Sheldon Press, 1981), 149–50 and 197–99.

65. Bhabha, 86.

6. RESISTING OTHERNESS

1. The choice of the period following the Middle Ages (the "Renaissance") as the origination and container for the rest of "modern" Arabic literature is interesting, since it is precisely at this point that—at least according to conventional historical accounts—Islamic civilization begins to decline and Western civilization begins to rise. Thus it could be argued that this periodization is empowering and necessary insofar as it allows Arabic literary history to enact a trajectory no less complete than that of Western literary history.

2. Samuel Taylor Coleridge, *Biographia Literaria, or Biographical Sketches of My Literary Life and Opinions* (New York: Leavitt, Lord and Co., 1834), 55–56.

3. This was a primarily Egyptian poetic school whose members were deeply influenced by the writers of English romanticism.

4. 'Aqqād and Māzinī, *Dīwān*, 20.

5. Jonathan Arac, *Critical Genealogies: Historical Situations for Postmodern Literary Studies* (New York: Columbia University Press, 1987), 55. For a detailed discussion of the romantic focus on "self-making" and its relationship to the use of "psychology" and "psychological" in literary contexts, see Arac, 53–55.

6. Until the end of World War I both modern-day states were part of a single Ottoman province, the province of Syria.

7. In Arabic, Gibran's name would be rendered Jubrān Khalīl Jubrān, but he officially changed it as a young man and his name is entered in most research materials as Gibran Kahlil Gibran, so I have used that form throughout.

8. See Jean Gibran and Kahlil Gibran, *Kahlil Gibran: His Life and World* (New York: Interlink Books, 1991), 211–12.

9. Jean Gibran and Kahlil Gibran, 252.

10. Ṭaha Ḥusayn is probably most notable for his insistence on freedom as an important value espoused by his generation of writers, but see also Aḥmad Zakī Abū Shādī, commenting about Khalīl Muṭrān's love of freedom and his attention to it as a theme in his poetry, "Khalīl Muṭrān," *Al-Adīb* 12, no. 10 (October 1953): 3; Ma'rūf al-Ruṣāfī's poems about freedom are quoted in Jalāl al-Ḥanafī, *Al-Ruṣāfī fī Awjihi wa-Ḥadīdih,* (Baghdad: Maṭba'at al-'Ānī, 1962), 107, and 'Aqqād, *Shu'arā' Miṣr*, 15–16 and 120.

11. But one should be aware that the use of biblical references in modern Arabic literature is by no means limited to Christian writers. Especially in Sayyāb's generation (and continuing to the present day) it was increasingly disassociated from any specifically sectarian religious linkage (though not from its numinousness as a religious document) and became a source for writers of quite varied backgrounds. This may perhaps be due to the rich potential of the biblical matrix as a counter-discourse to the Koranic bias of traditional Arabic literature. By Gibran, however, it was most often exploited as an authoritative source used to undercut what he saw as the totalizing discourses propounded by the official forms of Christianity found in Lebanon.

12. Since he only began writing in English following World War I, after having become well-known in the Arab world, Gibran's English works were usually translated into Arabic almost immediately after publication, to feed the public demand for his writings in the Middle East.

13. He spelled his name Naimy in English, but he never seems to have changed it officially, so most reference materials have it as "Nu'ayma" and that is the version I have adopted here. See the note by his nephew Nadeem Naimy in *Mikhail Naimy: An Introduction* (Beirut: American University in Beirut Press, 1967), 68, n. 1.

14. His poem "The Frozen River" was said to be modeled on Lermontov's work, and his first prose work, a drama, was entitled *Al-Ābā' wa-al-Banūn* (Fathers and Sons), thus evoking Turgenev's famous novel by that name. He was also apparently very fond of Tolstoy. See Nadeem Naimy, 87–93 and 97–103.

15. See 'Aqqād, *Shu'arā'* 192; and Ghālī Shukrī, *Shi'runā al-Ḥadīth: Ilā Ayn?* (Cairo: Dār al-Ma'ārif, 1968), 20.

16. See the connection made between Greek and Arabic in an article—a manifesto of sorts for the magazine—by 'Alī al-'Anānī, "Abūlūn wa-al-Shi'r al-Ḥayy," in *Abūllū* 1, no. 2 (October 1932): 123, where he says that Arabic culture should be seen as at least in part as "the fruit of the Greek mind (*'aql*)."

17. Apollo, of course, was the god of medicine as well as poetry in the classical Greek pantheon.

18. Some of the neoclassical poets, like Aḥmad Shawqī, had had a certain familiarity with, and interest in, French literature. Shawqī, for instance, had translated a number of La Fontaine's fables into Arabic verse. The Dīwān school,

however, had in turn differentiated themselves from their neoclassic predecessors in part by choosing to affiliate with the English romantics. See Shawqī Ḍayf, *Al-Adab al-'Arabī al-Mu'āṣir fī Miṣr* (Cairo: Dār al-Ma'ārif, 1988), 59–60.

19. Muḥammad Mandūr, *Al-Shi'r al-Miṣrī Ba'da Shawqī* (Cairo: Dār Nahḍat Miṣr, 1969), 2:7–8. Mandūr uses similar terminology in defining the Mahjar poets elsewhere in this volume, thus suggesting that he saw the three schools (since the linkage between Mahjar and Dīwān was already close, given 'Aqqād's role in spreading Nu'ayma's ideas in Egypt) as phases in a broader single development. See Mandūr, 36.

20. The sources, both in Arabic and in European languages, where this terminology appears are too many to catalog within the compass of a single footnote. Among them, only Ghālī Shukrī, in *Shi'runā al-Ḥadīth: Ilā Ayn?*, would seem to question, even briefly, its applicability, and he appears to do so ultimately in order to more firmly underwrite it (7–9).

21. Badawi, 262.

22. See Badawi, 263.

23. See his 1977 interview with the editorial collective of *Les révoltes logiques*, translated as "Powers and Strategies" in Michel Foucault, *Power/Knowledge*, 134–45.

24. Fredric Jameson, *The Political Unconscious: Narrative as Socially Symbolic Act* (Ithaca: Cornell University Press, 1981), 9–10.

25. Harlow, 14–17.

26. Following the publication of Harlow's book in 1987, Edward Said has taken up some of her ideas and discussed them in his recent study of *Culture and Imperialism.* See especially his chapter "Themes of Resistance Culture" (209–20), where he briefly, though perceptively, discusses the Sudanese novelist Al-Ṭayyib Ṣāliḥ's *Mawsim al-Hijra Ilā al-Shamāl* (*Season of Migration to the North*) as a resistance work. His main emphasis, however, is on resistance to colonialism as it is articulated within the metropolitan culture.

27. The single most important exception to this generalization is Mounah Khouri's informative, compelling, and finely nuanced study of the development of an Arabic poetry of resistance to colonialism during the neoclassic and early romantic period, *Poetry and the Making of Modern Egypt* (Leiden: E.J. Brill, 1971). His presentation of the subject matter has been an important source of information and model for much of what I have done in this chapter, though, of course, the emphases of my analysis may sometimes diverge from his (I have tried, for example, to concentrate on poets and schools that are not the main focus of his book in order to avoid duplication) and this has had an effect on the lessons drawn from the material. It should be noted, for example, that despite the insight, thoroughness and reliability of his work, even Khouri does not explicitly draw a connection in his conclusions between the pressures exerted by colonialism and the choice by Arab poets to make their works follow patterns that could be

characterized as analogous to either the neoclassicism or romanticism formulated in Western literary histories, which is a major part of what I hope to do here.

28. Even though the use of 1798 is now recognized to be decidedly "Egyptocentric," in that the main impact of Napoleon's invasion was felt there, the tendency toward using this event as a benchmark in accounts of modern Arabic literary history has continued to be noticeable even in the writings of non-Egyptians. This bias occurs from the time of Jurjī Zaydān, the Lebanese scholar and journalist who wrote the first comprehensive accounts of specifically modern Arabic literature (see the final part of his *Tārīkh Ādāb al-Lugha al-'Arabiyya* in *Mu'allifāt Jurjī Zaydān al-Kāmila* [Beirut: Dār al-Jīl, 1982], 15:11, where he says baldly: "this *nahḍa* [the renaissance of Arabic culture] began with the French exodus from Egypt in 1801"), and Buṭrūs al-Bustānī (who is quoted to this effect—and his chronology largely accepted—by Nadeem Naimy in *Mikhail Naimy*, 1–2 and 15–16) to the 1970s, and can be found in all the major literary histories and anthologies which appeared during that decade. It is only with the 1980s that this trend begins to change. A notable instance of this change is Salma Jayyusi's introduction to *Modern Arabic Poetry: An Anthology* (2) where she states openly that the *nahḍa* began first in Lebanon, a position that modifies considerably her stance in her earlier work *Trends and Movement in Modern Arabic Poetry*, where, although she notes that "Egyptian [literary critics] tend to overlook the great cultural activity in Syria and Lebanon in the nineteenth century and the vital importance of the pioneer role played by the Syro-Lebanese writers in the Arab literary renaissance in general" (1:16), she still gives pride of place to Egyptian achievements in her account, and says that "[t]here is ample evidence to show that the Napoleonic invasion of Egypt (1798–1801) marked the beginning of the national renaissance of the country" (1:15).

29. See the chapter "The Scope of Orientalism" in Edward Said, *Orientalism* (New York: Random House, 1978), and especially 79–89.

30. Jabrā Ibrāhīm Jabrā, *Al-Riḥla al-Thāmina*, 9.

31. Again, the major exception here would by Mounah Khouri's study in *Poetry and the Making of Modern Egypt*.

32. The entire passage runs: "When the light of this knowledge [of seafaring and navigation] died out among [the Arabs] and they ignored it—out of their disdain for it or some other reason—their voyages of exploration became few in number, and different groups of Europeans took their place and grew skillful at voyaging. Then the rulers and the ruled [of the European countries] took advantage of the enormous benefits [thus made available] in political and mercantile matters. The half-bestial peoples [of the New World] were assimilated into the Christian community—and Islam would have been more deserving of this distinction. Thus, our glorious sovereign has embarked upon the revival of this knowledge, from both ancient times and modern, so that the glad tidings of the sciences will become apparent and the pall of darkness will be lifted from knowledge" (Ṭahṭāwī, 155–56).

33. Ṭahṭāwī, 146. See also Ṭahṭāwī, 158. It should probably not be forgotten that one of the factors that led to the outbreak of the 1952 Revolution was the impasse reached in negotiations between the British and the Egyptians over the question of whether the Sudan should be given its independence or returned to Egyptian control after the British left.

34. 'Alī al-Ḥadīdī, *Maḥmūd Sāmī al-Bārūdī* (Cairo: Dār al-Kātib, 1967),78.

35. In 1956, Sayyāb wrote a poem in the traditional form, entitled "Būr Sa'īd" (Port Said) , praising Nasser's political victory in the Suez war and the determination shown by the Egyptian people in opposing the British, French, and Israeli invasion of the Suez Canal Zone. The poem is, in part, a *mu'āraḍa* of Abū Tammām's famous poem about al-Mu'tasim's conquest of the city of Amorium (for more information, see Tawfīq, 335–36).

36. Ismā'īl was apparently very well aware of the advantages of being able to manipulate public discourse to his own advantage, since he was the first Khedive to divert extensive subsidies to various private newspapers in Cairo and elsewhere in the Ottoman Empire (including Istanbul) in order to control their presentation of his activities. He was also quick to implement greater control of those whose loyalty he could not buy through more efficient enforcement of the censorship laws. See Juan Cole, *Colonialism and Revolution in the Middle East: Social and Cultural Origins of Egypt's Urabi Movement* (Princeton: Princeton University Press, 1993), 126, 223–26; and Khalīl Sabāt, *Tārīkh al-Ṭibā'a fī al-Sharq al-Awsaṭ* (Cairo: Dār al-Ma'ārif, 1958), 240–52.

37. For a description of this poem, see Ḥadīdī, 80–81.

38. Though Ismā'īl made no explicit comment alluding to his disenchantment, al-Bārūdī seems to have spent an inordinate amount of time in the late 1860s and in the 1870s abroad on military missions.

39. For a detailed description of this period in Ismā'īl's reign, see Juan Cole, *passim*, especially 234–49.

40. Al-Bārūdī, *Dīwān*, 217.

41. Alī al-Ḥadīdī, *al-Bārūdī*, 81; and *Dīwān*, 224.

42. The commentary on this line in the *dīwān* says: "After he mentions their [=the people's] acceptance of humiliation and contempt despite their huge numbers, he repeats the kind of expression used by someone who is sad or in despair, reminding himself that everyone returns to God, and one should accept His wise judgment, and by this it is as though he is alluding to the death of manly characteristics among them," *Dīwān*, 221, n. 40.

43. Bārūdī, *Dīwān*, 218 has part of the text of this speech by al-Ḥajjāj.

44. The Arabic reads: "Wa-mā l-ḥubbu 'illā ḥākimun ghayru 'ādilin // 'idhā rāma 'amran, lam yajid man yaṣudduhu."

45. The Arabic reads: "Ẓalūmun la-hu fī kulli ḥayyin jarīratun // yaḍijju la-hā ghawru l-faḍā'i wa-najduhu."

46. See Julie Meisami, *Medieval Persian Court Poetry* (Princeton: Princeton University Press, 1987), 24–25.

47. According to the commentary appended to the text of the poem in the *dīwān*, the foxes allude to base men, and the lions to noble ones.

48. According to the commentary, the second hemistich means: "this ordeal causes the swords to leap from their scabbards and demands resistance through fighting and war."

49. The references to "the hunt" and "the back of a thoroughbred" evoke similar images in Imru' al-Qays's "Mu'allaqa," and the image of birds circling above the battle field is a commonplace of the early Islamic poetry, used with great effect by Abū Tammām. Al-Āmidī in his *Muwāzana Bayna Abī Tammām wa-al-Buḥturi* traces it back through many intermediaries to al-Afwah al-Awdī (1: 65–67).

50. This would help explain al-Bārūdī's resort to praise for Pharaonic civilization, which is pursued by Shawqī as well. If the colonizer does not recognize Arab Islamic traditions as "civilized," perhaps he will be better constrained by the reminder that a civilization to which he traces his own cultural roots—Pharaonic Egypt—is a source for the Egyptian "national character" as well.

51. Nowhere can this shift be seen more clearly than in Sāṭi' al-Ḥuṣrī's book on his struggle to set up an educational system in Iraq following World War I and the establishment of the British mandate there.

52. Baring, Sir Evelyn (Lord Cromer), *Modern Egypt* (New York: The MacMillan Co., n.d.), 146.

53. Edward Said, *Orientalism*, 38.

54. "Egypt and India," *The Spectator*, no. 4737 (4/12/1919): 486.

55. "The Arab," *The Edinburgh Review* 201:412 (April 1905): 387–88.

56. "The Arab": 400.

57. "The Arab": 408.

58. Ernest Renan, *Histoire générale et système comparé des langues sémitiques* in *Oeuvres complètes* (Paris: Calmann-Levy, n.d.) 1:16.

59. See J.A. Spender, "The Egyptian Problem," *The Quarterly Review* 471 (April 1922): 425, where it is stated that the percentage of Egyptians employed in "the higher posts" of the Egyptian civil service declined from 27.7 percent in 1905 to 23 percent in 1920.

60. Quoted (and translated) in Khouri, *Poetry and the Making of Modern Egypt*, 186, where it is mentioned as being taken from 'Abd al-Raḥmān Shukrī, *Dīwān*, ed. Niqūlā Yūsuf (Alexandria: Munsha'at al-Ma'ārif, 1960), 71.

61. 'Abbās Maḥmūd al-'Aqqād, *Dīwān al-'Aqqād* (Aswan: Maṭba'at Waḥdat al-Ṣiyāna, 1967), 278.

62. Independence was only nominal because British troops remained in military occupation of many strategic sites, including Alexandria, the Suez Canal zone and downtown Cairo.

63. ‘Aqqād and Mazini, 36.

64. This would contrast with the modernist construct of identity, which, as one can see in such exemplars as T.S. Eliot's *The Waste Land* and Ezra Pound's *Cantos*, is an inherently fragmented and inchoate identity. This may explain why Arab poets of the 1920s and 1930s—even though they read the Anglo-American modernists—were unenthusiastic about adopting their point of view.

65. ‘Aqqād, *Shu‘arā’*, 196.

66. A translation of the poem, along with the original Arabic text, may be found in Mounah Khouri and Hamid Algar, *An Anthology of Modern Arabic Poetry* (Berkeley: University of California Press, 1974), 32–33.

67. Mikhā’īl Nu‘ayma, for example, roundly denounces the use of the *nasīb* as "old-fashioned" in *Al-Ghirbāl* (Cairo: Al-Maṭba‘a al-‘Aṣriyya, 1923), 147–48. And we have already seen ‘Aqqād's opinion of it in his article about Shawqī.

68. Badawi, 135–36. Badawi's analysis also incorporates a translation of a substantial portion of "Al-‘Awda."

69. "Sufism" (Islamic mysticism) is best approached as a portmanteau term used to describe a varied set of practices that have as a more or less common goal the development of the individual's personal awareness of, and sense of closeness to, God. Because it is an inward turning mode, devoted primarily to a process of remaking the self, romantics in the Arab world seem to have found it a fertile source of imagery for appropriation, just as their counterparts in the West did with the structuring categories of Christian mysticism.

70. That the words for "desire" (*hawā*) and "to fall" (*hawā*) form a paronomastic (*jinās*) pair also invokes the language of the poetic tradition, since this rhetorical figure was very popular in classical Arabic poetry.

71. This imagery can be found as early as the *mu‘allaqa* of Imru’ al-Qays, where he describes his tears as falling on his sword-belt and wetting the ground.

72. Arabic text is taken from Ṭaha Wādī, *Shi‘r Nājī* (Cairo: Kulliyat al-Ādāb, 1976), 155.

73. Nu‘ayma, 148 (emphasis added).

74. The Arabic literally says "rūḥ" here, which is usually translated as "spirit" or "soul." But Gabriel, who was frequently charged by God with delivering the revelation to Muḥammad, is often called a *rūḥ*, or "messenger-spirit" and Nājī appears to be alluding to this sense of the word here.

75. In Arabic the word "rūḥ" (soul) is feminine in gender. Its "femininity" is accentuated by the fact that it is one of a handful of feminine words in Arabic that lacks a standard feminine gender marker like *tā’ marbūṭa*, thus requiring an Arabic speaker to memorize (and thus to be more aware) that it is in fact feminine.

7. 1948

1. That Sayyāb himself was apparently a prime source for such retrospective attempts at imposing a fictive unitary vision on his life should perhaps not surprise us, given his characteristic attempts in other situations to make use of literary paradigms for the purposes of "self-fashioning." See 'Abbās, 340–41, where he indicates that Sayyāb was one of the first to attribute his growing ill health in 1961 (actually the initial symptoms of the incurable degenerative muscular disease amyotrophic lateral sclerosis [ALS]) to the time he had spent in Iraqi prisons: a cycle that began in 1949, when the government first identified him as a Communist.

2. Literally, the "Leap." Tawfīq (79) says that the term was first used by the Iraqi Communists and later became general.

3. The one absent grouping, of course, was the governing class: the old nationalist Free Officers and the great landowners, who owed their privileged status to their support of the British presence in Iraq.

4. Essentially, it seems to have been an extension of the 1930 Anglo-Iraqi Treaty, with mainly cosmetic improvements. See Batatu, 546.

5. Batatu, 551.

6. Batatu, 554.

7. Baḥr al-'Ulūm was the most famous "political" poet in Iraq after Jawāhirī during this period. For a description of his role in fomenting one of these demonstrations, see Batatu, 552–53. For Jawāhirī's role see Bullāṭa, 51–52.

8. The picture can be found in Fā'iq Buṭṭī, *Ṣiḥāfat al-'Irāq: Tārīkhuhā wa-Kifāḥ Ajyālihā* (Baghdad: Maṭba'at al-Adīb al-Baghdādiyya, 1968), 160.

9. Khāliṣ 'Azmī, *Ṣafaḥāt Maṭwīya min Adab al-Sayyāb*, 9–10; quoted in Tawfīq, 79.

10. See Bullāṭa, 51–52; for Sayyāb's own impressions of those days and the Communists' role in the Wathba, see 'Abbās, 102.

11. See Bullāṭa, 57; and Batatu, 615.

12. Lamī'a 'Abbās al-'Amāra was born in the Karkh district of Baghdad in 1929 to a family that has been described as "upper bourgeoisie." Her family moved to the town of 'Amāra, located on the Tigris River about midway between Baghdad and Baṣra, when Lamī'a was a young girl and she completed her primary school studies there. She returned to Baghdad for secondary school. When she finished, she wanted go abroad on an educational exchange, but her father died in September 1946, so she entered the Teachers College and graduated in 1950. While she was at the Teachers College she was a member of the Communist Party. A year after her graduation, she married. She has published four collections of poetry: (1) *Al-Zāwiya al-Khāliyya* (The Empty Corner) in 1958; (2) *'Awdat al-Rabī'* (The Return of Spring) in 1962; (3) *Aghānī 'Ishtār* (Songs of Ishtar) in 1969; and (4) *'Irāqiyya* (An Iraqi Woman) in 1971. Her work

has made her probably the best-known woman poet in Iraq after Nāzik al-Malā'ika. Recently, however, she has emigrated to the United States and currently lives in California. For more information about her, see Tawfīq, 146–57.

13. See Bullāṭa, 52–53; and Tawfīq, 147.

14. This religious group, also known as "Mandeans," include elements of both Christianity and Judaism in their doctrine. Along with Jews and Christians, they are mentioned in the Koran as "People of the Book," tolerated groups under Islamic law who are entitled to special protections. For a concise description of their beliefs and history, see *The Shorter Encyclopedia of Islam*, art. "al-Ṣābi'a."

15. See 'Abbās, 109–10; Tawfīq, "Introduction," *Azhār Dhābila wa-Qaṣā'id Majhūla*, 16.

16. *Azhār Dhābila*, 69: quoted in Tawfīq, *Sayyāb*, 268.

17. Having said this, it is necessary to point out that any resemblance between *al-shi'r al-ḥurr* and English "free verse" or French "*vers libre*" is merely incidental. Arabic "free verse" employs regular metrical feet throughout the poem (in fact, it insists, as a basic requirement of the form, that these feet be identical), and it generally has rhyme. What makes it "free" in relation to traditional Arabic prosody is that the number of feet used in each line may vary.

18. Both poets would later consistently deny that either one knew what the other was doing at this time. Since they freely admitted that they collaborated later on, in 1948, after free verse became popular, there does not appear to be any reason to disbelieve them.

19. Like Sayyāb, al-Malā'ika would go on to become a prominent poet in the Arab world on her merits, not just because of her association with free verse. She would also later become a university professor and pen several important literary critical studies, including one on the Egyptian romantic poet 'Alī Maḥmūd Ṭaha and an influential treatise on free verse.

20. See, for a typical assessment of the innovation's importance, Nāzik al-Malā'ika, *Qaḍāyā al-Shi'r al-Mu'āṣir* (Beirut: Dār al-'Ilm li-al-Malāyīn, 1962, 1978 rpt.), 37, and 51–52, where she also speaks about the negative reactions to the movement (which were equally vehement). The negative reaction of the Egyptian romantic poets to free verse (led by 'Abbās Maḥmūd al-'Aqqād) is presented in detail in Ghālī Shukrī, "Al-Mudhakkira al-Sawdā'," *Dhikriyāt al-Jīl al-Ḍā'i'* (Baghdad: Wizārat al-I'lām, 1972), 87–94.

21. Badawi, 225.

22. There have been a surprisingly (given the fact that the metrical aspect of poetry in various languages is usually the most difficult feature to appreciate in translation) large number of studies of Arabic free verse metrics in English. To be recommended for their thoroughness are Shmuel Moreh, *Modern Arabic Poetry: 1800–1970* (Leiden: E.J. Brill, 1976) and Salma Khadra Jayyusi, *Trends*, 2:605–40. In Arabic, the two most influential studies have been Nāzik al-

Malā'ika's *Qaḍāyā al-Shi'r al-Mu'āṣir* and Muḥammad Nuwayhī's *Qaḍiyyat al-Shi'r al-Jadīd* (Cairo: Institute of Higher Arabic Studies, 1964).

23. See Jayyusi, "Introduction," *Modern Arabic Poetry: An Anthology*, 8–13.

24. First published in *Al-Adīb* 11, no. 6 (June 1952): 11.

25. First published in *Al-Adīb* 11, no. 11 (November 1952): 40.

26. Abdul-Hai, 111–116.

27. Quoted in 'Abbās, 136.

28. Malā'ika, 55.

29. Even if it were written later, the absolute last date after which it could not have been composed would be October of 1947, since the October 20, 1947, issue of the Egyptian magazine *Al-Risāla* published one of the poems from the collection, saying that it was in the process of being printed (see Tawfīq, "Introduction," *Azhār Dhābila*, 15) and Rafā'īl Buṭṭī's introduction to the original edition of *Azhār Dhābila* is dated October 31 of that year. This would seem to be very persuasive evidence that the entire collection was complete and out of Sayyāb's hands for at least five months before he composed another free verse poem.

30. Interestingly, Sayyāb gives us some evidence that the two of them actively collaborated in writing free verse poems, but not until the early months of 1948. In a short autobiographical sketch published after his death in Jārjī, he says: "In 1948 I began to write nearly all of my poems in this way [i.e., in free verse]. In that year I was always meeting the poetess Nāzik al-Malā'ika, and I used to visit her—along with a number of male and female friends—at her house. Each of us benefited from these meetings and from the exchange of views. And we had agreed to publish a collection of free verse poetry jointly" (19). This would also seem to confirm that neither was particularly impressed with the potential of the free verse form until they saw how strong a reaction it provoked in the literary circles of Baghdad.

31. For the text of the entire poem, see Sayyāb, *Dīwān*, 1:33–37.

32. See Bullāṭa, 55; 'Abbās, 121 and 137 (where he equates "tyrant" with "father" thus making the referent entirely personal rather than ambivalent); and Tawfīq, 151–52.

33. Sayyāb, "Introduction," *Asāṭir*. The text of this introduction was republished in Sasson Somekh's article, "Asāṭīr al-Sayyāb: Thalāth Mutāba'āt," (published in *al-Karmil: Abḥāth fī al-Lugha wa-al-Adab* 8 [1987]:61–82) where he puts the introduction in its context and gives an illuminating analysis of its significance.

34. Fredric Jameson's characterization of "third-world" literary texts as being, in some sense, always "national allegories" should be seen as of utmost relevance here (see his article "Third-World Literature in the Era of Multinational Capitalism," in *Social Text* 15 (Fall 1986): 65–88). What I would argue with in such a characterization—at least insofar as Arabic literature is concerned—is its

relative lack of nuance (in reference to this, see Aijaz Ahmad's "Jameson's Rhetoric of Otherness and the 'National Allegory'" (*Social Text* 17 (Winter 1987): 3–25), which, though its criticisms are generally well-taken, suffers from a similar lack of discrimination in the area of identifying the functionality of individual texts within the larger paradigm). In Arabic literature during the modern period, poetry has been closely identified with the rise of nationalism. Thus, its main thrust has been to expose and critique instances where the ideals of the nationalist project have not been fulfilled, not to examine or interpellate those ideals themselves. This has been more the province of the novel, especially in the postwar period under the influence of Najīb Maḥfūẓ's writings.

35. See DeYoung, "Mu'āraḍa.": 231.

36. This anthology was well known to at least one Arab romantic poet, Aḥmad Zākī Abū Shādī. See Moreh, 165.

37. See 'Abbās, 68–69.

38. See my article, 235.

39. Harriet Monroe, *The New Poetry*, 7–8.

40. It is worth noting that Sayyāb will compose a poem in August 1948—like this one, with strongly imagist overtones—and give it the title "Ughniyya Qadīma" (An Ancient Song). See Sayyāb, *Dīwān*, 1: 70.

41. But even this may not be the case. Shmuel Moreh argues just as plausibly for the "Cowleyan ode," with its irregular line lengths, as the inspiration for Sayyāb's first experiment. See Moreh, 209. This, however, does not loom so importantly if we view the development of Arabic free verse as a slow process of many experiments, where Sayyāb's later acquaintance with the Imagists in early 1948 led him to look at the form in a different light.

42. But we can also look to more specific inversions of imagery. For example, in "Choricos," the "songs" move in a procession to the sea (water) and are associated with flowers (fertility) and the moon (non-threatening light). In Sayyāb's poem, the "decrepit" (i.e., nonfertile) myths are described as "[d]ragging the centuries (i.e., a procession) / In a chariot of flame" (opposite of water). The fact that these lines also evoke the story of how Phaeton died by driving his chariot too close to the sun (deadly light—opposite of the moon in Aldington's poem) sharpens the antithetical engagement of the two poems even more.

43. "Sirāb" (Mirage), dated March 27 (*Dīwān*, 1:54) and "Ughnīya Qadīma" (An Ancient Song), dated August 20 (*Dīwān*, 1:70).

44. For a discussion of the generic requirements of the dramatic monologue and the history of the form (Browning is usually credited with inventing it), the authoritative source is still Robert Langbaum, *The Poetry of Experience*, especially 75–82.

45. Langbaum, 76. This is not to speak of the possible influence of the other great Victorian writer of dramatic monologues, Tennyson, a poet whose presence (as we saw in chapter 4) seems to haunt Sayyāb's disposition of the mythic figure

of Odysseus/Ulysses. This early in Sayyāb's career, however, it is much more difficult to discern a current that can be connected with Tennyson than it will be later.

46. Langbaum, 77.

47. Mayer, 10.

48. Mayer, 10. See also Langbaum, 190.

49. We have already seen that Sayyāb would have had access to substantial portions of "Prufrock" in Arabic translation through Lūwīs 'Awaḍ's 1946 article about Eliot, which we know that Sayyāb read (see chapter 3 of this study). In addition, the poem "Malāl" (Boredom), composed in early May of 1948, has been recognized as having specific quotations taken from "Prufrock" (see 'Abbās, 145).

50. It should be noted that this is the one poem by Eliot that Harriet Monroe includes in her anthology.

51. T.S. Eliot, "Portrait of a Lady," in *Collected Poems*, 8.

52. It is worth noting that this uncanny mirroring effect would seem to be reflected, so to speak, in an image Sayyāb uses in his poem "Boredom," (the same poem that includes fairly specific allusions to "Prufrock") as his speaker inventories the meaningless objects that fill his lonely room and catches a reflection of himself in the mirror : "Nothing to do, . . . a window whose empty void makes the long road even longer / Nothing to do, and *a mirror where deep within a silent anguish yawns. . . .*" (emphasis added).

53. This poem is dated 2/30/1948 (February 30, 1948), which is of course impossible. So I would suggest an emended reading of March 30, substituting a "3" for the first "2," since that would require only a small change as the two numerals are very similar in form in Arabic.

54. Sayyāb, *Dīwān*, 1:47–48.

55. Sayyāb, *Dīwān*, 1:21–26.

56. See Iḥsān 'Abbās, *Ittijāhāt al-Shi'r al-'Arabī al-Mu'āṣir* (Kuwait: Al-Majlis al-Waṭanī li-al-Thaqāfa wa-al-Funūn wa-al-Adab, 1978), 43.

57. Sayyāb, *Dīwān*, 1:26–28.

58. Baṣrī, 9 [emphasis mine].

59. Moreh, 210.

60. See Buland al-Ḥaydarī, *Khaṭawāt fī al-Ghurba* (Beirut: Manshūrāt al-Maktaba al-'Aṣriyya, 1965), 58, 68, and 140.

61. Of the nine poems that Moreh lists, three—"Sūq al-Qarya," "Al-Abārīq al-Muhashshama," and "Fī al-Manfā"—fall into the category of full-blown *mu'āraḍa*. The inversion/engagement of Sayyāb's themes (as opposed to his imagery and poetic structure) is less clear with the other poems.

62. As noted earlier, this poem was published for the first time in the November 1952 issue of the Lebanese literary magazine *Al-Adīb*, where many of Bayyātī's poems later included in *Abārīq* can be found.

63. See ʻAbbās, *Ittijāhāt*, 48. ʻAbbās's reading of Bayyātī's poem is particularly important for my purpose. It takes place in a chapter called "Evidence of the Earliest Beginnings [of Modern Arabic Poetry], which looks closely at three early poems written in free verse, Nāzik al-Malā'ika's "Al-Khayṭ al-Mashdūd fī Shajarat al-Sarw" (The Thread Stretched Taut in the Cypress Tree), Sayyāb's "Fī al-Sūq al-Qadīm" and Bayyātī's "Fī Sūq al-Qarya." Although ʻAbbās never directly states that Bayyātī's poem is a *muʻāraḍa* of Sayyāb's, he nevertheless makes direct comparisons between the two in the course of his analysis. He probably comes closest to making the explicit connection when he says: "It is as though Bayyātī is saying in his poem: "Why does the poet [of "Fī al-Sūq al-Qadīm"] choose to walk alone at night in a market, empty of people, or nearly so, in order to dream of love . . . and he does not even attempt to see the market in its true reality, in the fullness of day, and in the village, not in the city, and listen to the dreams of the poor and wishes of those in need?" (49).

64. ʻAbbās, *Ittijāhāt*, 48.

65. ʻAbbās, *Ittijāhāt*, 56.

8. THE EPIC TURN

1. ʻAbbās, 128.

2. ʻAbbās, 129. The fact that Muṣṭafā became commissar is not as strange as it might sound. Batatu (569) calls this the period of the "Children Communists," when "many, if not most, of the primary party organizations were led by boys aged thirteen to seventeen." These teenagers were practically the only group in the Party whose numbers were not decimated by the government's sweeping arrests.

3. ʻAbbās (130) suggests that this slight may have sown the first doubts that Sayyāb had about his membership in the Party.

4. Bullāṭa (61) says that the move should be attributed to Sayyāb's desire for a better-paying job. ʻAbbās (131) suggests that the company fired him because they found out about his party connections. But he admits there is no proof of this.

5. Bullāṭa, 63.

6. See Bullāṭa, 63, and al-Baṣrī, 83. The Arabic translation was published by the group in a separate pamphlet around this time. This prepared the way for a collection of modern poetry, *Selections from World Poetry*, which included translations of poems by T.S. Eliot, Edith Sitwell, Arthur Rimbaud, Federico Garcia Lorca, Franz Kafka, Pablo Neruda, and Ezra Pound, among others. Sayyāb translated the non-English-speaking poets from English translations of their works. The collection was published in 1955. See Bullāṭa, 85; and Baṣrī, 83.

7. See Batatu, 666–67.

8. In the Iraqi magazine *Al-Taḍāmun*. See 'Abd al-Jabbār Da'ūd al-Baṣrī, 83.

9. The Peace Partisans published the poem twice as an independent pamphlet, the second time with an introduction, probably by Sayyāb himself, strongly endorsing the Peace movement platform (neither printing was dated). See Sayyāb, *Azhār*, ed. Tawfīq, 228.

10. Since the "Ban the Bomb" movement did not begin until March 19, 1950 and Sayyāb completed the poems in *Myths* in December 1948, there is a period of more than a year when we cannot establish what, if anything, he was writing. It is possible that he might have revised some of the poems in *Myths* during this period, but his correspondence suggests that he had given the collection to the publisher long before its September 1950 publication date. See Sayyāb, *Rasā'il*, 54. The dating of this particular letter, however, presents something of a problem. It is given as May 7, 1947, but internal references (to *Myths*, which we know was not begun until 1948, and to the publication of Nāzik al-Malā'ika's collection *Shaẓāyā wa-Ramād* (Shrapnel and Ashes), which was not published until 1949) indicate that it was more likely written on May 7, *1949*. Even if it was written on this later date, there is still a long gap between May 1949 and September 1950.

11. Bullāṭa mentions it under the title "Ajniḥat al-Salām" (Wings of Peace). See Bullāṭa, 64. The published version was 143 lines, but the (apparently) manuscript version Bullāṭa saw in the keeping of Sayyāb's brother-in-law was approximately 400 lines.

12. Sayyāb, *Dīwān* 2:247.

13. 'Abbās, 155.

14. To be sure, much of the political poetry I will be speaking about was not collected (most from back issues of Iraqi newspapers) until the early 1970s. Thus, 'Abbās could very well have been unaware of its existence (or at least the existence of much of it) when he was writing in the late 1960s.

15. This was later collected and published after Sayyāb's death in the *dīwān* entitled *A'āṣīr* (Storms). For more information on this collection (as well as others published after the poet's death), see Tawfīq, 121.

16. Jārjī, 117.

17. I am not suggesting that this would be the only Marxist "take" possible on this literature. What Sayyāb would have absorbed from his sources was the particular form of Stalinist-dominated Soviet Marxist ideology officially endorsed from 1934 to 1953. See Terry Eagleton, *Marxism and Literary Criticism* (Berkeley: University of California Press, 1976), 37–40, and Dave Laing, *The Marxist Theory of Art* (Atlantic Highlands, New Jersey: Humanities Press, 1978), 34–45, for descriptions and critiques of what most contemporary Marxist theorists dismiss as "vulgar" distortions of true Marxist positions under the influence of Stalin and the socialist realism he promulgated from the 1930s to the 1950s.

18. Maḥmūd al-'Abṭa, 88 (quoted in 'Abbās, 155).

19. This text was rescued from oblivion by 'Īsā Bullāṭa. Some portions of it were published in an appendix to his biography of the poet (202–4). See also the discussion of the discovery of the poem (64).

20. For a detailed study of this use of epic, see David Quint, *Epic and Empire: Politics and Generic Form from Virgil to Milton* (Princeton: Princeton University Press, 1993), especially chapter six, "Tasso, Milton, and the Boat of Romance," 248–67.

21. For details of this incident, see Quint, 343–55.

22. 'Abbās, 157.

23. A few of the more useful books dealing with this subject include: Brian Wilkie, *Romantic Poets and Epic Tradition* (Madison: University of Wisconsin Press, 1965); Balachandra Rajan, *The Form of the Unfinished: English Poetics from Spenser to Pound* (Princeton: Princeton University Press, 1985); and Thomas McFarland, *Romanticism and the Forms of Ruin: Wordsworth, Coleridge and the Modalities of Fragmentation* (Princeton: Princeton University Press, 1981).

24. See M.H. Abrams, *Natural Supernaturalism*, 21–30.

25. Though that success, especially in terms of closure, can be disputed. See Balachandra Rajan, 126.

26. *Letters of John Keats to His Family and Friends*, ed. Sidney Colvin (London: MacMillan and Co., 1925), 321.

27. Edgar Allan Poe, *The Literary Criticism of Edgar Allan Poe*, ed. Robert L. Hough (Lincoln: University of Nebraska Press, 1965), 33–34.

28. See *Iliyādhat Hūmīrūs*, trans. by Sulaymān al-Bustānī (Beirut: Dār al-Ma'rifa, rpt. n.d.) 1: 164. The influence of Bustānī's position may be reflected in the fact that the issue is framed in virtually identical terms in Ḥasan Muḥsin, *Al-Shi'r al-Qiṣaṣī* (Cairo: Dār al-Nahḍa al-'Arabiyya, 1980), 127.

29. See *Modern French Poets on Poetry*, ed. Robert Gibson (Cambridge: Cambridge University Press, 1979), 8–13 and 147–49.

30. For background on these developments see Margaret Dickie, *On the Modernist Long Poem* (Iowa City: University of Iowa Press, 1986) and the special issue of *Genre* 11, no. 4 (Winter 1978), especially Joseph N. Riddel, "A Somewhat Polemical Introduction: The Elliptical Poem": 459–78.

31. See the quotation from Ernest Renan in this chapter (and n. 39 below) as a paradigmatic example of such a judgment. Such categorical pronouncements, of course, tell us a great deal more about the limitations of Western critical understanding than it does about Arabic literature—especially since the whole notion of epic as a viable genre was under attack by poets themselves at precisely the same time Renan and his ilk were issuing their condemnations of Arabic literature.

32. Adel S. Gamal, in his article "Narrative Poetry in Classical Arabic Literature" (in *In Quest of an Islamic Humanism: Arabic and Islamic Studies in Memory of Mohamed al-Nowaihi*, ed. A.H. Green [Cairo: American University in

Cairo Press, 1984], 25–38) makes a very convincing case for the contention that Arab poets—when they chose to do so (and this is the operative proviso)—were quite capable of incorporating narrative into their work as an effective technique of literary representation. In his preface to the centerpiece of the article, a close analysis of a fine poem by the early Umayyad poet 'Umar ibn abī Rabī'a, Gamal's observation that this is "one of 'Umar's most outstanding poems, *albeit one of the least appreciated*" (29—emphasis mine), would, however, seem to support my contention that the value placed on narrative poetry by its audience in the medieval period was not very high.

33. It is important to differentiate here between literature composed in the classical Koranic language and folk literature composed in the various colloquials. These latter contain many poems that certainly qualify as long narrative—if not epic—poems. Recently, these poems have attracted the attention of many scholars, both Arab and non-Arab, but even as early as 1936, Ṭaha Ḥusayn was calling upon his fellow critics to pay more attention to the stories of 'Antara and Abū Zayd al-Hilālī, since he felt it was "this literature which we leave to the coffeehouses of the common people and treat with scorn," that could be used as a basis for the creation of epics in Arabic (Ṭaha Ḥusayn, *Min Ḥadīth al-Shi'r wa-al-Nathr* (Cairo: Dār al-Ma'ārif, n.d.), 14–16.

34. The Arabic uses the same word here as is translated as "slaughtering" the riding camel in line 11.

35. Al-Khaṭīb al-Tibrīzī, comp., *Sharḥ al-Qaṣā'id al-'Ashr*, ed. Fakhr al-Dīn Qabāwa (Beirut: Dār al-Āfāq al-Jadīda, 1980), 33–43. The translation is adapted from that found in *Al-Sab' al-Mu'allaqāt, The Seven Poems, Suspended in the Temple at Mecca*, trans. Frank E. Johnson (Bombay: Educational Society's Steam Press, 1893), 2–30.

36. This version of the story can be found in al-Tibrīzī, 37–38.

37. It is important to recognize, however, that this "refusal to narrate" on Imru' al-Qays's part is not simply negative—it does allow him to focus on other modes of representation in this section of poem: (1) the descriptive metaphor (as with the reference to the fat on the camel meat being like "fringes of twisted silk") that celebrates the power of the poet's language to transform the contingent and mutable into the permanent and aesthetically appreciable; and (2) the immediacy of dialogic give-and-take between 'Unayza and Imru' al-Qays that portrays their relationship as one that involves reciprocity and the potential for incommensurability.

38. The Arabic word means, in its most literal sense, "a making *true*" or "a showing (something) to *be true*."

39. Renan, 16. Bustānī, in his translation of *The Iliad*, seems to be well aware of judgments like Renan's (165).

40. More common, actually, was the strategy of pointing out that it had appeared previously in numerous works that had not been for one reason or

another fully assimilated into the high tradition. For an exhaustive treatment of the subject, see Muḥsin, *Al-Shi'r al-Qiṣaṣī*, especially his first chapter. It should also be noted that, in an objective sense, Renan was wrong. In *colloquial* as opposed to standard Arabic, the epics of Abū Zayd al-Hilālī, 'Antara, and others continue as one of the few living oral epic traditions in the world today. As such, they are the object of much interest among folklorists and students of oral literature. See 'Abd al-Raḥmān 'Abnūdī's many works on the subject, as well as Susan Slyomovics, *The Merchant of Art: An Egyptian Hilali Oral Epic Poet in Performance* (Berkeley: University of California Press, 1987), and Bridget Connelly, *Arab Folk Epic and Identity* (Berkeley: University of California Press, 1986), for more information on the recent "discovery" of this epic poetry. On the other hand, as was mentioned in n. 33, earlier, Ṭaha Ḥusayn already recognizes in the 1930s the importance of the colloquial epics and suggests that poets writing in the classical language should adapt and use them as a source of inspiration. See Ḥusayn, 16.

41. See Muḥsin, 176.

42. For a brief but lucid discussion of the relationship between Muṭrān and Bustānī, and the influence of both on epic in Arabic, see Khouri, *Poetry and the Making of Modern Egypt*, 155–58. Muṭrān's comments on the necessity of changing the form of the poetry in order to make epic possible are translated on page 155 of Professor Khouri's book. For similar comments by Bustānī, see *Iliyādha*, introduction, 165–68.

43. See Khouri, *Making*, 157–58.

44. See Muḥsin, 257–58.

45. See, for example, the opinions of Muḥammad Mandūr, the most influential critic of that period concerning Abū Shādī's experiments in *Al-Shi'r al-Miṣrī Ba'da Shawqī al-Ḥalqa al-Thāniya: Jamā'at Abūllū*, 28–32.

46. Sayyāb, *Dīwān*, 2:334–36. Sayyāb sent the original manuscript of the poem to Ṭaha at his home in Egypt, but the older poet died shortly thereafter (1947), and the manuscript was never returned. Since that was the only complete copy, what has been printed in the *Dīwān* consists of fragments found among Sayyāb's notes after his death.

47. See Nāzik al-Malā'ika's biography of 'Alī Maḥmūd Ṭaha (*Shi'r 'Alī Maḥmūd Ṭaha* [Cairo: Al-Mu'assasa li-al-Dirāsāt al-'Arabiyya al-'Ulyā, 1965]), 343; Badawi, 145; and Jayyusi, *Trends*, 2:406.

48. "Ḥuffār al-Qubūr" was announced as forthcoming work at the end of *Asāṭīr* (Myths) that had been sent to the publisher sometime early in 1949, but it was not actually published until late in 1950. It is impossible to tell for certain, but it would seem likely that over this nearly two-year period, Sayyāb would taken the opportunity to revise "Ḥuffār al-Qubūr," and would not have just left it alone. Thus, there was plenty of time for him to change it from a traditional form (like the other 1950 poems) to free verse.

49. Bullāṭa, 64, quoting a letter from Muḥyī al-Dīn Isma'īl.

50. This area is vividly described by Sayyāb's friend Jabrā Ibrāhīm Jabrā in his English-language novel *Hunters in a Narrow Street* (Washington, D.C.: Three Continents Press, 1990), 23–25. According to Jabrā, the district could only be entered through doors where the patrons were frisked for weapons by policemen, because so many of the women who worked in the brothels had been murdered by their outraged male relatives, seeking to restore the family honor.

51. "In the Greek myths, the eyes of Medusa turn everyone who encounters them to stone."—poet's note.

52. "In the Koran, the crow is the one who shows Cain how to bury his brother after he kills him."—poet's note.

53. "Oedipus married his mother Jocaste, not knowing that she was his mother. Thebes is the city which he entered after he killed his father the king of Thebes; then he married his mother, the wife of the murdered king. The Sphinx used to guard the entrance to the city, and he asked every stranger who sought to come in the following question: 'What being walks on four [legs] at dawn, two at noon, and three in the evening?' Oedipus solved this riddle, and the answer is 'man.'"—poet's note.

54. Sayyāb, *Dīwān*, 1: 509–11.

55. Sayyāb makes this connection more explicit in lines 76–85, analyzed below, which directly mention Faust, and contain a footnote that directly ties his poem to Goethe's version of the legend.

56. Quint, 24.

57. Sayyāb, *Dīwān*, 1: 514.

58. Sayyāb, *Dīwān*, 1: 521–22.

59. "God and Satan made a wager over Faust. Satan claimed that he could corrupt him body and spirit. Faust agreed to sell his soul and Satan put himself at Faust's disposal in return for this. He gave Faust back his youth, and pearls and money, and showed him the ghost of the Greek Helen."—poet's note.

60. "In the end Satan only obtains Faust's body, while his soul ascends to heaven"—poet's note.

61. "The line is from Faust by Goethe in a speech Satan makes to Faust when he is visiting Marguerite (whom he deceived and killed her brother and she bore a child and then killed it) while she is in prison."—poet's note.

62. "Daphne was the daughter of a demigod of the rivers. Apollo, the sun-god, saw her and fell in love with her and chased her, trying to capture her. She sought help from her father, who sprayed her with a handful of water and changed her into a laurel tree, whose branches they use to make heroes' crowns. As for the arrows of gold, they were shot by Cupid into Apollo's heart to inflame his love, and we have borrowed them as a symbol for the power of money."—poet's note.

63. Sayyāb, *Dīwān*, 1: 515–17.

64. The most notable example of this is in Khalīl Ḥāwī's poem "Al-Baḥḥār wa-al-Darwīsh (The Mariner and the Dervish)," where the author speaks of his hero in the epigraph as having "wandered with Ulysses in the unknown and with Faust he sacrificed his soul for knowledge." (*An Anthology of Modern Arabic Poetry*, trans. Khouri and Algar, 61).

65. Sayyāb, *Dīwān*, 1: 519–20.

66. Sayyāb, *Dīwān*, 1: 522–24.

67. This Arabic word, often used a woman's name, literally means "morning."

68. Sayyāb, *Dīwān*, 1: 524–25.

69. Sayyāb, *Dīwān*, 1: 525.

70. The connection of second-person pronouns with religious discourse is particularly strong in Islam, because so much of the Koran is couched in this form—as the direct address of God to either Muḥammad personally, or to the community of believers in general.

71. Jonathan Culler, "Apostrophe," in *The Pursuit of Signs: Semiotics, Literature, Deconstruction* (Ithaca: Cornell University Press, 1981), 149.

72. Culler, 142.

73. "Everyone who has read the Koran knows the story of Yagog and Magog, but the popular tales add that the two of them would lick the wall with their tongues every day until it became as thin as an onion skin. Then they would be overcome by weariness, and they would say 'We will finish the job tomorrow.' But the next day they would find the wall as firm and strong as ever . . . and thus it would continue until a child was born to the two of them whom they would name "God Willing," and he would destroy the wall."—poet's note.

74. Sayyāb, *Dīwān*, 1: 529–530.

75. The name literally means "the two-horned one," and it is traditionally linked to the figure of Alexander the Great, the world-conquering Greek king.

76. See Sayyāb's note to the poem about Yagog and Magog (earlier, n. 71) for comparison. By phrasing his comment as he does, he draws attention to the discrepancy between traditional versions of the story and Salīma's.

77. Sayyāb, *Dīwān*, 1: 537–38.

78. Sayyāb, *Dīwān*, 1: 539–42.

79. Sayyāb, *Dīwān*, 1:542.

80. See Dickie, 2.

81. Sayyāb, *Rasā'il* (letter to Suhayl Idrīs dated 3/25/1954), 59.

82. A measure of the importance attached to length can be seen in the fact that in October, 1954, *Al-Ādāb* held a contest for poetry in which one of the major criteria was that the poem be "not less than 30 lines, and not more than 100 lines." (*Al-Ādāb* 2, no. 10 [October 1954]: 17).

83. Jārjī, 54.

9. CONCLUSION

1. "Unshūdat al-Maṭar" was published in June 1954 in *Al-Ādāb* (18). Although it eventually became the best-known of Sayyāb's poems, and one of his most highly regarded, it was by no means an instant success. 'Abd al-Laṭīf Sharāra, who wrote the review "Qara'tu al-'Adad al-Māḍī" the following month (*Al-Ādāb* 2, no. 7 [July 1954]: 63–68), compared it unfavorably to two politically "committed" poems contributed to the same issue by Fadwā Ṭūqān and Nāzik al-Malā'ika, saying: "The poetic experience is authentic and real, Badr al-Sayyāb feels it deeply, his attitudes are sound, that is, the poem is unmarred by any traces of artificiality or affectation, but it fails in the end, and after every effort at influence, to move your emotions at their source, in contrast to what Fadwā Ṭūqān and Nāzik al-Malā'ika have accomplished" (65).

2. Both this poem and "Unshūdat al-Maṭar" are briefly discussed in chapter 1 of this study. For more information on "Madīna Bilā Maṭar," see DeYoung, "And Thereby Hangs a Tale," 154–68.

3. The collection was first published in Beirut in 1964. The poems in this collection were later incorporated into Sayyāb's *Dīwān* (1:597–723). "*Shināshīl*" is the local Iraqi name for a type of enclosed wooden balcony or alcove also common in Egypt (where it is known as *mashrabiyya*), screened by carved panels that are usually open latticework but can also incorporate inlays of stained glass. Bullāṭa tells us that there was such a window in the principal's office of Sayyāb's first school (which was the converted residence of a wealthy landowner from Abū al-Khaṣīb), and that it was decorated with "blue, red, green and orange" stained glass, as well as "carved wooden panels ornamented with delicate motifs of Arabic [calligraphy]." There was a similar *shināshīl* attached to a house next to the school, which belonged to 'Abd al-Wahhāb Jalabī al-'Abd al-Wāḥid, a local magnate who sometimes employed Badr's father as his agent or overseer in business affairs (Bullāṭa, 22–23).

The word *jalabī* (possibly from Persian *chalabī*) is also from the local Iraqi dialect, and is a courtesy title used in referring to wealthy local notables.

4. The word Sayyāb uses here is *jawsaq*, which is an arabized term from the Persian word *kūshk*, "a palace, villa, or mansion." It is used in Arabic as a synonym for *qaṣr*, "palace," but its specific local meanings vary, so that it can often mean something more like a pavilion in a garden or on a terrace, rather than a large official dwelling. Since the context in which Sayyāb uses it suggests a rough, unfinished temporary kind of shelter, I have chosen to translate the word as "reed pavilion" to give a sense of both its real functionality and the evocative associations of past splendor the word also conveys.

5. The word used by Sayyāb is *nāṭūr*, who was a retainer employed by wealthy landowners to keep watch over their crops, especially at night, and keep them from being stolen by thieves. Such a person would usually not be of the

same social class as his employers, but he would live on terms of some intimacy with them and their families, very much like a "hired man" on American farms before World War II.

6. "'And shake the palm tree's trunk, so that ripe dates will upon you' (Sūrat Maryām—The Koran)."—Sayyāb's note. This is intended to remind the reader of the charming story in the Koran (which echoes that of Christian folklore about the birth of Jesus), where the pregnant Virgin Mary, feeling her labor pains coming on, takes shelter beneath a date-palm tree that drops its ripe dates at her feet so that she will have nourishment (19:23–27).

7. Literally "O rain, O my milk / Make the daughters of the jalabī weep. / O rain, O muslin / Make the daughters of the Pasha weep / O rain of gold." Bullāṭa says that this is a children's song for rainy days that Sayyāb learned when he was a child at the school in Abū al-Khaṣīb (22).

8. Sayyāb, *Dīwān*, 1:597–601.

9. Wordsworth 4:47.

Bibliography

‘Abbās, Iḥsān. *Badr Shākir al-Sayyāb: Dirāsatun fī Ḥayātihi wa-Shi‘rih*. Beirut: Dār al-Thaqāfa, 1969.

———. *Ittijāhāt al-Shi‘r al-‘Arabī al-Mu‘āṣir*. Kuwait: Al-Majlis al-Waṭanī li-al-Thaqāfa wa-al-Funūn wa-al-Adab, 1978.

Abdul-Hai, Muhammad. *Tradition and English and American Influence in Arabic Romantic Poetry*. London: Ithaca Press, 1982.

Abrams, M[eyer] H. *The Mirror and the Lamp: Romantic Theory and the Critical Tradition*. Oxford: Oxford University Press, 1953.

———. "Structure and Style in the Greater Romantic Lyric." In *Romanticism and Consciousness*, ed. Harold Bloom, 201–29. New York: W.W. Norton, 1970.

———. *Natural Supernaturalism: Tradition and Revolution in Romantic Literature*. New York: W.W. Norton, 1971.

Abū Shādī, Aḥmad Zākī. "Khalīl Muṭrān." *Al-Adīb* 12, no. 10 (October 1953): 3–4 and 73–74.

Ackerman, Robert. "The Cambridge Group: Origins and Composition." In *The Cambridge Ritualists Reconsidered*, ed. William M. Calder III, 1–19. Atlanta: Scholars Press, 1991.

Adūnīs (‘Alī Aḥmad Sa‘īd). "Muḥāwala fī Ta‘rīf al-Shi‘r al-Ḥadīth" (An Attempt to Define Modern Poetry). *Majallat Shi‘r* (Beirut) 2, no. 3 (Summer 1959): 79–90.

Ahmad, Aijaz. "Jameson's Rhetoric of Otherness and the 'National Allegory'." *Social Text* 17 (Winter 1987): 3–25.

"Akhbār wa-Qadāyā." *Majallat Shi‘r* 1, no. 2 (Summer 1957): 111–16.

‘Alawī, Hādī al-. "Min Riḥlat al-Fikr wa-al-Taḥawwul." In *Muḥammad Mahdī al-Jawāhirī: Dirāsāt Naqdiyya*, ed. Hādī al-‘Alawī, 11–39. Baghdad/Najaf: Maṭba‘at al-Nu‘mān, 1969.

‘Alī, ‘Abd al-Riḍā. *Al-Usṭūra fī Shi‘r al-Sayyāb*. Beirut: Dār al-Rā’id al-‘Arabī, 1978.

'Ālim, Maḥmūd Amīn al-. "Qara'tu al-'Adad al-Māḍī." *Al-Ādāb* 3, no. 3 (March 1955): 65–73.

Āmidī, Abū al-Qāsim al-Ḥasan ibn Bishr al-. *Al-Muwāzana bayna Abī Tammām wa-al-Buḥturī*. Cairo: Dār al-Ma'ārif, 1972.

'Anānī, 'Alī al-. "Abūlūn wa-al-Shi'r al-Ḥayy." *Abūllū* 1, no. 2 (October 1932): 113–24.

An Anthology of Modern Arabic Poetry. Ed. Mounah A.Khouri and Hamid Algar. Berkeley: University of California Press, 1974.

'Aqqād, 'Abbās Maḥmūd al-. *Shu'arā' Miṣr wa-Bī'ātuhum fī al-Jīl al-Māḍī*. Cairo: Maktabat al-Nahḍa, 1937.

———. *Dīwān al-'Aqqād*. Aswan: Maṭba'at Waḥdat al-Ṣiyāna, 1967.

'Aqqād, 'Abbās Maḥmūd al-, and Ibrāhīm 'Abd al-Qādir al-Māzinī, *Al-Dīwān*. Cairo: Dār al-Sha'b, n.d.

"The Arab." *The Edinburgh Review* 412 (April 1905): 386–409.

Arac, Jonathan. *Critical Genealogies: Historical Situations for Postmodern Literary Studies*. New York: Columbia University Press, 1987.

Ashcroft, Bill, Gareth Griffiths, and Helen Tiffin. *The Empire Writes Back: Theory and Practice in Post-Colonial Literatures*. London: Routledge, 1989.

'Awaḍ, Lūwīs. "T.S. Iliyūt." *Al-Kātib al-Miṣrī* 1, no. 4 (January 1946): 557–68.

———. *Al-Thawra wa-al-Adab*. Cairo: Dār al-Kitāb al-'Arabī, 1967.

'Awaḍayn, Ibrāhīm. *Al-Mu'āraḍa fī al-Adab al-'Arabī*. Cairo: Maṭba'at al-Sa'āda, 1981.

'Azzāwī, 'Abbās al-. *Tārīkh al-'Irāq Bayna al-Iḥtilālayn*, vol. 6. Baghdad: Sharikat al-Tijāra wa-al-Ṭibā'a, 1954.

———. *Tārīkh al-'Irāq Bayna al-Iḥtilālayn*, vol. 8. Baghdad: Sharikat al-Tijāra wa-al-Ṭibā'a, 1956.

Badawi, M[uhammad] M. *A Critical Introduction to Modern Arabic Poetry*. Cambridge: Cambridge University Press, 1975.

"Baghdad Railway, The." *The Edinburgh Review* 422 (October 1907):371–98.

Bakhtin, Mikhail. *Dialogic Imagination*. Ed. and trans. Michael Holquist and Caryl Emerson. Austin: University of Texas Press, 1981.

Barakāt, Rajab. *Ṣiḥāfat al-Khalīj al-'Arabī*. Baghdad: Maṭba'at al-Irshād, 1977.

Baram, Amatzia. *Culture, History and Ideology in the Formation of Ba'thist Iraq, 1968–89*. Oxford: St. Anthony's College in association with Macmillan, 1991.

Baring, Sir Evelyn (Lord Cromer). *Modern Egypt*. New York: The Macmillan Co., n.d.

Bārūdī, Maḥmūd Sāmī al-. *Dīwān*, 2 vols. Cairo: Dār al-Kutub, 1940.

Baṣrī, 'Abd al-Jabbār Dā'ūd al-. *Badr Shākir al-Sayyāb: Rā'id al-Shi'r al-Ḥurr*. Baghdad: Dār al-Jumhūriyya, 1966.

Batatu, Hanna. *The Old Social Classes and the Revolutionary Movements of Iraq: A Study of Iraq's Old Landed and Commercial Classes and of its*

Communists, Ba'thists, and Free Officers. Princeton: Princeton University Press, 1978.

Bayyātī, 'Abd al-Wahhāb al-. "Fī Sūq al-Qarya." *Al-Adīb* 11, no. 11 (November 1952): 40.

Bāzī, Ḥāmid al-. *Al-Baṣra Fī al-Fatra al-Muẓlima*. Baghdād: Dār Manshūrāt al-Baṣrī, 1969.

Bedient, Calvin. *He Do the Police in Different Voices:* The Waste Land *and Its Protagonist*. Chicago: The University of Chicago Press, 1986.

Bell, Gertrude. *Letters*. 2 vols. Ed. Lady Bell. New York: Boni and Liverwright, n.d.

Bender, Robert M., ed. "Joseph Conrad: Introduction." *The Shaping of Fiction*. New York: Washington Square Press, 1970.

Bergonzi, Bernard. *T.S. Eliot*. New York: Collier Books, 1972.

Bhabha, Homi. *The Location of Culture*. London: Routledge, 1994.

Bigongiari, Dino. "Dante's Ulysses and Columbus." In *Columbus, America, and the World*, ed. Anne Paolucci and Henry Paolucci, 103–19. Review of National Literatures, no. 16. New York: Griffon House Publications, 1992.

Bloom, Harold. "The Internalization of Quest Romance." In *Romanticism and Consciousness*. Ed. Harold Bloom, 3–24. New York: W.W. Norton, 1970.

Boullata, Issa J. "The Poetic Technique of Badr Shākir al-Sayyāb (1926-1964)." In *Critical Perspectives on Modern Arabic Literature*. Ed. Issa J. Boullata, 232–43. Washington D.C.: Three Continents Press, 1980.

———. "Jabrā Ibrāhīm Jabrā." In *Encyclopedia of World Literature in the Twentieth Century*. Vol. 5: Supplement and Index. Ed. Steven R. Serafin, 329–30. New York: Continuum Publishing Company, 1993.

Brantlinger, Patrick. *Rule of Darkness: British Literature and Imperialism, 1830–1914*. Ithaca: Cornell University Press, 1988.

Brummett, Barry. *Contemporary Apocalyptic Rhetoric*.New York: Praeger, 1991.

Bullāṭa, 'Īsā. *Badr Shākir al-Sayyāb: Ḥayātuhu wa-Shi'ruh*. 1971. Reprint. Baghdad: Dār al-Shu'ūn al-Thaqāfiyya al-'Āmma, 1987.

Buṭṭī, Fā'iq. *Ṣiḥāfat al-'Irāq: Tārīkhuhā wa-Kifāḥ Ajyālihā*. Baghdad: Maṭba'at al-Adīb al-Baghdādiyya, 1968.

Byford, Cecil. *The Port of Basrah*. London: Waterlow and Sons, 1935.

[Cicero], *Ad Herennium*. Trans. Harry Caplan. Cambridge: Harvard University Press Loeb Classical Library, 1954.

Cleveland, William L. *The Making of an Arab Nationalist: Ottomanism and Arabism in the Life and Thought of Sati' al-Husri*. Princeton: Princeton University Press, 1971.

Cole, Juan. *Colonialism and Revolution in the Middle East: Social and Cultural Origins of Egypt's Urabi Movement*. Princeton: Princeton University Press, 1993.

Coleridge, Samuel Taylor. *Biographia Literaria, or Biographical Sketches of My Literary Life and Opinions*. New York: Leavitt, Lord and Co., 1834.

Connelly, Bridget. *Arab Folk Epic and Identity*. Berkeley: University of California Press, 1986.

Cordesman, Anthony. *The Iran-Iraq War and Western Security 1984–87: Strategic Implications and Policy Options*. London: Jane's Publishing Co., 1987.

Culler, Jonathan. "Apostrophe." In *The Pursuit of Signs: Semiotics, Literature, Deconstruction*, 135–54. Ithaca: Cornell University Press, 1981.

Curtius, E[rnst] R[obert]. *European Literature and the Latin Middle Ages*. Princeton: Princeton University Press, 1953.

Dante Alighieri, *The Inferno*. Trans. with notes by Allan Gilbert. Durham, N.C.: Duke University Press, 1969.

Darwaza, Muḥammad 'Izza. *Durūs al-Tārīkh al-'Arabī min Aqdam al-Azmina Ḥattā al-Ān*. In *Mukhtārāt Qawmiyya li-Muḥammad 'Izza Darwaza*, ed. Nājī 'Alūsh, 55–217. Beirut: Markaz Dirāsāt al-Waḥda al-'Arabiyya, 1988.

Ḍayf, Shawqī. *Al-Adab al-'Arabī al-Mu'āṣir fī Miṣr*. Cairo: Dār al-Ma'ārif, 1988.

Deleuze, Giles. *A Deleuze Reader*. Ed. Constantin V. Boundas. New York: Columbia University Press, 1993.

Derrida, Jacques. *Of Grammatology*. Trans. Gayatri Chakravorty Spivak. Baltimore: Johns Hopkins University Press, 1976.

DeYoung, Terri. "And Thereby Hangs a Tale: A Study of Myth in Modern Arabic Poetry." Ph.D. diss., University of California, Berkeley, 1988.

———. "A New Reading of Badr Shākir al-Sayyāb's 'Hymn of the Rain.'" *Journal of Arabic Literature* 24, no. 1 (March 1993): 39–61.

———. "Mu'āraḍa and Modern Arabic Poetry: Some Examples from the work of Badr Shākir al-Sayyāb." *Edebiyat* n.s. 5 (1994): 222–29.

Dickie, Margaret. *On the Modernist Long Poem*. Iowa City: University of Iowa Press, 1986.

Duncan, Joseph. *Milton's Earthly Paradise: A Historical Study Of Eden*. Minneapolis: University of Minnesota Press, 1972.

Eagleton, Terry. *Marxism and Literary Criticism*. Berkeley: University of California Press, 1976.

"Egypt and India." *The Spectator*, no. 4737 (4/12/1919): 486–87.

Elborn, Geoffrey. *Edith Sitwell: A Biography*. London: Sheldon Press, 1981.

Eliot, T[homas] S. *After Strange Gods: A Primer of Modern Heresy*. New York: Harcourt, Brace, and Company, 1933.

———. *Collected Poems: 1909–1962*. New York: Harcourt Brace & Co., 1963.

Fiedler, Leslie. *The Stranger in Shakespeare*. New York: Stein and Day, 1972.

Foucault, Michel. *Power/Knowledge: Selected Interviews and Other Writings 1972–1977*. Ed. Colin Gordon. New York: Pantheon Books, 1980.

———. *Technologies of the Self: A Seminar with Michel Foucault*. Eds. Luther H. Martin, Huck Gutman, and Patrick H. Hutton. Amherst: University of Massachusetts Press, 1988.

Frazer, James. *The Golden Bough Part IV: Adonis, Attis Osiris*. 3rd ed. New York: The Macmillan Company, 1935.

Gamal, Adel S. "Narrative Poetry in Classical Arabic Literature." In *In Quest of an Islamic Humanism: Arabic and Islamic Studies in Memory of Mohamed al-Nowaihi*, ed. A.H. Green, 25–38. Cairo: American University in Cairo Press, 1984.

Gibran, Jean, and Kahlil Gibran. *Kahlil Gibran: His Life and World*. New York: Interlink Books, 1991.

Greenblatt, Stephen. *Marvellous Possessions: The Wonder of the New World*. Chicago: University of Chicago Press, 1991.

Ḥadīdī, 'Alī al-. *Maḥmūd Sāmī al-Bārūdī*. Cairo: Dār al-Kātib, 1967.

Ḥanafī, Jalāl al-. *Al-Ruṣāfī fī Awjihi wa-Ḥadīḍih*. Baghdad: Maṭba'at al-'Ānī, 1962.

Harlow, Barbara. *Resistance Literature*. New York: Methuen, 1987.

Hodgson, Marshall. *The Venture of Islam*. 3 vols. Chicago: University of Chicago Press, 1974.

Homer, *Iliyādhat Hūmīrūs*. Trans. by Sulaymān al-Bustānī. 2 vols. 1904. Reprint. Beirut: Dār al-Ma'rifa, n.d.

Houston, John Porter. *French Symbolism and the Modernist Movement*. Baton Rouge: Louisiana State University Press, 1980.

Ḥusayn, Ṭaha. *Min Ḥadīth al-Shi'r wa al-Nathr*. Cairo: Dār al-Ma'ārif, n.d.

Ḥuṣrī, Abū Khaldūn Sāṭi' al-. *Mudhakkirātī fī al-'Irāq*. 2 vols. Beirut: Dār al-Ṭalī'a, 1968.

Hutcheon, Linda. "Circling the Downspout of Empire: Post-Colonialism and Post-modernism." *Ariel* 20, no. 4 (October 1989): 149–75.

Ibn al-Muqaffa'. *Al-Adab al-Kabīr*. Beirut: Dār Ṣādir, 1987.

Ibn Qutayba. *Kitāb al-Shi'r wa-al-Shu'arā'*. Leiden: E.J. Brill, 1904.

Ismā'īl, Muḥyī al-Dīn. "Al-Shi'r al-'Irāqī al-Ḥadīth." *Al-Ādāb* 3, no. 1 (January 1955): 49–57.

'Izz al-Dīn, Yūsuf. *Al-Shi'r al-'Irāqī Ahdafuhu wa-Khaṣā'iṣhu fī al-Qarn al-Tāsi' 'Ashar*. Cairo: al-Dār al-Qawmiyya li-al-Ṭibā'a wa-al-Nashr, 1965.

———. *Al-Shi'r al-'Irāqī al-Ḥadīth*. Cairo: Dār al-Ma'ārif, 1960.

Jabrā, Jabrā Ibrāhīm. *Hunters in a Narrow Street*. Washington, D.C.: Three Continents Press, 1990.

———. *Al-Riḥla al-Thāmina*. Beirut: Al-Maktaba al-'Aṣriyya, 1967.

———. "Al-Shā'ir, wa-al-Ḥākim wa-al-Madīna." In *Muḥammad Mahdī al-Jawāhirī: Dirāsāt Naqdiyya*, ed. Hādī al-'Alawī, 43–80. Baghdad/Najaf: Maṭba'at al-Nu'mān, 1969.

Jameson, Fredric. *The Political Unconscious: Narrative as Socially Symbolic Act*. Ithaca: Cornell University Press, 1981.

———. "Third-World Literature in the Era of Multinational Capitalism." *Social Text* 15 (Fall 1986): 65–88.

———. *Postmodernism Or, the Cultural Logic of Late Capitalism*. Durham, NC: Duke University Press, 1991.

Jārjī, Sīmūn. *Badr Shākir al-Sayyāb fī Ḥayātihi wa-Shi'rih*. N.p.: Manshūrāt Aḍwā', 1966.

Jay, Gregory S. "Postmodernism in *The Waste Land*: Women, Mass Culture, and Others." In *Rereading the New: A Backward Glance at Modernism*, ed. Kevin J.H. Dettmar, 221–46. Ann Arbor: University of Michigan Press, 1992.

Jayyusi, Salma Khadra. *Trends and Movements in Modern Arabic Poetry*. 2 vols. Leiden: E.J. Brill, 1977.

Jurjānī, 'Abd al-Qāhir al-."Al-Risāla al-Shāfiya fī al-I'jāz." In *Thalāth Rasā'il fī I'jāz al-Qur'ān*, eds. Muḥammad Khalafallah and Muḥammad Zaghlūl Sallām, 117–58. Cairo: Dār al-Ma'ārif, 1968.

Kamāl al-Dīn, Jalīl. "Bayna al-Sayyāb wa-Dustīyūsfskī." *Al-Ādāb*, 22, nos. 7–8 (July–August 1975): 37–43.

Kayālī, 'Abd al-Raḥmān Rabāḥ al-. "Hawla Qara'tu al-'Adad al-Māḍī." *Al-Ādāb* 3, no. 6 (June 1955): 68.

Keats, John. *Letters of John Keats to His Family and Friends*. Ed. Sidney Colvin. London: MacMillan and Co., 1925.

Kemp, Penny. "For Generations to Come: The Environmental Catastrophe." In *Beyond the Storm: A Gulf Crisis Reader*, ed. Phyllis Bennis and Michel Moushabeck, 325–34. New York: Olive Branch Press, 1991.

Kenner, Hugh. *The Invisible Poet: T.S. Eliot*. New York: McDowell, Obolensky, 1959.

Khairallah, As'ad . "The Greek Cultural Heritage and the Odyssey of Modern Arab Poets." In *Tradition and Modernity in Arabic Literature*, ed. Issa Boullata and Terri DeYoung, 23–41. Fayetteville: University of Arkansas Press, 1997.

Khalil, Samir al-. *Republic of Fear*. Berkeley: University of California Press, 1989.

Khaṭṭābī, Abū Sulaymān al-. "I'jāz al-Qur'ān." In *Thalāth Rasā'il fī I'jāz al-Qur'ān*, ed. Muḥammad Khalafallah and Muḥammad Zaghlūl Sallām, 21–71. Cairo: Dār al-Ma'ārif, 1968.

Khaṭṭāṭ, Qāsim al-, Muṣṭafā 'Abd al-Laṭīf al-Saḥaratī, and Muḥammad 'Abd al-Mun'im al-Khafājī. *Ma'rūf al-Ruṣāfī: Shā'ir al-'Arab al-Kabīr*. Cairo: Al-Hay'a al-Miṣriyya al-'Āmma li-al-Ta'līf wa-al-Nashr, 1971.

Khouri, Mounah A. *Poetry and the Making of Modern Egypt*. Leiden: E.J. Brill, 1971.

Khūrī, Ra'īf al-. "Qara'tu al-'Adad al-Māḍī." *Al-Ādāb* 3, no. 2 (February 1955): 65.

Laing, Dave. *The Marxist Theory of Art*. New Jersey: Humanities Press, 1978.

Langbaum, Robert. *The Poetry of Experience: The Dramatic Monologue in Modern Literary Tradition*. New York: W.W. Norton, 1957.

Larkin, Margaret. "Two Examples of *Rithā'*: A Comparison between Aḥmad Shawqī and al-Mutanabbī." *Journal of Arabic Literature*, 16 (1985): 18–39.

Leavis, F[rank].R[aymond]. *New Bearings in English Poetry: A Study of the Contemporary Situation*. London: Chatto and Windus, 1942.

Levin, Harry. "What Was Modernism?" *Refractions: Essays in Comparative Literature*, 271–95. London: Oxford University Press, 1966.

Lewis, C[ecil]. Day. *A Hope for Poetry*. 1934. Reprint. Oxford: Basil Blackwell, 1945.

Malā'ika, Nāzik al-. *Qaḍāyā al-Shi'r al-Mu'āṣir*. 1962. Reprint. Beirut: Dār al-'Ilm li-al-Malāyīn, 1978.

———. *Shi'r 'Alī Maḥmūd Ṭaha*. Cairo: Institute of Higher Arabic Studies, 1965.

Mandūr, Muḥammad. *Al-Shi'r al-Miṣrī Ba'da Shawqī*. 2 vols. Cairo: Dār Nahḍat Miṣr, 1969.

Marsot, Afaf Lutfi al-Sayyid-. *Egypt's Liberal Experiment: 1922–1936*. Berkeley: University of California Press, 1977.

Matthews, D.J., C. Shackle, and Shahrukh Husain. *Urdu Literature*. London: Urdu Markaz, 1985.

Matthews, Roderic D., and Matta Akrawi. *Education in Arab Countries of the Near East*. Washington D.C.: American Council on Education, 1949.

Matthiessen, F[rancis].O. *The Achievement of T.S. Eliot: An Essay on the Nature of Poetry*. Oxford: Oxford University Press, 1935.

Maxwell, Donald. *A Dweller in Mesopotamia: Being the Adventures of an Official Artist in the Garden of Eden*. London: John Lane, 1921.

Mayer, John T. *T.S. Eliot's Silent Voices*. Oxford: Oxford University Press, 1989.

McFarland, Thomas. *Romanticism and the Forms of Ruin: Wordsworth, Coleridge and the Modalities of Fragmentation*. Princeton: Princeton University Press, 1981.

Meisami, Julie. *Medieval Persian Court Poetry*. Princeton: Princeton University Press, 1987.

Modern Arabic Poetry: An Anthology. Ed. Salma Khadra Jayyusi. New York: Columbia University Press, 1987.

Modern French Poets on Poetry. Ed. Robert Gibson. Cambridge: Cambridge University Press, 1979.

Monroe, Harriet, and Alice Corbin Henderson, eds. *The New Poetry*. New York: The Macmillan Company, 1920.

Moreh, Shmuel. *Modern Arabic Poetry: 1800–1970*. Leiden: E.J. Brill, 1976.

Mortier, Roland. *La poétique des ruines en France*. Geneva: Droz, 1974.

Muḥsin, Ḥasan. *Al-Shi'r al-Qiṣaṣī*. Cairo: Dār al-Nahḍa al-'Arabiyya, 1980.

Naimy, Nadeem. *Mikhail Naimy: An Introduction*. Beirut: American University in Beirut Press, 1967.

Nation and Narration, ed. Homi K. Bhabha. London: Routledge, 1990.

Nawfal, Muḥammad Maḥmūd Qāsim. *Tarīkh al-Mu'āraḍāt fī al-Shi'r al-'Arabī.* Beirut: Dār al-Furqān, 1983.
Nu'ayma, Mīkhā'īl. *Al-Ghirbāl.* Cairo: Al-Maṭba'a al-'Aṣriyya, 1923.
Nuwayhī, Muḥammad. *Qaḍiyyat al-Shi'r al-Jadīd.* Cairo: Institute of Higher Arabic Studies, 1964.
Palgrave, Francis T. *The Golden Treasury of Songs and Poems, Selected by Francis T. Palgrave, Revised and Englarged with Additional Poems.* New York: Thomas W. Crowell Co., 1924.
Poe, Edgar Allan. *The Literary Criticism of Edgar Allan Poe.* Ed. Robert L. Hough. Lincoln: University of Nebraska Press, 1965.
Qabbānī, Nizār. "Ḥublā." *Al-Adīb* 11, no. 6 (June 1952): 11.
Quint, David. *Epic and Empire: Politics and Generic Form from Virgil to Milton.* Princeton: Princeton University Press, 1993.
Qurṭubī, Abū 'Abd Allāh al-. *Al-Jāmi' li-Aḥkām al-Qur'ān*, 12 vols. Cairo: Dār al-Kātib al-'Arabī, 1967.
Rajan, Balachandra. *The Form of the Unfinished: English Poetics from Spenser to Pound.* Princeton: Princeton University Press, 1985.
Renan, Ernest. *Histoire générale et système comparé des langues sémitiques* in *Oeuvres complètes.* 10 vols. Paris: Calmann-Levy, n.d.
Riddel, Joseph N. "A Somewhat Polemical Introduction: The Elliptical Poem." *Genre* 11, no. 4 (Winter 1978): 459–78.
Robbin, Tony. "Tennyson's 'Ulysses': The Significance of the Homeric and Dantesque Backgrounds." *Victorian Poetry* 11, no. 3 (Autumn 1973): 177–193.
Rowlinson, Matthew. "The Ideological Moment of Tennyson's 'Ulysses'." *Victorian Poetry* 30, nos. 3–4 (Autumn–Winter 1992): 265–67.
Rummānī, Abū al-Ḥasan 'Alī ibn 'Īsā al-. "Al-Nukat fī I'jāz al-Qur'ān." In *Thalāth Rasā'il fī I'jāz al-Qur'ān*, ed. Muḥammad Khalafallah and Muḥammad Zaghlūl Sallām, 75–113. Cairo: Dār al-Ma'ārif, 1968.
Ruṣāfī, Ma'rūf al-. *Dīwān al-Ruṣāfī.* Cairo: Al-Maktaba al-Tijāriyya al-Kubrā, 1963.
Al-Sab' al-Mu'allaqāt, The Seven Poems, Suspended in the Temple at Mecca. Trans. Frank E. Johnson. Bombay: Educational Society's Steam Press, 1893.
Sabāt, Khalīl. *Tārīkh al-Ṭibā'a fī al-Sharq al-Awsaṭ.* Cairo: Dār al-Ma'ārif, 1958.
Said, Edward. *Orientalism.* New York: Random House, 1978.
———. *The World, the Text and the Critic.* Cambridge: Harvard University Press, 1983.
———. "Yeats and Decolonization." In *Nationalism, Colonialism and Literature*, 69–95. Minneapolis: University of Minnesota Press, 1990.
———. "Foreword." In *Beyond the Storm: A Gulf Crisis Reader*, ed. Phyllis Bennis and Michel Moushabeck, 1–6. New York: Olive Branch Press, 1991.
———. *Culture and Imperialism.* New York: Vintage Books, 1994.

Sāmarrā'ī, Ibrāhīm al-. *Lughat al-Shi'r Bayna Jīlayn*. Beirut: Al-Mu'assasa al-'Arabiyya li-al-Dirāsāt wa-al-Nashr, 1980.

Sayyāb, Badr Shākir al-. "Wasā'il Ta'rīf al-'Arab bi-Nitājihim al-Adabī al-Ḥadīth." *Al-Ādāb* 4, no. 10 (October 1956): 22–24 and 100–1.

———. *Dīwān*. 2 vols. Beirut: Dār al-'Awda, 1971.

———. *Rasā'il al-Sayyāb*. Beirut: Dār al-Ṭāli'a, 1975.

———. *Azhār Dhābila wa-Qaṣā'id Majhūla*. Intro. Rafā'īl Buṭṭī, ed. Ḥasan Tawfīq. Beirut: Al-Mu'assasa al-'Arabiyya li-al-Dirāsāt wa-al-Nashr, 1981.

Segal, Charles. *Singers, Heroes, and Gods in the Odyssey*. Cornell: Cornell University Press, 1994.

Sharāra, 'Abd al-Laṭīf. "Qara'tu al-'Adad al-Māḍī." *Al-Ādāb* 2, no. 7 (July 1954): 63–68.

Sharett, Christopher. "Introduction: Crisis Cinema." In *Crisis Cinema: The Apocalytic Idea in Postmodern Narrative Film*, ed. Christopher Sharett, 1–9. Washington, D.C.: Maisonneuve Press, 1993.

Shawqī, Aḥmad. *Al-Shawqiyyāt*, 4 vols. Cairo: Maṭba'at Al-Istiqāma, 1964.

Shāyib, Aḥmad. *Tārīkh al-Naqā'iḍ fī al-Shi'r al-'Arabī*. Cairo: Maktabat al-Nahḍa,1954.

Shukrī, Ghālī. *Shi'runā al-Ḥadīth: Ilā Ayn?* Cairo: Dār al-Ma'ārif, 1968.

———. *Dhikriyāt al-Jīl al-Ḍā'i'*. Baghdad: Wizārat al-I'lām, 1972.

Simon, Reeva. *Iraq Between the Two World Wars: The Creation and Implementation of a Nationalist Ideology*. New York: Columbia University Press, 1986.

Slemon, Stephen. "Magic Realism as Post-Colonial Discourse." *Canadian Literature* 116 (Spring 1988): 9–24.

Sluglett, Peter. *Britain in Iraq: 1914–1932*. London: Ithaca Press, 1976.

Slyomovics, Susan. *The Merchant of Art: An Egyptian Hilali Oral Epic Poet in Performance*. Berkeley: University of California Press, 1987.

Smith, Sidonie, and Julia Watson. "Introduction: De/Colonization and the Politics of Discourse in Women's Autobiographical Practices." In *De/Colonizing the Subject: The Politics of Gender in Women's Autobiography*, ed. Sidonie Smith and Julia Watson, xiii-xxxi. Minneapolis: University of Minnesota Press, 1992.

Somekh, Sasson. "The Neo-Classical Arab Poets." In *Modern Arabic Literature*, ed. M. M. Badawi, 36-81. Cambridge: Cambridge University Press, 1992.

Spender, J.A. "The Egyptian Problem." *The Quarterly Review* 471 (April 1922): 415–29.

Spender, Stephen. "Remembering Eliot." *Encounter* 24, no. 4 (April 1965), 3–14.

Spivak, Gayatri Chakravorty. "Neocolonialism and the Secret Agent of Knowledge: An Interview with Gayatri Spivak." *Oxford Literary Review* 13 (1991): 220–51.

———. "The Rani of Sirmur." In *Europe and Its Others*, vol. 1, ed. Francis Barker et al., 128–51. Essex: University of Essex, 1985.

Stanford, W[illiam] B. *The Ulysses Theme: A Study in the Adaptability of a Traditional Hero*. Oxford: Basil Blackwell, 1954.

Stark, Freya. *East is West*. London: John Murray, 1945.

Studies in Modern Bengali Poetry. Ed. Nirmal Ghose. Calcutta: Novela, 1968.

Sulaiman, Khalid. *Palestine and Modern Arabic Poetry*. London: Zed Books, 1984.

Suleri, Sara. *The Rhetoric of English India*. Chicago: University of Chicago Press, 1992.

Sūmīkh, Sāsūn. "Asāṭīr al-Sayyāb: Thalāth Mutāba'āt." *Al-Karmil: Abḥāth fī al-Lugha wa-al-Adab* 8 (1987):61–82.

Ṭabari, Abū Ja'far Muḥammad ibn Jarīr al-. *The Commentary on the Qur'ān*. Trans. J[ohn] Cooper. Oxford: Oxford University Press, 1987.

Ṭaha, 'Alī Maḥmūd. *Dīwān*. Damascus: Al-Mu'assasa al-Thaqāfiyya li-al-Nashr wa-al-Tawzī', 1962.

Ṭahṭāwī, Rifā'a al-. *Takhlīṣ al-Ibrīz fī Talkhīṣ Bārīz* in *Uṣūl al-Fikr al-'Arabī al-Ḥadīth 'Ind al-Ṭahṭāwī, Ma' al-Naṣṣ al-Kāmil li-Kitābih: 'Takhlīs al-Ibrīz'*. Ed. Maḥmūd Fahmī Ḥijāzī. Cairo: Al-Hay'a al-Miṣriyya al-'Āmma li-al-Kitāb, 1974.

Tawfīq, Ḥasan. *Shi'r Badr Shākir al-Sayyāb: Dirāsa Fanniyya wa-Fikriyya*. Beirut: Al-Mu'assasa al-'Arabiyya li-al-Dirāsāt wa-al-Nashr, 1979.

Tennyson, Alfred, Lord. *Complete Poems*. New York: R. Worthington, 1885.

———. *The Poems of Tennyson in Three Volumes*. Ed. Christopher Ricks. London: Longman, 1987.

Terdiman, Richard. *Discourse Counter-Discourse: The Theory and Practice of Symbolic Resistance in Nineteenth-Century France*. Ithaca: Cornell University Press, 1985.

———. *Present Past: Modernity and the Memory Crisis*. Ithaca: Cornell University Press, 1993.

Tibrīzī, Al-Khaṭīb al-, comp. *Sharḥ al-Qaṣā'id al-'Ashr*. Ed. Fakhr al-Dīn Qabāwa. Beirut: Dār al-Āfāq al-Jadīda, 1980.

Tramontini, Leslie. *Badr Šākir as-Sayyāb: Untersuchungen zum poetischen Konzept in den Diwanen azhār wa-asāṭīr und unšūdat al-maṭar*. Wiesbaden: Otto Harrassowitz, 1991.

Vickery, John. *The Literary Impact of* The Golden Bough. Princeton: Princeton University Press, 1973.

Viorst, Milton. "A Reporter at Large: The View from the Mustansiriyah—II." *The New Yorker* (October 19, 1987): 76–96.

Wādī, Ṭaha. *Shi'r Nājī*. Cairo: Kulliyat al-Ādāb, 1976.

Wā'ilī, Ibrāhīm al-. *Al-Shi'r al-Siyāsī al-'Irāqī fī al-Qarn al-Tāsi' 'Ashar*. Baghdad: Maṭba'at al-'Ānī, 1961.

White, Hayden. *Tropics of Discourse: Essays in Cultural Criticism*. Baltimore: Johns Hopkins University Press, 1978.

Wilkenfeld, Roger B. "'Columbus' and 'Ulysses': Notes on the Development of a Tennysonian Theme." *Victorian Poetry* 12, no. 2 (Summer 1974): 170–74.

Wilkie, Brian. *Romantic Poets and Epic Tradition*. Madison: The University of Wisconsin Press, 1965.

Wordsworth, William. "Preface to the Second Edition of *Lyrical Ballads* (1800)." In *The Poetical Works of William Wordsworth*, 11 vols., ed. William Knight, 4:275–305. Edinburgh: William Paterson, 1883.

Ya'qūb, Imīl Badī'. *Jubrān wa-al-Lugha al-'Arabiyya*. Tripoli, Lebanon: Jarrūs, 1985.

Zaydān, Jurjī. *Tārīkh Ādāb al-Lugha al-'Arabiyya*. 1914. Reprint in *Mu'allifāt Jurjī Zaydān al-Kāmila*, 20 vols., 15:9–419. Beirut: Dār al-Jīl, 1982.

Index

Abbasid dynasty, 14, 129, 272n. 15
'Abbās, Iḥsān, 4, 82, 127, 213, 217, 218, 219, 224, 267n. 16, 283n. 46, 286n. 7, 306n. 63
Abrams, M.H., description of "greater romantic lyric," 284n. 51
Abū Shādī, Aḥmad Zākī, 156–157, 232
Abū Tammām, 132; bird imagery of, 299n. 49; contrafacted in Sayyāb's poetry, 298n. 35; *Hamāsa* of, 173; influence on Sayyāb, 128
Ādāb, al- (Beirut literary magazine), 46, 79, 81, 91, 122, 252, 255, 256, 282n. 36, 312n. 82
Adam and Eve, story of, 24, 31, 57, 91, 141, 293n. 51; in Koran, 278n. 78; in Sayyāb's poetry, 28, 54, 56, 57, 58, 86, 102, 236, 247
Adonis, myth of, 73, 74, 77, 86, 88, 91
Aeneid. See Virgil
Aldington, Richard, 200–01, 209, 304n. 42
Algeria: in Sayyāb's poetry, 81–82
Alhambra: as a symbol in Sayyāb's poetry, 84, 88, 284n. 49
'Alqama, 133–34
'Amāra, Lamī'a 'Abbās al-, 191, 198, 208; biography of, 301n. 12
'Antara, 120; contrafacted in Sayyāb's poetry, 49, 277n. 70, 290n. 25
apocalyptic, 11–12, 30; animal imagery in, 7, 28; defined, 270n. 37, in *Heart of Darkness*, 7; in Koran, 12–16, 25, 247; placelessness of, 8; and postmodernism, 17,78; and prophetic eschatology 19; in Sayyāb's writings, 1, 4, 15–16, 19–20, 23, 27–28, 97, 98, 103, 243–44, 251, 255; temporal emphasis in, 1, 11–13
Apollo school, 156–58, 159; narrative poetry of 232
'Aqqād, 'Abbās Maḥmūd al-, 45, 148, 153, 155, 176–80, 275n. 54, 276n. 55
Arabic language: in Iran, 34; in Iraq, 34–36, 39, 42; revival of, in modern times, 33; in Sayyāb's poetry, 51
Arabic literature: and epic, 220, 308n. 32, 309n. 33, 309n. 40; modern period of, 136, 151, 158–159; neoclassical period of, 153–53, 159, 169, 174, 177–78, 180; periodization of, 151–52, 161–62, 294n. 1, 297n. 28; and theme of freedom, 295n. 10. *See also* nahḍa; qaṣīda
Arab-Israeli wars, 10, 209–10; in Sayyāb's poetry, 83
Aragon, Louis: influence on Sayyāb's poetry, 223
atomic bomb, 46, 77, 125; and Peace Partisans group, 223, 307n. 9
Awaḍ, Lūwīs (Lewis), 4, 68–70, 281n. 14, 281n. 16; biography, 68

Babylon, 7–9, 16–17, 92–94, 103, 234, 235, 255
Badawī, M.M., 158, 181
Baghdad, vii, 11, 16, 32, 35, 36, 120, 129, 235; "triple tragedy" of, 14
Baḥr al-'Ulūm, Muḥammad, 189, 301n. 7
Bārūdī, Maḥmūd Sāmī al-, 140, 152–53, 163–70, 174, 175, 185, 195, 298n. 38, 298n. 42; fluency in Persian and Turkish, 163
Bashīr, al-Tījānī Yūsuf, 157
Basra, 11, 30, 31, 32, 222, 224, 272n. 12, 275n. 52; winged horse of, 119–21